The Truth of Chasing Rainbows

Escaping Suburbia for the Dream Life in Costa Rica

Anne Beaudoin

The Truth of Chasing Rainbows

*Escaping Suburbia for
the Dream Life in Costa Rica*

Anne Beaudoin

The Awakened Press

The Awakened Press
www.theawakenedpress.com
Copyright © Anne Beaudoin, 2024, 2025

For additional information, please contact
The Awakened Press at books@theawakenedpress.com.

The Awakened Press can bring authors to your live event.
For more information or to book an event contact
books@theawakenedpress.com or visit our website at
www.theawakenedpress.com.

Editing and book development, Lindsay R.A. Dierking
Cover and book design, Kurt A. Dierking II

Printed in the United States of America and Canada
Distributed throughout the United States of America, Canada, and worldwide
First The Awakened Press edition

E-Book ISBN: 979-8-9912770-7-5
Paperback ISBN: 979-8-9912770-8-2

To you, dear dreamer, who dares to listen to your inner voice
and follow what tugs at your soul.

Contents

Part III: Real, Raw, and Remote

Introduction
Landed

We'd done it. We'd made it to Costa Rica.

We made our way from the San José airport to our new home in the remote Dota mountains two hours away. I sat in silence as an overwhelming surge of, Oh God, what have we done? swallowed me up. Kevin sat up front as our shuttle driver, Minor, accelerated and braked intermittently in gridlocked, rush-hour traffic. With our Miniature Dachshund, Frankie, snoozing in her cozy carrying case beside me, I sat in the back seat and braced myself for a slow, jerky, miserable ride. We'd be lucky to get to the farm before dark.

Part I

Stuck in Suburbia

One
It All Started When

1987-2011

I lived through a whirlwind of adventures with my first husband in my twenties. After more than a dozen moves across Canada — from province to province, big cities to small towns, remote cabins to flimsy tents — we eventually settled down near family and friends in Burlington, a suburb of Toronto in the province of Ontario, where I got a well-paid corporate job as an account manager in the graphic design industry.

By my early thirties, after a tumultuous eleven-year marriage, I had sole custody of my eight-year-old daughter, Phoenix, and two-year-old son, Jude. Without any child support, I was on my own. Desperate to provide a safe, healthy environment for them, I convinced myself I needed to work hard and stay the course. And I did. For thirteen years.

Over time, though, no amount of money, encouragement from friends and coworkers, vacation time, or office perks was enough. I felt simultaneously stressed and lethargic, comfortable yet dissatisfied. Clutching in and out of first gear on the hour-long commute to work wore me out. My senses dulled as if engaged only through muscle memory.

Where had my adventurous life gone?

I wanted so many more experiences. I couldn't afford to quit my job, so instead, I read. I lost myself in travel memoirs. Books like *Eat Pray Love, Under the Tuscan Sun*, and the yellowing pages of one of my all-time favourites, *Walk Across America,* kept me going. They kept me dreaming.

In 2003, five years after my divorce, I met the man who would become my second husband. Kevin moved in directly across the street and we started dating a year later. Three years after that, I sold my house, and the kids and I moved into his modest white bungalow.

In September 2007, Kevin and I flew to England for a short holiday to visit his parents. One day during our stay, we took the train into London. We browsed in Harrods and Harvey Nichols, walked by Buckingham Palace and Trafalgar Square, and stopped for lunch at a quaint pub. Although we were having a lovely time, I was suffering from a head cold and walking all day had tired me out. I was desperate for a nap and wanted to head back to his parents' place so I could rest up before heading out for dinner. Instead, Kevin convinced me to detour to Piccadilly Circus. I'd mentioned that morning I wanted to see this famous tourist attraction, and, seeing how keen Kevin was to show me, I didn't have the heart to refuse. Kevin grabbed my hand tightly and, with a huge grin on his face, whisked me up the stairs to the fountain of Eros. My head was in such a fog I thought he was looking for a good spot to take a picture. To my surprise, he got down on one knee and proposed, with the god of love as our witness. Exactly one year later, on September 27, 2008, we said *I do*.

In the early years of our marriage, Kevin and I often dreamt about living abroad someday. We were drawn to the adventure of seeing new places, meeting new people, and acquiring new skills. I found the thought of fleeing our *long* Canadian winters (and my annual bout of Seasonal Affective Disorder) especially enticing.

We spent our honeymoon scoping out southern France as a possible relocation destination. We loved the country but ultimately decided it wasn't the right time. Instead, we bought an original 1950s bungalow back in Burlington and determined that renovating it would become our adventure. Together, we gutted the house and created what I thought was our dream home. That was why, when Kevin suggested halfway through the transformation process that we should flip it and start another project, I snapped without faltering, "Hell no!"

"We'll see," he replied under his breath.

Between March 2009 and September 2011, we were so consumed with the renovation that we were too exhausted to think of much else. We hired an architect to design the cathedral ceiling, a contractor to install the structural beams, and an electrician and plumber to meet specific building codes, but Kevin had the tools and the know-how to do the majority of the work. He poured his heart and brawn into it and loved it. With Kevin's raw building talent and my affinity for design, we discovered we made quite a team on this house transformation. And yet...

Spring and Summer 2011
First Musings

I should have known better. A perfectly renovated house couldn't possibly compete with the wanderlust that ran through my veins. Our dream home didn't appease my desire for a dream life, no matter how much I tried to convince myself otherwise. Luckily, Kevin felt the same way.

In the early spring of 2011, Kevin started a part-time job as an electrical technician at a solar panel company. He needed a break from the day-to-day of our remodel and his paycheque helped with the never-ending renovation bills. Sometime in May, Kevin returned home from work and mentioned that he and his coworkers had bantered over which country they'd want to move to and live — if they could choose only one in the world. Many of Kevin's coworkers were immigrants as it was, including him, so he found the conversation fascinating. One of the guys, Bashir, had waxed poetic about Costa Rica, extolling the virtues of the small Central American country. Bashir was from Nigeria and had never been to Costa Rica, but he was nevertheless obsessed and seemed to have done his homework, according to Kevin.

Intrigued, I did what any curious person would do — I started Googling. Sitting across from me with his laptop, Kevin did the same. We investigated...examined... considered. For two months, we spent evening after evening researching Costa Rica's climate, healthcare and education systems, political and social infrastructures, and residency rules. Bashir was right: Costa Rica seemed idyllic in every way.

"It's so central, kind of the hub of Central and South America. Just think, we could explore lots of other countries so easily from there. Visit places we'd probably never see otherwise," Kevin suggested.

"Bocas del Toro in Panama for instance and Belize. Just a hop and a skip by plane. Oh, and I've always wanted to hike up to the ruins of Machu Picchu in Peru."

There was no denying that I was lured into the fantasy. I was no longer looking at Costa Rica and what it had to offer within the confines of its borders but was becoming enamoured by its proximity to what felt like complete freedom.

One day in late July, Kevin sent me a picture of a beautiful oceanfront property. Then he sent another...then ten, twenty, fifty more. The pictures and descriptions were inviting, but I knew they showed a limited perspective.

If we were truly thinking about relocating, the next logical step was to see Costa Rica for ourselves. I was due some vacation time, so we booked our flight for mid-September, knowing it would be the rainy season. Seeing Costa Rica at its worst, we reasoned, might inject a healthy dose of reality into our imaginings. We planned on renting a vehicle and going on a two-week road trip to scope out the culture and lifestyle. That was the plan —

no other agenda — and I loved the spontaneous feeling of it all. It felt like an adventure!

September couldn't come soon enough.

Headline Scoop

We hadn't told the kids about our thoughts of relocating during the search phase, but with our trip to Costa Rica just around the corner, it was time to come clean. I didn't want to tell anyone about the possibility of relocating; not my parents, not friends, and especially not coworkers until I knew for sure it was actually happening. So many things could stop us from moving forward with this dream. There wasn't any point in stirring the waters if nothing was going to come of it. But, I felt compelled to let the kids know our plan.

"Hey Phoenix... Jude... Can you come here, please?" I called out.

Phoenix emerged from her room, and Jude walked down from the bedroom we'd built for him over the garage. It was his pad, his den...he loved it in there. I knew it would be difficult to sell him on giving it up for something unknown. My fifteen-year-old was averse to change.

They approached from opposite sides of the house, converging in the middle of the living room.

"What's up?" Jude asked before he crossed the large open-concept space.

"Sit down for a minute, I need to tell you both something."

"Who died?" Phoenix sat on the puffy couch, smoothing out her silky auburn hair. Jude sprawled next to her.

"No one died. Kevin and I have been doing some research for the last couple of months and we're thinking we might want to move to Costa Rica. Our upcoming trip is not just a holiday, it's a bit of a scouting expedition to see if we like it."

"Really? Wow! Costa Rica? That's so cool!" Phoenix squealed.

"Well, it's early days yet, and the stars will have to align. We're giving ourselves a year to find the right place. Who knows if we'll like it enough to live there," I continued, looking at both of them. Then I turned to Phoenix. "I want to give you enough time to sort yourself out financially just in case it does happen. So that you're well prepared to move out on your own again. I don't want to pull the rug from under you."

Her smile dropped. Her brow furrowed. I could see her confusion, which then confused me. "Mum, it's Costa Rica! I want to come with you!"

"You're twenty-one and, unfortunately, you don't qualify under the dependent status. You'd need two hundred thousand dollars to apply for permanent residency. Besides, I thought you couldn't wait to get out of here?" I added. It never once occurred to me that she would consider coming with us.

Phoenix had moved out when she was eighteen and for three years had lived as an independent adult, splitting expenses with roommates. But things got financially hard when those roommates became unreliable, so I suggested she move back in with us until she could get back on her feet. Just temporarily. She agreed, but she'd done so reluctantly. She didn't want to live under the same roof as Kevin. Their relationship had been rocky from the start. They were civil, but for my sake, mostly. When Kevin came onto the scene, Phoenix was fourteen. Her dad had committed suicide two years earlier, resulting in Phoenix behaving somewhat like...*a cat*. If a father figure had come along and earned her trust, then she would have been open and loving. Deep down, she wanted to feel that warm bond again. But she needed to feel safe first. Kevin was a dog person, however. He expected my kids to accept him right off the hop and when Phoenix was reticent, he seemed to blame the awkwardness on her not displaying friendly canine traits. Cats and dogs have very different communication styles and due to Kevin's inability to grasp where Phoenix was coming from, my fourteen-year-old daughter didn't feel lovable. With the combination of her grieving process, being bullied at school, and her mother falling in love with someone she didn't get along with, her world had come crashing down. Strong-willed by nature, she put up walls and shut down. She didn't talk about any of it with me. She was happy that I was happy, but a wedge had been created. In her eyes, she was losing me to Kevin and that came with a lot of complicated feelings. She showed me what she wanted me to see: an independent, freedom-seeking, I-can-do-it-on-my-own iron will. She had developed a hard, protective shell, and I had failed to understand that shell was insulating her tender, sensitive heart.

Phoenix was a young child when she caught the wanderlust bug. We had moved thirteen times by the time she entered the second grade, and she felt restless most of her life. She was always talking about the places she would go someday.

"Knapsack on my back, I'm outta here when I'm eighteen," ten-year-old Phoenix had told me once with longing in her eyes.

"Oh, Mummy, don't worry, I will live with you forever and ever," four-year-old Jude had chimed in, utterly shocked by his sister's proclamation.

I didn't know what concerned me more — having a daughter so eager to spread her wings at such a young age or having a son who never wanted to leave my side.

Phoenix's first big trip was to New Zealand with her high-school class. She enjoyed it but confessed she would have enjoyed it more if the chaperones, who were intent on enforcing the rules, hadn't been there. She wasn't a rule breaker by nature, but she didn't like to feel hemmed in. She wanted to be trusted for the responsible teenager she was and resented anyone doubting her good character. When I asked her what her favourite part of the trip was, she replied, "I liked exploring the streets when we were left alone to shop in Christchurch. And, bungee jumping. I *loved* that!"

At seventeen, Phoenix flew to Japan on her own to visit her then-boyfriend for a month. And just a few weeks before our big announcement about Costa Rica, she had mentioned she'd been invited to go to Brazil for two months in March. Our house was just a place for her to crash and lay her head for a little while, or so I thought. Not having to worry about the Phoenix factor was one of the reasons I could even remotely entertain such a big move. My mind was reeling.

I was raised by parents from a generation that believed parenting duties stopped at eighteen. Once I moved out, never in a million years would I have expected my parents to include me in any of their plans going forward. Perpetuating this parenting style to some degree, I figured once my kids moved out, they'd be on their own. Phoenix had already moved out once, moved back in, and was eager to be out on her own again. I also thought our being far away would support her sense of independence. All she ever talked about was wanting to be free.

I'm her mother. How could I have gotten it so wrong?

"Well, I don't have two hundred thousand dollars. And living with Kevin would be hard, but Costa Rica! How could you think I'd want to stay behind? I *love* to travel! Damn. You're so lucky, Jude!"

"Whatever," was Jude's retort. "All I hear is *if*. It seems like there's a good chance this won't happen. You haven't even finished the renovations yet. What the hell? But of all the random places you could choose, at least you picked a country with a primary forest. That's pretty cool." I suspected Jude was trying to find a pro amid the cons. He wasn't a get-up-and-go kind of guy. He wasn't impulsive like his sister. He needed a lot of time to process.

"Well, you're right. It might not happen at all," I answered. "All I know is I've been stressed at work for some time, and I need a change. Kevin is ready for a change too. And honestly, Jude, I don't see you thriving in the school system here. Maybe a change of scenery and culture would do you good. Lots of reptiles and bugs, and stuff — "

"Oh my God, I hope you get to do it, Jude!" Phoenix interrupted with envy before turning to me. "I'm sad I can't go, but I do think you totally deserve to do this. You've worked hard your whole life. It's exciting. Can I come visit?" she asked sheepishly.

"You better! And we'll come back and visit, too. I'm not abandoning you," I reassured her. Or maybe — guilt still gnawing at me — I was trying to reassure myself. "Besides, knowing you, you'll go to Brazil and end up staying there."

"True. You've got a point. That could happen," Phoenix laughed, lightening the mood.

"Please keep this to yourselves for now," I finished. "I'm giving you the headline scoop, but I want it kept under wraps until we know for sure it's happening. Okay?"

Sister Gladys

When Carlos, another of Kevin's coworkers, heard we had decided to visit Costa Rica, he was excited for us and insisted we stay with Sister Gladys, a relative of his who lived in the capital not far from the airport. Kevin learned that in her mid-seventies, the nun ran a daycare program for underprivileged children out of an old school.

"I thanked him, of course, but told him we couldn't possibly impose like that," Kevin relayed back to me.

"How thoughtful of him, but I totally agree."

"I'm sure nothing will come from it. It's just something people say to be nice," he added, downplaying the likelihood Carlos would contact the nun.

A few days later, Kevin came home from work, his lips curled inward in a tight grimace. He was massaging his shaved head — a tell-tale sign something was on his mind — and it was obvious he wasn't sure how to go about telling me.

"What's up?" I asked.

"Carlos contacted Sister Gladys."

"Oh yeah... And?" I waited for him to expound.

"He's arranged to have her pick us up at the airport and for us to stay with her."

"What? Are you serious?" I was more than a little surprised. I hesitated, not wanting to sound inflexible. "Um, don't you think staying with a complete stranger who doesn't speak English might feel a bit awkward? I thought you said nothing would come of it."

"Yeah, well, refusing the invitation now feels even more awkward. He sounded so happy that he could do this for us. I don't want to offend the guy. Let's just consider it part of *the adventure*," Kevin said, emphasizing the last part. Whether he meant it or not, he tried to sound like he was all in.

When the word *adventure* was thrown on the table like a bargaining chip, I flat-out folded.

Well played, Kevin. Well played.

Two
Spiders, Sloths, and Rainbows, Oh My!

September 2011

Two weeks later, Sister Gladys stood squarely outside the terminal in matronly black shoes. The short but stocky woman wasn't hard to spot against the white stippled concrete wall in her well-pressed veil and smooth navy habit. A slightly taller nun in a matching habit and a black-moustached man in a beige suit stood behind her, the way back up singers do behind their lead vocalist. As we approached them, our luggage in tow, the smile that accentuated Sister Gladys's cherub cheeks grew wider, and her bright eyes beamed with kindness. The other two emanated just as much warmth. Despite our earlier reservations, seeing their good-natured faces was comforting. Through the introductory exchange, we learned the second nun was Sister Gladys's biological sister, Sister Gloria. And the man was their good friend and driver, Jorge.

We arrived in San José in the late afternoon on September 15, which happened to be Independence Day. Considering all the research we had done, the fact that we'd be landing on a day that meant there'd be chaos in the streets with parades and drunken celebrations had been lost on us when we had booked the plane tickets. It wasn't until crowds of people walking amid beeping cars — singing and waving blue-, white-, and red-striped flags — that Jorge explained what was going on.

Seeing the joy on the citizens' faces and their sheer exuberance certainly made for a high-vibe first impression, but I don't mind admitting I felt relieved we didn't have to rent a vehicle near the airport and attempt to crawl across that bustling city. It didn't take long for nightfall to obscure the landscape, which would have made it even harder for us to navigate and find our way.

As we left the heavy congestion, glaring billboards and neon marquees that vied for attention blurred outside the van window. Like a swarm of fireflies, glowing headlights came and went much faster in every direction. Jorge was obviously a pro and handled the mayhem with adept skill.

Sister Gladys understood more English than she could speak while I grasped enough French/Spanish cognates to get the main points. It was hit or miss, but we managed half the time. *"Muy despacio, por favor,"* was my new mantra when I needed her to slow down. During our ride from the airport to her place, Sister Gladys pointed to landmarks, explaining in two-word bursts what things were. *"El estadio... La iglesia... Pollo campero..."*

The stadium and church were obvious, but I didn't know what *pollo campero* was. I remembered that *pollo* meant *chicken* and I was trying to follow her finger to see what she was pointing at. Finally, I noticed the bright yellow sign with "Pollo Compero" written across it. It was a fast-food chicken joint. Apparently it was a modern landmark, but important just the same, according to Sister Gladys.

An hour-and-a-half later, hugging the curb, Jorge parked on a dark narrow street where it was difficult to see where one building ended and the other began. As we stepped out of the minivan, a diesel odour filled the air and sirens screamed close by.

Jorge removed our suitcases from the trunk then shook Kevin's hand.

"Muchas gracias, señor," Kevin and I said in union.

Then we followed Sister Gladys to a locked wrought-iron gate. She jiggled the key — more by feel than by sight — until we heard it click. The gate swung open. She led us a short distance under a covered walkway. She unlocked and opened the front door with a different key. As soon as we walked in, Sister Gladys gestured for us to wait and then scampered off. We stood there with our luggage by our sides while our eyes adjusted to the moonlit room. A few minutes later, we heard the buzzing of the fluorescent light overhead as it struggled to illuminate the foyer. The blue glow revealed bare floor tiles and what I could only assume were chocolate-brown wood-panelled walls. Sister Gladys poked her head around the corner and smiled with satisfaction. Then she combed through her keychain again to find a third key and unlocked the next door. My curiosity piqued. I couldn't help but wonder what was on the other side of door number two. Like in a suspenseful thriller movie, the hinges creaked when Sister Gladys opened the door. I could sense her waddling gait as she ushered us into yet another shadowy room.

Because she was ever so quiet and it was ever so dark, Kevin and I had forgotten that Sister Gloria was tagging behind us. I turned to close the door and accidentally buried my face directly into her ample bosom. Startled, I shrieked. Sister Gloria giggled as if this was a prank she liked to play on unsuspecting visitors.

There's a little dickens in this glorified soul. I like her.

Sister Gladys switched on a second set of lights while Sister Gloria bid us goodnight and moseyed down the dim-lit hallway.

Carlos had mentioned that Sisters Gladys and Gloria shared an apartment above the school and that we'd be staying in a spare room on the main floor. Our room, we discovered, was tucked behind a spacious play area and beside a row of washing machines. It was so crammed with furniture that it could have easily been confused for a storage closet. Crooked frames of Mother Mary and baby Jesus hung precariously on the pale hospital-green walls and a strong scent of ammonia attempted to mask the musty smell. Exhausted from our day of travel, we reframed the clutter as *old-world charm* and inhaled a lungful of gratitude.

As Kevin flopped onto the thin, lumpy mattress, the springs squeaked. "This double bed feels more twin-sized. Where are you sleeping?" Kevin quipped.

"Haha, very funny. And check out how slanted the floor is. We'll have to be careful not to roll out of bed in the middle of the night," I laughed. Then, eyeing Jesus looking down on me from one of the many crosses, I immediately felt guilty for my sass.

We woke the next morning at 6:00 a.m. to honking cars, muffled voices outside our window, and tiny high-pitched screams just beyond our door. Although my back was stiff and my left hand felt cramped from gripping the edge of the mattress all night, I saw it as part of the adventure. I could have been stuck in suburbia commuting to work, but instead, I was in Costa Rica. *And*, I'd managed not to fall out of bed.

No small miracle, I assure you.

Jorge was already sitting and sipping a cup of coffee when Kevin and I entered the kitchen. After breakfast, once we finished eating our fried eggs and toast with melon on the side, Jorge had been tasked to drive us to the car rental company where we'd pick up an all-wheel-drive vehicle for the rest of our trip.

We were rested and well-fed. Despite our initial uneasiness and the language barrier, we were glad we'd accepted the invitation and appreciated Sister Gladys's sweet charity.

An absolute angel.

With promises to visit her again if we moved to Costa Rica and a chorus of, "*Muchas gracias, muchas gracias,*" Kevin and I took turns hugging her squat figure.

"*Adíos. Bendiciones para ustedes dos,*" she nodded, as she waved us goodbye with God's blessings.

El Castillo

Armed with the handy-dandy *Lonely Planet* guidebook we'd purchased during our layover in Miami, we felt ready to tackle the first day of our scouting expedition.

"Let's travel north toward Arenal Volcano," I suggested.

"Sure. The guidebook," Kevin pointed to an open page, "recommends we avoid staying in the town of La Fortuna though. Too touristy."

We took the guidebook's advice and headed up to El Castillo instead — and when I say *up,* I mean straight up, vertical, bolt upright — on a very rough, unpaved road. I quietly mouthed a prayer as we made the steep climb to Essence, the recommended boutique hotel.

If they can run a business out here in the middle of nowhere and make a living, then anything is possible.

As we reached the crest, a magnificent volcano, boastful from our vantage point, dwarfed everything around it. The hill we had just climbed felt insignificant next to Arenal's imposing eminence. Fluffy white clouds danced around its vent, unafraid of the possible consequences.

"The book says it used to spew lava almost nightly, and the odds of glimpsing it in action were fairly high. That went on for decades," I mentioned as I read. "But the volcano has been dormant since 2010. Looks like we're a year too late for the big show."

"That's a drag. Never know, though, we could get lucky."

"Yup, I suppose. But I'm not holding my breath," I sighed.

Kevin parked our grey Nissan Pathfinder, and we made our way up to the office.

"One room, please. For two adults," Kevin requested.

The medium-height, medium-build, thirty-something man standing on the other side of the counter — who later introduced himself as Kelly — nodded without looking at the booking log in front of him.

"If this was the high season, you would've had to call us at least a week ago. We're always booked solid," Kelly said as he handed us a key to one of the rooms and ran through the hotel rules. Since he was clearly an expat, we wondered how he had ended up working in such a remote location. Kelly, we discovered, who was originally from the U.S., owned the hotel. He had fallen in love with Costa Rica during a visit and decided to stay. He struck me as low-key and easy to talk to. We told him we were from Canada and that we were looking to relocate, too.

"Oh yeah? What are you looking to do, exactly? And where would you like to settle?" he inquired.

"Not sure. We're here to explore all possibilities," Kevin said honestly.

"Right on."

I've come across plenty of people, from all walks of life, who see themselves as uniquely qualified to take on certain challenges while viewing everyone else as spineless wannabes. Talking to Kelly, I detected no whiff of the bristling that might suggest he was one of those people.

"Your room is just across the way," Kelly pointed to the structure directly in front of us, closest to the parking lot.

We thanked him, got our bags from the trunk of the trusty ride, and found our room. It was stark: four unadorned walls with cold, bare terracotta floor tiles housed a solitary queen-sized bed with white sheets and an orange covering barely thick enough to be called a covering.

What do we expect for fourteen bucks a night?

But the floors were level, which was a bonus, and as we drew the curtains open, the awe-inspiring volcano astounded us, even without spewing lava. The room might not have been fancy, but we'd scored a million-dollar view.

The next morning, we bumped into Kelly as he carried a basket of freshly picked vegetables and herbs.

"Morning!" Kelly projected. "Want a tour of the property? We've got organic gardens and trails. Then if you want, I can show you a couple of properties up for sale in the area."

"That sounds awesome, thanks!" I replied.

"Great. Give me two minutes to drop this off in the kitchen," Kelly hefted the basket. "I'll be right back."

As Kevin and I waited, the looming silhouette against a beryl-blue sky stared us down. Arenal was so damn impressive regardless of the lighting and bearing witness to its majesty never seemed to get old. I tried to imagine living in such a captivating place. It felt like we had climbed a magic beanstalk, and we were waiting for a giant to *fee-fi-fo-fum* us.

Are we going to find our golden egg in this magical place?

Kelly returned — *not a giant* — and guided us down the sloping terrain while pointing to a hodgepodge of herbs and vegetables growing out of dirt and rock. No uniform rows as far as the eye could see.

"We're working to be as sustainable as possible," Kelly started. "Ninety percent of our energy is solar, and we source our water from local natural springs."

"Wow! That's amazing," Kevin enthused.

"When we took over in the late nineties, the land was an overgrazed cattle ranch. So much of it was stripped away," Kelly described as he walked, and we followed. "I'm sure our permaculture farming practices are the reason we have such a vibrant, medicinal food forest today. It takes a lot of patience, but it's worth it," Kelly noted with a hint of pride in his voice.

We learned that Kelly and his team had planted over 9,000 trees on the 22 hectares to combat deforestation. And even with all those trees, the sun still blazed down on us. Beads of sweat dripped from Kevin's sunburned scalp and my sodden bra stuck to my chest. An ever-growing sweat stain grew on my T-shirt from where my unfashionable but practical travel pack sat around my waist.

When we were done touring the property, we were only too happy to ride in Kelly's covered Jeep as he chauffeured us around El Castillo.

From afar, the vegetation looked verdant. From a closer view through Kelly's Jeep windows, however, the land appeared parched. Dry wind whipped through our hair, which seemed contradictory, considering it was the rainy season.

"The air feels drier because of the altitude. It never feels as humid up here as it does at lower elevations. And this is the driest wet season we've had in years," Kelly explained as we drove up and down the hilly landscape.

The two houses Kelly showed us had magnificent vistas of Lake Arenal, but both were built on cliffs with virtually no land. Either would have been worth considering for the views alone, but neither ticked the *what would we do for a living?* box.

I was also concerned about finding a school for Jude. Being close to an international school where lessons were taught in English was what we were also looking for.

"Yeah, that's a bit of a problem. The school in this village and the one in La Fortuna are Spanish-only," Kelly confirmed. I felt deflated and started to tune out after that bit of news.

When he showed us a larger piece of property with business-conversion opportunities, Kevin was weighing the possibilities. He kept suggesting ideas, but all I heard was *whah, whah, whah* like the teacher in Charlie Brown's classroom. I had already made up my mind that El Castillo was not the place for us.

It was important to me that the Costa Rica experience be positive for Jude. Kevin's attitude, however, was that we were the adults and Jude was the child, and within that dynamic Jude would simply have to *get with the program*. Kevin wasn't wrong and to some extent, I agreed with him. I certainly hadn't been raised with any say in such important matters. But Jude required routine and order — any kind of change was a struggle for him — and he was too smart for his own good, making school a daily challenge. So as the mother of a sensitive soul, I felt protective and wanted to do what was best for him.

"Thanks so much for showing us around and sharing so many valuable tidbits. We really appreciate it," Kevin said.

"Yeah, it was great. You've given us a lot to think about," I added, trying not to sound dismissive.

"No problem. My pleasure... Oh, before I forget, spaghetti's on the menu tonight," Kelly mentioned as we slid out of his dusty vehicle. My mind was whirling and my stomach grumbled. After an active day, some of that comfort food sure sounded good.

"At Essence, if you want dinner, you've got to help make it," Kelly informed us. "It's a good way to meet and bond with other travellers, y'know? When you're this far off the beaten path, it's nice to build a sense of community, and those who make it up here all have at least one thing in common." He paused, pointing to the steeply graded road we all had to navigate to get here. "Besides, it's fun," he added before he turned and walked toward the office.

An hour later, freshly showered and ravenous, Kevin and I entered the office building where the dinner-making extravaganza would take place. Just beyond the intake desk, above a free-standing sink, a sign asked — in a few different languages — "Please wash your hands before sitting down."

We had just washed our hands, but we dutifully lathered up again and patted them dry, then walked through the entryway into an open-concept space.

To the left, in the kitchen, three chefs in crisp white aprons busied themselves with setting up. To the right, in the dining room, a few people had already selected their seats from the three rustic picnic tables that had been jammed in side by side.

"Looks like we're in for a treat," Kevin commented as we surveyed to see where we'd like to sit. We turned and stopped at the table closest to the door. Kevin scooched down the long wooden bench and I followed, settling in next to him. The middle table was empty, but not for long. Within minutes, dishes and chairs scraped and clattered, and the room bustled. The last four guests shuffled in and looked around to assess their limited options.

"Can we sit here?" one of the young ladies asked, pointing to our table.

"Sure!" I said and gestured for them to make themselves at home.

"Thank you. We are Soleil and François," she greeted, her index finger moving like the pendulum of a metronome between herself and the guy towering over her. "From France."

"Hanne and Hendrik," the other young man chimed in, then cleared his throat. "From Belgium. Much better than France." He grinned and threw Soleil and François a knowing look as if it were already an ongoing inside joke.

"Oooh, fighting words, *mon ami*," François called Hendrik out and laughed.

"I'm Anne," I pressed my palm to my chest. "And this is my husband, Kevin," I said with a side wave of my hand. "I'm originally from Québec, Canada, and Kevin's from England."

"But we live in Ontario... Canada," Kevin clarified. "Nice to meet you."

Both in their late twenties and both on their honeymoon, the couples were both in Costa Rica by coincidence. They had met one another earlier in the week in Tortuguero, on the eastern side of the country, and had been travelling together ever since.

As the conversation ebbed and flowed, I glanced around the room. Knowing the hotel was half empty, I couldn't imagine what a tight squeeze it must be during the high season when the hotel was fully booked. As it was, we had to be careful we didn't elbow our fellow diners.

Once we were all seated, Chef Number One came out from behind the counter. *"Pura Vida, amigos. Mi nombre es Felipe. Bienvenidos a todos,"* he welcomed us.

Felipe held a ramekin for each ingredient and placed them, one by one, on the wooden surface in front of us.

"Un po-co de ha-ri-na... Un hu-e-vo... Agua... Sal... Y un cu-chi-llo." He enunciated each syllable as if we were all concussion patients.

It was easy to understand with such clear visual cues. The ingredients spoke for themselves. Behind the counter, Chef Number Two stood waiting. She had all the same ingredients in front of her.

Once the ramekins were delivered to all the guests and we were ready, Chef Number Two began the lesson. "Hello. My name is Gaby. I will be explaining what you have to do," she said with a Spanish inflection. "Let's start. Make a volcano shape with the flour," she instructed.

We spread the white mound and created a crater.

"Then put the egg so the yolk goes in the middle," she pointed to the hole.

We cracked the shell, and the yellow centre plopped into the hollow.

"Muy bien! Add a bit of water and salt and mix it up."

Using our fingers, we mixed everything together, added a bit of water, and sprinkled a pinch of salt, as directed.

"Mix until it becomes sticky," she continued. "Okay, now keep adding flour until it feels a bit more firm... Like this," she stopped kneading and then poked her springy mound. "We're almost done. Now flatten your masterpieces." She pounded her mound of pasta dough down and patted it flat.

We followed her lead and walloped ours onto the table. Smacks, splats, and thuds resounded in the room in a syncopated beat. We then patted them flat with a polite *tap tap tap.*

"Now, cut thin strips, *por favor,*" Gaby added.

At first, I assumed Felipe, the first chef, would keep tabs on our pasta portions and would serve them back to us accordingly. I didn't worry too much that my strips were imperfect. But minutes later, as Felipe gathered up everyone's pasta onto one large platter, I realized he was adding them all into one common pot of boiling water. There was no way of knowing which noodle belonged to whom.

Sure hope everyone washed their hands!

While we'd been engrossed in pasta-making, the third chef had prepared a savoury vegetarian sauce with garden-fresh herbs. The delicious aromas of thyme, oregano, and rosemary wafted through the snug room. My mouth watered nearly to the point of drooling as we waited in a conga line to serve ourselves like one does at a buffet. Back at our table, we all dug in and slurped our spaghetti as if we hadn't eaten in days.

Between delectable mouthfuls, François tried to persuade us to climb the smaller, extinct volcano beside Arenal.

"It's called Cerro Chato," Soleil said after swallowing a bite of her dinner.

"I heard it's pretty tough," Hendrik remarked and sipped his drink.

"Come on, it won't be too *difficile*. We go up, we go down. It has a beautiful *lac turquoise* at the bottom," François reported.

Oooh, an easy hike with the promise of a turquoise lake! Clearly, an adventure we should not pass up.

François managed to convince Hanne, Hendrik, Kevin, and me to meet him and Soleil outside the hotel at the crack of dawn. Kevin and I had had a long day, and we knew we'd need to be well-rested for the hike the next day. We finished our dinner, said goodnight, and made an early night of it.

True to our word, as the amber sun was rising over the cone-shaped mountain and cheerful chirps from flitting birds greeted the day, we showed up in front of the office. Soleil and François were already waiting, steaming coffees in hand. Hanne and Hendrik turned up minutes later, carrying a backpack similar to ours with water bottles clipped on either side.

Kelly's mouth lifted with a grin as he walked by and overheard our plans. "Just make sure you don't grab any tree limbs on the way up because, y'know...snakes. They blend into the environment and some are poisonous."

Oh great, thanks for putting that into my head.

It took a half hour or so to get from the hotel to the edge of Cerro Chato where its trail — if you could call it that — began. It was another vertical climb, but this time we had to get to the top under our own steam.

So, this is what you call easy, eh François? Duly noted.

François and Soleil led the pack, bouncing and bounding up the uneven terrain with cat-like agility. Hanne and Hendrik trailed behind them. They were not as agile as the buoyant French couple, but close.

Then came Kevin and me. We huffed and we puffed the whole way up, red-faced with embarrassment and exertion. I chalked it up to us not having a long leg span. Not grabbing on to branches to hoist ourselves — a warning we took to heart — handicapped us further. Our desperation to save face was the only reason we hadn't turned back during the first ten minutes of this beastly trek. I couldn't be sure if it was naïve determination or middle-aged stubbornness that propelled us forward, but Kevin and I pressed on. We didn't give up.

Our feet crunched through the thick brown duff and overgrown foliage covering the forest floor. The overhanging boughs created a dense ceiling of green, but on occasion the sun cut through the dappled shade, providing rays of hope. It was magical...until a Bocce ball-sized tarantula smack dab in the centre of our path brought us to a screaming halt.

No one moved. Not even the hot-shot French couple. The orange and black spider was as effective a roadblock, as if a tree had fallen across the path.

"What if we toss some rocks near it?" Hanne suggested.

"Oui, bonne idée, the vibrations will wake it up," François agreed.

"It's worth a try," I said squeamishly.

Like the big babies that we all were, we started throwing rocks near but not at it. We intended to herd it, not harm it. We were hoping the reverberations of the rocks landing on the ground would encourage the creature to move along...away from us.

"Ah, merde!" Soleil griped out of frustration.

Is it dead? Maybe it's dead.

We inched closer to check on it. Then closer still. The stunning yet creepier-than-creepy arachnid went from Sleeping Beauty to Speedy Gonzales in the blink of an eye, suddenly scuttling under the brush.

Nope, not dead!

Six adults shrieked and jumped back a few paces.

Where'd it go?

Knowing it was out there, somewhere, gave me serious spine shivers. We gave it a minute, then continued on our way, stomping loudly as we passed the spot where we saw it disappear.

The second half of our hike was thankfully downhill to the bottom of the crater.

"Et voilà," François gloated as though he'd painted the canvas himself. A serene turquoise lake glistened before us as though it had a glossy lacquered coating. Golden orbs waltzed across the surface of the water and created a sparkly haze against the emerald vegetation.

First to strip down to their bathing suits, François and Hendrik splashed into the water to cool off. Then, holding their breath, Hanne and Soleil both waded out until the water reached their thighs. Mirroring each other, they slapped water over their arms and shoulders, then dove in.

While Kevin went in for a quick dip, too, I rested on a hollow log and eavesdropped on the warbles coming from the treetops. I inhaled the combined scent of moisture, humus, and wood...the sweet smell of life.

And yes, you better believe I was keeping an eye out for spiders and snakes!

While Soleil and François continued to enjoy their swim, the others dried off. That was when we got to know Hanne and Hendrik a little better.

"We were married in a civil wedding ceremony last May but delayed our honeymoon until now." Hanne dabbed her lily-white skin and scrunched her shoulder-grazing locks with a small microfibre towel. "We met — "

"Ten years ago at Ghent University, a Dutch-speaking uni," Hendrik volleyed back, as only couples who have been together a long time can do.

I craned my neck skyward, shading my squinty eyes with my right hand. "How many languages do you speak?" I asked.

"Dutch, French, German, and English," he said, wiping his glasses clean.

"Only? No Spanish?" I teased.

"No, I wish. It would come in handy, for sure."

"That's impressive. What did you study?" Kevin asked next.

"We both graduated as bioengineers," Hanne picked up from there, as she grabbed her dry T-shirt from their pack and pulled it over her damp blonde hair. "And we live and work in Antwerp now."

Everything about their calm, reserved, well-spoken demeanour exuded *smart* to me. And though we'd gotten a glimpse of their sense of humour at dinner the night before, Kevin decided to put it to the test. As he finished off a chocolate bar, he mischievously — but nonchalantly — threw the wrapper on the ground.

The place was pristine and natural. In fact, an hour earlier one of us had mentioned how wonderful it was that people had shown so much restraint from littering. Even though I knew Kevin was poking fun and was only trying to provoke a reaction, the wrapper's soft landing on the forest floor felt sacrilege.

At first, Kevin kept walking as if nothing had happened, trying to stretch his shenanigan a little longer. But I laughed and ruined the joke. I sensed Hanne and Hendrik's immediate relief and they laughed, too. In that shared moment, we forged a bond. No longer mere acquaintances, a friendship was forming. Kevin promptly picked up the wrapper and stuffed it into his pocket. He left no further evidence of that memorable prank.

Feeling somewhat refreshed by our time at the lake, Kevin and I dug deep to muster enough energy to head back the way we came. It was just as hard, but we survived with our pride intact.

El Castillo provided so much more than the average sightseeing destination, but knowing in my heart that it wasn't the place for us long term, I was eager to continue down the road and see what else we might discover. And so was Kevin.

Our goal was to travel to the Monteverde Cloud Forest, reach its mountaintop village, Santa Elena, and explore what that area had to offer. Hanne, Hendrik, Soleil, and François decided to hang back another day, but they expected their next stop would be Santa Elena as well. We gave them the name of the hotel where we intended to stay and made tentative plans to meet in a day or two.

Monteverde Cloud Forest

Our guidebook noted that it was only a three-hour drive from El Castillo to Santa Elena, but we wanted to allow enough time for us to stop along the way or veer off course if we felt tugged to do so. Not wanting to rush, we left soon after breakfast with the expectation of arriving at our next hotel by early afternoon.

Driving west around Lake Arenal, every turn uncovered a scrumptious surprise with undulating pastures as fresh and luminous as a watercolour painting. As we took our time, we took it all in.

Although it was the rainy season, so far it had been sunny during most days. The rain fell only in the late afternoon for an hour or two, then subsided by early evening — a pattern we mistakenly believed would continue. By about noon, however, as we were winding our way up the rutted road through the Cloud Forest, the skies opened up. We were caught in an unexpected deluge. Brown, muddy torrents gushed down the hillside. The windows fogged up while the windshield wipers moaned at full speed. It was hard to see where the road ended and the cliff started. Kevin steered the Pathfinder as close to the mountainside as possible while trying to avoid the water-filled gullies. This was our first taste of a white-knuckle adventure.

Backtracking was too dangerous; a three-point turn on the slippery gravel could mean backing over the cliff's edge. Forward was the only option. Kevin and I were always quiet and taciturn when we were stressed — and we were definitely stressed — so for the remainder of the drive, neither of us uttered a word.

Not one word.

As we made it up the mountainside, the rain eased to a drizzle and a kaleidoscope of greens shimmered below us. Raindrops on the leaves reflected the sunbeam that poked through the misty plumes. I couldn't see any signs of houses or people, just nature at its most spectacular. I half expected gorillas to appear out of the cool mist.

I know, wrong continent, but from what I'd seen as a kid in my dad's National

Geographic *magazines, we could just as easily have been in the Virunga cloud forests of Central Africa.*

Once we reached the small town of Santa Elena, we wasted no time finding La Pensión, located in the heart of the downtown area. Calling it *downtown* might be a stretch. Perhaps *hub* would be more appropriate since Santa Elena only consisted of three main streets that formed a triangle.

With the Pathfinder parked, we left our stuff in the trunk and ran across puddles. Upon entering the hotel lobby and wiping our feet on the welcome mat, we took in — with one sweeping glance — the chill bohemian vibe. Calling it a hotel was a stretch, too, certainly by North American standards. I would have leaned into the word *hostel*, myself. Thick wooden beams crisscrossed above us, holding up the high ceiling. A handful of free-spirited travellers — the ones who seem to make a career of travelling the world on a shoestring budget — lounged on couches and hammocks. Others congregated at bistro tables in the centre of the open space, drinking coffee. A few more stood at a bar-height counter that supported a couple of antiquated desktop computers located at the other side of the room.

I can never figure out if they exude freedom or a lack of direction. That's probably why I'm so drawn to them.

I'd read in our guidebook that siblings from Texas owned the hotel. We were hoping to meet them and pick their brains for information, but first, we needed a minute to collect ourselves after our harrowing expedition.

Standing behind the office desk, a staff member suspended her conversation with one of the super groovy dudes standing next to her. "Hi, how can I help you?" she turned to us in a friendly tone, her sleek chestnut hair fluttering from the cross breeze. Her English was crystal clear. My shoulders dropped with relief.

"We'd like to book a room, please," I responded while Kevin remained distracted by how the ceiling was constructed. I could see his mind swirling with new building ideas.

"Sure thing. Would you like a room with a queen bed and your own private bathroom, or two bunks in one of the dorms with shared bathrooms?"

"We'll take a private room, please," I replied without consulting Kevin, knowing he'd appreciate having a room with its own bathroom, then continued. "We'd also like to chat with the owners at some point, if that's possible. Do you know when they'll be around?"

"Yeah, one of them will be covering for me after my shift. I'm done at six. Come back after that and I'm sure Shannon or Ran will be here. Probably both, actually," she said without vetting us and handed me the key.

Kevin and I hauled our suitcases up the metal stairs to the second-floor room and dropped them next to the bed. While we waited for the rain to stop, Kevin took a nap. I was tired but not sleepy, so to pass the time, I thumbed through the free pamphlets I had taken from the office.

An hour or so later, the rain finally stopped. Feeling calmer, we strolled around the tiny town investigating the small number of businesses: a few restaurants, a bar, a grocery store, and a variety of lodging options. Based on the flashy, attention-seeking awnings, the rest of the businesses were dedicated to tourism: coffee and chocolate tours, wildlife nature walks, whitewater rafting, and the ever-popular ziplining.

The epicentre of eco-fun.

When we returned to the hotel, we noticed there had been a shift change. A blue-eyed woman in her late thirties with a pleasant but no-nonsense quality — and the tattoos to prove it — sat on the other side of the desk. I supposed it was the sister-owner, Shannon. A tall, sturdy man wearing blue jeans and a white T-shirt emblazoned with *Pura Vida* came in just then, too. I assumed this was her brother, Ran, not only because he spoke to her in a familial manner, but because his subtle Texan twang gave him away. We walked over, introduced ourselves, and revealed our plan to relocate to Costa Rica. They were only too happy to answer any questions we had. So we peppered them.

"How easy is it to run a business in Costa Rica as an expat?" Kevin fired question number one.

"We've been running this business since 2004. It's been great, but we're in a great location. We're literally on the main drag in a high-traffic tourist area," boomed Ran as he stood with his hands on his hips.

"Like any business owner, if you treat your staff right and you know what you're doing, you can do well," Shannon added. "Being a permanent resident helps, of course, with taxes and all that."

"But don't kid yourself if you think there's less red tape than in the U.S....and Canada, I assume. This is a socialist country, so the government favours the labourer over the employer. And labour ain't cheap. You have to pay for each employee's pension, healthcare, Christmas bonus, and vacation time. ...And then there's the stuff no one tells you," Ran slid in.

Our ears perked up.

"Oh yeah, like what?" Kevin inquired.

"Well, for one, if someone sells you his business, you have to make sure that he officially lets his workers go and pays them the severance they're owed before *you* take over. Otherwise, the government sees it as a continuous period, and if you ever fire someone, you'll be responsible for paying not only from the time *you* became owner but all the years they worked for the other guy. I'm telling you, if you buy any business in this country, no matter what it is, make sure you get everything in writing. And make sure the books are clean and up to date so that you know you're starting fresh," Ran warned. "No one tells anyone this shit. Oh, and get a good lawyer, too."

"How do you go about finding a good lawyer?" I asked.

"Ours is in San José. He's good. We won't deal with any lawyers in Monteverde, not because they're not good, but because small towns, here — like anywhere — are gossip dens. We just feel better knowing our stuff is kept private," Shannon answered.

"If we ever get as far as wanting to buy something, would you mind if we reached out to you for your lawyer's contact info?" I pumped, hoping I didn't sound too forward.

"Sure — "

"I'd recommend you sign up through ARCR," Ran jumped in as he raked his wavy brown hair back with his fingers.

"What's ARCR?" asked Kevin.

"The Association of Residents of Costa Rica. It's the agency that helps foreigners immigrate. They offer all kinds of services. They'll even appoint you a lawyer so you don't have to worry about finding one yourself. They'll help y'all fill out the paperwork when you're ready to become residents. In English. Stuff like that," Ran explained.

"Thanks, this is *really* helpful, we appreciate you taking the time to talk with us," Kevin said.

"We're straight shooters, man. We don't sugarcoat things. We're not about to give you a bunch of bullshit. Don't get us wrong, we're both married and have our families here. We love it," Ran took a breath, then continued with verve. "I don't know if it's the same in Canada, but I highly recommend leaving the hustle of the so-called 'American Dream.'" Ran tilted his head and made exaggerated air quotes with his fingers.

"It's smart to do your homework. No matter where you go, there's good stuff and shitty stuff. Most people romanticize what it'll be like, y'know? They think running away from their problems will magically make those problems disappear. Some will, but new ones will crop up," Shannon chimed in, clicking the top of her pen mindlessly. *Click, click-click, click.*

We were grateful for their encouragement, but even more grateful for their candour. With so much to consider, still, nothing they shared fazed us. Where others might have felt overwhelmed, we felt emboldened.

I squeezed in one more question, "And about schools? We have a fifteen-year-old son, and we'd want him to attend an English-speaking school. I read there's one in Monteverde. Do you know anything about it?"

"Yup, the Friends School. Our kids go there and the teachers are fabulous. American Quakers founded the school in the early 1950s. They were looking for a non-militaristic society. Since Costa Rica had given up its military in 1948, they ended up settling here," Shannon combed the desk, looking for something. After she found a blank piece of paper, she clicked her pen again and started drawing a map. "You just go down here, then turn left. Keep going, you'll go by a few houses." She drew lines and boxes. "You can't miss it; it'll be on your left." *Click*. Shannon handed me her map.

"Thanks so much, we'll definitely go have a look. It sounds perfect," I replied.

Feeling satisfied with the intel we'd gathered and armed with knowledge, we thanked them.

El Castillo wasn't right for Jude, but maybe Monteverde would be. When we left the hotel, we took a left and roamed the other side of town to see if any property or business opportunity jumped out at us. We noticed a serpentarium down the road with a red sign on the door that read "*CERRADO*." My intuition told me that word meant *closed*, but just to make sure, we walked up to the glass door and pulled on the handle to see if it would open. It didn't.

I know where Jude would be hanging out if we lived here.

On our way back, we spotted a "*SE VENDE*" sign nailed to a barbed wire fence in front of an empty building.

"Hey look, a bar for sale. We could always run a bar. Tourists like to drink. In fact, I could go for a drink just about now, myself," I said to my teetotaler husband who preferred to avoid drunks.

"Or turn it into a pool hall. That could be fun." Kevin would try to repurpose the building into a business he'd actually enjoy running.

Back in our room, we spent the evening discussing every idea we could come up with...and spent the same amount of time tearing each one apart to see if any held up to scrutiny. Nothing we came up with sparked any real interest. Tired, we turned out the light and fell asleep.

On Shannon's enthusiastic recommendation, the next day we visited the Friends School just outside of town. We followed her hand-drawn directions and found ourselves in the school's parking lot fifteen minutes later.

We were greeted by an affable-looking teenager sweeping the porch. "Hello. I'm Jeremiah, but everyone calls me Jerry. Do you have an appointment?"

"Hi, Jerry. No, we don't. Would it be possible to speak to the director of the school?" Kevin stepped forward.

"Sure, I'll go get him. Please make yourselves comfortable on the couch, and I'll be right back," he leaned the broom on the wood cladding. I was struck by his calm energy and maturity.

As Kevin and I waited, we snooped around a bit, peering through glass windows into empty classes. I wondered where the kids were but then heard the clacking of hard-soled shoes coming closer. We stepped away and sat back down quickly on the couch to avoid being caught snooping.

"Good morning, welcome. My name is John. How can I help you?" the director smiled and shook our hands.

John was another expat from the U.S., so we were able to conduct our inquiries in English without any miscommunication, which was ideal.

"It's recess, so the kids are outside in the back field right now. I can show you the classrooms upstairs if you'd like."

"Thank you, we'd love that," I smiled.

John gave us a tour of the school and we shadowed him like excited puppies. "The school consists of small classes and the lessons are primarily taught in English," John informed us, "but no matter the students' native language, they all graduate speaking and reading Spanish."

Just then, we could see Jerry sweeping the hallway outside the classroom and John took the opportunity to inform us of the school's culture. "As you can see, students are expected to participate in housekeeping duties as well, where they learn to cook meals, mop and sweep the floors, and tend to our school garden. It's a holistic kind of learning, not strictly academic."

So dazzled, I was speechless. I couldn't think of any more questions to ask. It felt as if with each new piece of information the director shared, he was giving me a yummy treat to devour. I didn't care what subjects were being taught because it seemed like everything that was important was covered. And then, there was Jerry.

Jerry had me at hello.

"When are you thinking of relocating?" John quizzed.

We explained that we were in the first stages of scoping things out to see if relocating was even an option for us. We thanked the director for the guided tour and assured him that we'd be in touch if we decided to enroll Jude.

We drove away with lots to think about.

"I think the individual attention Jude would receive by being in smaller classes would benefit him," Kevin admitted as we drove back into town.

Right? I love it when we're on the same page.

As Kevin wedged the SUV into the last parking space in the hotel lot, we noticed Hanne and Hendrik standing on the sidewalk. I gave them a spirited wave as we walked over to them, then extended our arms for a heartwarming embrace.

"When'd you get here?" asked Kevin.

Hendrik looked at his watch. "About an hour ago."

"Where are Soleil and François?" I wondered.

"They're busy doing laundry, but later we're all going for dinner at that pizzeria up the road. You'll come, yes?" Hanne had a natural expectation in her tone of voice as though we couldn't possibly refuse...in a nice way. Anyone else might have sounded pushy, but not Hanne.

"Of course. That sounds great!" I accepted the invitation on behalf of Kevin as well.

"Did you get a room here?" Hendrik's eyes pointed to the building.

"Yeah, we're on the second floor, number five," Kevin pointed up toward our room.

"Oh cool. François wanted to go to a different hotel. Since he drove us up here, that's where we are, too. It's just a few blocks away," Hendrik motioned to the right. "We came to see if we could find you to let you know we had arrived."

"We've just come back from touring a school," I said.

"Was it any good?" Hanne seemed genuinely interested.

"Yeah, I loved it. It would be perfect for Jude. He wouldn't get gobbled up in a big system like back home. The classes are so much smaller and the teenager we met seemed happy to be there. Jude's not crazy about school, but I think this is the type of environment where he could thrive," I mused with confidence.

"How exciting. So, you like Monteverde then? Enough to move here?" Hendrik grinned.

"Well, there are definitely more business opportunities for us to consider compared to El Castillo, but we've only just started looking. We'll need to see more of the country before we can make any decisions," Kevin's tone was neutral, keeping his enthusiasm in check.

Later, when we got to the restaurant, we ordered our choice of pizza toppings, a pitcher of beer, and a Coke for Kevin. As we waited for our food, François recounted a nerve-racking adventure they'd had the night before, when a flat tire had resulted in them sleeping in their stranded rental. It was getting dark and without a jack to hoist and fix it, they decided it was safer to stay put.

"With four *persons* crammed inside, it was getting hot. So, we rolled down our windows to get some fresh air," François started.

Hanne confirmed it had been warm and clammy and the most uncomfortable sleep she'd ever had.

"It was so dark we couldn't see past our noses, but man that forest was loud! Everyone was sleeping, except me. I kept hearing weird noises, but not in the *distance*. Really close. I was flipping out," François described, more animated.

Hooked, Kevin and I sat on the edge of our seats and listened intently.

"My head was hanging out the window to cool off and I felt an animal brush against the car, something *sauvage*. I could feel the wildness, y'know? I turned my head and a jaguar was watching me! I almost *sheet* myself."

Kevin and I gasped.

"I stuck my head back in and rolled up my window so fast! My *panique* scared the jaguar and woke the others," François pantomimed excitedly to emphasize his words.

"We didn't see the jaguar, but we all screamed and rolled up our windows too," Hendrik laughed.

"Yeah, no one slept a wink after that," muttered Hanne.

"In the morning, I asked a farmer to help with the flat tire. The farmer was so nice and helpful, but he said it was probably just a house cat," François said, sounding incredulous. "But *non non non,* I swear to you," holding his hand on his heart, "it wasn't."

I could tell François would be sharing this story many more times, possibly adding more details, more suspense, and more creative creatures. Regardless, Kevin and I were highly entertained.

Minutes later, we were devouring our pizza and downing our drinks. Between bites and gulps, the gang planned to play tourist and take advantage of the eco-tours. We landed on ziplining and the suspension bridge tour and then meandered back to our hotels.

We spent the next day following a tour guide under the peaceful rainforest canopy learning about the native flora and fauna, then ripping and roaring over it with our hearts in our mouths. You would have thought that was enough for one day, but with the rush of exhilaration, we were ready for more, and, at the last minute, signed up for a fascinating night-walk tour.

As the guide flashed his light high up a tree, I spied my first sloth. Captivated by his long hook-like fingers wrapped around the trunk as he moved down, hand over foot, I lingered to watch his slow-motion progress.

I also got a close-up peek at my second tarantula. This one had purple stripes and crawled out from an inconspicuous hole on the side of a hill. None of us would have noticed it if it weren't for our guide's blinding light provoking it. Although our guide informed us that tarantulas are one of the least dangerous spiders in the world, it still didn't cure my spontaneous full-body squirms. But Jude was an arachnophile, and I couldn't help but think how stoked he'd be to play in a backyard such as this one, with all its critters.

The following day, we went on a fascinating coffee tour with Hanne and Hendrik. I'd never realized the coffee *bean* was actually a fruit that started out green and ripened to a deep red. It only became dark brown once it had been roasted.

The farm was a family operation handed down from one generation to another, and everything was processed by hand. They even had a wooden cart pulled by a lumbering ox. I thought it would be fun to ride in one. I was wrong. It was rickety with no shock absorbers and unforgiving on my tailbone. My joints ached riding on it, and I couldn't wait to get off. Some adventures aren't meant to be repeated, and this was one of them.

Despite hating the ox-cart ride, I fell in love with Monteverde. Kevin was less sure. He liked it as a tourist, but he couldn't wrap his head around what we would do for a living. *Something to do with tourism, I guess. The school, remember the school?*

I wasn't getting distracted by the nuts and bolts just yet. Kevin was the worrier — or perhaps the realist — whereas I tended to soak everything in on an experiential level.

"We'll figure it out," I tried to reassure him.

After a few days of taking in the sights in Monteverde, Kevin and I were ready to move on. We were on a mission, after all.

Hanne and Hendrik were ready to leave Monteverde, too, and resume their plan to bus across the country. As we were comparing maps, we realized we were going in the same general direction, so we invited them to ride along with us.

"We would love to tag along if it's no trouble," Hendrik replied.

But first, we met up with Soleil and François for breakfast. They had already made plans to travel in the opposite direction, so this was our last meal together. As we finished eating, the jovial mood turned quiet. The time had come. After exchanging hugs, Kevin and I climbed into the front seats of the Pathfinder while Hanne and Hendrik made themselves comfortable in the back. Soleil and François stood on the sidewalk and waved us off.

"Bye," we all cried out our open windows.

"*Au revoir,*" Soleil and François chimed, their voices trailing as we drove away.

The bittersweet reality of being a world traveller is that sometimes the bonds that are formed last a lifetime and other times they only last for a short season. In the case of Soleil and François, sadly, we never saw them again.

Pacific Coast

We left the mountainous area and drove west toward the Pacific Coast. We stopped in Liberia for lunch before reaching Tamarindo, a small surfing town known for having good swell conditions. From the car window, we watched the white lapping waves build momentum and then crash onto the shoreline. From a distance, it looked so inviting. The temperature was much hotter than up in the mountains, and, lucky for us, our hotel faced the beachfront. Having been sitting in the car for most of the morning, we couldn't wait to change into our bathing suits and go for a swim.

As we approached the water, I noticed the charcoal beach. "What the hell? Where's the postcard-perfect, champagne-coloured sand?" I said to no one in particular. It wasn't manicured or combed neatly, either. It wasn't littered with garbage, but it looked messy.

Fallen coconuts and palm tree fronds were strewn everywhere.

"*Ow!* These sticks and stones are sharp. Be careful, guys," Hendrik cautioned as we all walked barefoot on the gritty ground.

It was a perfect natural mess in a perfect natural setting, but not what I was expecting and it kind of bummed me out. Later, I read that the colour of the sand is the result of eroded lava erupting from nearby volcanoes over thousands of years. Costa Rica has six active volcanoes and sixty-one that are considered dormant. It made perfect sense that the sand would be so dark, but I longed for stretches of that sand-washed silk feeling between my toes, as promised in glossy travel brochures.

As we continued south, we were struck by the sheer number of "*SE VENDE*" placards in Tamarindo. It seemed like every other property was advertising a purchase opportunity. I was encouraged that we had lots of options to choose from, but also wondered if it was a warning sign.

Is there a mass exodus happening? If so, why? And where is everyone going?

We stayed in the more well-known towns dotted along the seashore — the ones we had read about during our research phase: Samára, Montezuma, Jacó, Quepos, Manuel Antonio, Dominical, and Uvita. Each one seemed overrun by expats, and if we decided to move to this area, we would be adding to those numbers.

Having a ready-made community of English speakers would make it easier, but it wouldn't be the cultural experience Kevin and I were hoping for. Itsy-bitsy villages that sprinkled the countryside between the larger towns did attract fewer expats, but they offered no respite from the heat or the critters that came with it.

We were having a wonderful time in spite of the sweltering conditions...just as long as we weren't trying to imagine ourselves living and working in 34°C (93°F) every day. I was sure the insufferable buzzing flies would become annoying too. I'd be reduced to slapping myself silly to kill them. It would be miserable. I would be miserable.

The more we travelled down the coast, the more we realized a beach lifestyle was not for us. What had started out as a focused scouting expedition became a fun road trip with new friends. We lost interest in looking at properties and became full-fledged tourists instead, which was okay by me as it made Monteverde the only contender. In terms of climate, it was the clear winner in my mind.

Kevin and I had never travelled with anyone else before, and Hanne and Hendrik were easy-going companions. They didn't get frustrated with us, nor did they get on our nerves, as can so easily happen when sharing the same space day after day. We pressed onward toward Puerto Jiménez.

While in Puerto Jiménez, we decided to visit the OSA Wildlife Sanctuary across the bay as bona fide tourists. We purchased a packaged deal and boarded a motorboat named *La Sirena*.

As our skipper, Pedro, pointed to a pod of dolphins swimming starboard side, the refreshing wind on our faces whistled loudly. We couldn't hear a word he was saying so we simply nodded politely. Once we reached the Gulfo Dulce shore, we gathered with the other sightseers who had arrived on their own hired boats from other hotels.

"Hi. I'm Carol, co-owner of the sanctuary. Welcome." Tall and toned, Carol was clearly a roll-up-her-sleeves, no-nonsense, speaks-her-mind kind of woman and I sensed everyone on the tour was a bit intimidated by her.

Everyone hushed as she explained the purpose and mission of the sanctuary.

"My husband, Earl, and I created this place to rehabilitate mostly monkeys and birds that have been injured or orphaned. Our goal is to release them once they're healthy, but when that's not possible, they remain in the sanctuary for the rest of their lives. Like Sweetie here," Carol added, glancing over at the cheeky primate perched on her left shoulder. "Sadly, a large percentage of the animals we rescue fall victim to the illegal pet trade that goes on here. They're captured young, often neglected or abused, and then abandoned once they become too big to manage. Some people don't realize wild animals belong in the wild."

The crowd moaned in shock and disgust. Humans can be so cruel.

We spent the day hanging on Carol's every word and meeting toucans, parrots, sloths, peccaries, and more monkeys. Some monkeys roamed freely but others lived in enclosures so large we couldn't see the chain-link fence on the other side. Having all that space allowed them to socialize and forage for food in their natural habitat while still being protected. Many showed off their lively personality while the shy ones retreated and hid.

Sweetie, however, was my favourite; she was precocious, funny, and highly entertaining. At one point, she came right up to me and pulled my hand down straight onto her head. I played along and scratched her behind the ears. After a minute or so, I stopped and pulled myself up from my crouching position. Although this was a cute interaction, I thought we were done.

Oh no, not a chance.

Sweetie grabbed my hand and begged for more affection, urging me to tickle her under one arm. I complied, but after a few minutes, stopped again. Unrelenting, she coerced me into tickling under the other arm, stroking below her shoulder, then rubbing under her chin. There was no escaping her demands. Every time I stopped, she insisted I continue. She wouldn't take *no* for an answer. Then, with a saucy squint, Sweetie looked over at the amused onlookers and emitted a squeaky snickering sound as only spider monkeys can. I was obviously the object of her ridicule. Everyone laughed. There was no denying she was the master of her well-trained pet.

Me!

After the excursion ended, we made our way back to our rendezvous spot on the beach. The *thrum-thump-thud* of the outboard engine signalled Pedro was ready and waiting. Hanne, Hendrik, Kevin, and I climbed aboard *La Sirena* one by one. Facing the back of the boat, we watched the endless white foam trailing behind us while the sun drifted lower onto the horizon. When we reached the other side of the bay, Pedro manoeuvred the boat parallel to the dock and hopped out quickly to secure the bow line. Then Hendrik swung the stern line so Pedro could fasten it to the mooring ring. The engine was now *spit-squirt-spurting*. The wake pounding against the side of the hull exaggerated the rhythmic sway and we could barely keep our balance.

"Gracias, Pedro!" we yelped, one after another, wobbling out of the boat and feeling a little off kilter.

We toddled over the sand dunes to the hotel and got cleaned up for dinner.

As we ate our meal and recapped our time together, the orange sun disappeared. And while we raised our half-empty glasses and toasted to our friendship, none of us could hide our exhaustion. We all anticipated the eight-hour drive north to San José the next morning and needed a good night's sleep, so called it an early night.

At the crack of dawn, all packed and ready to go, we loaded our bags and weary selves into the SUV. From Puerto Jiménez, we backtracked to Dominical. From there, we turned east to San Isidro de El General, then north up the Pan-American Highway, stopping to stretch our legs and grab snacks along the way. As we climbed higher in elevation, the air became crisp, clean, and cool.

For our last pit stop before reaching the city limits, Kevin pulled over on the side of the road. It felt like we were sitting on top of the world. The four of us got out of the SUV and spun 360°, taking in the panoramic view.

Before us, in a valley between two mountains like something out of a children's book, a vibrant rainbow stretched across the large divide, which was stacked above an equally vivid second arc directly below it.

A double rainbow! My symbol of hope and good luck.

Feeling disappointed that we hadn't found a place to call home during our travels, I wished we had had more time to explore this particular area. However tempting, we needed to get back to the city to catch our flight the next day. There was no time, and I felt gutted. I regretted spending so much time on the hot, sticky coast where we knew we'd never want to live. Why did we stop our scouting expedition?

I pressed my heavy head against the passenger window for the rest of the drive. The dramatic contrast of beautiful green countryside rolling into the grim, grey city punctuated the stress of driving our rental between zooming cars in pot-holed streets. As we dropped Hanne and Hendrik off at their hotel, gratitude mixed with a twinge of sadness bubbled up. We wrapped our arms around each other and promised we would keep in touch

Flight Home

Our round-trip foray through Costa Rica had covered 1,865 km, or 1,158 miles, but we'd only skimmed the surface.

How can such a small country also be so vast?

Kevin and I were quiet on the plane home as we pondered our past two weeks. Although we didn't speak, my mind whirred.

Can we parachute into a foreign land where we don't have a clue how we'd make a living, uproot one child who doesn't like change, leave behind the child who thrives on it, and leave all the security and comforts we're accustomed to? Sure, we made good friends, and we saw spectacular sights, but are we really prepared to pull the ripcord?

Regardless of all my uncertainty, I had enough sense to know that if we didn't do something drastic soon, we never would.

By the time we were deliberating about Costa Rica, Kevin had transplanted himself twice. He had moved from England to Canada when he was twenty-one and stayed four years, moved back to England for twelve, then returned to Canada when he was thirty-seven. Moving internationally didn't faze him, but moving to a country where English was not the primary language did. With my French-Canadian background and a couple of years of Spanish and other languages under my belt, I felt less daunted about the language barrier. I was confident, whether justified or not, that given the necessity to communicate, I'd pick up Spanish again relatively quickly.

As I turned over considerations in my head, I was sure Kevin was doing the same. Although I knew the language barrier would be a factor, I braced myself to hear his other concerns once he was done contemplating silently.

We landed, sailed through customs, and picked up our luggage from the rolling carousel. Canada's deep autumn colours greeted us outside the airport's sliding doors. As we waited for the shuttle to drive us back to our vehicle, Kevin turned to me and said, "I know we didn't find what we were looking for and it felt more like a holiday, but if we can find the right property in the right location for the right price, I think we should go for it."

I was more than a little shocked. We hadn't fallen head-over-heels in love with any property that whispered, *"This is it."* And despite my attempts to convince Kevin that Monteverde could work, it had been futile. He wasn't feeling inspired to settle there. So I thought the trip had been downgraded to a pleasant diversion, nothing more.

The dream was still alive!

Three
First Contact

October 2011

O nly two days later, the Costa Rica house-hunting agenda began in earnest. Armed with a better idea of which areas we would consider moving to — and more importantly, which ones we wouldn't — Kevin started looking online at real estate properties. First, he searched for parcels of land with no buildings because they were always so much cheaper. Having renovated our home from top to bottom, he wasn't daunted by having to start from scratch and looked forward to the challenge. He also searched for farms, small businesses, and hotels. Neither of us had reached retirement age and we couldn't rely on savings. Whatever we decided to do, we'd have to make an income.

A lot would depend on how much someone was willing to pay for our Canadian suburban home. People tend to overestimate the worth of their house because they're so attached — *sentimentality is priceless*. With all the work we'd done to reimagine and modernize our outdated 1950s post-war dwelling, we were no exception to that rule.

Kevin stumbled upon an internet site advertising properties for sale in Costa Rica. However, it didn't show the date the listings were posted, so we weren't sure if we were looking at something current or wasting our time on something that had long been sold. Kevin scanned hundreds of listings. The gorgeous properties with their infinity pools, endless sunsets, and ever-present views were way over our price range. Those that fit within our budget offered uninspired shacks with no land or business opportunities.

But one listing was different.

Really different.

"Hey hon, come take a look at this," Kevin called me over.

I moved from the couch and snuggled beside him on the loveseat.

"It's an old trout farm with seven ponds and a river that flows through the property. Remember when we were obsessed with finding a property with a river or lake in France?"

"Yeah, we couldn't find the right property in France, but maybe that's because our river was in Costa Rica all along," I mused.

"It'd be pretty cool to live by a river. And seven ponds, that'd be even more awesome. Here's the main house," he clicked open the picture file to enlarge it so we could have a closer look.

"Whoa, look at that huge fireplace. And there's a loft too. Nice!"

"Vegetable and flower gardens. A guesthouse. There's so much potential. We could grow our own food and maybe sell it at markets." Kevin clicked from one picture to the next, then read the marketing blurb that boasted, "Spring-like weather all year round with no mosquitoes."

"Music to my ears, baby, music to my ears!" I said.

It seemed too good to be true. The mountain paradise was located in a natural preserve and listed at a price low enough that we might be able to afford it with a little negotiation.

"Should we find out if it's still for sale?" I pressed.

"Sure. There's no point dreaming about it if it's no longer on the market."

It took me an hour to compose a note. At first, I bombarded the seller with questions. Then I edited, trying not to sound too eager. I agonized over how to strike the right tone...friendly and sincere, but not too desperate.

"Anne, what are you doing?" Kevin questioned, slightly exasperated. "Just ask if the property is still for sale. That's all we need to know right now. They don't need to know our life story."

Kevin didn't like typing so he left the correspondence task to me, but I tend to overthink and overwrite. I backspaced and deleted everything I'd written. I went against every fibre of my being and kept it brief:

Hello.

My husband, Kevin, and I are inquiring about your Costa Rica property. It's beautiful. Is it still for sale?

Kind regards,
Anne

I pressed the *send* button before I could embellish it further.

I waited.

I checked my inbox every few minutes, half-expecting to receive an immediate response. After a couple of hours, I got bored and assumed my note was sitting in an abandoned inbox somewhere in cyberspace.

Hours became days.

We went to work during the day and continued the search during the evening. It was torture. Nothing compared to the trout farm, and we now measured every property against it. We wouldn't consider anything less. I wanted to see more of the trout farm, not more listings. And there was no one to blame but myself. A glutton for punishment, I had pored over each picture uploaded on the sales website. It's like those few pictures were transporting me to the centre of my soul. I couldn't shake the feeling.

Four days later, as I filtered through several unread messages, I zeroed in on a reply email to our inquiry.

I inhaled, trying to slow my heart rate.

Rubbing my palms on my jeans, I swallowed and stared. Bracing myself, I clicked on the email:

Dear Anne,

Thanks for contacting me about the farm. Yes, it's still on the market. My wife, Mona, and I are retired folks from the U.S. We've spent the last fifteen winters in Costa Rica, getting away from the Pacific West Coast's cold, damp weather. We only live in Costa Rica from January to early April, so we're available to show you the property between those months if you're serious buyers. Please keep me posted.

Kind regards,
Rick

"IT'S STILL FOR SALE! IT'S STILL FOR SALE! IT'S STILL FOR SALE!" I sang while dancing around the living room.

Kevin walked in on me during my happy dance. He hugged me, then pulled away as he looked directly into my eyes. Then he spoke to me in a tone intended to calm a skittish horse down. "That's great news, but — "

"But what?" I worried Kevin had experienced a change of heart.

"But let's just take one step at a time and make sure we're crossing our Ts and dotting our Is, okay?"

We emailed Rick several times, asking more questions. My overthinking and over-writing came in handy. None of his answers raised any red flags. In fact, they clinched our resolve to investigate further. Rick's emails were much more succinct than mine, but he usually attached a batch of pictures, which was even better than words. In one email he included pictures of the land survey, showing where the river flowed in relation to the land and outbuildings. We tried to piece everything together in our minds and to ensure we weren't being duped, Kevin looked up the property on Google Maps, then on Bing. It appeared to be legit. Nestled in a small, rural community called Río Blanco, the beautiful 37-acre property sat at 2,045 metres, or 6,710 ft, in elevation within the Dota mountain range. It was real.

"Hey, that's where we saw the double rainbow!" I blurted out.

What are the chances? What does it mean?

I was quietly optimistic but restless too. Rick insisted that if we were truly interested, we needed to travel south and spend a few days on the farm to have a proper look. He wouldn't entertain making any kind of deal over the internet, and neither would we.

In my last exchange, I told Rick:

We'll think about it and get back to you soon.

Staying focused and motivated at work became nearly impossible. I made mistakes and forgot the most obvious things. With the lure of a dream life, I became easy bait. Of course, much of this was my own doing. I had screen-captured my favourite pictures of the river, ponds, and serene pastures, then designed a wallpaper montage for my desktop. Every time I glanced at my screen, it glowed with hypnotizing pictures that shaped a new perspective of my future.

Our future.

At the time, I couldn't pinpoint whether I was drawn to the photos due to the culmination of stress and fatigue or if the adventurous spirit I'd stuffed deep inside me was busting to the surface. Either way, I knew something had to change.

Marvelling at each additional picture Rick sent us, Kevin and I mulled things over... *and over...and over...* together and separately. From one minute to the next, my stomach either fluttered or flip-flopped. Meanwhile, Kevin's furrowed brow contradicted his boyish grin. Sitting on the couch late one night, my right index finger, which had only recently been resting on my laptop's touchpad, glided the cursor up and opened a new tab. In the search bar, I tapped the keys and spelled *E-x-p-e-d-i-a.* As if possessed, my fingers were scrolling and clicking. They landed on a flight itinerary for the week between Jude's last exam in late January and the beginning of his second semester. I was about to click...

What am I doing?

I snapped out of my trance and looked up at Kevin. "What do you say we spend a week in Costa Rica the first week of February?" I asked, continuing before I let him answer. "We'll bring Jude. By that time, we'll all need a holiday from the winter blahs and we can go have a look at this property. I'm done hanging in the balance. We're either doing this, or we're not."

"Sounds good, Costa Rica in February it is," Kevin said without wavering.

Woohoo!

Four
Property Visit

February 2012

Dan the Passport Man

Having left home at 3:30 a.m. and driven an hour and a half, we arrived at the Buffalo, New York airport before daybreak. Without another soul in line, Kevin, Jude, and I breezed on through to the American Airlines check-in counter. The man standing on the other side greeted us with a perky smile as he took our passports. He looked up at the screen, then down again. He scrutinized one of the passports, then placed it on the counter before taking a long look at the other two. Without explanation, he left his post. Finally, he returned, looked directly at me, and said, "I cannot let you board the plane. Although your passport is considered valid in the U.S., your passport must be valid for ninety days to enter Costa Rica. Unfortunately, yours is only seventy-five days. The good news is Mr. Lawrence and the young man may board."

What? Are you kidding me?

For a moment, I wondered if I was still fast asleep having one of those pesky nightmares before a big trip. Oh, it was a nightmare all right, but the very-much-awake kind.

Now what?

Kevin and Jude waffled and nearly didn't board, not wanting to leave me behind. Our trip, however, wasn't a relax-in-the-sun vacation. This trip was the kind that could change *everything*.

Kevin had no choice. He and Jude had to get on the plane. Besides, our tickets were non-refundable. We would lose not only the opportunity to see the paradise we'd been dreaming about for the last four months, but several thousand dollars' worth of plane tickets too.

Double whammy, but not in the colourful rainbow kind of way.

I'd be damned if we wasted that much money.

"If you can get your passport renewed by tomorrow morning, I can get you on the seven o'clock flight at no extra charge," the gate agent informed me in an encouraging tone.

"Thank you," I said, then turned to Kevin, "but even if I can't, you need to go so you can report back."

"Yeah, I suppose," Kevin reasoned.

I wished them a safe flight and Kevin tossed me the keys to the 4Runner before he and Jude walked through security.

I jogged back to the parking lot. The frigid air bit my face and the sky was just as dark as when we'd first arrived. I turned on the ignition, cranked up the heat, and breathed into my cupped hands while I waited for the GPS to guide me home. I watched it search for a satellite signal, loading to 99%. Then, *nothing*. It was stuck.

Come on, don't do this.

Kevin had driven to the airport that morning and I had barely been conscious at that god-awful hour. I needed GPS. I decided to check my phone's Google Maps app and found instead that my phone had 8% battery life remaining. My charger was in Kevin's bag.

Jesus!

I studied the route on Google Maps, memorizing the highway names and numbers, and whether to drive east or west, north or south. Just as I began to feel confident I had it all straight in my head, I remembered I'd left my driver's license back in Burlington. Kevin had planned to drive, so I did the responsible thing and emptied my wallet of all supposed non-essential cards.

Well, I thought it was a good idea at the time.

Feeling like an outlaw, I steeled myself and started driving regardless of my precarious situation. I kept to the speed limit as I imagined calling Kevin: "Hi honey, I didn't *quite* get to the passport office as planned. I'm calling you from a holding cell. I'm being detained for driving without a license in the U.S. So, *how's Costa Rica?*"

Thankfully, the roads were still empty. Although I felt anxious about a hundred different things, the highway gods were watching over me. Miraculously, I found my way back to the border and presented my passport without incident.

Oh, Canada. From nervous outlaw to strong and free!

I paid the toll and exhaled with relief, but I was only halfway off the hook. I was still driving without a license, but I hoped if an officer stopped me at that point, I'd merely get a ticket. Nevertheless, I continued to drive just under the speed limit. I drove straight home, picked up my driver's license, and headed off to the passport office in Mississauga. This particular passport office was forty-five minutes from our house in a mall with easy parking.

I arrived at the passport office at 8:00 a.m., just as the doors opened and the lines were short. Things were looking up! After hearing a quick explanation of my predicament, the clerk instructed, "Go downstairs and get your picture taken first, then while you're waiting for the photos to be processed, fill out this form. It will save you time."

One of the sections asked for the names, addresses, phone numbers, and employment information of two people who had known me for over two years, who would vouch for me, and were not family members. I knew lots of people, but I could barely remember my own name at that point, let alone *their* names and contact info. I started to panic but focused and regained my composure. I decided to call two colleagues from my workplace. They had both known me for well over a decade and I could ask them for their details at the same time. I grabbed my cell phone.

A remaining battery life of 3%.

Trying to stay calm, I called the office. Lisa, the receptionist, answered. I wasted no time chitchatting and asked for what I needed. She gave me her details and then — like a baton in a relay race — she passed me over to the second coworker. Thankfully, Laura was happy to help too.

Just as I finished filling out the form, the photographer handed me my official passport photos. I paid, thanked him, and rushed to the second floor, taking a number and sitting down with my documentation ready. Considering the craziness of it all, everything was going smoothly.

Within a few minutes, clerk number two, Dan, called me over to his wicket. Sick of repeating myself, I was sure it was written all over my face, but Dan was kind and empathetic. After examining my paperwork, he said he needed just one last thing to be able to rush it through same-day delivery.

My flight itinerary.

"I have a confirmation number, does that count?" I asked, rummaging for the piece of paper. Dan insisted he must see the itinerary.

"If I can get on the internet and show you the itinerary on my phone, would that be good enough?"

Please say yes.

Dan looked furtively right, then left, checking for eavesdroppers, then whispered, "Normally, we wouldn't be allowed to accept that, but okay."

Oh my God, what a nice guy.

My hands shook as I tapped furiously...*tap tap tap*. I was on the airline's website... *tap tap tap*. Under my account...*tap tap tap*. Nearly there...

Got it!

Grinning ear to ear, I turned the phone to my new best friend and the screen went... *Black.*

A little empty battery icon showed 0%. I wanted to cry, but if I had let myself shed even one tear that would have been the end. That one trickle would have become a waterfall, and I would have dissolved into its pool right there on the floor.

So dramatic. How badly do you want this new life? Pull yourself together!

"Can you get to a computer, print out the itinerary, and return it to me?" Dan asked with a hopeful look. "Or to save time, just fax it to me?" he added, opening his eyes wide with this stellar idea. Time was ticking. I had two hours to meet the eleven o'clock deadline for same-day processing.

"Yes, I think I can do that."

Just as I readied myself to leave, Dan dropped a bomb. "When I call both your contacts, they must pick up." He stressed the point by deepening his voice an octave. "I can't leave a message and won't call twice due to time constraints."

Dan gave me the opportunity to change my contact information or add more names. I frantically started writing a list of a dozen other coworkers but realized it would take too long to get all their details now that my phone was dead. So I stopped. With the newly scribbled names crossed out, I returned the form unchanged. I gathered my things, fled the mall, and drove like hell to the office.

Fifteen minutes later, the elevator doors opened, and through the glass door, I saw Lisa behind her desk. I nearly kissed her. I quickly ran through the plan, and she promised she wouldn't budge. As I ran down the hallway, stunned coworkers called out questions as I passed, but I shook my head — *not now* — and kept running. I found a cell phone charger and then printed and faxed my itinerary. I may have sent some of my colleagues into a tizzy, but I was calm, focused, and on a mission. *Operation: Get My Passport* was a go!

When Dan called to confirm he'd received my fax and intended to start calling my contacts, I felt prepared. By the time I reached the reception area, Lisa was already talking on the phone, signalling with a thumbs-up that it was Dan. I felt dizzy with relief and a little queasy too.

So much for being calm.

I dashed back to warn Laura but found her office empty. Thirty long seconds later, she sauntered down the hall with a mug of coffee in her hand while I gesticulated wildly for her to get back to her seat. I'd barely finished begging her to stay put when the phone rang.

Nothing to do but go to my office and collapse on my swivel chair.

Passport buddy Dan called a few minutes later to confirm he had everything he needed. He couldn't guarantee my passport would be ready by 4:00 p.m., but he put my chances at 95%. I couldn't help but fixate on the other 5%. The whole rigamarole took over two hours. It was 11:30 a.m. — thirty minutes past Dan's stated deadline. All I could do was show up at the passport office at 4:00 p.m. There was nothing left for Dan to do but wish me luck.

In an effort to whittle away the time, I waited for my phone to fully charge, told Lisa and Laura the saga without divulging the underlying reason for the Costa Rica trip, and finally addressed other coworkers' curiosity. Then I wandered aimlessly, trying to stay out of the way, until it was time to head back to the passport office.

I arrived not a minute early, not a minute late. While my mind ruminated about whether to give it another few minutes, my feet edged forward toward the counter. The pleasant young woman who greeted me there sifted through a grey metal box.

Nothing with my name on it.

I started to sweat a little, but denial had always served me well and I refused to believe that I wouldn't be on that plane. I closed my eyes and willed my passport to be ready.

My pulse hammered in my temples as she got up from her stool, exchanged a few words with one of her colleagues, then returned and checked the drawer under her desk.

And voilà! Come to mama, you sweet thing.

After paying $150 (rush delivery has its price), the navy-blue booklet recognized worldwide as proof of Canadian citizenship was finally in my possession.

For the second time that day, I exhaled deeply.

Déjà Vu

My "impossible" mission was accomplished. With my passport finally in hand, I was running on fumes. My stomach growled — an angry reminder that I hadn't had anything to eat or drink since leaving the house at 3:30 that morning. A celebratory dinner of eggs on toast was in order.

I pulled into the driveway, feeling like a lifetime had passed since I'd run in to grab my license.

What a whirlwind.

I unlocked the door, walked into our quiet home, and set my purse on the credenza. "Honey, I'm home!" I called out, cracking myself up. My voice carried through the open space and bounced off the cathedral ceiling.

As I sat on the couch in the echoing emptiness, I worried about how Kevin and Jude were getting along. Things hadn't been smooth; the blended family dynamic that plagued so many families had been a bubbling undercurrent in our household for some time. They rarely spent any time together and barely spoke. I was caught in the middle. I tried to be present, tried to understand, and tried to support my husband *and* my son. It seemed like I failed them both most days.

When we told Jude about the farm in Costa Rica, he didn't quite know what to make of it. I showed him pictures and drew him in with talks of reptiles and insects. He didn't show any visible resistance, but I knew I would have to tread lightly. I couldn't oversell it; he would smell the desperation. I needed to make the features and benefits attractive enough for him to feel like he was making his own decision. I started to feel anxious thinking about the two of them spending so much time together without me as a buffer.

I was also worried about their plane landing safely. I hadn't been in touch with them since they left. I hadn't been listening to the news. The whole day had been about me and my bloody passport.

What if I wasn't meant to be on that plane? What if something bad happened to them?

At 7:00 p.m., I logged onto my laptop to video chat with Kevin and Jude, hoping to pacify my active imagination. My heart pounded in my ears.

Then, at long last, I heard Kevin's voice, "Hello, sweetie."

My eyes welled up. "Hey guys," I sniffed. "How did everything go?"

"Our flights and layover were tiring but uneventful," Kevin replied tiredly, then continued. "Flying without you, not knowing what was happening back home, wondering what we'd do if you couldn't renew your passport, was stressful."

"So, Mum, don't keep us hanging over here, did you get it?" Jude jumped in, impatient with the small talk.

They were both waiting to hear my news, and I didn't have it in me to tease them. Smiling, I held the brand-spanking-new passport up to the tiny camera lens. They whooped and hollered with relief.

"It's been quite a day. I'm exhausted. But I'll be on that plane first thing tomorrow morning," I declared like my life depended on it.

We ran through the new plan: Kevin and Jude would leave San José and drive to the farm to meet Rick. And I'd meet them there with a little help from Sister Gladys. She was arranging for her personal driver, Alex, to pick me up at the airport.

Bless her! Bless Alex! Bless Dan, the Passport Man!

From the airport, Alex would drive me directly to El Empalme, a small village right on the Pan-American Highway about thirty minutes away from Rick's property. Jude and Kevin would come and pick me up in our rental. With our strategy in place, Kevin, Jude, and I said goodnight and logged off. Knowing they'd landed safely, seeing that they looked positively jovial with one another, and knowing what the next steps entailed, the adrenaline quickly wore off. I felt shattered. I dozed until my alarm went off at 3:30 a.m. Despite beginning with a bad case of déjà vu, the endgame would be different this time.

First Impression

My flights were on time…albeit twenty-four hours later. As promised, Sister Gladys' driver, Alex, greeted me at the airport at 2:30 p.m. and drove me the two hours it took to get to El Empalme, where Kevin, Jude, and I reunited according to Plan B.

Amen!

Whatever drama I lived through the day before didn't seem to matter anymore amid the fabulous vistas. We drove from El Empalme to La Trinidad, a little pueblo that was barely a spit on the map. If you blinked, you'd miss it. La Trinidad consisted of a convenience store, a school, and a church — *that was it*. The descent from La Trinidad to the property was 5 km, or 3 miles, on a winding dirt road with magnificent panoramic views. The word *remote* came to mind.

"Wow, this really is out of the way, isn't it?"

"It sure is," Kevin replied.

"Any idea what the population of Río Blanco is? That's one question I never asked Rick."

"If we move here, we'll be bumping it up to sixty-three," Kevin laughed, keeping his eyes on the road as we dipped and turned, the SUV bobbing up and down the rough terrain.

"Oh wow, that's less than the number of people who live on our street," I mused. Then, eager to know, I asked, "Tell me about your day so far."

"We arrived at noon, met Rick, and basically spent the last four hours chatting. Rick arrived alone a few weeks ago to open up the house," Kevin responded.

Rick had mentioned in one of our last emails that his son and daughter-in-law were expecting their first child in mid-February. Not wanting to miss the birth of her grandchild, his wife, Mona, had stayed behind to lend a helping hand. Whatever questions we had during our stay, Rick would have to be the one to answer them.

"Rick didn't waste any time showing us the property," Kevin carried on.

"Yeah, and then about an hour later, we went fishing," Jude interjected from the back seat.

"In the river?"

"No, in the big pond behind the house. It was pretty cool. I caught a fish," he informed me with more enthusiasm than I'd heard in quite some time.

That's not saying much but I'll take it.

I guessed that was when Jude had caught his sunburn, too. "You've caught some colour already."

"Yeah, no more pale, pasty boy," Jude chuckled.

There was no denying his mood was more relaxed than it had been in some time. He and Kevin were bantering like old friends. A pleasant surprise.

"So what are your initial thoughts?" I poked, looking over at Kevin from the front passenger seat.

"I don't want to say. I want you to see it the way Jude and I saw it for the first time. I don't want to taint your first impression," Kevin was trying to keep his cool, but I could tell he was excited. I thought he was going to burst.

We had seen many pictures over the last few months but still didn't know exactly how everything fit together. Like a puzzle, we had all the pieces and while some pieces fit in obvious ways, others were harder to figure out. Back home, Kevin had searched the property on Bing Maps from the survey Rick had sent us. Looking for ways to be as informed as possible, Kevin took the time to calculate the size of each pond based on the acreage. It appeared the ponds were significantly smaller than what Rick had claimed on the real estate listing and Kevin was prepared to use the discrepancy as a negotiation tactic. He had done his homework and would not be taken advantage of or lied to.

We drove up to the entrance. Already familiar with the routine, Jude got out of the all-wheel-drive Mitsubishi and opened the old worn gate while Kevin drove through. Jude secured the gate behind us with the wooden latch and climbed back into the back seat.

Immediately to the left of the driveway, a patch of lawn — no buildings, just green space — had been mowed. As the driveway veered to the right, under the shade of towering trees, dense moss draped over the craggy ground. Then the road, as though carved right out of the hillside, cut through a tiny orchard of peach, plum, and avocado trees, before curving around a bend.

From this vantage point, the mystery unfolded before me with a view that took my breath away. The fertile valley revealed more avocado trees tucked into the undulating slopes and clumps of swaying cedar, alder, and bamboo that lined the edge of the river below. Beyond the rushing water, another lush hillside stretched up to the clear blue sky. Straight in front of me stood a grandiose two-storey chalet — unlike the humble homes we had seen on the way down. With its sharp-pitched roof, protruding gables, and a balcony jutting out and balancing on pillars, it looked like it had been transplanted from the Swiss Alps. The only hint that I was still in Costa Rica was its yellow paint and green trim, which infused a distinct tropical feel.

We descended down...down...down...until we reached a flat interlocking brick section. Gardens filled with flowers in magnificent shades of yellow, orange, purple, pink, white, red, and blue bordered this parking area. The guesthouse where Kevin and I would be sleeping was to our left, and beyond it, I could hear the river.

Things looked familiar. We had studied the pictures a thousand times. As soon as we got out of the SUV, Kevin and Jude led me around to the back of the main house.

"Holy guacamole!" my jaw dropped. Whatever paradise I had conjured up based on the photos Rick had sent was a lackluster version of what surrounded me.

A rounded outdoor bread oven and an in-ground, concrete hot tub flanked the large terracotta-tiled terrace. Both were handmade, and both were wood-burning. The terrace connected the main house to the largest of the trout ponds.

The pond's quaint little island looked like a mirage. A footpath followed the length of the pond on its left side, with the river directly below to the left of the footpath. Orange, lemon, and lime trees lined the right bank. A forest and a pasture extended beyond all of this.

I was speechless.

My mind whirled and everything felt rather surreal. It didn't feel like the Costa Rica we had visited just five months earlier: There were no monkeys, no scorpions, no scary snakes, no big hairy spiders, and no sloths. And, as promised, there were no blood-sucking mosquitoes! The high altitude offered a completely different wildlife experience from the lowlands. This was bird country.

Rick came out of the house and Kevin introduced us. Rick was a charismatic fellow, tall with a booming voice. He heard us talking about birds and informed us that the elusive resplendent quetzal lived on the property and had been spotted on several occasions.

"That's where it makes its home," he pointed to a tree. "This exquisite bird also has a distinctive call that helps birdwatchers pinpoint where it's perched before ever seeing it." Rick narrated his lines like a well-rehearsed David Attenborough script.

This was exciting news; however, both Kevin and I commented on how quiet it was. We didn't see or hear many birds except for a few hummingbirds.

Not sure if I believe the glowing sales pitch.

Once the pleasantries were out of the way, Kevin and I excused ourselves.

"It'll be dark soon. I'll show you the rest of the property in the morning," Kevin said to me as he lugged my suitcase into the guesthouse.

After I freshened up, we met up with Rick and Jude in the main house for dinner. The house had one master bedroom and a loft where Jude would sleep during our visit. As Jude sat on a stool at the kitchen island, I noticed he had changed into long pants and his fleece hoodie.

As the sun went down, so did the temperature. Rick lit a large log in the huge fireplace. The fireplace was so big he had to crawl into it to light it. And the log was so large, Rick had to dowse it with kerosene to get it to ignite. That sucker burned all night without having to be poked or prodded, and it kept the house toasty warm.

Rick baked the trout with lemon and rosemary — both from the garden — in the small toaster oven that rested on top of the small fridge.

So fresh and tasty.

We had so many questions. After each bite, we'd pump Rick for more information. I was especially interested in how this property had been developed into a commercial fish farm. We knew from basic email correspondence that Rick and Mona had bought the property from the man who had started the rainbow trout business. The property boasted a hatchery with seven ponds — all interconnected by an aqueduct system. Rick had mentioned in passing that this section of the property was engineered by a gentleman from Switzerland years earlier and I wanted to know more.

"Developing this hilly landscape into a trout farm seems like it would need a certain kind of vision. It's pretty amazing the engineering that went into it. Do you know what made the Swiss guy go to all the trouble?"

"He married a Tica and needed to make money to provide for his family up here. He was pretty smart and since the property butted against the downflow of the river, he figured a way to use it to his advantage," Rick explained.

Trout farming in mountainous regions that have sustainable water resources was an enticing employment solution in areas where income-generating options were limited. Swiss Man was the first habitant to bring trout farming not only to Río Blanco but to the Dota mountains. Or so we were told.

Swiss Man devised an efficient, gravity-fed system. The property was topographically higher in elevation at one end and sloped down at just the right pitch to the other end. The diverted river water rushed through a concrete channel at the one end of the property where it gushed into the first two cascading ponds, one after the other. These shallow ponds acted as filters specifically designed to collect dirt and sediment. The clean water then flowed down a manmade canal, was redirected into metal pipes that extended above each pond, and spilled onto the surface with a splash. This canal came down the whole length of the property and ended up reconnecting to the river at the other end.

There was also an underground conduit system that started at the sediment ponds. This kept the water flowing continuously from one pond to another, creating lovely waterfalls. Water pressure and gravity did all the work. Each pond had two gates: one to let the water flow in and another at the opposite end to let the water flow out. The gates could be adjusted in a way that allowed more or less water to flow or completely shut them to prevent any water from going in or out. Why couldn't the ponds simply be filled once and leave it at that? Well, trout are finicky creatures; they need cold, clean, oxygenated water to grow healthily. If the water is too warm or dirty, they will die. If it's stagnant, they will die. Splashing water creates bubbles and aerates the ponds. It was a clever system.

It wasn't hard for us to imagine ourselves living like this, away from our hectic lives back home, away from the cold, harsh Canadian winters, and living off the land. Selling rainbow trout was a key piece of the puzzle on how we could earn money in Costa Rica.

The house itself had a cottage feel. Nothing seemed completely straight or sufficiently sealed. The decor was a hodgepodge of homespun tin-can-and-beer-cap light fixtures, bright tapestries, eclectic artwork, and family photos. We were almost done with our own renovations back in Canada and we'd spent the last three years making sure everything was done right, not only to our taste and within our budget, but to municipal building codes. Nothing had been slapped together haphazardly, nothing had been left to chance, and we'd been wound up pretty tightly about it. So seeing the gaps between the walls and the uneven door frames of Rick and Mona's home had a three-fold effect on us: We started hyperventilating a little; we envisioned all the potential improvements we could add; and, we realized we both needed to learn to relax and let go of perfection.

The paradise property, with its rustic charm, had made a lasting first impression.

Five
Easy to Imagine

Rick was surprised we were considering moving to Costa Rica permanently. He'd assumed we wanted a holiday home even though I'd gone to great lengths in my emails to explain how important it was to find a suitable school for Jude. Río Blanco seemed rather remote, and I knew from my research there were no international schools nearby, but Rick had mentioned there was a high school and an English learning centre in the next town, which sounded promising at the time. Rick also pointed out that there was an English teacher who lived in Río Blanco, which was intriguing.

Finding the right academic environment was going to be our biggest challenge. Jude didn't care much for school, and unless he found what he was learning meaningful, no amount of nagging, threatening, or failing motivated him to do the work. I wanted to see him get back to nature, which he loved so much as a young child. The Canadian education system didn't seem to be the right fit and I feared he was losing the insatiable appetite for knowledge he'd once had. I clung to the hope that Costa Rica would feed his hunger once again.

"The schools are closed for the summer," Rick informed us. "Just like North American schools shut down in July and August, Costa Rican schools close from mid-December to mid-February during the summer season."

"That's too bad. It would have been helpful to chat with the principal and have a look around," I sighed, wishing we had known before booking our flight for early February.

"Well, we should scope out the neighbouring towns, regardless," Kevin encouraged me, before turning to Rick. "Should we drive back up to La Trinidad?"

"No, go over the little dirt bridge at the bottom of the hill," he began, "then drive a little bit, then turn right when you see the one-room school and the community centre..." Rick shared a series of instructions. All his directions were based on landmarks rather than street names or set distances until he concluded, "That's Copey. That's where the closest high school is and the English learning centre. You'll see the soccer field on the left and the church on the right... Turn left and follow the paved road. That road will get you to Santa María. The same main road continues to San Marcos if y'all want to go that far." As Rick rattled on, I hoped Kevin was paying close attention because I wasn't taking any notes. It seemed straightforward enough, but one wrong turn could get us lost since our GPS proved useless on these unmapped roads.

After a 4-km or 2.5-mile drive down the gravel road that led to the sleepy village of Copey, we stopped at the red octagonal "ALTO" sign. We turned right and drove by a small grocery store and an empty restaurant with a "CERRADO" sign in the window, which I remembered from the serpentarium in Santa Elena on our first visit meant closed. We drove past a bright blue, single-story building with a corrugated tin roof and a cheerful mural of flowers, trees, and clouds on the outside wall. There were no children — or adults, for that matter — anywhere to be seen, but it was obvious that this was the primary school. Not only was the school deserted, but the entire village felt like a ghost town. A pale-yellow church with a tall steeple and one of the most well-maintained soccer pitches I'd ever seen completed the town.

From Copey, we followed the paved road as Rick had instructed. Cutting through the mountain range, the journey gradually brought us lower in elevation. Copey sat in a valley 375 m (1230 ft) lower than Río Blanco. And Santa María was another 300 m (984 ft) lower than Copey. Kevin was getting the hang of driving on twisty roads, but one section of the ride between Copey and Santa María revealed not only a drop-dead gorgeous view, but also a precipitous cliff with the tightest switchback we'd encountered so far and no guardrail to prevent us from driving over the edge. I pressed both feet into the floorboard — as if that would help somehow — and my fingernails bore into the passenger door's armrest. Drop dead was literal in this case. Thank God it wasn't raining and that no other cars were coming in the opposite direction. I'm sure Kevin was relieved too. But no one said a word. Not even Jude. Kevin shifted into first gear and inched the SUV down the steep slope and around the corner. Nice and easy.

The rest of the trip was far more subdued, bringing our heart rates back to normal. We reached Santa María a few minutes later...just as the yearly horse parade got underway. As a result, we came across a traffic jam.

Police vehicles barricaded the main road and diverted drivers onto secondary roads to the left and to the right. Kevin turned right and, after a few minutes of looking for a parking spot, squeezed our rental between an old, dented Honda sedan and a shiny new Suzuki SUV.

People walked by wearing light summer clothes and I quickly understood why. As I slid out of the Mitsubishi, by reflex, I screwed up my eyes to avoid the blinding sun, then stretched my shoulders back and inhaled deeply. Hot dry air seared my nostrils and choked my lungs. The temperature had risen by several degrees compared to Río Blanco. The three of us wasted no time removing our fleece jackets before locking up.

A large, white church with a lovely park across the street signalled we had arrived in the centre of town. Santa María was made up of a smattering of shops and restaurants, a bank and a pharmacy, and two schools. It was also home to the world's first carbon-neutral coffee plantation and processing plant.

Hundreds of equestrians — or maybe *cowboys* was a more accurate term — from all over the country were in Santa María that day to show off their horse-riding skills. Thousands of onlookers lined the sidewalks. That was a lot of people in the centre of one small town.

So that's why the entire village of Copey felt abandoned. Everyone must be here.

We watched the parade for a while until pangs of hunger hit. Finding a place to eat without having to wait in line for an hour seemed impossible, so we weaved our way back to the Mitsubishi, then zigzagged through the streets and headed to San Marcos 6 km (3.7 mi) farther down the road. Between Santa María and San Marcos, Kevin coasted 120 m or 393 ft downhill, rarely having to accelerate or brake.

Just as we parked, it started to pour. The three of us ran into the first restaurant we saw and sat down at an empty table. Like many of the restaurants in Costa Rica, it was a hybrid indoor/outdoor space. Three sides of the building consisted of solid walls, while the fourth was a large pillar at the front with wide openings on either side to walk through. No doors. People scurried by with their umbrellas, wet stray dogs wandered the streets, and old pick-up trucks full of lumber or livestock rumbled through the busy intersection. Motorcyclists sped between people and vehicles as if the rules of the road didn't apply to them. It was a bit like watching a live-action movie and feeling relief that no one got hurt.

Kevin and I ordered a typical Costa Rican lunch: chicken, rice and beans called *gallo pinto*, fried plantain, and salad. The Spanish menu stumped Jude, but he understood *hamburguesa*.

"Hamburger and *papas fritas, por favor*," Jude said as he pointed to the menu. His effort to order in Spanish floored me.

Is this a sign of acceptance? Is he warming up to the idea of living here?

Jude received his meal and dug in. Kevin's food came ten minutes later, and mine ten minutes after his.

"Hmm, interesting how meals don't come to the table all at once, eh?" I commented.

Experiencing the meaning of *Tico time* firsthand, we took it in stride and chalked it up to cultural differences.

Stay home if you want first-world service.

By the time we finished our lunch, the sun had come out. We paid the bill and headed back to Río Blanco.

The rest of the day was spent looking around the property, weighing out the possibilities, and trying to be realistic about the pitfalls. The more we saw, the more we fell in love with the place and the lifestyle.

What's not to love?

"The guesthouse would make a lovely lodge for a bed and breakfast. Rural tourism is the new trend," I commented.

"Yeah, our guests could fish for their dinner, and we could serve them a home-cooked meal like Rick did for us," Kevin noted, hopping on the idea.

"Just think, the vegetables would come from our organic garden and maybe we could get some chickens and goats," I filled in. I wasn't sure what we would do with goats, but it was fun spit-balling ideas.

"Maybe we can grow enough vegetables to sell at markets? And revive the avocado trees and create a business selling avocados? Of course, there's the trout, too. There's just so much opportunity. I think we could make something work here," Kevin said with a glint in his eye.

These thoughts were outrageously at odds with our suburban reality, but somehow, they felt feasible. Whether these feelings of everything falling into place were just symptoms of romantic escapism or heartfelt signs of things to come, I couldn't be sure. Kevin and I both seemed to be thinking big, we were clear we needed a change, and this sure fit the definition of *big change*.

Neighbours

Since schools were closed, Rick arranged for us to meet Adriana, the "English teacher" he had implied might be available to help with Jude's studies. We were investigating all options at that point and wondered if she would consider teaching Jude privately. Homeschooling with structured accountability seemed perfect for a kid who didn't always mesh with public school.

At breakfast, Rick had explained that Adriana was married to Roberto, the son of Río Blanco's renowned cheesemaker, Abel. Abel happened to be the son of Abel Pacheco Sr., Costa Rica's president between 2002 and 2006. I felt a little starstruck knowing our possible future neighbours were related to such a high-ranking official, but I kept that to myself when they came by for a visit.

As we sat on the terrace eating breakfast and chatting with Rick, we heard a vehicle engine rattle, then doors opening and closing. Before seeing anyone, we heard, "*Hola*!" A woman and a man, both lean with dark brown hair, soon rounded the corner.

"Roberto! Adriana! Hi. Thanks for coming over. I'd like you to meet Kevin, Angela, and Jade," Rick said. We all shook hands.

"It's Anne, actually," I told them.

They both nodded, acknowledging the correction.

"Hi, and my name is Jude, not Jade," Jude politely added.

Adriana giggled a little as if she felt embarrassed for Rick on getting not one name wrong, but two. We smiled back at her, appreciating her good humour. Rick, on the other hand, seemed blissfully unaware of the awkwardness.

"They're the ones who are looking to buy the property," Rick clarified, as though he'd already mentioned us in some previous conversation.

In his late twenties or early thirties, Roberto towered over his short-statured wife. Adriana wore glasses and I guessed was about the same age as Roberto.

"Adriana and Roberto live on Abel's farm on the other side of the river. Remember when you turned right at the community centre to go down to Copey? Well, if you turn left and drive straight up, you end up on Abel's property," Rick explained.

"Yes, that's right. We live in a little domed house on my father's property. If you have time before you return to Canada, please come and visit. It would be my pleasure to show you the cheesemaking process," Roberto offered. Though kind, Roberto's reserved manner was surprisingly formal as if he was conducting important business rather than meeting potential neighbours. I wondered if he was worried he would say something that might discourage us from buying the property.

Adriana was timid, sweet, and possibly a teacher…but not an *English* teacher, as she spoke very little English. Roberto translated a lot of what we said so she could keep up with the conversation as he told us their story. Roberto's father, Abel, was Costa Rican and his mother, Elly, was originally from the U.S., which explained Roberto's proficiency in both languages. Abel learned English and Elly learned Spanish. The whole family, including Roberto's brother and sister, was bilingual. Abel had started a dairy farm decades earlier and that's how Roberto learned cheesemaking. And although Adriana had taught Spanish for a few years, she'd switched to graphic design and fine arts illustration.

It was a pleasure to meet them both and it was easy to imagine becoming friends if we moved, but we had to scrap the notion that Adriana would be Jude's English teacher. How did Rick get it so wrong? I didn't know. But I didn't want to antagonize him by pressing for an answer. We'd gotten the information we needed and would have to figure out how to move forward from there.

After lunch, we met Rick's hired help, Martín and Clara, who lived the same distance as Roberto and Adriana, but in the opposite direction. Martín had been working on the farm for over fifteen years by this time, so he knew the ins and outs, and the dos and don'ts. Clara, his wife, helped Mona by weeding the flowerbeds a few hours a week. They didn't speak English and Rick knew only a few words of Spanish, but somehow, they managed to communicate. Kevin felt more at ease and a little less worried about his Spanish skills — or lack thereof — after seeing that Rick had managed well without being fluent.

Martín and Clara had no idea Rick was trying to sell the property and he offered no explanation for why we were visiting. It was clear they were wondering why Rick was having them meet us, but they smiled, nodded pleasantly, and made us feel welcomed. The whole interaction felt stilted. We didn't appreciate being accomplices in this cover-up that, once disclosed, might leave a bad taste in their mouths. If we bought the property, we'd need all the help we could get, and we didn't want to ruin our chances of Martín and Clara agreeing to work for us. Trust is king in rural villages so if they felt duped before we even landed, it wouldn't bode well for us in this tiny community.

We knew Rick had had the property on the market for a couple of years and was motivated to sell. On the one hand, Rick was trying to bait, hook, and reel us in as any seller would. On the other, I assumed he didn't want to worry Martín and Clara unnecessarily. That was probably why he only advertised on U.S. websites. Sharing information on a need-to-know basis had its purpose, of course, but while we sat with Martín and Clara, it felt underhanded. If he wasn't being honest with workers who had been loyal to him for nearly two decades, then there was little hope he would feel qualms about withholding information from us...*about anything*. We took note and reminded ourselves to stay vigilant, as any buyer should. Then again, maybe he was being tight-lipped for reasons we couldn't understand yet and maybe we were simply feeling hypersensitive from our swirling emotions of the last few days.

Next Stop...Monteverde

We thanked Rick for his hospitality and told him that if we could sell our house for the right price and could sort out Jude's schooling, we'd consider purchasing his property. I think he took it all with a grain of salt; he'd heard it all before.

I thought Jude might like to see the ocean and spend some time at the beach before heading up to Monteverde. Rick told us there was a shortcut to get to Quepos and offered directions since it was down another unmapped, unnavigable road where GPS wouldn't work. Rick's directions were basically, "Go to San Marcos, drive down the road that leads to the big hardware store, and keep going straight. You'll get to a large river, just keep going until you reach the ocean." That was it. It sounded easy enough, except for all the forks in the road where we had to guess which way Rick considered *straight*. We guessed for the most part, but twice we ended up having to stop and ask people to point us in the right direction. Out there, above the clouds in this unpopulated heaven, these people were like angels sent by God.

Ticos are the nicest!

From the arid wide-open mountaintop, we travelled down to where the impenetrable jungle encroached onto the road. The rougher and more off-the-beaten-path we drove, the more I appreciated this treasure trove for the soul — the purity, the solitude, the connection to something greater than myself. It sure was remote; the type of road Robert Frost would surely deem *less travelled*. I imagine few tourists stumble upon such hidden gems unless they are willing to diverge from the usual mainstream sights. A great metaphor for life.

The Mitsubishi wasn't rugged, but it had four-wheel drive, and it did the job. We reached the large river, but when Rick said to *keep going* it didn't occur to us that he meant *through* it. We continued following the road alongside the river, which seemed like the logical thing to do. We soon ended up in a palm tree plantation with rows...*and rows...and rows...*of palm trees. It was a lovely sight and the shade the fronds provided was a welcome relief from the searing temperature, but it was a maze. Everything looked exactly the same. We went this way, then that way...

"Weren't we just here?" Jude asked, looking around.

We kept backtracking to avoid getting completely lost, but we got lost anyway.

I want out!

Kevin noticed one road ever so slightly more trodden than the others and figured it might be a thruway.

Luckily, it was, and five minutes later the highway came into view. Our unintended adventure through this palm labyrinth set us back a couple of hours. Frustrated and hungry, we stopped for a bite to eat at the country's number one fast-food chicken restaurant, Pollo Compero. This was the one and the same franchise that Sister Gladys had pointed out when we first came to Costa Rica back in September — it seemed fitting.

After we wolfed down our lunch, we realized we'd have to forego the beach if we wanted to reach Monteverde before dark. I'd promised Jude we would go ziplining in Monteverde, so he didn't seem too disappointed. And, without air conditioning in the rental, we were looking forward to getting to higher ground where the temperature promised to be cooler.

We arrived in Monteverde just as the sun dropped below the tree line and drove directly to La Pensión hotel to ask about vacancies. It had been the low season the last time we'd stayed there, so we'd had no trouble getting a room. Now, peak season had arrived, and the place was overflowing with people.

We scanned the lobby to see if we could see the sister-brother team from Texas, but neither was around. I went up to the front desk and asked for two rooms. The young lady said that we were in luck. Most of their guests were backpackers on lean budgets and had chosen to sleep on bunk beds in shared dorms. Two private rooms, each with its own shower and toilet, cost $40 a night. I didn't hesitate and signed on the dotted line.

Kevin, Jude, and I unloaded our stuff, got changed, and headed over to the same pizzeria we'd gone to with Hanne, Hendrik, Soleil, and François. We recognized the server who'd helped us in September, and the sense of familiarity, superficial as it was, felt comforting.

Monteverde was not a sleepy little town. It wasn't a big town, but there was a constant buzz in the air. The warm feeling I'd experienced when we visited in September greeted me like an old friend. Jude perked up, too. He seemed to enjoy the energy of the place...or maybe he was just happy the hotel had internet.

We shared a pizza and then walked back to our rooms. Kevin and I were wiped and fell asleep early. I learned the next day that Jude had stayed up and hung out in the lobby, chatting with other travellers while he waited his turn to use one of the two computers available to guests. As soon as one was free, he logged in on Facebook and caught up with his friends back home.

Ziplining with Jude

In the morning, Jude and I went on an hour-long suspended bridge walk, the same tour Kevin and I had done in September. This time though, we had the guide all to ourselves. Our guide, Lorenzo, took his time and educated us on the biodiversity of Costa Rica, which Jude enjoyed. I knew this to be true because he was slinging one question after another at our guide, and unless Jude was interested in the subject, he wouldn't have bothered. Lorenzo was not dodging any of them; he seemed happy to indulge in every single question.

"Do you have poison arrow frogs in this area?"

"*Sí muchacho*," Lorenzo nodded, smiling.

"How about the leopard and crowned frogs?"

"Yes, *mi amigo*, we do. This place is full of amazing animals, but you seem to like the *ranas*. Come with me."

Jude and I followed Lorenzo down a passageway through the dense forest that hugged a rock wall. I remembered it from my first visit but this time it was just us. No other tourists. It was dark and cavernous and the rocks surrounding us were cold and sweaty with condensation. I got goosebumps from the chill in the air. A small pond covered with lily pads and algae sat in the middle of this circular trail.

Lorenzo put his right index finger to his lips, whispered, "*Shhh*," and then stared into the pond. I wasn't sure what we were looking at, but Jude's energy matched Lorenzo's.

Jude's gaze said it all; he was in his element. And I was in mine merely by observing him in his. While the ancient forest rustled beyond us, we were quiet and still in this wet womb. Waiting.

Then, Jude's eyes widened. "Is that a red-eyed tree frog?" Jude pointed somewhere specific yet too general for me to track.

"You have eagle eyes, my friend. *Sí*, it is. I knew you would like this pond," Lorenzo laughed and put one arm around Jude, giving him a squeeze as if welcoming him into a secret frog fraternity. We could have gone home right then and Jude would have thought this was the best day of his life. It couldn't get much better than seeing his favourite frog in its natural habitat. However, the day wasn't over. Not by a long shot.

As promised, we went ziplining. Jude was excited to conquer all fifteen platforms. We had fun zipping through the shorter, less daunting lines. Jude loved the adrenaline rush and wanted more. He couldn't wait for the line where the cable is attached to the back of the harness and folks zip over the canopy high above the ground, arms spread like Superman's. Kevin and I had done it and had told Jude about it, but the sky had been clear during our adventure. On this day, the clouds, thick as pea soup, rolled in just as we reached the platform.

"Okay, friends, due to the high winds today, please do not spread your arms wide. Instead, tuck them close to your bodies," the guide at the cast-off tower shouted so the group could hear. So much for the Superman stance, but the wind was our kryptonite, and we weren't going to mess with it.

The first time I'd tried this line, I could see just how high up I was. I had soared above the trees. Anyone afraid of heights would no doubt have soiled themselves. But not this time. Although we were still just as high, the nebulous haze created the illusion that there was not much of anything in front of us or below. The guide hooked the first person in line to the cable and gently pushed him into the abyss. We heard him yell a few colourful expletives, but I wasn't sure if it was from elation or fear. The moment he slipped out of sight everything went completely quiet, as though he was sucked into an alternate dimension. The same eerie thing happened as the second and third people flew down the line. I had signed the consent form and promised Jude, so it was too late to call the whole thing off. Besides, let's face it, telling my teenage son — who was having the time of his life — that I was pulling the plug would have been way scarier.

Next, it was Jude's turn to be hooked up and pushed out. I watched my baby boy disappear like all the others...into nothingness. Since I couldn't see the other side, I prayed he made it all the way.

I was next. I kept my arms folded across my chest and felt the water droplets sting my face as my body careened through the air. I didn't holler with excitement. I didn't make a sound. I knew I was moving — *moving fast*. Yet for a split second, it felt like I was suspended, not only in mid-air but in time as well. It was magical. Then, as I head-butted through the mist, the landing strip was suddenly visible. And just like that, it was over.

I met up with Jude and the others. As we made our way to the last platform, the wind died down and the dense clouds evaporated.

The last platform was the Tarzan swing. It had sounded fun until we were standing on the edge of a 143 m, or 470 ft, platform with the cable hooked to the front of our harnesses. Once we stepped off the platform, we could expect the swing motion to span 90 m or 295 ft. For context, that's higher than London's clock tower, Big Ben!

I went first. On the platform, one of the guides held on to the back of my harness with one hand while opening the security gate with the other. Then, he counted in my ear, "*Uno... Dos... Tres.*" On *tres*, I jumped. It was exactly the same concept as bungee jumping; except I was doing it right-side up.

When I jumped, the slackened cable unravelled above me. I fell freely, no resistance. I screamed from sheer terror just as I had the first time, back in September. When I reached the length of the cable, the bungee sprung back, preventing me from smacking the ground. I screamed in relief as I swung to and fro.

Jude soon followed. One by one, the rest of the group jumped, crying out like Tarzan.

While Jude and I played tourists, Kevin spent the day investigating business opportunities and chatting with Shannon, the co-owner of the hotel. By the time Jude and I got back, it was time to go meet the director at the Friends School. I couldn't wait for Jude to see the school. I thought once he met a few of the students and saw how the classes were set up, he'd be just as excited about it as I was.

I'm not entirely sure why I thought my skeptical teenager would suddenly morph into someone who didn't question every possible outcome, weighing out the pros and cons. I can only attribute my speculation to being a hopeful idealist.

John, the director we had met before, was there to greet us. He introduced us to his co-director, Audrey, who took over the tour. She covered much of the same information John had provided, but this time the students were in class. We got to observe groups of them working on computers conducting a chemistry experiment and discussing environmental issues. The pervading mood was one of collaboration, as if the students had ownership of their education and the teachers were there to support their individual processes. The teachers and students emanated mutual respect. To me, the smaller classes seemed more expansive than restrictive.

"If you move to Costa Rica, will you be living in Monteverde?" Audrey asked.

"We're not sure. We're currently looking at a property in the Dota mountains five hours away from here," I answered.

"Oh, that's a beautiful area, but quite a commute," she said. "We do have a program where Jude could stay with a host family. We have a few families who take advantage of this program. It's a great way to get immersed into the culture and it speeds up learning Spanish, too."

"That's great news, I was hoping that would be the case," I said to Audrey, then looked at Jude with raised eyebrows. *Well, what do you think? It's great, right?*

Jude met my parental prodding with stiff, closed-off body language. If I could redo my schooling, I'd want to go to this school in a heartbeat, but Jude didn't look the least bit impressed.

Later, when pressed, he disclosed that the small classes reminded him of elementary school, which was not a selling point. Although he admitted everyone seemed friendly. Jude often resisted change, so I hoped this was just too much for him to take in and he'd come around once he had time to think of all the other great things Costa Rica had to offer.

Like red-eyed tree frogs and ziplining.

If Jude boarded with a host family, he'd be far enough from us to feel independent but close enough to get on a bus and visit on weekends, holidays, and summer vacations. I thought of myself at Jude's age and knew I would have loved this kind of arrangement. But I also knew my son. If I pressed too hard, Jude would automatically dig his heels in. So, I left it alone. I figured there was no point in trying to convince him of something that may not even happen. It would be just my luck to get Jude revved up only to tell him this whole moving idea wasn't in the cards after all. I decided to worry about the logistics once we knew for sure it was one hundred percent real. By then, Jude would have had time to let it sink in.

Ever the optimist.

Six
Decision Made

By the time we landed back in Canada, Kevin and I had made our decision. If we could sell the house for a good price, we were going to reinvent ourselves in Costa Rica. Río Blanco, specifically.

Dream life, here we come.

We'd completed the big renovations in the main living area, but we still had work to do. And the list was long: finish the basement, stain and install baseboards in every room, build stairs so we could walk out of the sliding door down into the backyard, clean up the yard and flowerbeds, hang our favourite pictures and artwork, and go through our stuff and purge what we didn't need. It was going to be a lot of work.

If we intended to put the Burlington house up for sale, we'd need to have it on the market within six to ten weeks to capitalize on the peak Canadian real estate season. *Spring is king!* Six weeks would be pushing it, and after all the love and attention we'd put into doing things right, there wasn't much point in rushing if it meant compromising on quality. If for whatever reason we couldn't sell it, we'd have to live with the finished product. Ten weeks seemed more realistic.

We gave ourselves until mid-April. I was overwhelmed, but it was also nice to have something pushing us forward in the final stages of the renovation. After three years of breathing life back into the bungalow, our momentum had waned. There is nothing quite like a deadline to rekindle that spark of passion and determination. I love decluttering, moving furniture around, and finding the right place for things. I find the staging process creative and fun. I couldn't wait.

Brazil

While we faced the enormous task of completing the renovations, and then all the packing that would come afterwards, Phoenix was getting ready for her big trip to Brazil. She crammed her knapsack with everything she would need and boxed up the rest of her things. We needed her stuff put away for staging purposes.

Phoenix had worked at a summer camp, teaching a photography class to teenagers from Brazil. Her love of travel had been a topic of conversation, and their chaperone, Mario, blurted out that she should visit his beautiful country. She was welcome to stay with his family.

"I told him not to toy with me unless he was serious about me landing on his doorstep," Phoenix recounted, chuckling.

"I'm totally serious. Please come. You can stay with us. My parents would be happy to host you," had been Mario's response.

Phoenix, who never leaves an adventure *un-adventured*, jumped at the chance. After August, when I had told her of our plans and she understood moving to Costa Rica with us wasn't an option, she had become more motivated than ever to make the Brazil trip happen. With free accommodations, she only needed enough money to pay for her plane ticket, meals, and entertainment. She knew this offer might never come again and wasted no time looking into flight costs. She worked two jobs and saved up. She was pumped. She was focused. And she rose to the challenge. In January, she bought the cheapest plane tickets she could find and, based on her projected savings, planned on staying for two months.

Two months! In Brazil! Staying with someone she barely knows. Give me strength.

I'd seen the movie *City of God* years before, which was enough to worry any mother, but a documentary I'd watched more recently had me scared shitless. It depicted Sao Paulo's *Carnival*, and although *Carnival* looked fun, the film also focused on Brazil's high crime rate and the seedy and dangerous side of Sao Paulo — they had a name for it, but I'd forgotten.

I'd also watched a documentary on human trafficking shortly before Phoenix announced her plans to travel. In it, single women travelling alone were lured to parties by handsome men, given drugs, and sold as sex slaves, never to return home. Although human trafficking is a global problem, not a Brazil-specific one, I felt panicked. I had no idea who this Mario was. This was completely different from her trips to New Zealand and Japan. She was older now and more experienced, sure, but the stakes felt so much higher.

How is this different from when I was twenty-one and hitchhiked all over Europe during a time when there was no internet or cell phones, and I never wrote home?

Evidently, my hypocrisy knew no bounds. I could hardly deny Phoenix her own adventure. Not only had I been on several adventures in my twenties, but I was embarking on another one at forty-seven. I was leaving it all in search of more. I had no idea how it would all turn out. The risks were different, but they were risks, nonetheless. It wasn't fair to freak her out with my fears.

"So Mario is a teacher and lives with his parents?"

"Yup, he said it's not uncommon for adult kids to live with their parents until they get married. It's kind of expected. He's engaged and said he'll introduce me to his fiancée. She knows that I'm coming. His parents know that I'm coming. It's all good. What are you worried about?"

"Well, I guess I'm worried about the unknown. I've never met this guy."

"Says the woman who's moving to a Central American country to be a trout farmer in the middle of nowhere. You're funny. Mario is great. Besides, you know me, I'll be posting pictures every day on social media, so you'll be able to follow along and see that I'm safe. And we can video chat, too. You've always taught me to take calculated risks. I feel like this is the best possible scenario to experience Brazil. The way I see it, there's zero risk."

Good point. We have so many ways to keep in touch. And how is this any different from allowing her — no, encouraging her — to go to Japan for a month to meet up with a boyfriend she had only been dating for a few weeks before he left to study Qigong? And that went well.

Phoenix was smart and capable. I trusted that she had good instincts. She was calculating the risks. So what was my issue?

Guilt. Shame. And the fear of losing her.

She was rising to the challenge of sorting out the details by herself, for which I was proud. But to me, there was an undercurrent of pain and resentment, as if she was rising from the ashes of what felt to her like abandonment. Was she flying to Brazil in search of a new family to replace the one she felt was kicking her out of the nest? Maybe she wouldn't come back.

Back where though?

Costa Rica is closer to Brazil than it is to Canada. If I was going to be in Costa Rica, what did it matter?

She might not come back...to me. No matter where I live.

As I was packing up my possessions, I realized there was a lot of emotional baggage that I needed to unpack.

On February 25, Phoenix, her best friend, Kaila, and I walked through the airport together looking for the Air Canada marquee. It was time to see Phoenix off. Kaila and

I were by her side when she stood at the counter to check in.

"Passport, please."

Phoenix handed the agent her passport.

"Please put your luggage on the scale."

Phoenix placed her knapsack on the flat metal surface in front of her. The agent then handed her three boarding passes. A different agent pulled the knapsack off the scale and loaded it onto the baggage conveyor where it rolled out of sight.

"Don't lose these. This one is from Toronto to Chicago. And this one is from Chicago to Sao Paulo. And this last one is for your last flight to Belo Horizonte. You're going to walk down to the end and go through security. Look for this gate," the agent told her as she circled Gate 19.

Now that Phoenix didn't have to lug her knapsack around, she felt lighter. And she was determined to keep the mood light, too, by making lighthearted jokes and talking a mile a minute about how excited she was. No big blubbering scenes. So, I held back my tears.

"I miss you already. Have the best time *evah*," Kaila said. "I'll be checking Facebook every day so you better post lots of pictures."

"I will, for sure." Phoenix hugged Kaila and then turned to me. "I'm so excited about this trip."

"I'm excited for you, too. It's going to be amazing. Skype with me as soon as you get there, okay?"

"I promise. And good luck selling the house."

"Thanks."

"I won't lie, I'm glad I won't be there for all the open houses and having to keep everything even tidier than usual. You're going to be a nightmare, aren't you?"

"Most definitely," I played along, keeping everything *light, light, light.*

"Poor Jude. Sucker!" she laughed. I laughed, too.

"I love you, Mum."

"I love you more."

We hugged. There was no guilt, no shame, no pain or resentment. Just love. *And maybe a little fear.*

Seven
Keeping Secrets

March 2012

I was on guard at the office; I hadn't told a soul. I felt it was better to wait until we knew our house was sold.

Oh, the irony!

I may have judged Rick too harshly about not coming clean to Martín and Clara, because there I was, walking in the same dirty shoes.

Part of me enjoyed keeping this secret to myself. I felt giddy, even. When a crisis hit, I breathed deeply and gazed at the pictures of the farm pasted on my desktop background and thought, *It won't be long.* But the better part of me hated it. I was interacting with people I'd known for over a decade, many of whom I considered friends. Holding back the truth every day made me feel slimy. I was a fraud.

I could only help Kevin after work and on weekends. He did the heavy lifting during the week. He worked non-stop on the house, putting all this effort into a place we were never going to fully appreciate.

"I feel attached and detached at the same time. Happy and sad," he admitted.

Over the weeks, we slowly let our parents and siblings in on our secret, then a few close friends, then a handful of neighbours. Their responses fell between enthusiastic encouragement — *That's awesome, I wish I could do that!* — and questioning our sanity... *What the hell are you thinking?* and, *You've just finished your renovation!* were common themes. The encouragement lifted our spirits and strengthened our mettle. The heaviness of the doubts, however, infiltrated our thoughts and challenged our resolve.

It felt shitty. And it was hard.

Calculated Risks

I always looked forward to Phoenix's updates from Brazil. She was having a much better time than I was. I loved how she rambled with excitement when we caught up on Skype. And she *did* post on social media almost daily; her beaming smile in all her pictures reassured me that she was having a wonderful time.

At her age, I had bought a one-year open ticket to Europe. When my parents dropped me off at the airport, all they had said was, "See you when you get back." They had no idea when that would be. They didn't even know which countries I had planned to visit. All they knew was that I was landing at Heathrow in London, England. This made sense to me at the time. Whether they went on a weekend getaway or a three-week holiday — leaving my sisters and me at home with a guardian — my parents never called to let us know how they were doing or to see how we were doing. They left and, after a period of time, they came back with tacky souvenirs. I imagine it was their way of nipping separation anxiety in the bud and fostering independence. Or maybe that was what I wanted to believe. Maybe it was just their way.

I had come by my parenting style naturally. I'd even adopted sayings I promised myself I would never say and behaviours I claimed I would never repeat. Like most parents, I leaned into what was familiar. I, too, raised my children to be self-sufficient. As a single mother working full-time, I would drop Phoenix and Jude off at my parents' place three hours away for two weeks every summer. Although I worked during those two weeks, I didn't have to pay for summer camp or daycare. I appreciated Mum and Dad's help. It was good for the kids to spend some time with their grandparents, too. They didn't see each other often.

My parents softened a little with age, but not much. They still had strict rules, and the kids were expected to listen. I reminded Phoenix and Jude to behave, gave them big hugs and kisses, told them I would miss them, and said, "See you in two weeks."

Although I'm Canadian, I was not immune to the influences of American news. At the time, I leaned into Hillary Clinton's catchphrase: "It takes a village to raise a child." So I didn't call them once during those two weeks. I figured Phoenix and Jude would settle in and if things were unmanageable, my parents would call me. That's only half true though. The other part of this equation was that I wanted them to feel grateful to be back home. I wanted my kids to experience my parents' toughness.

They think I'm strict?

I'm not sure I would have been able to drop my twenty-one-year-old daughter off at the airport without having a clue where she was going or what she was doing. Nor would I have considered moving to Costa Rica if it weren't for the fact that easy communication was possible.

Phoenix had flown from Toronto to Chicago and then from there to Sao Paulo, and everything had gone smoothly. She hadn't realized, however, that her third flight was taking off from an entirely different airport across the city.

"It was scary, but I figured it out," she said. "Before I left, I did my research on which taxi companies were legit."

You did? Good thinking. Smart girl!

"I showed the cab driver my boarding pass and pointed to where I needed to go. He drove like a maniac but got me there just in time." It was the first of her many adventures in Brazil. I listened and smiled, trying not to show my panic.

"And Mario and his fiancée were there waiting for me when I landed."

Phew!

"Apparently, I just missed *Carnival*, which is a drag. It's a huge deal here and lasts for, like, six days or something."

"That's too bad, it would have been a cool cultural experience."

Was it too bad, though? All those millions of people swarming the streets, wearing masked costumes, dancing and drinking, and God knows what else.

"Oh, for sure, but it's all good. Belo Horizonte is a cool place. Mario's family is *so* great, too. They treat me like an adult and let me do whatever I want. There are no rules I have to follow or anything."

Ouch.

"Mario teaches during the day so I don't really spend that much time with him, but his fiancée introduced me to her sister, Calista. She's super nice. And Calista introduced me to a bunch of her friends, so I mostly hang out with all of them."

"Aren't they in school?"

"The high school students are, but college students are on some kind of break this time of year, which is lucky for me."

"How do you spend your time?"

"Well, the other day Calista and her friends took me to see the *favela*, which is on the poor side of the city."

"*Favela*!" *That's what it's called. Yes, I remember now.*

"The houses are on top of each other and there are no streets, just alleyways. It was eye-opening. Not a place to wander alone, that's for sure. And we didn't actually go there, we just saw them from a hill across a lake. Belo Horizonte, though, is mostly like Burlington, with a suburban feel. And so far, we've mostly been going to coffee shops during the day and on hikes, visiting parks, sightseeing on the bus, and going, like, to nightclubs in the evening. I'm having so much fun."

Please be safe, keep an eye on your drink... Better yet, don't drink... Stay alert... Are you staying alert? Calculating the risks? Stop it! She's fine. She's got this.

"That sounds awesome, hon. I'm envious."

"Oh, I forgot to tell you that I met this guy, Santiago, on the second leg of my trip. He was in Chicago on a vacation and flying back home. He's twenty-seven. A lawyer. Really sweet. Anyway, he invited me to spend the weekend with him and get a tour of Sao Paulo."

Tell me you are not going to accept that invitation, young lady! Remember that guys prey on young, vulnerable, single women. Sex trafficking is a real thing. Don't do it!

"I just got back, actually. I spent the weekend with him."

What? Are you kidding me? Holy shit. What part of sex trafficking don't you understand?

"He lives with his sister, but she was on a business trip."

Breathe. Just breathe and listen.

"We ended up spending most of the weekend with his parents and cousins. Brazilians are so welcoming. I want to learn to speak Portuguese now. I love it here."

"I'm glad you're meeting such friendly people."

"Friendly? That's an understatement. When Santiago and I were messaging each other on Facebook, he asked me what types of things I like to do. I told him I love to go whitewater rafting and ziplining, and that's what we did! I just thought he was asking a general question. But he organized it all. And his whole family came, too. And he also showed me around Sao Paulo. My personal tour guide. It was so awesome, Mum. Best weekend ever. I probably should have let you know that I was going to do that."

You think?!

"But I didn't want to worry you or have you talk me out of it."

I'm so upset with you. The point of keeping in touch and letting me know where you are is so that I know what coordinates to give the police if you go missing.

"I did my homework though. When we became friends on Facebook, I lurked on his page to see what kind of vibe his posts were giving me. He seemed wholesome. Lots of pictures of him with his sister and parents. Big smiles. Nothing weird. Everything he told me matched his bio and stuff like that. Then I asked Mario what he thought about me meeting Santiago in Sao Paulo. Mario said that it wasn't unusual for Brazilians to invite strangers into their homes and didn't seem concerned. I had a good feeling, so I went for it."

I am proud of you for being so independent and capable. I'm impressed yet conflicted. Do I ream you out or cheer you on?

"Sounds like you had a great weekend. I'm glad you had such an amazing experience. Just remember to be careful, eh hon? Keep your wits about you."

"Yeah, I am. Calista and her friends have warned me where it's safe to go on my own in Belo Horizonte and where it's not. I don't go out on my own at night, like ever. I'm not looking for trouble, but I'm not locking myself away in my room either. I'm doing what you taught me. I'm taking calculated risks."

Touché.

I wasn't the only person Phoenix was staying in contact with back home. As her trip was winding down and her return flight loomed, she let me know that she had been reaching out to possible roommates. The two months away made her realize just how much she cherished her independence. The idea of living under our roof and following our rules turned her off.

One of Phoenix's friends mentioned that her brother was looking for a roommate. Ben lived in a basement apartment and the shared rent fell within Phoenix's budget. She had met Ben at a few parties and liked his mellow vibe. She seemed confident they'd make good housemates. Another calculated risk. She hadn't had good luck with roommates — some were downright scary and abusive — so I was praying this would work out for her. The fact that Phoenix would be living only ten minutes away from her grandmother also felt comforting. For her sake.

Who am I kidding?

"Hey, I have something to ask you," Phoenix said a week before she intended to return to Canada.

"Go on." I held my breath, waiting for her to ask me if I thought it would be a good idea to stay in Brazil forever with her new-found family.

"I was wondering if you'd be willing to move my stuff over to Ben's apartment before I arrive. That way when I land you can drop me off there. Probably easier for everyone concerned."

She's coming back! Woohoo! She's coming back!

"Sure, I can do that for you. Send me the address and Ben's phone number so I can make plans for him to let me in."

I didn't mind helping her out and moving her stuff. She didn't have a whole lot to her name, so it wouldn't take me long. And, it would give me the chance to suss out her new digs and meet Ben.

"Ben works the graveyard shift and sleeps in the daytime. He said he'll leave the door unlocked and you can just go in and out whenever you want. He said he sleeps like a rock, so don't worry about making noise. He won't hear you. My room is going to be the one on the right after you pass the living room."

"I'm just supposed to walk in, unannounced? That feels awkward. But sure, I'll get it done this weekend."

"Thanks so much. I really appreciate your help, Mum. I'll chat with you next

Monday to, like, make sure there are no changes to my flights and stuff. You've got all my flight numbers, right?"

"I do and I'll be checking them on this end, too."

"I can't believe I'll be home next week. These two months have flown by. This is one trip I'll never forget. I love travelling so much! I love being immersed in a different culture. I've met so many amazing people. I love Brazil! And the food... I *love* the food. I wouldn't hesitate to come back. There's so much more to see. Like the Amazon rainforest! How cool would that be? Can you imagine whitewater rafting down the Amazon River? Thanks for raising me to take calculated risks and to follow my tug."

"I never doubted that this trip would provide lots of interesting experiences and life lessons."

I just never realized how many of those lessons would be mine.

Eight

House of Our Dreams

April 2012

I t was the last push to get the house ready. We spent the whole weekend cleaning the oven and stovetop, tidying, ironing curtains, washing windows, mowing the lawn, planting flowers, staining and installing the last few baseboards, and dusting.

Who needs to go to the gym with all that lunging, squatting, stretching, and lifting?

Every part of my body ached. And I do mean every inch of it...even my eyelashes hurt. But boy, did our house ever clean up nicely. We had been living in upheaval for nearly three years so seeing it in mint condition was a welcomed change. It was a little too magazine-perfect for day-to-day living, but to see our vision finally realized gave us a sense of accomplishment. Together, Kevin and I had built the house of our dreams and now we were selling it.

Are we completely crazy?

First Showing

I am good at ignoring my body's warning signs. Too often, when I push myself for an extended period of time, I throw self-care out the window. So, true to form, after a month of eighteen-hour days of constant hustle, topped off with our punishing weekend, I became sick. The head fog progressed into a full-blown headache, the tickle in my throat developed into a sandpaper scratch that made it painful to swallow, and the sniffles were running amok. I called the office to let them know I wouldn't be in, then pulled the covers over my head. Medicated with Benylin, I drifted back to sleep.

The ringing woke me up. "Hello," I said, groggily.

The woman on the other end of the line introduced herself as Trish. She was a real estate agent and a friend of one of our neighbours up the street. Trish had two clients who were actively looking for properties and wondered if she could pop by the house at noon.

"Today? In an hour?" I asked, gravel-voiced. "Yes, of course."

I'd had no intention of crawling out of bed that day, but adrenaline kicked in. I made the bed and shoved whatever clothes that had been flung casually onto the armchair the night before into our dresser drawers. After showering quickly, I made sure to fold the towels neatly and clear the counter of any personal items and get the bathroom back to its Pinterest-worthy state.

While I rubbed the fingerprint smudges off the stainless-steel appliances, Kevin put away the dog paraphernalia and wiped Frankie's slobber off the front window. She liked to perch herself on the back of the couch and look out. Frankie barked at anything that moved and made a fine mess of the pane with her wet nose. I fluffed the throw pillows and turned on all the lights. With two minutes to spare, we sat down and waited. When the doorbell chimed, Kevin opened the front door.

"Hi, I'm Trish."

"Please come in," Kevin welcomed.

All smiles, Trish walked in and, before she took another step, said, "Oh wow, this is beautiful. It's so unassuming from the outside, but boy, what a great job you've done. I love the open concept. And how unusual to have added black window and door frames! It has that loft feeling."

"Thank you. Let me take your coat. We'll take you through room by room," I said.

"Everything is done to code. We got a permit to build over the garage, too," Kevin started as I was hanging up her coat. "I did most of the work myself. It was a labour of love."

"Who's your designer? I'm always looking for good interior designers for my clients."

"We didn't hire anyone to help us with that. Anne had the vision and we worked together to make it happen."

"Well, great job guys. I can't wait to see more."

We led her down the hallway to my favourite room in the house: the bathroom.

"I love to take baths, so we spared no expense," I informed her. "This Amalfi bathtub is made of volcanic limestone, and it keeps the water hot for up to forty-five minutes without needing to top it up. The high backrest makes taking baths so much more comfortable. Kevin never sees me anymore because I'm always in here, soaking. And look," I walked over to the tub and turned the faucet to the left, "the water pours out from the ceiling."

"Wow, of all the homes I've been into, I've never seen that. That's really cool. So luxurious. And I love that you continued the exposed brick wall in here like in the kitchen and dining room, it really warms up the space. Very spa-like."

"And then over here, we have a separate shower stall. I installed the tile and the pebble flooring," Kevin demonstrated.

"You thought of everything. The devil's in the detail, eh?"

"Speaking of details, we have some fun unexpected features, too."

"Oh yeah? Like what?"

We showed her the tall barn doors for the office Kevin had made. Although sliding barn doors became trendy later, at the time it was a means to solve a space issue. And I was always looking for ways to balance the stark loft feeling by adding warm, textured elements. The honey-stained wooden doors helped with that, as did the floor-to-ceiling fieldstone fireplace and exposed brick on the west-facing wall.

"On the island, we noticed there was some wasted space on the stool side, so we asked the manufacturer to add shelving, and, instead of faux panelling, we got them to add functioning doors. They're easy to get to, but out of sight to keep things from looking cluttered," Kevin opened one of the doors to reveal our CD collection.

"That's so clever."

"And over here," I walked over and opened the broom closet, "is probably my favourite hack. Kevin thought I was crazy when I asked him to add an outlet here so that we can charge the Dustbuster out of sight."

"Get out! What a great idea. Everyone likes open concept homes these days, but they forget about all this stuff."

Trish was blonde and bubbly in a Theresa Caputo — AKA the Long Island Medium — sort of way. I half expected her to start channelling my dead relatives as we moved from room to room. She didn't, which was disappointing. However, my mood perked up when she started talking about price. Kevin and I had a ballpark figure we had tossed around, but her number was out of the park. If we could get her price for the house, we'd be thrilled. Her verve was infectious.

Trish had two motivated clients at her fingertips, primed to buy, she told us. But Trish wasn't our agent, which threw a wrench into things. We hadn't officially signed any agreements yet, but our intention was to give the listing to our previous realtor, Liane. Since Trish was ready, right then and there, we made her a deal. If she could sell our house within the next week, we'd give her the commission. If no deal was made, then Liane would get the listing. Trish confidently agreed to the terms and said she'd be back at 2:00 p.m. with her first client. Although this curveball was unexpected, we enjoyed the good vibes it brought. I was feeling much better, despite my cold.

A few minutes before 2:00 p.m., we locked up, put Frankie in the back of the 4Runner, and drove to the dump to get rid of a load of garbage.

When we got back, Nora, our neighbour across the street, had clocked that Trish and her client were in the house for fifty minutes. It was a good sign, we thought. We waited for the call, which came about an hour later.

"My client loves the house and wants to come back with her husband tonight."

We tried to contain our excitement but failed as we broke out into a happy dance.

Once again, Kevin went around wiping everything down as I fluffed up the pillows and turned the lights back on. Five minutes before 7:00 p.m., we were out the door and walked Frankie around our neighbourhood. An hour later, as we strolled back towards the house, we recognized the white Audi backing out of our driveway and driving off in the opposite direction. We waited for the call. And waited.

Two hours later, the phone rang.

"My client's husband loves the house as much as she does, no flinching at the price, except," Trish began, then tempered her high energy, "your house is located two streets east of their child's school catchment. It's a special school for gifted kids with two hundred names on the waiting list. The school is strict and won't bend the rules so they can't make an offer. I'm so sorry. I was so sure we would be selling your house tonight."

Although frustrated, we decided to take it as a good sign that the house showed well and was priced right. We didn't despair. Trish was showing the house to her second client later in the week. We were still hopeful.

Trish called the next day to inform us that her second client had decided not to view the house because she needed two bathrooms on the main floor and ours only had one. *Damn.*

We called Liane and told her to draw up a contract. The *"FOR SALE"* sign went into the ground on Monday, April 16, 2012, based on the original plan. We never heard from Trish again.

May 2012

Bombshell

I remember it was raining. That's why I offered Jude a ride to school. He was quiet on the way there, but that didn't raise any suspicion. It was early and he looked tired, most likely from staying up too late playing video games. Sitting next to my son, who was on the cusp of turning sixteen, it felt like a typical morning.

Then Jude declared, without even a quiver in his voice, "Mum, if you sell the house, I won't be moving to Costa Rica with you and Kevin." He didn't ramble trying to explain himself or defend his decision. Unlike his mother, Jude knew how to take a dramatic pause. He said nothing else. I sensed he was serious.

Shocked, I continued to drive in silence, feverishly collecting my thoughts and feelings while trying to avoid ramming into a telephone pole. I needed a minute to process. I reached the school lot and found an empty space to park.

Processing...processing...not computing...processing...

When I was Jude's age, it never would have occurred to me that I had a choice. When my parents moved from Québec to Ontario, I followed them automatically. Period. No discussion. As much as I wanted to play the too-bad-so-sad-you're-going-anyway card, part of me understood where Jude was coming from. Although I wasn't prepared to have my teenager dictate what we were going to do with our lives and change our trajectory, I was willing to listen. I braced myself and gently asked, "What do you mean you won't be moving with us? What's your plan?"

Please don't tell me your solution is to couch surf from one friend's house to another.

"I'll ask Nan if I can live with her and Dean."

His paternal grandmother, Jan, lived twenty minutes up the road and had recently reconciled with her ex-husband. Dean had caused her unimaginable emotional and psychological torment, and they had divorced thirty years earlier. I believe many of my ex-husband's mental health issues were a result of living in such a toxic environment. Dean was no saint, but Jan was convinced he had found redemption and had changed.

Family meant everything to Jan. She had been adopted as a newborn and was an only child. Feelings of abandonment plagued her. As it happened, Dean was also an only child. His alcoholic mother had dropped him off at her parents' one day and didn't come back. He spent his formative years living a healthy, stable life with his grandparents. Then, out of the blue, when he was eleven, his mother returned and whisked him away. From that day on, he lived on *the wrong side of the tracks*, experiencing turmoil and uncertainty. He channelled his energies into sports and became a great athlete. Being the captain of the hockey team suited his broad shoulders and square jaw. He also became a bad boy, a player, and a smooth talker.

Young girls swooned, so I was told, and Jan had been no exception. She wanted a large family to compensate for the loneliness she had felt throughout her life. Then, once she and Dean were married, she found herself more alone than ever. He was more often on the road travelling for business than at home. As the story goes, Dean was home just long enough to impregnate her before leaving again. She was desperate to fill the void. Unfortunately, she suffered several miscarriages. When Jan carried her son, Christopher, to term, she considered him a miracle. There were complications though;

the umbilical cord coiled around his neck and was strangling him. The doctors had to perform an emergency C-section to save his life and hers. Doctors had cautioned her that trying to have another child would be dangerous, dashing her dreams of having a large family. She poured all of her maternal identity into Christopher. When her only son committed suicide in his late thirties, Jan's identity shattered.

Maybe Dean represented a sliver of hope in Jan's old age? I don't know. Dean had been the love of her life once and maybe she was still clinging to a fragment of *happily ever after.*

Phoenix and Jude grew up seeing their grandmother regularly and affectionately called her *Nan.* They had not, however, fostered any kind of relationship with their grandfather. The last time Dean had seen his grandson, Jude was three months old. So, Jude wasn't about to start calling him *Granddad* anytime soon. He hadn't earned it. But that didn't mean Jude wasn't intrigued; he'd lost his father when he was six. Dean didn't feel like family, but he was blood. Jude had heard the stories. He was curious about the man and the myth.

"Nan and Dean? Well, I'm sure Nan would love it. But there are pros and cons in every situation. Don't expect that living with her will be easy, especially now that Dean is on the scene."

"I know, but if he's a changed man, then maybe it's not too late to get to know my grandfather. If he hasn't changed, then maybe it will be good for me to be around to keep an eye on him. Help keep Nan safe."

"Well, I hope he has changed, but for the record, I don't trust him. And keeping your Nan safe isn't your responsibility."

"I know, but they're both getting older. Maybe having me around will make it easier on them. I can help around the house and stuff."

"You'll have to change schools."

"Well, I'd have to change schools anyway if I move to Costa Rica. And stay with a host family that I don't even know. And go to a school I don't want to go to."

Damn it, damn it, damn it! Way to use my own argument against me. That's what you get for raising smart, critical thinkers, Anne. Shit! Shit! Shit!

"You're making an adult decision here. You're going to have to prove to me that you can take on the responsibility that goes with it. You'll have to ask your Nan and Dean; I'm not doing it. And if they agree, I'll sign whatever papers need signing for your transfer, but you'll have to do the work. You'll have to get the forms, fill them out, and meet with the principal. I'm assuming you'll be going to MM Robinson?"

"Pearson, actually."

"Why? MM Robinson is literally across the street. You can't expect Nan to drive you to school in the mornings and pick you up at the end of the day."

"I have friends at Pearson. I'll walk, ride my bike, or longboard to school. Pearson is closer to Nan's than my school is to our house and I don't ask for rides, you offer them," he justified, then added, "I'll do the work." He was calm and clear-headed. There was no drama.

With a last-ditch effort, I appealed to his little boy self, "But what about the red-eyed tree frogs? And the spiders? And all the creepy crawlies you love so much?"

"I guess they'll have to manage without me. Nice try, though," he smirked, then his eyes softened. "This is your dream, Mum, not mine. I don't want to go. But *you* should *definitely* go."

But when you were four, you said you'd live with me forever and ever. What do I do now? I'm damned if I do, damned if I don't. First, Phoenix shocks me by telling me she wants to come with us so now I feel I'm abandoning her. Jude can go — and should — but is now declaring that he won't! So essentially, I'll be leaving him behind as well. Where do I collect my Mother-of-the-Year award?

Leaving me to pick up the shrapnel from this bomb, he hugged me. "I love you, Mum."

Jude got out of the car, flung his satchel over one shoulder, and walked away. His posture was straighter than usual, and he didn't look back to wave. I don't know how he was feeling at that moment, but his stride was sure.

My baby boy felt ready to make his way in the world without me, and that stung. As I drove to work with my hands gripped around the steering wheel to help steady my nerves, I grappled with Jude's decision. "I'm not abandoning him, staying behind is *his* choice," I repeated to myself, as tears ran down my face.

Living with his grandparents could be good for him — and them — and Phoenix will only be ten minutes away. Knowing her brother is just up the road might help her feel less orphaned. This scenario could nurture a deeper bond between them. This could be fine... just fine.

No matter how much I believed Costa Rica would be an amazing experience for Jude, there was no point dragging him there. I knew my son. He would dig his heels in and make life miserable.

Besides, I was getting way ahead of myself. The house wasn't sold yet and who knew if it would sell? The lump in my throat might have been for nothing.

Nine
From Dream to Reality

June 2012

For six weeks our life consisted of open houses every weekend, keeping the house and yard spotless, and going to Frankie-friendly places while the house was being viewed. It was inconvenient with our four-legged girl. Thank goodness the weather was sunny and warm most of the time so we could take her on long walks.

We received amazing feedback on the house, but no offers. We had people come for second and third viewings, but still no offers. Maybe we got caught up in the fact that the TV show *Urban/Suburban* selected our house to be featured in one of its episodes, maybe we chose to believe Trish when she told us our house was worth more than it truly was, and just maybe our pride was getting in the way.

Just maybe.

Our agent, Liane, had hesitated to list so high, but we urged her to match Trish's sparkly appraisal. Liane agreed but warned us that the pool of potential buyers would be shallow in our price range. She didn't seem flustered that it was taking time. She reminded us of all the great comments. Even as Liane urged us to sit tight, I grew discouraged. I wondered if no offer was a sign that we weren't meant to move.

We'd purchased our ranch bungalow at a rock-bottom discount shortly after the 2008 economic crash. Over the three years we'd been working on the house, the real estate market had slowly recovered. There was no question we'd make our money back and then some, but whether we would make as much as we were led to believe — and enough to buy Rick's farm — seemed less certain. Kevin and I decided to reduce the price.

Open houses... Second viewings... Love-gushing fests... Wait, wait, wait... Zero, zilch, nada... Soul-crushing test of our patience. Rinse and repeat.

We reduced the price yet again. The second drop was where we initially thought the house should have been listed, with a little wiggle room for negotiation. If we couldn't sell at that price, then we wouldn't sell — not yet anyway. The Costa Rica deal would be off the table, and we'd have to rethink our future. I believe things happen as they should and the reasons aren't always obvious in the moment, but depression set in, nevertheless.

How much longer can this go on?

To avoid having to answer questions, I hadn't told people at work that our house was up for sale...another secret I was keeping. I was a mess. I hadn't had a good night's sleep in months. I was tired and fed up. Thank goodness Kevin was home to deal with the cleaning and tidying before each viewing. I surely would have cracked.

July 2012
Done Deal

"Today's the day, I can feel it in my water," Kevin boasted as he sprang out of bed. I rolled my eyes at the old English expression that meant he felt something big was about to happen. I, on the other hand, did not jump out of bed. The only thing I could predict for sure was that I would be sleeping in a little longer. July 1, Canada Day, landed on a Sunday that year, which meant government agencies and most corporate businesses were closed on the Monday. I had the day off work and for the first time in months, I had no plans. I simply turned over and buried myself deeper under the covers for a while longer. When I finally woke up mid-morning, I lounged in bed reading a book.

At noon, we received a phone call.

"Hi. My name is Chad. I work with Liana. Normally she would call you, but as you know she's away at her cottage for the long weekend. I called her just now and she mentioned she won't be home until later this afternoon. She told me to call you directly. I'm sorry for the short notice, but I was wondering if I could show your house to my clients today at one?"

It didn't leave us much time to tidy up, but we were so used to it by this time, we had it down to a science.

"Yes, of course, see you then." I placed the receiver down in its cradle.

Frankie was limping from a sore paw so we couldn't go for our usual long walk. Instead, with permission, we backed the 4Runner into Nora's driveway across the street. From that vantage point, we could appreciate our thick, green lawn and the colorful flowers that added curb appeal. The house showed well. What a transformation from where it all started three years earlier. We sat and admired what we had accomplished and talked about the *what-ifs*. Nora's driveway also provided the best view to keep track of how long Chad's clients would take to view the house.

You're off the hook, Nora, we're doing our own surveillance now.

The middle-aged couple, with no kids in tow, was thorough. They remained inside the house for a long time.

I wish we had bugged the house so we could listen in.

When they came outside, they kept walking between the front and back yards. The measuring tape came out. They would divide and look around on their own, then huddle back together. Chad, the agent, wasn't sure who to follow so he gave up and leaned on his car. We couldn't hear a word they were saying, but their gestures were animated with a lot of finger-pointing and head bobbing. They stayed longer than their allotted hour and Frankie was getting antsy so when they weren't looking in our direction, we got out of the 4Runner and moseyed on over. We pretended we were coming back from walking Frankie and introduced ourselves.

Bryn was originally from England and Michel was from Québec.

Interesting, since Kevin is originally from England and I'm from Québec. Kismet?

We invited Bryn, Michel, and Chad back into the house. Since Kevin did most of the work himself, he was able to squash any concerns they had and put their minds at ease. The smiles got wider with every question answered while they mentally moved in.

"The room over the garage is perfect for my daughter," Bryn mentioned. "I'll repaint the walls a soft blue, though, because army green isn't her colour."

"I love the huge island, but we'll definitely replace this with granite," Michel included, tapping the butcher-block countertop that Kevin built and installed himself.

"Our table will look great here, and you know that crystal chandelier we have in storage?" Bryn gestured to Michel, looking up at our pewter light fixture. "We can finally bring it out. It'll look great over our table, hanging from this cathedral ceiling." Then, looking a little embarrassed, as if she had just remembered that we were still in the room, she turned back to us and said, "Our design preference is more traditional; less contemporary rustic."

I know you discarded the gorgeous butcher-block countertops without blinking, but did you notice the contemporary rustic exposed brick wall, the fieldstone fireplace, the wooden beams and ceiling, the huge industrial stainless steel pendant lights over the island, and the sliding barn doors?

I know it's a good sign when people can see themselves in an environment, but I was confused.

Why buy a newly renovated house if you don't care for its design style?

I refused to get excited. Kevin, on the other hand, was one hundred percent convinced that not only would we get an offer, but that we would accept the offer that day. He counted on his fingers, "One: they've basically moved in already. Two: they've been looking for some time. Three: they admitted to being picky and they said they appreciated the quality of the work. Four: the sale of their house is closing soon so they're feeling the pressure of having to find something quickly. And five: I have goosebumps." He came closer and showed me the raised hair on his arm.

Bryn and Michel left our place at a quarter to three. I called Liane to give her a heads-up on what had transpired. I thought I might have to leave a message, but she picked up and let me know that she had just gotten home from her weekend away. I told her about how Chad's clients were at the house for nearly two hours and how we ended up meeting them and answering their questions. She said it all sounded positive and that she'd call Chad and would get back to us once she knew more.

Liane called back fifteen minutes later to inform us that Chad was drawing up an offer.

An hour after that, Liane knocked on our front door. "Let the games begin," she winked.

I invited Liane to make herself comfortable in the living room. While Kevin and I sat side by side on the sage couch, Liane sat in the timeworn patina leather chair and presented their formal offer. Liane advised us to think it over, to remember that there was no rush, and to know it was okay to let them wait. Making them sweat a little wasn't a bad tactic. Although the offer was too low, it was worth going a few rounds to see if they were flexible with their price. We needed them to come up to match our *we're-moving-to-Costa Rica* number.

Counteroffer... Tick, tock, tick, tock... Revised offer... Tick, tock, tick, tock... Counteroffer.

The negotiation process went on for two hours. Finally, by 6:00 p.m., we agreed on a price. The house was sold: two-and-a-half months after the *"FOR SALE"* sign went into the ground, five months after we fell in love with the farm and decided to buy it, nine months after Kevin found the property online and we first contacted Rick, ten months after we'd first scoped out Costa Rica and saw the double rainbow and a year after our first musings tugged us to leave the grind in search of a dream life.

Sometimes, the transformation from dream to reality takes time.

Standing at the kitchen island, Liane spread multiple copies of the final purchase agreement across the counter. Each page had tiny yellow stickies, and Liane explained the gist of what each section meant. She advised us to read it through on our own, but we trusted it was in order. Well, we hoped it was.

Instead of slowing down with some pretense of perusing the legal jargon, we picked up the pace. We inked our full names and initials in all the required spots, as fast as possible, so that Bryn and Michel couldn't change their minds. I didn't recognize my illegible signature on the page, but I didn't care.

As soon as I was done, I turned and walked away as if afraid the beautiful butcher-block wood underneath the stack of papers would turn to stone before my eyes. And then, I sobbed. Kevin wondered if I was having second thoughts. I wasn't. A profound sense of relief washed over me. We were moving to Costa Rica.

Costa Rica!

It was really happening. I could *finally* tell the world.

Ten
Stress of a Different Kind

Within one short week, our house had gone to the dogs. How quickly things changed. We no longer lived in a pristine, tidy home. Papers were scattered everywhere, shoes were piled near the front door, and none of the throw pillows had been fluffed for days. We no longer stressed over keeping everything in its place, how many people came to each open house, or if there would be an offer. Instead, the stress was of a different kind: One of the conditions of the sale was that we be packed and out of the house within forty-five days.

Can we get what we need to get done in such a short amount of time?

It was quite daunting and a little scary too.

Although all conditions on the sale of our house were met, we still needed to iron out the details of the Río Blanco property deal. And when I say *we*, I mean Kevin. I was still at work dealing with hectic deadlines. I was of no help to him with this stuff. I would come home every evening, and he would update me on what he'd been able to accomplish, how far he'd gotten in the process, and what more needed to be done.

We had signed up as members of the Association of Residents of Costa Rica (ARCR) as Ran from La Pensíon in Monteverde had suggested. We'd figured we could find a lawyer through ARCR but learned that ARCR only assigns residency lawyers to its members, not real estate lawyers. The woman Kevin was in contact with was kind enough to share some links of possible lawyers, but she couldn't vouch for them. Rick said that his lawyer, Diego, was great, and suggested that we use him too. Dividing Diego's fee would save Rick and us money. Canadians would consider this a conflict of interest, but Rick assured us Costa Ricans wouldn't bat an eyelash.

Uneasy with this arrangement, we decided to ask Diego some questions first to see how he responded. Diego, who wrote English well, ensured our best interests would be served and he was always willing to chat on the phone when three-way emails got confusing. At one point, Rick attempted to add some contingencies to the original agreement. Kevin was livid. Diego jumped in and explained to Rick why he was advising us not to consent to the new provisos. I suppose Rick was pushing his luck to see what he could get away with, but since he didn't want to lose the sale, he retracted his demands, and everything was back on track. From that moment on, Kevin and I trusted that Diego had our backs. Once the mountain property deal was clinched, we tackled a mountain of paperwork.

For Costa Rica's immigration purposes, we had to get new birth certificates, a new marriage certificate, a police check form, and a veterinarian health approval for Frankie. The Costa Rican government required the long version of the original documents — no abbreviations or copies — and they all had to be notarized. Kevin had to get his birth certificate from England, which concerned us a bit. But none of these documents gave us as much aggravation as the paperwork we needed to organize for Frankie. Getting a straight answer from the airline seemed impossible.

Kevin spent two weeks on the phone trying to figure out how to fly Frankie down. He was given such inconsistent information he didn't know who to believe. The rules were vague. The airline's reservation department gave him one story, then their pet safety department gave him another. To fly in the cabin, dogs could not be more than a certain weight, but the weight criteria fluctuated depending on who he spoke to. Frankie had to go through customs... No, she didn't. We received quotes between $600 for a Costa Rican vet to check her on the other side and $4,100 for a broker to take care of all the paperwork. While Kevin spent all his time on the phone trying to sort it out and me being at work all day, nothing was getting packed.

Kevin's frustration mounted and he lost his patience. He suggested that the airline's reservation agent, pet safety agent, and he have a conference call to get some concrete answers. By the end of the conversation, they determined Frankie was able to fly with us in a collapsible crate stowed by our feet for $250. We just had to hand over the paperwork from our vet in Canada stating Frankie was healthy and sufficiently inoculated, and that would be it.

No need for a vet to check her on the other wise, no broker, no fuss. What a relief.

Handing in My Notice

Although I'd thought for sure I'd shout the good news from the rooftop as soon as we sold the house, I was unexpectedly cautious and waited to give my notice at work. I didn't realize it would take two weeks to finalize the deal with Rick and sort out Frankie's flight arrangements, and I'd wanted those loose ends tied up first. But it was time.

On Monday morning, July 16, 2012, I stood outside my manager's office. He was always in early and so was I. I thought it best to catch him before the whirlwind of the day wreaked havoc.

I took a few deep breaths and tried to slow my racing heartbeat. I knew I would be happy once the deed was done, but in that moment, all I felt was dread. Even though I knew leaving the stress behind was the right decision for me and even though I had been dreaming of a new life for over a year, handing in my letter of resignation would make it real. Although my written notice was short and to the point for HR purposes, I felt compelled to clarify my reasons and let my manager know I wasn't leaving to start a similar role at some other agency. I wasn't just leaving the company — rather, my life as I knew it.

I'm leaving it all in search of something more. More what? Not sure, but there's no debate. I have to trust the dream, the signs, and the lines I'm willing to cross to test the boundaries of my fate. I can do this.

My heart pounded louder than my knuckles did on his office door.

"Good morning, Lawrence," I greeted through a semi-open door, waiting to be invited in...and for my legs to stop shaking.

"Good morning, come on in," Lawrence said with his back to me, still typing.

I walked across his office. I remained standing and waited for him to turn and face me.

"Just give me one minute to finish this sentence..."

I waited, my mouth bone dry. I tried to swallow without making a sound.

"What's up?" Lawrence queried as he swivelled his chair around. He eyed the white business envelope in my hand. Then he looked up at me with a quizzical expression.

"I'm handing in my resignation. Kevin and I just sold the house and we're moving to Costa Rica."

"...You're kidding, right?"

"No, I'm not. I'm really quitting. We really did sell our house. And we're really moving to Costa Rica."

"You and Kevin sold your house? The house you spent three years renovating? Holy shit, when did all this happen? I didn't even know you had it up for sale!"

"No one did. I didn't want to say anything until I knew for sure it was happening. Remember when we went to Costa Rica in February? Well, we were actually checking out the property we ended up buying. And the vacation before that back in September? That was our first scoping expedition."

"You sneaky devil. Where in Costa Rica did you buy?"

"We bought thirty-seven acres up in the mountains in a remote community. We're going to be rainbow trout farmers."

Lawrence's eyebrows lifted. He was speechless for a few seconds before opening his mouth again. "Trout farmers? What do you know about trout farming?"

"Absolutely nothing."

"Well, aren't you full of surprises? But it's not like you haven't left us before. I remember when you left everything behind to walk across Canada and settled down in Regina for a couple of years. And then came back. Then drove across the country a few years later and ended up in Victoria, BC, wasn't it? But you came back. You see where I'm going with this?"

"Just call me Boomerang," I wisecracked. "It's time for me to move on again. I need a change. We need a change. We're seeking a different kind of challenge."

"Well, wow, what can I say? I'm sorry to see you go, but I'm thrilled for you guys. Sounds exciting. Do you have pictures?"

"Thanks, I appreciate your support. And yes, I have tons of pictures," I gushed.

"I'm sure it's all in this letter, but when's your last day?"

"August sixteenth."

"That's like five weeks — "

"I know we're really busy with the Kraft account right now, but if all goes well, the heaviest part of my projects should be wrapping up by the time I leave," I interrupted to reassure him that I had no intentions of dropping the ball. Then I added, "As long as I'm not given any new projects between now and then."

"That's amazing. I appreciate you giving me so much time to sort out your replacement. Thanks for not jumping ship during all the craziness."

"I'd never leave you high and dry. Besides, full disclosure, I don't want to burn any bridges. I might be asking for my job back in a few years," I laughed.

Throughout the day, I let my team and other coworkers know about the move as I met up with them in meetings or around the water cooler. The news spread fast. People that I hadn't told asked me for details. I was touched by everyone's interest, but they weren't all heartwarming responses.

"I hear you're leaving us again. Costa Rica, is it?" one coworker probed.

"Yes, that's right," I smiled.

"You can't stay put very long, can you? You're just not a long-term kind of person, huh? You can't commit. Isn't this your second marriage?" Judgement oozed out of his mouth. It wasn't uncommon for him to spew these types of comments under the guise of fun banter, but I never bantered back. I would slink away and keep my head down.

This time, however, I couldn't help myself. "Well, that's not entirely true. I'm definitely committed to personal growth. I was committed to my abusive first husband for fifteen years before I became committed to not being a victim. And this third stint at the company has lasted nearly a decade. That's pretty *long term*," I countered, then added, because I had nothing to lose, "At least I don't let fear stop me from stepping out of my comfort zone. When was the last time you did that?"

Well, there goes the bridge...up in glorious flames.

"I give it two years, then you'll be back. You always come back," he scoffed.

"You say that as if two years would indicate some kind of failure. I never said we'd be gone forever. If we manage to last six months, I'll consider it a success. At least we will have tried. We will have expanded our minds. Challenged ourselves."

"Don't get me wrong, I admire your sense of adventure," he said, treading more carefully. Then he added, "Just so you know, no matter how long you've worked here, whether it be one year, two, or ten, you've always done a great job. You're a hard worker. No complaints there. Worth every penny... I do wish you well. It takes guts."

Stuff

Finally, we could concentrate on packing. Kevin phoned and got several quotes from shipping and moving companies. The savings were significant if we did the packing ourselves.

"Sure, we can do that, no problem," I agreed.

What the hell am I thinking?

Before we could build a new life, we had to deconstruct our current one. The first plan of action was to get rid of as much stuff as possible. We assessed what was worth shipping and what wasn't. We gave lots of our belongings away to family and friends. There were things we wanted to keep but didn't want to ship to Costa Rica, which we stored in my parents' basement. We sold other stuff and threw out a bunch more.

So much stuff!

We were stripping the house down to the bare bones. And even though we'd reduced our belongings by two-thirds, we still needed a standard 20-ft shipping container to ship the pieces of furniture we knew would work well either in the house or the guesthouse. Our garden tools would be useful. Pots and pans, dishes, cutlery, linens, CDs, DVDs, books, pictures, and clothes all needed to be packed too.

One required task of an international move, which Kevin knew from previous experience, is for all items to be meticulously inventoried and assigned a value. That meant we had to count each knife, each spoon, each *everything* and guess what they were worth as a unit and then as a bundle. And when we didn't know, we had to look up the item online and calculate what it would cost us to buy new and then guess its depreciation. The process was tedious and time-consuming, and it became Kevin's full-time job. Although I helped after work and on weekends, I dreaded it.

We packed each box with extra paper and bubble wrap so nothing would shift or break during transport. We then attached a list of the contents on the outside of the box and labelled the box with a number, which corresponded to the spreadsheet. We also had to keep track of every serial number for every electronic device, from the toaster oven to Kevin's power tools. Despite their bulkiness, bringing the power tools made sense because we knew they'd come in handy on the farm. Besides, Kevin would lose money if he sold them in Canada only to repurchase them in Costa Rica. So yes, we would be shipping all of them. That was non-negotiable.

We lived in limbo. Although we had to get the packing done, we also had to live our day-to-day lives. I still needed access to my work clothes, laundry paraphernalia, and kitchenware to cook and eat our meals. Once we packed a box, the rule was that we wouldn't open it again. We simply had to learn to do without for the next few weeks… Except the boxes were right there in front of us. It was too easy to strip the tape off and find what we needed. We were packing and unpacking simultaneously.

One step forward, two steps back.

It was imperative that we put back whatever we took out of the boxes, and it was even more important that we not add anything extra to those boxes without updating the spreadsheet. Every item in every box had to be accounted for. The shipping company could not have put a finer point on that stipulation. Everything had to match when the customs agents inspected the container. Since we were doing the packing ourselves, the responsibility fell solely on us, and we took it seriously. Having our belongings confiscated would be an expensive mistake.

Dismantling our life at the Burlington address reminded me that a house, in and of itself, is devoid of heart and soul. I've always understood that it is the design style one chooses, the personal touches one adds, and the energy one imbues into a space that creates a feeling of home — and that *home* is an outward reflection of who we are. My desire to overhaul the old 1950s dwelling wasn't about keeping up with the Jones's but about keeping up with my own evolution. The house reflected who I was at that time — and where Kevin and I were at as a couple. The more stuff we packed up and the emptier the space became, the more detached and disconnected I felt from my identity as an exhausted, middle-aged suburbanite and corporate account manager.

I'm not a stagnant being by nature and never have been. My life's path has often been unclear, but longing to stretch and cultivate more self-awareness has always been at the root of my restlessness. The idea of reinventing myself as a trout farmer and bed-and-breakfast host in the remote mountains of Costa Rica invigorated my senses. Even with all the uncertainty ahead, I knew I had to choose the unknown over the familiar to keep my soul alive.

Eleven
Costa Rica, Here We Come!

A Curveball

Rick planned to meet us in Río Blanco to sign the purchase agreement, turn over the keys, introduce us to his network of friends, and run through the daily rhythm of the farm. For a 37-acre property with seven trout ponds and an aqueduct system...there was a lot to know. We felt grateful for this onboarding plan.

Then we got a call from Rick telling us he wouldn't be able to make it down in person. A curveball.

After a few minutes, Kevin put the landline on speaker so that I could listen too.

"What the hell, Rick? You agreed to meet us and stay a couple of days to walk us through all of the equipment and farm stuff."

"Well, yeah, but I booked a trip to Portugal with some friends and that's when they wanted to go," he said as though this reasoning would somehow absolve his lack of consideration toward us.

Kevin paused. Dead air. His hands clenched and I could sense he didn't want to say anything in case he said something he might regret.

"I'll make sure Martín is there to hand over the keys," Rick said, breaking the silence.

"So, Martín and Clara know you sold the farm to us?"

"Yeah, yeah. He and Clara know."

It seemed a bit callous to me that Rick would give Martín and Clara this type of news over the phone after fifteen years of service, but it was done.

"Are they willing to work for us?" Kevin asked.

"I told Martín you were the new boss. He was fine with it."

"You have to let them go, officially. You know that, right? You need to provide a written letter and pay their severance, and all that, remember?" Kevin said, stressing his words.

"Yeah, I'll do that," Rick didn't seem the least bit stressed, however.

"I've got to tell you, Rick, this change at the eleventh hour doesn't sit well. We're disappointed you won't be there in person."

"I'm afraid it can't be helped. Nathalie — a good friend of ours and my power of attorney down there — has the authority to sign for me. I spoke with her yesterday, and she will sign all the documents on my behalf. She'll meet you at Diego's office in San Marcos the day after you arrive. She's French but she speaks English and Spanish fluently, so it actually works out even better for you guys. She can translate anything Diego can't."

"I guess it is what it is," Kevin said with resignation. "What are we supposed to do with your belongings? We're knee-deep in packing our stuff over here, we're not keen on having to pack yours as well when we get there."

The sales agreement included all furniture, farm equipment, the Prado SUV, the Bombardier four-wheeler, and the kitchen appliances. However, we didn't want any of their personal belongings like their clothes, toiletries, framed family pictures, or trinkets. *Who would?*

"Don't worry. Nathalie will pack our personal stuff, and have it shipped to us before you get there. We'll leave you all the other items, as we discussed. We'll get Clara to clean the house and guesthouse, too."

"Thanks. How do we get a hold of Martín if we need to reach him before we land?"

"Nacho, one of his sons, works with Nathalie as a carpenter. He speaks English. I'll email you his contact information before I leave for Portugal. You can then reach Martín that way and let Nacho know when you'll be arriving. He can meet you at the house and give you the keys."

We weren't thrilled with this new development, but what could we do? We had to trust it would all work out.

August 2012
Ground Rush

I've never been skydiving, but I know that when you jump out of a plane and free fall, gravity pulls you down. That was a no-brainer. I'd experienced it in reality when I jumped off the Tarzan swing platform in Monteverde. A friend, who was an experienced skydiver, once told me about a scary moment when he'd waited a little too long to pull the ripcord.

"There's this strange phenomenon that happens when you jump out of a plane at high altitude and then pull the ripcord at a much lower altitude," he explained. "An optical illusion creates the feeling that the ground is rushing up to meet *you* and the sensation of sudden acceleration makes you feel completely out of control. They call that *ground rush*."

My friend's description of *ground rush* summed up how I was feeling. We were about to take the leap and plunge into a whole new life. We'd been focused on our target for months. We had planned, organized, and managed all our affairs. Free falling, yes, but with direction and with a modicum of control. Then, all of a sudden, that target was rushing towards us at lightning speed. There was only so much we could do ahead of time. For example, we needed to sell both our vehicles, but we also needed them daily up to the very end.

How long do we wait before we feel we can do without one or the other, then both, and not miss the selling window?

We didn't want to wait too long and find ourselves having to negotiate at a must-sell price. We knew we'd have to rent a vehicle at some point, but we didn't want to rent one for longer than necessary.

For items like our mattress, we wanted to sell but hoped we wouldn't need to sleep on the hard floor between the buyer picking it up and us leaving.

Perfect timing is crucial.

Don't Tell Me I'm Having a Heart Attack

We were so close. I could almost taste the fresh-caught rainbow trout and hear the ambling river. Utopia beckoned just past the horizon.

I'd envisioned the days winding down after I gave my notice, but instead, they ramped up. Client revisions challenged critical launch dates; changes needed to be made while the same deadlines needed to be met. My already hectic days turned into a pressure-cooker spectacle. Working overtime during these demanding times was the nature of the consumer package design industry. I knew it well, and yet, I hadn't accounted for it. I had somehow decided that a week between my last day of work and our flight out would be enough to wrap up final lawyer meetings, banking and police checks, and the selling of last-minute items, not to mention all the personal goodbyes. It wasn't.

I had been meeting friends for dinner and lunch since mid-July. To fit everyone in as the days on my calendar dwindled, I resorted to meeting some of them for breakfast. The fact that I had nurtured so many rich relationships was heartwarming, but I was growing frantic. There was still so much to do, and I feared I'd have to start telling friends, "No, sorry, I just don't have the time."

As I sat at my office desk in the midst of these frantic weeks, responding to another urgent email and doing my best to avert a crisis, I started to feel dizzy. My chest tightened. But I pushed on.

I'm probably just hungry. I haven't eaten anything all day.

I seldom ate when I was busy...*tap tap tap*. As I typed, my right arm started to tingle and go numb, so much so that I pumped my fingers open and closed to see if I could get some feeling back. Then, my breathing became short and shallow. I started gasping for air.

What happened to the air conditioning? Man, it's hot in here.

My peripheral vision narrowed, my heart palpitated, and my body trembled. I could hear people talking right outside my office, but their voices were unintelligible, as if they were speaking underwater. An intense feeling of doom overwhelmed me. It felt like someone was choking me or something was smothering me — that same claustrophobic sensation I sometimes experience when I feel trapped. I was scared I might pass out. I managed to stand up and steady myself, still pumping my fingers open and closed. My throat constricted, making it hard to swallow.

Fresh air, yes, that's what I need.

I can't remember making my way down the elevator, but I do remember sitting on a bench outside. The mirrored glass of the office building reflected an exceptionally pale version of me, clutching my chest and trying to inhale.

Oh Jesus, don't tell me I'm having a heart attack. Don't tell me I waited too long to quit my job and change my life. This can't be happening. I can't let it. Nope, nope, nope. Should I go to the hospital? No! The last thing I need is to have some doctor tell me I have to stay overnight for tests — or worse, tell me that he doesn't advise me to leave the country. There's no way I'm letting that happen. No way! This will pass. I just need to stay calm. And breathe... Keep breathing. Should I call Kevin? No, he's got enough on his plate to worry about. What can he do anyway? He would just tell me I'm being dramatic. Maybe I am. I'm tired, that's all it is. It's been quite a ride lately. I haven't stopped. I'll have plenty of time to rest once we're in Costa Rica. We won't even have internet for the first few weeks, so I'll have all the time in the world to relax. I'm okay. I'll be fine. Just breathe.

After about twenty minutes, my heart rate slowed. My arm was no longer sore. I calmed down. I had talked myself out of what I can only assume was a panic attack, *not* a heart attack.

Man, can you imagine if I died a week before my last day of work? I'd be so pissed off.

Jobless

I wasn't sad. I was ready. The day came when I said *adiós* to my colleagues at work. To be fair, it didn't feel final since there were so many ways to keep in touch with Facebook,

Skype, and email. Not to mention we were opening a B&B in a paradise setting, so I expected we'd be hosting some of them before too long. In their excitement for me, many implied they would come to visit — or maybe I just inferred it. Hope can sometimes blur nuances such as this one.

I took the elevator down, stepped into the underground garage, got into my car, and drove off. As the sun beamed through the wide-open windows and sunroof, the cross-breeze on my face felt invigorating. I felt free. It was hard to believe I didn't have a job anymore. My days of commuting through traffic and working long hours were over.

I thought it might take some getting used to. It didn't.

Leaving Canada

I spent the last afternoon in Canada with my kids. And how did we spend it? We went shopping at the mall.

I hate shopping. I hate malls. But not today.

They both needed winter jackets, and even though it was a sweltering August day, we managed to find some cold-weather apparel to match their tastes and my budget. Then I took them out for lunch, and I made sure to soak in every moment. As is often the case, I laughed until my insides hurt.

No one can make me laugh like Phoenix and Jude can.

Even though we had finished eating, we kept ordering more water, more pop, and more coffee — not wasting one drop of liquid or one minute of time together.

Sadness seeped in as I drove them home. Phoenix was first. I dropped her off at the low-rise building where she now lived with Ben — in the same apartment where I had moved her stuff before she came back from Brazil. We both got out of the rental car and held each other for a long time.

"Have a good life," she said with a semi-sarcastic tone.

I felt crushed by the weight of her words — felt her pain to the core of my existence — and pulled her in closer. I couldn't speak. When I let her go, she turned and walked away. I got back in the vehicle and started to reverse, but I just couldn't do it. I stopped and got out again, and to my surprise, Phoenix was running toward me. We clutched onto each other as though our lives depended on not letting go and cried our eyes out. It was excruciating. I was excited about starting my new life, but leaving my kids behind broke my heart...broke it in two. It was like I was betraying them and betraying myself. I couldn't bring myself to release my grip but knew I had to. Phoenix did, too. We said goodbye, for real this time.

Jude had moved all his things into his grandparents' place the week before, so I dropped him off there. I had sobbed through my goodbye with Phoenix and the waterfall continued to flow freely when I hugged Jude.

"Everything is going to be okay, Mum. For me and for you. Don't worry," he assured me.

After a long hug, I pulled away, feeling unsure I could go through with it. My head hurt. My heart hurt. I was in pieces. He was the strong one. Sniffling, I managed a shaky nod in agreement.

I drove off with tears clouding my vision.

I headed back to Nora's, the neighbour whose driveway we'd used to park the 4Runner and spy on the couple who bought our house. We stayed the last three nights with her while Bryn and Michel moved their stuff into their new home. It was weird not having the keys to that house anymore. And weirder still for Frankie when, after walking her, she would automatically strut up the driveway only to be pulled back and guided across the street. It was all very weird.

"Hey, how'd it go?" Nora asked as I walked through the door.

Eyes red and burning, I could barely look at her. She asked a bunch of other questions, but I couldn't absorb one word that she said to me. I had just gone *SPLAT!* from the ground rush.

An hour or so later, Kevin came back from having dinner with his sister, Kaz. He was in his own bewildered state. It had been a day of emotional and draining farewells. We were done *talking* about leaving; we wanted to concentrate on what we needed to do to get to the other side of this.

We sorted out our luggage. We weighed each of the four large suitcases and two were over the airline's allowance.

Damn it!

We shuffled some items around to even out the weight distribution and put them back on the scale to check if we had solved the issue.

"As long as we don't mess with anything, we're good to go," Kevin said, giving a thumbs-up.

Then I phoned the kids' grandmother, Jan, to say goodbye, since she hadn't been home when I had dropped Jude off earlier. Even if she had been, I was in no condition to face her.

"I'm sorry I missed you today. I have a piece of mail for you here. It got delivered today and I want to drop it off. Are you going to be up for a little while longer?" Jan asked.

"Yes, but it's nearly ten. I'm not expecting any important mail so don't worry about it."

"Oh, it's no problem. I want to say a proper goodbye to you and Kevin. I'll leave now and should be there in twenty minutes," she insisted.

"Okay, that'll be nice. Thank you. Don't forget we're staying with our neighbour across the street."

Jan arrived with our mail. As she was reassuring us not to worry about Jude, that she would take good care of him, she received a call on her ancient relic of a cell phone. She used it only for emergencies and outgoing calls. She was taken aback when it rang. I was taken aback that it could still ring.

How is that thing still working?

She fumbled. "Hello? Oh, hi. Is everything okay? ...Uh-huh... Okay, I'll tell her. Bye-bye," Jan cheeped like a baby bird, then squinted to find the disconnect button without her reading glasses. She slid her phone back into her purse pocket and then turned to me. "That was Dean. He called to say Jude is riding his bike down to say goodbye one last time. Dean sounded a little worried. It's been a while since he's lived with a teenager."

There were a lot of changes that everyone would have to get used to.

After handing over my mail and relaying Dean's message, Jan wished us well. But there was tension in her voice that I read as judgement and it made me feel uncomfortable. It's possible I was projecting my own sense of guilt onto her and it simply bounced back as judgement. At that moment though, I took the perceived disapproval personally. I forced a smile and thanked her. Although the smile was fake, my gratitude was genuine. I was grateful Jude would be safe. I was grateful I wouldn't worry about him every minute of every day while we were so far away. I was grateful he had a roof over his head, food to eat, and a soft place to land. I was deeply grateful for all of it.

Thank you, thank you, thank you, Jan.

Jude arrived on his bike forty-five minutes later. It meant a lot to me that he'd ridden halfway across town just for one last hug.

After some time chatting and playing with Frankie, I put Jude's bike in the back of the rental and drove him home. By the time I returned to Nora's, it was midnight. I was exhausted but wired too.

The alarm went off at 3:30 a.m. We showered and methodically loaded up the vehicle. The neighbourhood was calm and deserted. Crickets chirped in the distance. We took Frankie on a longer walk than usual so she would be fully exercised and emptied out before putting her into her snug crate; she would have to stay in it until we landed in San José. We prayed she'd be tired enough to sleep the whole way.

It's a lot to hope for, I know.

Since Kaz had kindly offered to return our rental vehicle for us, we made a small detour and picked her up on the way to the airport.

Next stop... *Costa Rica.*

Twelve
One-Way Ticket, Baby

We passed through customs and airport security without issue on the Canadian side. No problems with bringing Frankie whatsoever. They didn't even bother to check her paperwork.

We boarded the plane and followed the numbers until we found our row. Although I normally prefer an aisle seat, I had selected a window seat for this trip. I tucked the pliable crate under the seat in front of me, away from the aisle and all its distractions. Frankie had a tendency of whining incessantly when stressed so we'd braced ourselves for a long, embarrassing journey. But we didn't hear a peep out of her; she slept the whole way.

Perhaps the loud thrum of the engines is more soothing than scary.

The second leg of our trip, from Houston to San José, went equally well.

When we landed in Costa Rica, we went through customs without any incident. There was no need to show any documentation for Frankie yet. We picked up our suitcases and headed toward the luggage declaration scanner. This was where a gaunt, white-haired gentleman with a serious and authoritative demeanour looked at Frankie and motioned for — we could only guess — her health certificate. Kevin confidently handed him a wad of papers, signed by our vet and lawyer, all neatly stapled together.

No need to worry, sir. We're organized.

But the officer seemed confused. He wasn't sure why our lawyer had signed the document. This stumped him for a minute. Going over and above what we needed to do might have caused a needless snag. He shook his head.

That can't be good.

He then flipped through the pages as if he was looking for specific information. He'd stop to scan one page, then continue and examine another. Then another. My palms grew sweaty. Suddenly, the man who held Frankie's fate in his hands walked off with no explanation.

Where's he going? Is he coming back?

We weren't sure what was going on. We didn't move, convinced we were meant to wait. A few minutes later, he dawdled back with a three-inch thick, leather-bound, parchment paper-filled book under his skinny arm. It might have weighed as much as him. It looked like an old book of spells and potions from a sorcerer's library. Opening the book to the last page of what seemed to be a ledger with handwritten entries, he skimmed his index finger slowly up, then down, then up again, tapping it once in a while.

Our turn to be confused. We were feeling more and more uneasy.

He finally turned to Kevin and asked, "*¿Qué es la raza de su perro?*"

I caught the word *perro*, which I knew meant *dog*, and *raza* sounded a lot like *race* so I guessed he was asking us about her breed. Kevin blurted out, "Miniature Dachshund." A blank stare is all we got in response.

Kevin then wrote it on a piece of paper and drew a wiener dog stick figure. The old man grinned and returned to his book of spells. After what felt like an eternity, he found what he was looking for; Frankie was not on the list of dangerous breeds.

No shit!

The officer got his big old stamp and hesitantly squished it onto the ink pad, pressed down meticulously on the top page of the official document, then added his shaky scrawl inside the box. He handed the wad back to Kevin with a slight jerk of the head that signalled, "*It's all good. You can leave now.*"

Relieved, we kept repeating, "*Gracias, señor. Gracias.*"

It took every ounce of control to saunter outside the terminal. We had nothing to hide, and we had complied with all the Costa Rican rules, but it didn't feel that way. Even when we were innocent, I felt guilty. Kevin and I would make terrible criminals. All I could think was that Frankie better like living in Costa Rica.

Because this is a one-way ticket, baby!

We looked around to see if we could find our shuttle driver. Kevin had arranged for us to be picked up at the airport. Amid all the taxi and shuttle drivers holding signs with different last names, it only took a couple of seconds to spot ours. We rolled the sluggish luggage cart carrying our four suitcases, two carry-ons, and Frankie in her soft crate to the minivan. The shipping container with the rest of our stuff would arrive two months later.

"*Hola.* Kevin and Anne?" the shuttle driver asked as we approached.

"Yes. Hello," Kevin said, extending his right hand.

"Welcome to Costa Rica. My name — Minor. I drive you to La Trinidad," said the stocky man with a thick Spanish accent as if he had rehearsed every word beforehand. Then Minor motioned for us to hop aboard.

Before we climbed in, we pointed to Frankie's crate, gesturing that Frankie needed to relieve herself. Poor thing had been crossing her legs for nearly eleven hours. Surrounded by concrete ramps, sidewalks, parking lots, and paved roads, we opted for the sliver of grass on a narrow median. I expected Frankie to go *aaaahhh* right away, but we had to walk her up and down for several minutes before she finally squatted. I guess she'd been in shutdown mode for so long it took a little while to reboot her system.

After this short pit stop, we were on our way to the farm.

Our farm...in Costa Rica!

Would leaving all that was familiar to me for the unknown be my saving grace or a colossal mistake? Except for the emotional and mental chaos of leaving my kids behind, I had no doubts about giving up the rest of it. I was ready. I needed this change. In retrospect, ditching the grind was easy. But was I ready to face the days to come? The years to come? Would I be able to seize the adventure of a lifetime and attain some fantasy dream life, or was I about to face the ugly truth that I can't escape my own restlessness regardless of where I go? I didn't anticipate having so many questions. I thought I had answered them clearly in my head months ago. This self-interrogation seemed pointless as we drove across San José in rush-hour traffic.

We'd arrived. That was a fact. All the intellectual ping-ponging was useless. I had to buckle up, sit back, and enjoy the ride.

Part II
The Price of Paradise

Thirteen
The Veil Lifted

Thursday, August 23, 2012

The grey clouds hung low, creating a grim and heavy mood. But even on a sunny day, with its tropical yellow and orange birds of paradise plants perpetually flowering, San José was not a particularly charming city to me. It was dingy. Freshly washed clothes that hung across balconies on droopy ropes seemed to be getting instantly dirty in the smoggy air. And it was impossible to ignore the disorganized power lines crisscrossing the cityscape. Not to mention, most office buildings, restaurants, and houses were surrounded by galvanized steel fences, locked gates, and fortified by wrought iron bars on the windows. Even the most unassuming home seemed overburdened with an excessive degree of buffer between it and the outside world.

How do its citizens feel behind these impenetrable barricades? Secure or scared?

Looking around, the characteristics of our new country smacked me in the face...*hard*.

How dangerous is San José, anyway?

None of the sights were any different from what we had seen on our previous two trips. There were no surprises, but it was as though the veil had been lifted from my eyes, allowing reality to set in. I waited for the relief trapped deep inside me to bubble up into, *Ah, yes, Costa Rica. Home at last.* I waited, but no relief came.

Kevin and I weren't making eye contact, so I couldn't tell if he shared the same disillusionment. All I knew was that I needed to believe this visceral reaction was temporary and that I'd feel better after a good night's sleep.

First a drizzle, then larger raindrops slid down the foggy windows. I blamed my melancholy on pure exhaustion and the gloomy weather. Trying to keep the nagging question, *Was this a huge mistake?* at bay, I clutched onto the dog crate and shut my eyes in hopes that I would follow Frankie's example and fall asleep.

Awake Now

Half asleep, I felt the minivan slow down and make a hard right turn. I peeked through one eye and cheered up a little at the familiar sight of La Trinidad, the spit-on-the-map pueblo that marked the beginning of the 5-km, or 3-mile descent to our new home in Río Blanco.

The manager of the shuttle company had warned Kevin that their minivans were not all-wheel-drive and would not make it down any rough roads. For this reason, I had pre-arranged through email for Nacho — Martín and Clara's son — to come pick us up at the highway junction. Nacho had agreed to be on standby and wait for our call. However, the rain had stopped, and Minor felt confident the minivan would make it down the dirt road.

This new development concerned me. I knew from experience that the road got rougher with sharp turns and sudden dips. But sitting in the back seat and feeling a bit dozy from my nap, I felt removed from the decision-making process and surrendered. I said nothing. Clearly concerned too, Kevin cautioned Minor not to risk it. Our driver seemed unfazed, waving Kevin off as if he were swatting a fly. Minor was Costa Rican and drove a shuttle van for a living, dropping people off in various locations across this rugged country. Were these locations ever this remote? I didn't know, but I assumed he knew what he was getting himself into. His vibrato convinced me. And if Minor could give us door-to-door service, then we wouldn't have to bother Nacho. The non-confrontational, polite Canadian in me appreciated that.

Not too much further down the road, but far enough that I could no longer hear cars *whooshing* by on the highway while the distance between the humble homes tucked within the dense forest increased, Minor stopped the minivan. He shook his head at Kevin and mumbled under his bushy Tom Selleck moustache in his best English, "Sorry, no possible to go down more because no possible to come up." All his vibrato fell flat in an instant. I felt duped.

Now what?

Minor shifted into reverse and pressed the gas pedal into the floor as if he intended to back all the way up, but the wheels spun in place. Apparently, his assessment of our predicament came too late. He then attempted a three-point turn but the tires lost their grip, and the minivan slid sideways down the slope.

I'm awake now!

I sat ever so still — we all did — afraid any movement in the minivan might disturb the gravel beneath the tires and cause more slippage. Frankie whimpered. She was awake now, too.

We were at an impasse. Minor refused to drive us down the rest of the way, yet the minivan's tires didn't have enough tread to climb back up the dirt road. Minor was worried; the beads of sweat glistening around his right temple gave him away. Kevin reached over and handed our sweaty driver a piece of paper. With his thumb against his ear and pinky finger extending to his mouth, Kevin gestured to call the number. Minor nodded, produced his cell phone as if from thin air, and dialled. There was a short pause before he started speaking but then — in hurried, incomprehensible Spanish — I imagined he was explaining the situation to Nacho. He ended the call with "*Claro, gracias!*"

Reaching into his jacket's breast pocket, Minor pulled out a crumpled kerchief and wiped his ruddy forehead, then exhaled. He turned and gave us a tight-lipped smile and a thumbs-up. Pumping the air slowly with his outstretched hand as if to impress upon us to stay calm, he whispered, "*Esperamos.*" We didn't know at the time what that word meant but later learned that *esperamos* means *we wait* but also *we hope*. I remember doing both.

However, as one minute turned into two — then five — sitting in the minivan felt more and more precarious. Or maybe the uncomfortable silence between the three of us mobilized us into action. Or was it Frankie's annoying high-pitched whine? I couldn't be sure.

Careful not to jostle the van, we stepped out one at a time. Kevin and I had agreed to keep Frankie in her soft comfy crate until we were safely home. At least this way she was contained, and we could concentrate on solving the issue at hand. Letting her out would have added more chaos, which we didn't need.

While I swung Frankie back and forth in her carrying case like a parent trying to pacify a fussy infant, Kevin and Minor removed our luggage from the trunk. Their rationale was that a lighter minivan would be easier to move uphill.

My rationale? If the minivan rolls off the cliff, we won't lose all our stuff in the process.

Fifteen minutes or so later, an old khaki-green Toyota Land Cruiser came bounding up the hill like some animated cartoon. Three lanky, twenty-something guys hopped out with wide smiles. All three wore newish runners and baggy blue jeans — not baggy, down-to-their-knees that was hip-hop trendy at the time but in the well-worn, loose-fitting, manual-labour kind of way. No one was making a fashion statement, yet I noticed they each had their individual style. If I had been watching a movie, it would have been hard to figure out the climate from this scene.

Is it hot or cold up here?

The tallest of the three donned a sleeveless cotton-white undershirt, showing off his well-defined tanned biceps. The dirty-blond-haired one, however, wore an oversized camouflage-print hoodie that draped mid-thigh. The third had on a black graphic T-shirt with "Metallica" written across his upper chest and rows of white crosses — similar to the ones in the Arlington National Cemetery — dead centre. I could barely make out the faded lettering below the image that read *"Master of Puppets."* I wondered if he was a fan of the band or just the heavy metal look, but it wasn't the time nor the place to ask such questions. It was he who, like an ambassador, stepped up and made friendly but quick introductions.

"Hello, I'm Nacho. *Bienvenidos.* This is my brother Bryan," he motioned to the one in the sleeveless undershirt. It was easy to see the family resemblance. As Nacho's eyes directed us to the second guy, he added, "And our *amigo*, Charlie."

Without fanfare, swift handshakes were exchanged. Then the young men promptly helped Kevin push the minivan up the hill while Minor steered. The men's shoulders heaved as they grunted in unison. The harder they thrusted forward, the louder the grunts became. They had their work cut out for them; the incline was steep. My job? To stay with our luggage, pacify Frankie, and wait for this rescue mission to be over.

As I watched the men, the lesson on the importance of driving a 4x4 all-wheel-drive vehicle during the wet season was indelibly seared into my mind. When the men managed to push the minivan all the way to a safe plateau, I heard some victorious *whoops.*

Mission accomplished.

Waiting down below, I felt left out. Hunched sideways from lugging my dachshund — *miniature, my ass* — I hobbled up the road like Quasimodo and joined in on the high fives.

Minor apologized profusely for the scare and wished us, *"Buena suerte."* Remembering from my high-school Spanish class that *suerte* meant *luck*, I smiled at the irony that the bad luck we'd encountered was due to his poor judgement. Although I felt tired, stressed, hungry, and in need of a washroom, I did feel that good luck was on our side. The outcome could have been worse.

Kevin and I piled into the cramped Land Cruiser two-door wagon. Kevin up front with Nacho, I hunkered in the back seat with Frankie, her crate perched on my lap. Our luggage took up the rest of the back seat and trunk. Behind me, in the open trunk area, Bryan crouched crossed legged on top of our stuff. His pretzeled condition seemed exaggerated with his knees tucked so close to his chin. I surveyed the situation with some concern. It didn't look comfortable or safe. An unexpected slam of the brakes or pot-hole bounce could knock his teeth out. Nacho kept reassuring me not to worry; they did this sort of thing all the time.

I had no idea where Charlie disappeared to — one minute he was heaving the minivan up the hill with the others and the next minute he was gone. *Poof!* No matter: thanks to him and the two brothers, we survived our first Río Blanco wilderness adventure.

Home Sweet Home

We arrived on our new doorstep as the copper sun fell behind the tall, silhouetted trees. Sunsets up in the mountains are nothing like those by the ocean, but just as stunning against the dimming purple-pink sky...more enchanting, somehow.

As we turned into the driveway, butterflies in my stomach fluttered. All the excitement and trepidation from our first visit came rushing in as Kevin jumped out and opened the gate. This would be the first of a brand-new routine as residents of Costa Rica. The simple act of opening and closing our property gate would soon become second nature but in that moment, it seemed profoundly significant.

Nacho drove down the same driveway to the same house, yet everything felt different. It was too dark to see any details or be mesmerized by the view we had both fallen in love with back in February, but we could tell that the well-manicured property looked dishevelled and unkempt. The gardens were overgrown, and muddy craters pocked the landscape like bad acne; the ponds were empty of water and fish...of life. Our first visit was during the dry, sunny season. We had come when Rick had had time to clean up the place when the ponds were full, and when the gardens were brimming with colour.

As Nacho parked the Land Cruiser, we were met with the same pale-yellow house with its dark green roof and trim. The matching guesthouse stood to the left of the carport just as it did before. Had we arrived a few minutes later, they would have been obscured and swallowed up by the darkness. We had prepared ourselves for a letdown. We had talked about how this might happen and still, I was hit with an uneasiness. I knew we were in the right place, but I'd be lying if I didn't question our decision.

Nacho handed us the keys. There were four on the keychain and he explained what each key was for. One key unlocked the front door, another unlocked the French doors at the back of the house, the third small silver key opened the padlock to the garage, and the chunkier key was for the Prado SUV that was parked inside it. Well, Nacho made it sound like it was and I suppose since the key was branded with the Toyota logo, we trusted that it was. Besides, the bright yellow Bombardier four-wheeler was parked in plain sight under the carport, so nothing felt out of place.

"Martín, Clara, and I will come tomorrow morning. Is that good for you?" Nacho asked as he brushed his wavy raven-black hair off his forehead.

"Yes, that would be great. What time do Martín and Clara usually start?" Kevin inquired.

"Seven o'clock. It's okay? Is that too early for you?"

"Seven is perfect. See you then."

We thanked Nacho and Bryan again for saving the day, but they dismissed what we considered heroic action as everyday neighbourly help. The brothers jumped back into their father's vintage jalopy, extended their arms out open windows, and waved goodbye.

After we watched them drive off and round the corner out of sight, we finally released poor Frankie from captivity. For the first time since letting her out at the airport nearly four hours earlier, she was free. *Sniff, sniff, squat.*

As the sun dropped from the sky, so did the temperature by several degrees. The chill in the air formed goosebumps on my bare arms. Kevin and I had packed away our pullover fleece jackets because we knew it would be too hot in San José to wear anything more than a thin T-shirt. Waiting for Frankie to relieve herself, my shoulders automatically crept up to my ears as I rubbed my arms in attempts to warm up. I remember thinking, *How odd that I'm shivering in Costa Rica. It's not the usual image one would associate with this tropical country.* I imagined my friends howling at the irony that I left Canada to flee its cold climate.

When Frankie was done, I hurried her towards the back of the house and coaxed her to sit and wait in front of the French doors as Kevin inserted the key and unlocked the right door. We rolled our suitcases into the house and Frankie followed.

Once we were inside, Kevin found the light switch. I detected a faint bleach smell in the air. Someone must have mopped the floors earlier that day. And although we negotiated all of the furnishings and appliances into the purchase price, Rick and Mona's personal trinkets, artwork, and picture frames had been removed, as promised. Rick had mentioned they would leave a few extra pots and pans and whatever dishes they didn't want to bring back to the States, but we had no idea how much or little they would leave behind. I mused at how, during our visit, I had thought the house looked cluttered and how now it felt bare in comparison. It wasn't empty, but it felt devoid of personality. Without their personal flare creating visual distractions in every corner and on every surface, the colours of the walls, backsplash, and floor tiles seemed random with no cohesive connection. But I wasn't worried; transformation is my middle name. A roller and a can of paint were all I would need to make it feel like home. *Maybe two cans.* But I was getting ahead of myself. The first order of business was to warm up, feed Frankie, and make a snack for Kevin and me. We were famished.

When we had piled into the shuttle van at the airport, we had asked Minor if we could make a quick pit stop to buy some food. We knew we'd need a few things to tie us over until we could do a bigger shop in Santa María the next morning. Minor didn't hesitate. He knew just the place. There was a large grocery store on the other side of San José, the last big one before trekking into the mountains. He implied there would be more options for us there than the smaller family-owned shops sprinkled along the

Pan-American Highway. But we didn't need much; we kept it simple: milk, sugar, a box of tea bags, cereal, and a bag of dog food.

I rummaged through the kitchen cabinets to see what Rick and Mona had left behind. A lot more than I had expected, as it happened. We would have no problem getting by with those hand-me-downs until our own cookware and utensils arrived.

In the bottom cabinet, I found a kettle.

The prize of all prizes.

Then, standing on my tippy toes, I reached up and grabbed two mismatched cups from the open-faced shelves above the counter.

"Shall I put the kettle on?" I asked, already knowing the answer.

I adopted this expression from my English husband and no longer thought much about it. It was now something I said all the time. Drinking a cup of tea always seemed to make whatever you were going through better. If you are stressed or worried, have a cup of tea. If you are cold or bored, have a cup of tea. If you just landed in a new country and you are feeling tired and topsy-turvy with emotions, put the kettle on and brew yourself a cup of tea.

It was pitch dark outside by this time. Inside, the faint amber glow from Mona's tin-can-lamp creation cast bleak shadows. The phone line crackled when I picked up the receiver, so I put off calling the kids until morning. No SIM card for our cell phone, no internet, no TV, no radio... The lonely, isolated, unplugged sensation was real. It was only 6:30 p.m., but it might as well have been midnight.

How did it get so late so soon?

I was reminded that this was our new normal year-round living so close to the equator. No more summer twilight stretching into the late evening. I wondered if I would ever get used to it.

I sifted through our crammed luggage and found a cotton T-shirt, flannel pyjama bottoms, and my cozy pullover fleece to change into. Kevin did his own sifting and changed into one of a dozen soccer jerseys he had packed and his favourite faded-blue sweatpants. With our unzipped suitcases sprawled on the living room floor, we sat on the built-in couch with its custom-made rust-coloured cushions, taking turns snuggling Frankie and sipping our Tetley tea. Sitting there in silence, a bubbling of emotion rose up in me. It was in this quiet moment that I grasped the magnitude of this move.

Kevin and I were there because we had been compelled by a tiny tug propelled by curiosity. With steady momentum — like a small snowball that picks up more snow as it rolls downhill — our curiosity grew. And with every head-scratching *could we?* the answer somehow came up *yes*. There were a thousand little yeses along the way — most of them unspoken.

I felt unsettled, tired, and weary. But I also felt proud...and free. Kevin and I hadn't let fear of the unknown stop us. This was Day 1, with so many more adventurous days ahead of us.

Sip...snuggle...pet... Sip...snuggle...pet.

We put a whole lot of faith in Rick. Until the transfer of the property was finalized, we were merely guests. To be fair, Rick put just as much trust in us. Except for a modest downpayment, no significant money had exchanged hands yet and still he handed over the keys to his kingdom. I'm sure Kevin and I weren't the only ones hoping everything would go smoothly. We would be signing the legal paperwork the next day. Only then would Rick and Mona's half-empty holiday getaway retreat be ours.

Our home. *Our* property. *Our* new life.

Fourteen
Legally Ours

Friday, August 24, 2012

In the Light of Day

I hadn't slept that well in months. It must have been the combination of sleeping under the thermal duvet covers and the cool mountain air that knocked me out cold.

Even though it was the rainy season, the morning sky was bright blue without a cloud in sight when Kevin and I stepped out of the house at 6:00 a.m. Our disposition was sunnier, too. We were excited to explore the property before Martín, Clara, and Nacho showed up.

When we had visited six months earlier, we had fallen in love with the ponds, river, flowers, orchard, pasture, and the spring-like temperatures.

A paradise valley amid alder, cypress, and cedar trees.

Although Costa Rica is home to large primary jungles — true tropical vegetation at sea level — up there in the Dota mountain range, at such high elevation, the forests felt more like the ones in Canada — Northern Ontario, specifically. That was unexpected but comforting. We fell in love with that, too. But more than all that, we fell in love with the possibilities of what this place could be. We had tried to play it cool. We had tried not to get ahead of ourselves. Nothing was set in stone at that time. First, we had to sell our suburban dream house to make this dream life happen. I had to quit the security of my good-paying job to make this dream life happen. I had to leave Phoenix behind to make this dream life happen — and little did I know that I'd be leaving Jude behind, too. So many big decisions.

But there we were on Day 2, doing the rounds.

Standing outside the French doors, we stood on the terrace scanning the view. With relaxed shoulders and beaming smiles, Kevin and I took slow, soft steps and ambled our way through the dewy grass, pointing at things we hadn't noticed when we were there last. We *ooh*'d and *aah*'d with amazement mostly, but sometimes uttered a concerned *hmm*, making note of what needed fixing. Meanwhile, Frankie ran around on her stubby legs, stopping to sniff every new scent that caught her attention. Her ears flapped up and down as she bounced and *ruffed* at the wind. She was in dog heaven.

We had asked Rick not to fill the ponds so we could get a closer look at their depth, see how clean — or dirty — they were and whether the gates needed repair. The ponds were natural. Only the gates and the retaining wall that butted against the terrace next to the house were built from concrete. Without water, it's true the ugly mucky holes brought the look of the place down but everything else was so green and lush. In the light of day, we were back to being in awe of our surroundings.

Following the gentle slope, between the sediment ponds and the first small pond, the fish hatchery nestled inconspicuously. It wasn't an enclosed space but rather a narrow open-air structure sunken into the terrain. There were two long waist-high rectangular concrete tanks and eight smaller cylindrical ones further back. Metal beams supported a corrugated tin roof. This is where Swiss Man harvested the trout eggs and incubated them until they spawned. Each tank was used for different stages of the breeding process.

By the time we visited the property, the derelict building was reduced to a dumping ground for scraps of woods and junk — a long forgotten and unused operation. The half walls and tanks were still solid, but bits of dried concrete had cracked off and strewn on the floor. The emerald-green tin roof had no leaks that we could see, but the paint had peeled off, exposing patches of rust with a layer of fuzzy moss that blended into the surrounding forest. On the one hand it was an eyesore and on the other it was already so camouflaged that it would eventually, if left unattended, get swallowed up whole by the natural elements.

Because Rick and Mona used this place as a holiday home and only came down for three months in the wintertime, they had no use for the hatchery because they only ever filled the big pond with full-size rainbow trout. They were not running a business. They just wanted enough trout to feed themselves and any guests that might drop by for dinner. The other ponds were nice-to-look-at water features; whether they were kept clean or got dirty was of no consequence. Every year, when they returned to the United States, Rick had Martín drain all the ponds and empty the big pond of the remaining fish. The trout would flow through the canal that ran under the terrace and house and Martín would catch them with a net in the narrow channel. Once all the fish — about three hundred or so — were weighed, he'd put them into a large tank full of water and haul the tank in a trailer behind his Land Cruiser. Then Martín would transfer the fish into one of his own ponds beside his restaurant. They would get caught and eaten by his customers. The following January, just before Rick and Mona arrived for their three-month stay, Martín would fill the ponds with river water and replenish their big pond with the same amount of fish in weight. For the last fifteen years, the cycle repeated itself.

We looped back down and walked past the chicken coop, then followed the foot-path that led toward the house. There, we stopped for a moment, taking it all in. As we were admiring the beauty and power of the river — I was feeling true wonderment — Kevin turned to me with gentle eyes and said, "So, I'm thinking we live here a few years...clean the place up...create a world-class B&B vacation destination...sell trout... I don't know, maybe look into smoking it... Then we'll sell up and move on to our next adventure. What do you say?" His delivery did not match what I obviously mistook as wistful contemplation. His words sounded so practical, so detached. They took me by surprise and out of my reverie. It wasn't so much what Kevin said but *how* he said it that crushed me. Like it was no big thing. Like he was already over it.

When we embarked on this adventure, we never said it would be forever. And as experience has taught me, when I latch on to the *forever* idea, it doesn't take long for my tug to lead me in a different direction...a direction I can't possibly envision until it unfolds. I had been ready to make our last address in Canada our *forever home* and it only took three years to thwart me into a new reality.

It hadn't even been twenty-four hours and Kevin was already talking about leaving! The shipping container with our belongings was still in transit. Now that we were finally there, in paradise, I couldn't imagine feeling stuck there. I couldn't imagine ever wanting to leave.

So Boss

Martín, Clara, and Nacho turned up on the back terrace at 7:00 a.m. with their two little dogs, Flexo and Pulga, in tow. No leash, they just trotted a few steps behind, then calmly sat at Clara's feet. The pug, Flexo, possessed a short, stocky body and a squished muzzled face with a serious underbite where one solitary bottom tooth stuck out.

Mr. Personality!

Pulga, which means *flea* in Spanish, was a small ginger mutt, with no discernible characteristics. She was also so quiet that you barely noticed she was there.

When Frankie bolted towards them, I thought she was eager to meet new friends; to greet and welcome them as any gracious host should. With the mandatory butt sniffs out of the way, I was prematurely delighted she'd have her own kind to visit with.

But she was not impressed. Neither were Flexo and Pulga. They quickly got bored and proceeded to ignore each other.

All cultures have their quirks and traditions. I like to expose myself to different customs and social behaviours because I like how it expands my scope of understanding. It's one of the joys of travelling, I'd say. And as much as I don't like making sweeping generalizations, I couldn't help but notice that Costa Rican women — similar to my experience with Italians when I travelled through Italy — were demonstrative in a touchy-feely way. It wasn't unusual to see them hug and kiss on the cheek every time they saw each other while the men always shook hands. *Always.* So, when in Rome — *or Costa Rica* — as the saying goes, we followed the custom, then invited them inside for a chat.

While Frankie pranced in, hopped onto the couch, and hoisted herself up onto her new favourite perch beside the window — not unlike a smug cat — Flexo and Pulga remained on the terrace and waited. Another custom: pets are outdoor animals.

The first few minutes felt official: sitting up straight, minding we didn't say anything that might offend. I imagined they weren't sure what Rick relayed to us about them. And I wondered what Rick conveyed to them about us. Kevin and I couldn't assume we had been given correct information. We couldn't assume anything.

In the most basic English — and a lot of hand gestures, as if we were playing charades — we asked Martín and Clara if they wanted to continue working on the property. Nacho clarified in Spanish. They both nodded. Clara squeaked out, "Happy, happy, happy."

"Nacho, are you available to help out for a month or so?" asked Kevin. We had a long list of chores we wanted to catch up on and the extra hand would be appreciated.

"I'm a carpenter and usually busy but I don't have any work at the moment. I can help out until I'm called back to work," although Nacho's words came out as a warning that we shouldn't expect him to stay on the payroll, his grin indicated that he was happy the extra work would keep him busy while waiting for his next carpentry project.

We discussed wages and hoped the increase in pay we offered was agreeable. They beamed. We did our best to communicate, but it goes without saying we were relieved to have Nacho there to ensure nothing got lost in translation. More handshakes between the men and hugs and kisses between Clara and me confirmed we were in agreement.

So boss!

We all walked up and down the property together, prioritizing what we felt needed to get done. We shared our vision moving forward and they in turn told us their routine when they worked for Rick and Mona all those years. We were eager to hear if the information matched what Rick had told us.

Martín cut the grass with a heavy-duty weed whacker, chopped dead trees, mended fences, and worked on miscellaneous projects from 7:00 a.m. until noon, four or five times a week. It depended on what needed doing and his personal workload.

Martín had a small property with three trout ponds of his own to maintain and a rustic open-air restaurant they ran on weekends. People caught the trout from one of the small ponds, Martín gutted and cleaned their catch, and Clara fried it up. We had had the full experience when we visited in February. I remember I was taken aback when the fish I had caught minutes before — now lying next to a mound of rice and a simple salad on a white plate — was staring back at me. When I say Clara "fried it up" I mean she deep-fried the entire fish into a vat of oil until the skin was crispy. She served it with its head, spine, and tail attached. I also remember thinking that, although a cool cultural experience, if we were going to buy the property and create a B&B business, we would learn to gut, clean, and remove the head and tail. We would even go to the trouble of fileting it and removing the pinbones. I was thinking of our North American clientele, of course.

The restaurant was only open on weekends though, so Clara came by two or three mornings a week to weed the flower gardens from 7:00 a.m. to 9:00 a.m. Nacho explained the reason she left earlier than Martín was because every day she cooked hot lunches for the school kids and she needed time to shower and change.

In an earlier conversation, Nacho mentioned that he had two sisters. Paola, who was twenty-one, helped out at the restaurant and did odd jobs as a house cleaner. Nicole was eight and attended the one-room school with the other neighbouring kids. Clara was an active parent in the community, doing her part to help out.

Although I was grateful that Clara was willing to continue weeding the gardens — it was a big property — I was relieved she wasn't looking for more hours. After doing the math and calculating our monthly budget, I knew we couldn't afford to pay her more than the current deal stipulated. Besides, I would have a lot of time on my hands, so I'd be rolling up my sleeves and digging in, too.

It felt strange being employers, knowing people were depending on us to pay their wages. No more Monday-to-Friday jobs where we worked for someone else. The pressure was on to get the B&B and trout businesses up and running.

Although technically their boss, we wanted a friendly, let's-work-together type of relationship, especially since we were neighbours, too.

Too idealistic?

We knew building a trusting friendship would take time and we couldn't force it. We hoped everyone would get along and things would get done. Kevin and I knew that language barriers can muddy communication. We had to be careful that when we said *yes* to an idea to our friend and neighbour that it wouldn't be misconstrued as an employer/employee agreement. The line between friendship and employment had to be clearly defined, which would not always be easy. We had learned that employees could stretch the law to their own benefit. Time and experience would teach us how to walk this tightrope.

We inspected the empty, muddy ponds, too. Kevin and I had noticed several deep cracks in the big pond in particular and wanted to bring them to Martín and Nacho's attention. We stopped in front of it.

"How long will it take to seal the cracks and clean this pond?" Kevin asked.

Nacho turned to Martín, asked the question in Spanish, then turned back to us. "Martín says fixing the wall won't take too long, but cleaning this pond is a big job. It usually takes a few weeks with both of us working."

"Well, hopefully, it will go faster with the three of us," Kevin said.

"You will help us?"

"Yes, of course, I want to learn how to do all this stuff."

Kevin wanted to learn everything there was to know about the ponds and the aqueduct system. He wanted to be informed. He was a tool and dye maker by trade, mechanically inclined, and a natural-born inventor, so this stuff was his playground. He wasn't about to sit back and watch like some emperor overseeing his subjects. He was going to get his hands dirty, too. If he was going to run a trout business, he would do it from the ground up...*literally*.

"Wow, that's great," Nacho said. "Yes, it will go faster for sure."

When Nacho relayed this new information to his father, the energy shifted as if Martín was perusing a mental list of reasons why to like us. Martín smiled as his dark brown eyes softened. Working side by side with them seemed to have earned Kevin a positive check mark.

There was a lot to learn and there were some obvious issues that, to Kevin's astonishment, had not been resolved yet. For example, there was no gate at the mouth of the aqueduct that could be closed. When it rained a lot, the river got murky. Kevin knew that as soon as he arranged strategically placed rocks and logs, diverting the flowing river water through the aqueduct, the silt and sediment would flow through as well. Before we filled the ponds full of fish, we had to find a solution to keep the ponds as clean as possible all year round. But solving that issue would have to wait.

"Anne and I have an appointment in San Marcos this morning. Let's start fresh on Monday."

Shell-Shocked

It felt like we had already packed in a full day reacquainting ourselves with the property and figuring out next steps with Martín, Nacho, and Clara. After our morning walk-about, we filled up on hot tea and cold cereal. We showered and changed to look more presentable, too. We had serious business to attend to.

At 10:00 a.m., we set out to meet our lawyer, Diego. I found a few old blankets and made a nest for Frankie to lounge on while we were gone. With lots of under-the-ear scratches and forehead kisses, we reassured her we would be back soon.

We locked up and headed down to the garage. Kevin turned the key in the heavy padlock and the metal latch clicked. Much like French doors, I took hold of the right door and dragged it to one side and Kevin pulled on the left door, revealing Rick's gleaming, mint-condition, black Prado SUV inside. Although there was no reason to believe it wouldn't be there, I was relieved to see that it was. We had negotiated the SUV in the property purchase, but since Rick hadn't flown down to sign the final paperwork and provide the proper turnover, we didn't know what to expect. We were operating on the assumption that if Rick wanted the deal to go through, he wouldn't do anything to jeopardize it.

This was our first ride driving through Río Blanco as residents. We didn't need a map; we remembered the way. When we reached Copey, Kevin turned left at the soccer field without hesitation. We drove down the winding road that led through Santa María and I felt a twinge of familiarity. It felt good. We kept going until we reached San Marcos.

We found the lawyer's office and parked. We walked into a bare reception area with white walls and worn grey tiles. The waiting room chairs were all empty. Not a soul — not even the receptionist — was there. We waited for a minute, hoping we were in the right place. Soon a young woman came through a side door.

"*Hola. Diego? Por favor,*" I stammered.

"*Sí. Sígueme,*" the woman gestured for us to follow her.

Diego's parents were both lawyers and ran the law office in San Marcos while he lived in San José with his wife, and practiced real estate law there. He made a special trip so we wouldn't have to drive back into the big city. Diego had been a huge help in the negotiation process making this purchase possible, but this was customer service at its finest.

The receptionist directed us to one of the offices. A dark-haired man sitting behind a utilitarian metal desk that brought me back to the 1970s-office-cubicle era stood up with a bounce. His slender physique towered over us. With a wide smile and an extended right hand, Diego turned to me and shook my hand first, then Kevin's.

"Hi, I'm Diego. It's so good to finally meet you both," said our twenty-something lawyer with a lovely Latino accent.

Diego made us feel at ease. Thank goodness for his kindness and hospitality because we were alone in this transaction. Rick had assured us that his power of attorney, Nathalie — who spoke English fluently — would meet us at the lawyer's office to sign all the paperwork and help us with translation. But mere days before arriving in Costa Rica, Rick informed us that Nathalie had left for a month-long vacation in France and wouldn't be able to meet us in person after all. But not to worry, he had said, because she'd stopped by the San Marcos office to sign the documents on Rick's behalf.

Rick is out of the country. His power of attorney is out of the country. So grateful Diego had no travel plans.

After some small talk, Diego went through the house deed as well as both our vehicle purchase documents, which were written in Spanish. As he read each paragraph, he translated them into English for us. The English he had at his disposal, anyway. Diego highlighted the important parts to ensure we understood the implications, especially the large numbers relating to the amount we were paying. These documents could have said just about anything, and we wouldn't have known the difference. We had no choice but to trust him at that point.

Satisfied — or *resigned* might be more accurate — Kevin and I signed several copies of each document. Kevin called our Canadian bank, wiring the money to Rick's bank account. Everything went according to plan, which was a relief considering how much can go wrong with an international purchase. I thought I would have felt more anxious, but I didn't. Maybe I was shell-shocked. Or maybe, since Kevin was dealing with the banking and lawyer stuff back in Canada, I was relinquishing control. I was no stranger to taking on responsibility: I had purchased a home on my own before. I had worked and paid bills, counting and saving pennies to make ends meet. It felt empowering to know I could rely on myself and as a single mother provide for my kids. But in the same breath, I hadn't realized what a chokehold that responsibility had been. There was such a sense of relief at not having to be the one who had to manage the mental load of life's every detail. Although this was more than a detail — it was a huge transaction with huge financial implications — I was glad to loosen the grip of bookkeeping.

We were now proud owners of a 37-acre property in the remote mountains of Costa Rica. We kept smiling at each other in a giddy, teenage sort of way as if we had just gotten away with something.

Flipping Out

Kevin still owned one of those flip phones from the early 90s, which he had kept in his nightstand drawer because he kept everything *just in case*. It was the kind where to write a word you have to tap the number key and scroll to find the correct letter, then another number key for the next letter, and so on. No wonder people shortened everything to *brb* and *lol*. Who had the time or the patience to type out each and every word like that?

Despite the old-school design, Kevin thought the flip phone would be useful there. After all, we wouldn't have to worry about getting new cell phones. All it would need to function was a SIM card. We had already agreed before moving that we didn't want to be tethered to our devices and that we would share the one phone. And since our second phone was a landline, we wouldn't need the texting option anyway.

Thank God for that!

Since we were in San Marcos, we decided we would stop into one of the electronic shops and buy a SIM card before heading home. We didn't want a complicated phone plan. For $15, we could use a certain amount of minutes. When those minutes drained, we'd have to top it up. It was meant to be used locally: when we were in the SUV, and for emergency purposes. Who were we going to call anyway? We were always together, so we were in no rush for an upgrade.

Internet, on the other hand... Yes, please!

But we had had enough excitement for one day and it felt wrong to leave Frankie alone for long periods of time while she was settling in. We didn't want her to suffer from separation anxiety. We knew we'd be back to San Marcos to attend to one type of business or another every day for the next week, so we decided to tackle the internet task on one of those days.

Homesick

Although it had been a monumental day and one worth celebrating, it had been a long one. Not long as in hectic or exhausting, but rather in a so-many-new-and-exciting things-to-take-in sort of way. But the adrenaline rush was ebbing.

With dusk came a pang of sadness and it washed over me without warning. I'm not typically a homesick kind of gal. I've always loved changing things up. I hitchhiked across Europe when I was twenty-one and I moved many times all over Canada as a young adult. I lived in a tent for two-and-a-half months with my two-year-old daughter. I lived as a camp watcher in a remote heli-fishing resort in northern British Columbia. Not only did I welcome lifestyle changes, I sought them out. But this was the first time that I felt a deep, sinking feeling. I was grief-stricken about being separated from my kids. I wanted to call them, but the damned crackling phone line...

I suppose the altitude was adding to my funk and lethargy. The air at that elevation is fresh and clean, but it's thinner and it takes a few days to acclimate. But I wasn't thinking about the altitude effects at the time. No. All I could think about were Phoenix and Jude.

Earlier in the day, I felt crushed at the thought of leaving this place and now I felt crushed at the thought of staying. I wondered for the second time in two days if we had made the right decision. The contradiction filled my mind and heart with anguish. Laying on the couch in a fetal position, I wept like a baby.

Fifteen
Farm-Savvy First-World Expats

Saturday, August 25, 2012

The Highest Currency Exchange

Everything was calm, including my frame of mind.

After breakfast, Kevin and I drove back to San Marcos, but this time to meet Hugo, a reputable man in the community and manager of a small co-op bank. Rick had recommended we open bank accounts with Hugo because he spoke English and he'd be able to set us up without much fuss. Rick informed Hugo we were buying the property and was nice enough to make arrangements for us to connect.

We were pleasantly surprised the bank was open on a Saturday morning. We figured a predominantly Catholic, ultra conservative, rural town would have more conventional weekday business hours. It was closed on Sundays though; I guess the community wasn't prepared to trespass or bear the cross of that sin...*yet*.

The bank was its own cultural phenomenon. There was enough room in the large foyer for about five or six people to stand and wait inside; however, when we arrived, there was a lineup pouring outside onto the sidewalk. Apparently, the rain didn't deter those who needed to cash in their paycheques.

Wet umbrellas were leaned against the wall before each person was greeted by a sentry on duty who was blocking the door. Men got frisked on their way in, women's purses were checked, and hats were taken off so the strategically placed cameras tucked in the corners near the ceiling could clearly capture everyone's face. The institution may have been loosening its grip when it came to business hours, but it was definitely guarded when it came to security. It felt unnerving, but we soon learned it was everyday banking in Costa Rica.

The male tellers wore navy pants, and white shirts with blue- and green-striped ties, while the women were dressed with the same degree of professionalism in their navy skirts, white blouses, and blue and green scarves. Although it was clear that everyone was doing his or her best to look the part, I noticed they lacked a certain finesse; this person was missing a button, that person's hem was unravelling, and the shoes peeking under that desk over there were badly scuffed. When called over, the clients approached the partitioned desk and sat down in a chair across from the teller. Once seated, no one seemed in any rush to get up nor did anyone seem bothered that others were waiting in line for their turn.

We had read about the long lineups, so we were somewhat prepared. It seemed people used this time to socialize. It was a meet-and-greet-catch-up-on–all-the-gossip sort of thing. On this day though, Kevin and I didn't have to wait. The customer service clerk promptly ushered us into Hugo's office; he was expecting us.

A man with a thick head of jet-black hair looking like Erik Estrada's doppelgänger sat in a somber room behind an oversized oak desk. I actually had no idea if it was oak, but it was one of those traditional imposing dark-brown desks, one that declares *I'm important*. I couldn't help but compare the stark contrast to Diego's office the day before.

Hugo stood up. Where his physical stature fell short, his loose rolling gait oozed confidence as he strutted towards us. He possessed a certain swagger. He was the head honcho of this bank, make no mistake. He smiled and shook Kevin's hand, but not mine, which felt dismissive and chauvinistic. I was offended but tried to hide it by smiling back as I lowered my outstretched hand. Hugo then motioned for us to take a seat.

While poring over our documents, Hugo interrogated us about Canada and our motive to move to this part of Costa Rica. He seemed genuinely impressed with our sense of adventure and all the prep work we had done to get us there. Leaning back in his puffy leather chair, head cocked, making sure to remember every possible detail, he shared his own exploits of his younger days. His English was far better than our Spanish and it was clear he was taking control of the conversation. It's not that his stories weren't interesting. They were. But instead of bonding through our commonality, it felt more like a competition. The old, *Good for you, but wait 'till you hear what I did!* refrain. Regardless, he was welcoming and supportive, and I knew I was being too critical. I was probably holding a grudge because he didn't shake my hand. After an attitude adjustment, I felt grateful to have the head honcho of the bank in our corner and if listening to his rambling stories was the price, so be it.

After storytime was over, a good thirty minutes later, Hugo shifted in his chair and in subject matter. Sitting straighter with a more forward-facing posture, he explained the process of opening an account. He stressed how tricky it could be for foreigners. We nodded. Rick had warned us. Diego had warned us. And while doing our own research, we had read that bringing more than $10,000 into the country without being able to prove where it came from would be a problem.

Applying for residency had strict rules, too. Costa Rica welcomed expats as long as they weren't a burden on its healthcare system or taking employment opportunities away from its citizens. The government was protective that way. And we weren't looking to break any rules.

"People often land with their suitcases not thinking past the idea of having a grand adventure," Hugo remarked, shaking his head in disbelief. "They stroll into a bank, hand over their passport and a stack of cash, and figure it'll be that easy."

It wasn't that easy. Only legal residents were permitted to have Costa Rican bank accounts. We intended to apply for temporary residency under the *Rentista* status, which meant we had to prove we had a minimum of $2,500 of passive monthly income to last at least three years. This was over and above the amount we owed Rick for the property. We had considered applying under the *Inversionista* status, which allowed foreign nationals who were willing to immigrate to the country and invest at least $200,000 in an active business, real estate, stocks, or securities as a fast-track to permanent residency status. But that meant the money would have had to stay in Costa Rica. Rick wanted his money in the U.S. So, the *Rentista* option was the only way we could make the deal work.

"But I see you did your homework. Very good. Don't worry about a thing, we will take good care of you," Hugo finished as he closed the file folder with our stack of lawyer-stamped papers.

Since Hugo wouldn't always have the time to tend to our needs personally, he introduced us to Leo, the only bilingual teller. "Just ask for Leo next time you come in. He'll be happy to help you."

Having these connections in a developing Spanish-speaking bank was — to me — the highest currency exchange there was. It was humbling; I made sure I checked my first-world arrogance at the door as we left.

The Dirt on Clean Water

There were many differences between living in suburbia versus living on a 37-acre farm in the remote Dota mountains. One difference was the colour of the water coming out of the taps and silt deposits accumulating at the bottom of the toilet bowl. This wasn't an issue when we came to see the property six months prior. I would have noticed. In fact, I remembered the water being sparkling clear and Rick mentioning that the ponds and garden irrigation system were fed by the river, but that the house water came from a natural spring. Not only was it safe to drink, but it also didn't have fluoride or chlorine or whatever else a water processing plant of a big city added. It was pure, unadulterated H_2O like some elixir gifted by the mountain god. I saw this only as a benefit at the time. I didn't ask any more questions.

Rick and Mona only lived there three months out of the year... *The sunny, dry part of the year.* Chances are they never had to deal with dirty water because it so rarely rained during those months. Nothing got stirred up. Living on the farm full-time would bring different experiences and dirty water during the rainy season appeared to be one.

"Let's go up and check the water tank," Kevin urged.

"Good idea. Where is the tank anyway? I remember Rick talking about it but never showing us."

"It's just up the hill beside the pasture. Rick showed me the first afternoon we arrived. You were still en route with your new passport."

"Oh right, I missed out on Rick's grand tour."

"The water weeps right out of the side of the mountain into a large plastic tank, you'll see, it's pretty cool," Kevin smiled.

I couldn't picture it. *Water weeping? How does it get collected and into the tank? And how does it get from the tank to the house?* I was intrigued. As a suburbanite, I took a lot for granted. I turned the faucet on, and water poured out...like magic. I flushed the toilet and *whoosh*...never questioned the final destination. I didn't analyze it, I just let that shit go. If I'm honest, if it weren't for the dirty water, if there were never any issues, I may have never questioned it. But dirty water was an issue, and I was about to be educated on the force of gravity.

To the right of the house was the pasture. Or a portion of it anyway. Kevin opened the rickety wire gate and we both walked through it. I followed Kevin on a well-trodden path up the hillside. Beside the path I spied a black hose. Sometimes the serpentine tube was out in the open and easy to see and then I'd lose track of it like a snake following a rabbit into its burrow, only for the snake to pop out of the ground again a few feet away. I wasn't sure if this was intentional or if the earth had eroded over time, exposing the hose in random spots. More questions than answers swirled in my head, but I stayed focused and followed Kevin until we reached the tank.

Before me was akin to an elementary school science fair project. It's the only way I can describe it. The basic setup seemed cobbled together with gadgets, gizmos, and household items that were probably close at hand at the time. It lacked sophistication, but it did the job. Well, in the drier months it seemed to. But we weren't in the drier months.

"Let's see what's going on here," Kevin mused out loud, more to himself than to me. Then, looking at me, he explained, "Last February, I remember a steady trickle dripped down the mountain into this ditch over here." Kevin pointed to a shallow bowl-shaped hole directly below where the spring water was now flowing wildly. "You can't see it because it's too murky, but the bottom of this ditch is concrete to prevent the water from stagnating in mud. But it looks like the concrete might be cracked and the force of the splash is loosening the soil."

"The mud sliding down the hill into the ditch is not helping matters either," I added like a keen pupil.

"Exactly. And see the grey pipes over here?" he continued the lesson. "The natural spring water fills the ditch and the overflow then spills into these hoses, which trickles into the top of the tank and fills it up."

"I see. Then it travels all the way down the big black hose down to the house. But how does it get to our faucets? Our kitchen and washroom are higher than the bottom of the pasture."

"Gravity does the work to a certain point. The hose is buried underground and goes all the way through a hole in the foundation of the garage. You probably didn't notice it, but that's where the hose connects to the pump. The pump pushes the water into our plumbing pipes. I'll show you when we go back down."

Every April, when Rick and Mona went back to the States, Martín cleaned out the tank and disconnected the hose. I imagine the amount of residual sediment was minimal. Then, just before they arrived the following January, Martín reconnected everything. Rick had asked Martín to make sure the hose was reconnected for the new owners. For us. It was a considerate gesture.

What did we learn on our third day of being owners of a farm with a spring-fed water source? What was the dirt on clean water? Well, a mountain that wept in the dry months wailed during the wet ones. The force of the water hitting the cracked concrete and ditch walls was creating a mess. Oh, and the output valve of our tank was positioned too close to the bottom of the tank, not allowing enough space for the sediment carried in with the water to settle. There was too much dirty water flowing in...and out.

But Kevin had an idea. "If we tilt the tank so the output valve is angled higher, the sediment should have a chance to settle in the lowest part before the water flows out. It's just physics." Then, thinking it through some more, Kevin continued, "We should buy another tank so the water can settle in the first tank, then overflow into the second tank and settle some more before going down the hose. A double-filtering system. That way we'd get the cleanest water possible in the rainy season."

"And in the dry season we would have double the water capacity, which would be helpful with all the extra laundry and dishwashing when guests are here," I added. I felt proud that I followed the logic. Physics was never my strong suit, but having clean water — and as much of it as possible — was an easy concept to grasp.

I shed some of my suburbanite ignorance and gained some farming savvy. It felt like magic.

Sunday, August 26, 2012
Calling Home

Snap, crackle, pop.

The landline in the house was full of static and making it hard to hear the person on the other end. Although I picked up the receiver and checked it every day, I kept putting off calling the kids and my parents until there was a clear line. We had landed three days before... *Three days ago!* I hadn't yet shown any sign of life.

I would have been sick with worry had the situation been reversed. If I'm honest, being in Costa Rica, learning so many new things and feeling mentally drained, I felt like I was living in a different dimension. Time was at a standstill, not going fast or slow. Not going forward or backward. I could see how easy it would be to lose all track of days...then weeks. Time strung together only by loops of light and darkness, sunshine and rain. It was a bit Twilight Zone-ish.

That day, for some reason, the phone reception was better, so I jumped at the chance to call the kids. I spoke with Jude only for a few minutes. He didn't have much to say and the lack of inflection in his voice exuded an energy level that was neither high nor low, but I think he was happy to hear from me. It was hard to tell with his monotone delivery — a symptom that afflicted so many teenagers, it seemed.

Jude's life hadn't changed one iota since he rode his bike from his grandparents' house to say goodbye on Wednesday evening. He was settling into his own Twilight Zone dimension.

I didn't want to rattle on just to fill up the dead air — long-distance charges were accumulating — and he seemed fine keeping this chat brief.

"Well, bye for now. I love you."

"I love you, too, Mum."

Then I called Phoenix. I was disappointed when she didn't pick up, but I left a message and within a few minutes she returned my call. Our conversation was animated, the cheerleading lilt in her voice was infectious, and I felt my spirits instantly lift. But then it happened...

"I — *snap!*...pr — *crackle!*...y' — *pop!*"

"Sorry, pardon? I can't hear you, hon," I yelled into the mouthpiece.

We had to end the call sooner than I would have wanted because the phone gremlins had returned.

Connecting with them — even for just a few minutes — soothed my soul.

Monday, August 27, 2012
Martín's Approval

Before continuing working on the ponds, Kevin wanted to show Martín and Nacho his solution to slow down the dirty spring water. He led them both up to the tank.

While Clara and I waited for the men, we talked about less dire things like gardening. Well, we smiled and pointed, mostly. It became clear that learning Spanish was going to be a priority for me. All the smiles and head nodding felt positive with Clara regularly chiming in with, "*Sí*, happy, happy, happy," but I couldn't presume I was being understood.

The men came back down fifteen minutes or so later, looking pleased. Glancing in my direction, Martín gave me the thumbs-up. Then while pointing at Kevin, he squinted his eyes and tapped his index finger on the side of his right temple a few times. Grinning from ear to ear, it was obvious Martín acknowledged Kevin's cleverness.

Tilting the current tank and buying a second should solve our problem.

I felt yet another box on Martín's mental list being checked off.

Between Clara being *happy, happy, happy* and Martín giving us his seal of approval, I felt their acceptance as their new employers...their new neighbours...their new friends.

SIXTEEN
Between Worlds

Tuesday, August 28, 2012

First Grader

We lived out of four suitcases. We used dishes, cutlery, pots and pans left behind. There was nothing to clearly indicate all this was ours and I was looking forward to creating daily habits to help me feel more settled and less like a stranger in a foreign land.

Learning Spanish was one of the first items on my agenda. I decided to introduce myself to the teacher at the tiny, one-room elementary school. It would be fun to sit in on the classes with the neighbourhood kids and it would provide the routine I was craving. If I got to know the kids, I'd soon get to meet their parents, too. I believed it was a good way to integrate into the community in a humble way.

This gringa has a lot to learn from the locals.

Besides, up there in the middle of nowhere, there weren't any adult classes being offered. This felt like my only option.

I walked up to the school — just 500 m or 546 yards from our front door — and met the teacher, Elizabeth. Slightly confused at first, she thought I was kidding. She didn't speak a word of English, and my poor Spanish skills didn't help matters.

My point exactly... That is why I'm here.

Chuckling, she eventually understood what I was trying to say and agreed to let me attend school.

My new classmates were sweet and bashful. They kept staring at me, pointing and giggling. Having a grown-up in first grade must have felt peculiar to them. They introduced themselves one at a time and I tried to remember not only their names but also how they pronounced them.

The letter *V* is pronounced *B*, so when it was time for my classmate Kevin to introduce himself, without seeing his name written down, I automatically thought his name was spelled *Kebin* and continued to write it this way long after I knew better just so I could differentiate him from my Kevin. The letter *R* was a troublesome one and tripped me up. The Costa Rican *R* is different from how we francophones from Québec roll our *R*s. I was brought up speaking French and didn't realize there were so many different ways to sound out the same letter. I imagine most people don't think much about what their tongue is doing in their mouth when they talk. It just goes where it needs to go to make the sounds they were taught to make from the time they were a toddler. I was no different. I had no idea that my francophone *R* was so ingrained. As a teenager, when my family moved from the province of Québec to the province of Ontario, I had worked hard to learn English and get rid of my francophone accent. Somehow, I learned to subdue the guttural sound. Today, most people cannot detect any hint of my native language when I speak English.

I assumed the Spanish *R* was closer to the French *R* than it was to the English letter and that I could tap into the correct resonance with confidence. I was wrong. First, there are two different *R* sounds. One sounds like a cat's vibrating *purr* and the other is softer and much more similar to the English *R*. To manage the first stronger *R*, I had to roll my tongue against the back of my front teeth. I struggled. I rarely did it correctly. My tongue would naturally fall to the back of my throat and make the familiar Québécois raspy sound. The worst part was that I couldn't hear the difference. I kept thinking I had mastered it until the kids would snicker. It was clear that I was providing endless comic relief for them. I had no problem pronouncing names without an *R* though. However, out of seven students, four names contained that cursed letter.

Grade 1: Tamara and Kebin.

Grade 2: Nicole, Sharon, and Emilio.

Grade 5: Marco and Gabriela.

As a first grader, I sat between Tamara and Kebin in the front row closest to the chalkboard. I learned new vocabulary and how to pronounce words the Costa Rican way because it's different to the Spanish from Spain, of course.

Learning how to pronounce R *wasn't enough of a challenge for one day, apparently.*

Doing My Head In

As Sharon was reading a story to the class, loud banging noises from the other side of the wall interrupted her flow. She started again, raising her voice to the point of shouting. Elizabeth explained that workers were building a kitchen next door. All this time, Clara had been cooking lunch in a room not much bigger than a broom closet, which was dark and grungy, and the kids had to eat their meals at their desks in the crammed classroom.

The Costa Rican government paid for hot meals to be served at all schools across the country. It was considered an important program because many young children in the rural areas would otherwise go without lunch. The government also paid for school renovations when deemed necessary. However, from what I understood, the government would only pay for upgrades as long as twelve or more children were enrolled in a school. And since only seven students attended Río Blanco's, it did not meet the government's criteria and therefore would not be eligible for funding to build the much-needed kitchen. The Ministry of Education was willing to pay a teacher to teach the children, pay for the groceries, and cover Clara's hourly wage to cook the children's meals, but it drew the line at footing the bill for building supplies and construction workers. I suppose the government agency believed the children of our community could walk the forty-five minutes down to Copey to attend the primary school there and walk the forty-five minutes back up. Keeping the Río Blanco school open wasn't financially viable if the building also needed structural repairs or expansion for so few students. The parents of Río Blanco were busy tending to their farms and buses wouldn't be able to manage the rutted roads, so reliable transportation to Copey wasn't an option. And because the parents felt the distance was too far for their young kids to walk every day on their own, the parents formed a coalition and chose to keep them closer to home, which meant the cost of any improvements to the one-room school fell on our little community's shoulders to bear.

The community had had many fundraising events to help build a proper kitchen. They worked until the money ran out, then rallied and raised more. This small addition to the school had taken three years and it still wasn't finished. And when they did work on it, they did it during school hours. I didn't know how Elizabeth and the kids could hear themselves think with this racket. It was doing my head in and I couldn't concentrate. I barely lasted two hours.

I was happy to get home but the idea of the kitchen taking so long to complete irked me. Elizabeth mentioned they were running out of money again. Although a promise of some peace and quiet sounded divine, I wanted to help speed up the process. Kevin and I couldn't afford to hand over a wad of money, so I knew that wasn't the answer.

Definition of Progress

After school, we went to San Marcos again to put money in the bank and this time we did have to wait in line. It took about twenty-five minutes, which was nothing in Costa Rica. We were lucky enough to get Leo to serve us. *Phew!* Simple, everyday Spanish was hard enough to wrap my head around, but all things technical or important like banking made me sweat. I felt anxious and frustrated that I couldn't converse fluently. Kevin seemed to think I was crushing the whole language thing, but honestly, just because I knew a hundred more words than him didn't make me a Spanish maestro. He didn't seem to appreciate the anxiety I felt with every transaction; that all communication fell on me, whether it be writing, speaking, or interpreting. It was taxing. Sometimes I was up to the task and the words came to mind easily enough. Other times, it was like my brain data had been wiped clean and I drew a blank on even the most basic words.

"Can you call the bank to let them know we're coming?" he asked as though it was no big deal...as though I could break the language barrier through a form of mental telepathy. Even if I practiced what I wanted to say, that wasn't what brought on my anxiety. It was having to decipher their response...*on the phone...without hand gestures... and without visual cues.* Not to mention the staticky phone line I would have to contend with — it was hard enough to understand English, let alone Spanish.

"No, I don't think I can," I said.

"I can't believe you won't even try," he countered in a miffed tone.

It was exasperating.

No one was put more at ease than me to have Leo serve us. After exchanging pleasantries, Kevin handed him our traveller's cheques to deposit into our account. Leo stared blankly at them. The confused expression on Leo's face did not bode well.

"I've never seen these before. One moment, please. I will ask my manager," Leo said, taking the stack of the cheques with him. His professional demeanour never wavered.

When he came back, he didn't seem any wiser.

"My manager has never seen these before."

"I have to sign them. Once they are signed, they become the same as cash," Kevin explained.

Leo accepted our guidance since, clearly, he had no clue of the procedure. We were grateful he didn't refuse them altogether and he probably would have if we hadn't received special treatment from the big boss a few days earlier. We exercised extreme patience as I quietly murmured to myself, "Costa Rica, baby."

Considering it was its level of technology, decent education, and good healthcare that attracted us to come in the first place, compared to Canada, Costa Rica seemed so backward to me at times. I felt like we were living between worlds...between the old and the new, between established practices and modern-day advancements. Steeped in tradition, the older generation didn't seem to have much need for First World progress. At least not in the rural towns from what I could tell. Meanwhile, those under twenty-five were consumed — through the internet and satellite TV — by promises of what the developed countries had to offer. Most of them walked with their heads down, fingers tapping on their cell phones, which was not much different from the kids or adults in Canada.

What's the definition of progress, anyway?

Thank goodness there were chairs at each of the tellers' desks because we sat and watched Leo type each serial number for each of the sixty traveller's cheques, onto a data sheet on the computer, scroll his finger across each number on the screen checking that he typed each number correctly, then manually record them into a physical ledger... *one...at...a...time.* I hesitated but inquired about wiring money from Canada to Costa Rica. Hesitated not because I feared the answer but because I feared how long it would take to get the answer.

Leo was quick to answer though. "You have to go to a big bank to have money wired. At the Banco Nacional across the street."

We didn't have any contacts at that big bank — no one to coddle us. Since it was getting late, we decided to tackle it in a day or two. I had to go to school and ask Elizabeth to teach me more banking terminology.

With $10,000 worth of traveller's cheques deposited in our U.S. funds account, we transferred $1,000 into our Costa Rican colón account. By withdrawing the equivalent of $500, we left with 250,000 colones in our pockets. All those zeros made me feel instantly rich and suddenly this developing country didn't feel so backward at all.

Internet Junkie... Just Need a Little Fix

Sorting out our banking requirements was first on our long list of things to do, but getting some internet was a close second. I didn't want to be rude and use Leo as our personal concierge, but I asked him another question, "Is there a store in San Marcos where we can speak to someone about internet connection?"

"For your house? In Río Blanco...?" Leo asked, pausing to think. "Hmm, there is a little store...very small...bright yellow...on the corner of the main street, not far from here. They sell many different things. Maybe you can ask them?"

True to his word, we found the bright-yellow kiosk just up the road. It sold cell phones, electronic gadgets, and computerized cigarettes next to doughnuts, chips, and fruit smoothies. And I'm not sure, but I think they sold cars in their back parking lot, too.

At the kiosk, no one spoke English, but the word "internet" was universal and pricked one of the teenager's ears. He came out of the kiosk and motioned us to follow him. So we did.

Leading us down the street and up two flights of stairs to an internet café, our mute guide pointed to a sun-kissed Tica with silky ebony hair that trailed down to her elbows. I guessed she was the gal we needed to speak with. I turned around to thank the nameless teenager from the yellow kiosk, but he had vanished. This was the second time someone seemed to evaporate into thin air. Charlie had helped Kevin, Nacho, and Bryan push the shuttle van up the hill, then *poof!* And now this guy. I wondered if they were related and if this was a family superpower. Either way, both heroes in my book.

I returned my attention to the young lady behind the counter and inhaled before speaking. I knew Kevin expected me to take over from there. The pressure was on. I tried to line up the Spanish words in my head so they would spill out of my mouth in some coherent order. "*Hola. Mi nombre es Anne. Habla inglés?*"

"*Hola. Soy Milagro. No, solamente español,*" said the Tica.

"Tell her we need high-speed internet," Kevin prodded me.

"*Necesitamos internet rápido, por favor.*"

Milagro spoke Spanish at breakneck speed. That must have been *her* superpower. But with Kevin bending my ear with what he wanted me to ask her, me striving to collect my thoughts and translate them, her brain-twisting pace, and me having to unriddle her reply, to say I was struggling doesn't begin to describe how I was feeling. Communication came to a halt. The point was to leave the stress behind. I didn't come to Costa Rica to have a meltdown. And yet, there I was feeling overwhelmed and out of my depth.

Then, I had an idea.

We were in an internet café, after all. I went to one of the many computers, sat down, and used a translation app. Unfortunately, back then, the translation apps only got half of it right. Between my meagre Spanish skills, the half-baked translation, and a lot of hand gestures, we somehow managed. The glimmer in Milagro's eyes revealed that she understood, and she motioned for us to follow her.

Another follow-the-leader adventure.

We chased Milagro down the main street, took a left at the T-intersection, then up a couple of blocks — the grade of the road was steep enough that my glutes ached, and my breath shortened. Milagro walked as fast as she spoke. Thank goodness wherever it was that she was leading us wasn't much further. She turned right, then without warning, stopped. We nearly plowed into her. In front of us was a building with big "*I-C-E*" letters in blue. ICE (pronounced *ee-say*) was the national phone and internet company that also provided data cards for cell phones and laptop computers.

Just like at the bank, a security guard dressed in a bulletproof vest blocked the ICE building entrance. We all stood in line outside. For each person who walked out of the ICE office, the guard would wave another person in. Twenty minutes or so later, we reached the door.

Once the guard checked my knapsack and deemed we posed no threat, we entered a large open space. Directly in front of us were four rows lined with ten assembly-style chairs. To our right, there was a ticket dispenser and four white commercial desks with large computer screens. Opposite the desks, and just like at the bank, there were two chairs for customers to make themselves comfortable.

That day there were only two clerks on hand to serve the sea of seated people, all waiting their turn. Milagro pulled on the tab that revealed #146 and found three empty chairs. It was becoming clear that achieving more than one major task per day would be ambitious.

We waited another half hour, watching the electronic counter go up with every cluster of customers that left. Sometimes it was a single individual, other times a family of four or five. Although I couldn't be sure, I got the impression the clerks weren't just attending to each customer's immediate needs, but they were tasked to upsell, too. This took some explaining, some persuading...which meant more time, more patience. I was amazed that Milagro would take time from her job to wait with us. I couldn't imagine this scenario in Canada, but she didn't seem concerned or agitated in any way. In fact, she seemed relaxed and happy to do it.

Finally, #146 flashed with an arrow directing us to the next available clerk. Milagro seemed to know him and chattered on. The clerk spoke much slower than Milagro and although I still had no idea what Milagro was saying, I surmised from the way the clerk responded that he could schedule a crew to drop by our property to assess whether we lived close enough to get service through the Copey internet hub, but that could take a couple of weeks. In the meantime, if our cell phone showed three bars when we were on our property, then our laptops should be able to connect to the internet with a data card.

Although I wasn't thrilled about having to wait for wired high-speed connectivity, I felt strangely convinced that the data card would work despite not having any rational reason to indicate that it would. The fact that cell phone reception on our property was spotty was an understatement. There was one place at the very top of our property — way above the pasture — where we'd seen a signal with four bars...*once*. There was zero signal anywhere else on the property, but I felt a dash of possibility run through my veins.

After relaying to Kevin what I thought was being conveyed, I nodded enthusiastically and gave the clerk and Milagro a thumbs-up.

As we walked Milagro back to the internet café, she suggested we come back *mañana* with our *computadoras*, and she'd make sure we bought the right data cards.

"*Muchas muchas gracias,*" I mustered with sincere gratitude. I couldn't believe our luck at finding such helpful people. Everyone we had met so far had been so kind and generous with their time. But Milagro had gone above and beyond.

Before leaving San Marcos, I wasn't going to pass up the opportunity to check my emails and Facebook. It was the first time since arriving that I'd been online. The irony was not lost on me. We'd moved from our busy, hectic, *plugged-in* lives for a quiet, *unplugged* lifestyle and I was antsy — like an addict needing a fix — to get connected. I paid for half an hour. I had several messages — from Phoenix as well as all the Facebook comments since leaving Canada — to read through.

Euphoria!

It really perked me up. I posted a Facebook update letting people know we had arrived safely, describing in point form what our first week had been like. I also emailed our Belgian travelling companions, Hanne and Hendrik, letting them know that we did indeed relocate to a paradise property in Costa Rica. I explained that it was not far from where we saw the double rainbow — I was sure they'd remember that special moment. It was a full-circle story, and I imagined they'd be pleased for us. I was buzzing and the high kept me going for the rest of the day and night. We had to return the next day, and I relished the anticipation.

Wednesday, August 29, 2012
In Search of a Miracle

Would this whole data card thing work? The euphoria from the day before had waned and I now had my doubts. Solving our internet connection woes felt like it might take a small miracle. Kevin and I went back to San Marcos, as planned, in search of that miracle. And because I didn't want to misunderstand anything Milagro had to say, I asked Nacho to join us so he could help interpret.

"We'll pay you for your time, of course."

"Sure, I can go with you. No need to pay me. I know Milagro. She's very nice," he said.

When we got to the internet café, I scanned the dimly lit room. There were a few people already at the counter and a different young lady was serving them. Not Milagro. My heart sank. *Did I misunderstand what she had said? Was she not working today? Did she not say* mañana? I was sure she had. I was starting to feel bad that we might have asked Nacho to come to San Marcos for nothing. I could feel Kevin's frustration, too.

A few moments later, Milagro came through a door located at the back of the store. She must have been on her break.

As Milagro came closer, she gave a broad, toothy smile. "*Hola, amigos!*"

I felt relieved she recognized us. Next, this is what I heard Nacho say: "*Hola Milagro... Cómo estás* (how are you)...? Blah blah blah...*amigos*...blah blah...*Río Blanco... vecinos* (neighbours)...*necesitan* (need)...blah blah blah...internet...*rapido* (fast...hopefully meaning both high-speed internet and needing it quickly)... Blah blah blah...*por favor.*"

This is what I heard Milagro say: "*Hola*... Blah blah blah...blah blah blah blah blah blah...*computadora*...blah blah blah blah...*no problema*... Blah blah blah...*una hora*."

Nacho turned to us and said, "Milagro will install the data card software onto both your laptops and make sure everything is working correctly. She said to come back in one hour."

Since it was going to take an hour, Kevin asked Nacho if he'd like to grab some lunch as a thank-you for helping us. Nacho accepted the invitation and said he was happy to suggest a good restaurant. I decided to stay behind. I would have rather gone hungry than miss out on an hour of internet access. *No contest.*

I paid some final bills and got on Facebook again. I even had a live chat with Phoenix who happened to be online at the same time. I couldn't reach Jude because he was at school. Well, that was my theory, anyway.

My internet spree was over just as Kevin and Nacho came back. I gathered my sweater and knapsack and joined them at the front counter. Handing over our laptops, Milagro spoke at her usual lightning speed. I hoped I would know enough Spanish one day to understand her. This was my new goal. But in the meantime, Nacho translated for us. Well, some abbreviated version.

"She says as long as you can find a strong enough signal somewhere on the property, this should work."

"*Muchas gracias*," Kevin and I sang in chorus.

As we walked out of the internet café, I crossed my fingers and said a little prayer.

"Do you know what the name Milagro means?" Nacho asked as we drove back to Río Blanco.

"I have no idea."

"It means...miracle."

We set out in search of a miracle and found Milagro. You can't make this stuff up.

Finding the Sweet Spot

Once home, I got my laptop and jammed the data card in its socket. As Kevin drove the all-terrain four-wheeler at a snail's pace up and down the driveway, I sat behind him gripping my opened laptop for fear of dropping it, keeping an eye out for the stealthy signal. We found it, but within seconds it cut out. After several attempts, we decided to ride up the mountain. We had seen four bars on our phone once, but not today. If not at the top of our property, then maybe at the base. We drove down and stopped in front of Martín and Clara's restaurant, but still no luck.

We then rode over to the one-room school. It was 2:30 p.m. and the kids had long gone home. The soccer field behind the school was deserted. We rode around in circles, backed up, went forward a little...and repeated that pattern several times.

"Stop, stop, stop, stop, stop!" I cried out.

We finally hit four bars, which was equivalent to striking gold at this point! It was so sunny, though, I could barely see the computer screen. But after all that effort, I decided to try to log onto the internet anyway. Just as I finished typing in the username and password, dark clouds rolled in and it started to spit. We quickly packed up and headed home.

Doing all this on the four-wheeler is probably not the best idea.

We exchanged the four-wheeler for the SUV and drove back to the soccer field. The locals must have thought we were completely *loco*. We parked in that same sweet spot and connected to the internet again. *Eureka!*

In the distance, sheets of lightning played hopscotch behind the dense clouds, then loud rumblings followed. Since it had gotten so dark from the rain, I was able to see the computer screen much more clearly. I wrote a comment on Facebook about the adventure we were having and messaged back and forth with Jude. It was pretty bizarre to be sitting in an SUV...in the middle of a field on a mountaintop...in Costa Rica... typing on Facebook. Driving around looking for a signal certainly wasn't ideal, and we hoped we'd be able to get high-speed internet at the house in the next couple of weeks. But until that happened, this was how we rolled.

Seventeen
Transplanted Suburbanites

Thursday, August 30, 2012

Fingerlings

Although Swiss Man built a hatchery and raised his own rainbow trout successfully, we had no intention of incubating trout eggs. At least, not right away. There were enough variables coming at us all at once. We didn't need the extra stress of being on high alert monitoring the breeding process 24/7. Although we didn't know the exact process, we knew there was a lot of math involved — fiddling with pH levels and maintaining specific temperatures. It would have put me over the edge.

Achieving the correct clean water-to-oxygenation ratio for hardy, mature fish seemed challenging enough. But if we were going to sell trout, we'd have to get some fingerlings. We would buy a few hundred to start out with and go from there. With so many different pond sizes, we would raise each batch together and when they got too big for the smallest pond, we would transfer them into the next larger one. We would repeat the process until all the ponds were full of trout.

Different buyers might be interested in different fish weights depending on their end use. Restaurants might want smaller trout whereas a canning business might prefer much larger ones.

We didn't know what to expect yet. We didn't even know if running a trout business was viable. The only way we'd find out was by giving it a try with the setup we had. It all seemed doable, but honestly, what did we transplanted suburbanites know? We weren't exactly fishing enthusiasts. Kevin went fishing a couple of times as a kid and I had only gone ice fishing once in my life. We were simply riding the high vibe of possibility.

Rick had mentioned that there was a government facility up on the Pan-American Highway between La Trinidad and San Gerardo that imported rainbow trout eggs from Canada. Kevin and I decided to look for it and see if we could learn more about the procedure and if we might be able to buy fingerlings from their operation.

When we reached the Institute of Fisheries and Aquaculture (INCOPESCA), two squat men, who seemed suspicious of us poking around, greeted us outside.

"Hello. How can we help you?" said the first man in Spanish, as he pulled one last drag of a cigarette and stuffed the butt into an old empty pop bottle.

"We have a trout farm in Río Blanco. We want to buy baby trout. Maybe in November. You sell them here?" I replied in broken Spanish.

"Yes. We grow them from eggs until they are about this size," the other man nodded as he spoke while spreading his thumb and index finger about the length of a pink eraser. I looked over at Kevin to translate but he seemed to be understanding the Spanish *show and tell*.

"Would you like to come and see?" signalled the first man, opening the door to the building.

"*Sí, gracias,*" I nodded.

The building didn't look as sterile or clinical as I expected it would, but the distinct odour of disinfectant permeated the air. The concrete floor was sopping wet from the constant management of water. It was either being piped in and splashing in the tanks or sloshing from handheld buckets, I imagined.

Cigarette Man took the lead, washing his hands, then pulling on latex gloves. The other man kept walking and before disappearing into a room on the left further up the hallway, he stepped into a foot bath and rinsed his boots to prevent contamination, I assumed.

The tour started in the incubator room where a row of black floor-to-ceiling filing-type cabinets stood at attention. He opened a door and revealed shallow trays stacked one on top of the other on rolling shelves, like corpses on morgue slabs. Cigarette Man rolled one tray out and lifted the lid where two or three layers of tiny circular globs appeared. Although they looked slimy sitting in what looked like a gelatin substance, we didn't get a chance to inspect the contents carefully. Cigarette Man shut the lid almost as fast as he opened it.

"Very important to keep the eggs in complete darkness until they hatch. Important to keep trays clean, no fungus. Water is re-aerated as it flows through the stack of trays. Ten to fourteen days later, the eggs hatch and become sac fry which are transferred from here to over there," Cigarette Man said with animated pantomime.

Kevin and I got the gist. Seeing how things work in person is always so much better than just reading words on a page. And Cigarette Man's explanation of the process corroborated the research we had already done.

"Come with me," Cigarette Man gestured as he peeled off his gloves and disposed of them in a blue sanitary bin on the way out.

Although the entire conversation was in Spanish, it was like watching the simplest of Spanish-speaking movies without needing the subtitles. Kevin was enthralled but wasn't pressing me to ask a lot of questions. This was a visual lesson mostly and we were catching on to enough of the Spanish words in context. Had we been having the same conversation in a restaurant or bank line, I'm sure Kevin would have asked a whole lot of questions and I'd be stumped and useless at translating in Spanish or in English.

From the cramped incubator room, the man led us into a large spacious room with six or seven round waist-high above-ground pools and stopped at a long narrow trough where up to 30,000 sac fry started their growing journey.

"We feed them every fifteen minutes at this stage," Cigarette Man held a bucket of starter mash and sprinkled it over the water. All the fry swarmed to the surface.

In about two weeks, when the fry grow to 2.5 centimetres in length, or almost an inch, they would be ready to be moved to the larger tanks. They would be stronger by then and would need more room.

"It's not healthy to overcrowd them. No, no, no," Cigarette Man explained with an emphatic wag of his yellow-stained index finger.

In those big tanks, the tiny fry transform into fingerlings where they gain weight and grow to the length of a bobby pin.

"*Muy muy interesante*," Kevin said, enthused.

I could tell Kevin was relieved that Rick had been right about this facility, that it solved the question of where we would buy fingerlings, and that we were one step closer to being more informed, if nothing else.

We didn't need to be part of a cooperative or have an official business number. When we were ready to buy fingerlings, we would call them up and give them our order. Simple as that. They would collect however many we requested into big clear poly bags. We would have to keep them in those bags and let the bags float on the surface of our holding tank full of fresh, clean river water for twenty-four hours — a way of transitioning them from one water temperature to another without shocking them.

Even though both Kevin and I felt confident we understood the process, when November came, we would be sure to ask Nacho or Martín to call for us just to be sure we ordered hundreds, not *millions*.

> *Numbers are not my strong suit in English, let alone Spanish.*

Don't Bank on It

The day before we had bathed in Cigarette Man's welcome. Although sterile by design, the INCOPESCA's facility never felt clinical or impersonal. It had a grassroots quality about it and the atmosphere was a far cry from the Banco Nacional building... No warm fuzzy feeling there.

When we strolled up to the bank's metal-framed glass door and pulled, it didn't budge. The stern-faced security guard standing inside — who was far more imposing than the men at Hugo's bank and the ICE building — unlocked the door to let us in, then locked it again behind us. Without saying a word, without cracking a smile, he waved a beeping wand up and down our bodies like the ones used at airports, presumably checking for hidden weapons. It seemed a bit excessive.

But as I would find out a few weeks later, the Banco Nacional branch in Santa María, which was a much smaller bank, took security to a whole new level. It had a guard *and* a monitored lock-you-in security entrance. By that I mean, you had to open the first door, wait for it to close behind you and lock, then walk through a metal detector and wait for the green light before the second door unlocked. Only one person was allowed through at one time. If the door didn't open and the light remained red, as I experienced the first time, a muffled voice came over the intercom, which sounded a lot like someone talking underwater. I had no idea what the voice was trying to tell me. I couldn't even recognize what language it was.

I was stuck between two glass doors with a woman repeating the same thing over and over in a monotone voice. For someone who suffers from claustrophobia like I do, this scenario was pretty darn close to my worst nightmare. I could see the security guard standing there looking at me as if watching a confined animal at the zoo. I'm sure panic was written all over my face, but he didn't move a muscle. Suddenly, I heard one of the doors unlock. It wasn't the door leading into the bank as that light was still red. I quickly turned around and realized it was the outside door. I bolted. Freed from my glass cage, I calmed myself down. Kevin had gotten in, no problem; he was inside waiting for me to figure out what I had done wrong. I saw lockers to my left and to my right. Putting two and two together, it occurred to me that my knapsack was the culprit and something so bulky would not be allowed in this bank. I had brought a few purses with me, but I hadn't bothered to unpack them. My catch-all bag was more practical and had become my everyday go-to accessory. I removed my wallet and passport (because foreigners had to show their passport as proof of identity), then stuffed my knapsack in one of the small cubbies.

I had to dig deep and try again. The second attempt was smoother. I didn't have any problems going through those doors after that, but I still got nervous every time.

The length to which the banks went to flex the image of authority just looked like pomp and circumstance to me. San Marcos was a small, rural town. People wandered around in farm clothes with black knee-high rubber boots and straw hats or baseball caps. The men greeted each other with a friendly smile and a heartfelt handshake everywhere they went. The women were busy chatting about someone's cousin's nephew's daughter. All very benign. Although no one appeared super rich based on our North American standards, everyone appeared to have what they needed. Maybe I was looking at it with the wrong lens. Maybe it was simply a way to provide employment — having a security guard at the front door gave someone a job. *Maybe it's as simple as that.*

But I digress. The spacious lobby in the Banco Nacional in San Marcos felt sterile and all-business with a sea of white walls, white melamine counters, and white flooring. The hum of machines, the droning of background chatter, and the *click-clack* of high heels crossing the hard tiles echoed. Really high ceilings tend to have that effect, and those ceilings were pretty high. More rows of chairs for people to sit and wait — the usual affair. We didn't understand the directional signs so we took a seat and hoped when it was our turn to be served someone would speak a little English and could help us out.

Central and South America had a serious problem with money laundering while we were there and although Costa Rica had stiff penalties, it was not immune to criminal activity. Costa Rica was cracking down on the problem and rules were tightening up, we were told. If you had all your financial paperwork in order, there *should* be no surprises. If you didn't, then you could expect a long, drawn-out process. Kevin brought the document proving the sale of our Burlington house, signed by our Canadian lawyer. No matter how prepared we were, regardless of all the research and homework we'd done, when it came to the moment of truth, the uncertainty was stressful.

Forty minutes after sitting down, we walked up to the next available teller's desk and sat down *again*. In order to wire our money from Canada, we needed to open two bank accounts: one for U.S. currency and one for Costa Rican colón. Tried as I might to communicate with the teller, whose name tag read *"Miguel,"* I wasn't equipped with enough Spanish banking terminology to make myself understood.

"Alguien aquí habla inglés?" I asked, biting my lip, hoping Miguel could find someone who spoke English. Miguel seemed nice enough and willing to help. He pointed his index finger up in the air, the international symbol for *wait one minute*. About fifteen minutes later (yeah, in Costa Rica, we learned it takes the time it takes and you just have to learn to be good with it), Miguel came back with a young woman.

"Hello. My name is Valería. How can I help you?"

Relieved to hear that Valería spoke English, Kevin and I gave her our widest smile.

"Hello. We are Kevin and Anne," I said. "We bought a property in Río Blanco and moved here last week. We need to wire money from Canada. Hugo from the bank down the street told us to come here."

"You left Canada to live here? You will be living here full time? Permanently? I see."

I couldn't be sure whether she thought we had made the worst decision of our lives or the best. Her questioning tone sounded incredulous, yet her beaming smile seemed pleased.

Still standing in her form-fitting navy skirt, flouncy white blouse, and flight-attendant-style scarf around her neck in the complimentary bank's blue and green brand colours, Valería reached over to the mesh pen holder with her nail-bitten fingers and selected a blue one with the Banco Nacional logo on it. On a scrap piece of paper, she wrote a list. It appeared she had done this before and was ready for a quick conversation.

"Before you can wire your money, you'll need all of these things," Valería handed the piece of paper to Kevin.

I suppose she assumed we'd have to go collect the documents and come back another day. Kevin studied the list and checked it against ours — my heart pounding. I wondered if we had missed something important. But Kevin looked pleased. He unzipped our soft canvas pouch and handed her each document. Valería's eyebrows lifted in surprise. She clutched our paperwork, rolled out the low-back office chair with casters from under the desk, swivelled it, and plopped herself down.

Valería reviewed everything, and like Hugo, appeared impressed with our thoroughness. But it also meant we weren't leaving anytime soon. Miguel grabbed another chair and sat down beside her.

"I work in the loans department. There aren't many wire transfers needed in this region. Not many foreigners move this far up from the beach so most of my colleagues don't know the process," Valería explained, pulling her blonde shoulder-length hair and tucking it around her right ear.

Nothing was simple. Valería made several phone calls. Miguel watched and listened like an interested apprentice. Between calls, she got up several times — flitted and fluttered like a butterfly — walking out of view for several minutes.

Meanwhile, Miguel was left there looking at us with a *so, this is awkward* look on his face. Valería was pleasant and never made us feel like we were inconveniencing her, but we couldn't help but feel we were. This was taking much longer than she had anticipated it would.

Finally, Valería hung up the phone and turned to us, "Sorry but there's another document the bank needs before I can open your accounts."

We've been in the bank three hours and this information only comes to light now?

When things weren't done in a logical or service-oriented way to which we were accustomed, we repeated the same, "Costa Rica, baby!" refrain. It lightened the mood and reminded us that if we wanted Canadian efficiency then we should have stayed in Canada.

"You need to go to an accountant and have him create a business plan to explain how you're going to support yourselves," Valería informed us.

We could own a business in Costa Rica, but we could not be employed collecting a wage until we were permanent residents. We knew that.

"We'll be living off our savings for the next two years, at least. Our banking information signed by our lawyer is all in order, in there," Kevin zeroed in on the blue pouch in front of her.

Even though there would be no income to speak of for a while, it didn't seem to matter; we still needed an income projection.

However, as a representative of the bank, Valería couldn't recommend an accountant due to a conflict of interest or something like that, and since we didn't know any accountants there, we suggested perhaps our lawyer, Diego, might be able to help. Kevin gave her Diego's phone number, and she called him for a recommendation in the San Marcos area.

As she was talking, Valería scribbled the name *Samuel* and a phone number on a piece of paper. When she put the receiver down, she then called the number on the piece of paper. More quick chatter. After a few minutes, she placed the receiver down.

"Okay, Señor Samuel, the accountant Diego recommends, is available to see you right now," Valería said.

"Right now? This instant? That's lucky," my heart lifted.

And a little suspicious considering it's late Friday afternoon.

Valería drew a simple map on how to get to Señor Samuel's office and handed it to us. She added, "As soon as you have the final document, come back here. Go to that customer service desk over there and ask for me. You don't have to wait in the line again. I will complete the transaction for you."

We thanked her for all the time she spent helping us and off we went. We followed her scribbles on the yellow sticky note; it only took five minutes to get to our destination. However, the sign read "*CoopeSantos,*" which was the electric company. We checked the map again because it seemed a little odd to us that we would find a private accountant there.

Maybe he's moonlighting?

The first thing I noticed when we entered the building was that there weren't any chairs, not one, anywhere. Nor were there any lineups of people waiting. There was a strange echo-y emptiness. We walked through a long dark corridor before we reached the reception area. We told the woman sitting behind the orphaned desk that we had an appointment with Señor Samuel. Just Samuel, no last name. Or maybe that was his last name? With a stoic expression, she picked up the receiver from one of those multi-line office phones and pressed a grey button. She spoke briefly then said to us, "*Uno momento.*"

Several minutes later, a gaunt man with rounded shoulders and white tousled hair came around the corner.

"*Hola. Soy Samuel,*" he said as he met Kevin's firm grip with long limp fingers. I didn't bother stretching out mine; only a week in and I was getting the hang of being a Tica and knew my place.

Samuel didn't speak English, but he prattled on in Spanish to us as he shuffled down the hallway, up the creaky narrow staircase, and into a poorly lit room. He motioned for us to sit down. Kevin and I both hesitated for a split second. It felt like we were entering a tense interrogation scene in a Hollywood movie.

The walls were covered with dark wood panelling and a single naked lightbulb swung from a long, black cable poking through the ceiling. I wasn't sure if the desired effect was to strike fear in us; if so, it worked. The room was quiet except for the hypnotic whir of a solitary fan propped in one corner. Although the blades were spinning, they failed miserably at circulating the stale, stuffy air. It was...

The word that comes to mind is "bleak."

Feeling uneasy, Kevin and I inched our way into this dreary room and settled in side by side at the conference room table while Samuel toddled around and sat across from us. The table took up most of the space and its exaggerated width created a large gap between him and us. His already slight frame appeared even smaller. Then Samuel opened a coil-bound notebook and started to write one word per line. It could have been his grocery list for all I knew. Kevin and I sat there staring at him in complete silence for what felt like eternity.

We better not be paying by the hour!

Finally, Samuel put his pen down and looked up. He seemed a bit bewildered as though he'd forgotten we were there and threw us a sheepish grin. Then he narrowed his focus and flung some jazz hands our way as if to say, "Okay, so, what can I do for you folks?"

We were a little confused and we weren't really sure how to respond. I thought Valería had explained our situation. I began to speak in my staccato Spanish in attempts to clarify what we needed. Repeating words like *banco, nos documentos, de Canada.* Clearly, that wasn't helping our cause.

The old man got up and ambled to the door and opened it. Without a word, he waved as if he were flagging down a taxi. I assumed he was trying to get someone's attention but I couldn't see anyone from my vantage point.

Samuel tottered back to his seat. More uncomfortable eye contact...more silence...
more waiting. Eventually, a younger man came in.

"Hello. My name is Anton," the younger man said in English, shaking Kevin's
hand. "How can I help you?"

This was how it went; there always seemed to be one person in each building who
spoke enough English to be able to help us out.

"We were just at the Banco Nacional and a woman named Valería called here. She
said that we needed to speak with Señor Samuel about a business plan. Do you know
anything about this?" Kevin asked.

Anton turned to Samuel. They bantered in their mother tongue. There were nods,
smiles, and even some light laughter. The good-natured exchange was a stark contrast
against the gloomy backdrop. Then Anton turned to us with acknowledgment.

"For us to prepare a business plan, we need to know more about how you are going
to make money while you're living in Costa Rica," Anton replied.

"We intend to live off our savings for the first couple of years because we know that
as foreigners, we're not allowed to make an income," Kevin said.

"But you bought a trout farm, yes? In Río Blanco? What a beautiful village."

"Yes, that's right," Kevin confirmed.

"Are you applying under *Pensionado*?"

"No, under the *Rentista* category," I interjected.

"Ah, well, that's why you require a business plan because you will need to prove that
you can create an income at some point and since you bought a *trucha* farm, the bank
probably thinks this is how you will make money."

"Well, we hope to create a trout business, but we have no idea if we will be successful at growing this kind of commercial business or how much we can make," Kevin
warned, hesitantly.

"We're also hoping to open a bed and breakfast," I added.

Then I explained that we only arrived a week ago and suggested a business plan
was premature. Anton translated our intentions and concerns. Samuel bobbed his head
sagely but maintained we still needed to document our projections as best we could for
the bank's purposes. Since we couldn't predict the success of the B&B or the selling of
trout, our projections were pure pie-in-the-sky fantasy. We came to Costa Rica with
enough savings to last a while. We didn't have enough to retire on, so the goal was to
make money, but not necessarily in the first week...or first year, even. Anton urged us
not to worry; they'd take care of *everything*. If we weren't so desperate to hear something
hopeful, his words might have sounded intimidating.

Anton made copies of our documents, including our passports. I always felt nervous
when someone asked for my passport and then casually walked away with it. My passport

represented more than my identity and citizenship; it epitomized my sense of freedom. Each time I'd wonder if I'd get it back. So far, I had, but there's a first time for everything. I might have felt overly protective considering what it took to get this specific passport the previous February. The pit in my stomach didn't dissolve until Anton returned and it was safely back in my possession.

After a lot of back and forth about cash flow and yearly expenses, they told us to come back on Monday morning. To be fair, we didn't know why the bank needed this information. It felt like an add-on for the expat suckers. But what could we do? We didn't speak the language so it goes without saying we couldn't argue our case with any credible persuasion. The rules changed like the wind, and it was highly possible a new rule was instated between the time we did our research and the time we arrived at the bank.

Who knows?

We weren't in any position to bang our fists on the table, demanding justice. We could barely ask for a glass of *agua* without getting it wrong. Anton explained that this service would usually cost over $1,000 especially since they'd have to work all weekend on it. Our jaws dropped. However, he added that since they liked us and wanted us to be successful, they had decided to give us a break and only charge $300.

I felt angry and relieved all at once. We had no way of knowing if any of the figures would be accurate, but on Monday morning, we would pick up our so-called business plan with Samuel and Anton's best-guessed projections based on our goals and hoped it would appease the administrators at the Banco Nacional. We just wanted to wire some money so we could get on with living our dream life. But nothing about this day was simple. Nothing.

When we got home, we spoke to Diego about this new accounting requirement. He'd never heard of it and admitted expats often have extra conditions. A Tico didn't have to jump through these hoops to open a simple account. His expertise was in real estate, not immigration, but he didn't seem fazed this procedure was now in place. He suspected it was a money-laundering safeguard.

I suspect it's a cash-grab scheme.

Saturday, September 1, 2012
Welcome to Hush Valley Lodge

The river slapped against the rocks. Standing on the bank in my bright yellow raincoat with my face buried in its hood, I listened to the wind whistle through the swaying trees. The valley wasn't this loud when we came to visit back in February. I was sure of it. The name *Hush* now seemed ironic.

Should we rethink the name?

Our B&B wasn't open for business yet so changing the name wouldn't have been a big deal, but I had grown fond of it. Kevin liked it, too. It rolled off the tongue as though it was meant to be. I had designed a website and postcards promoting our new home and business as *Hush Valley Lodge*. I was determined to keep the name. Context was for me to decide.

Looking around, feeling clammy in my rubber gear but happy, I was reminded just how special this place was regardless of the weather patterns.

Regardless of the noise level.

One can always hear the river…like the lapping ocean waves on its shore. This type of white noise brings a *hush* to one's spirit. The broader definition of the word *hush* felt poignant…meaningful.

As droplets dripped from my hood's rim onto my cool cheeks and sniffly nose, I found myself grateful for the wet season and accepted that the river would inevitably calm down and go back to the *hush* that first tugged at my soul.

Sunday, September 2, 2012
An Imprint of My Own

It was Sunday and it felt like a Sunday.

At first, I thought Kevin was preparing his list of chores for the next day as he was strolling up and down the property. He liked to have clear directions for Martín and Nacho when they arrived each weekday morning. There was plenty to do beyond pond cleanup — weed whacking the pasture, mending broken fences, and clearing trails. Martín loved wielding his machete and never seemed to tire of chores that required him to use it. Kevin knew getting the big pond ready for water and trout was the priority, but he also knew that mixing it up with lighter tasks was a good idea…to give everyone's back a break instead of breaking everyone's back. His included. But from where I stood, I saw him pacing with his right hand up near his mouth — a sure sign that thoughts were whirling. When Kevin was problem-solving, he either bit his nails to the nub or absent-mindedly tapped his teeth with his fingertips as if they were piano keys. I was sure he was lost in his imagination. He wasn't working, he was inventing. What, I didn't know, but I let him be.

While Kevin was outside, I putzed around the house aimlessly…sitting, getting up, sitting back down. I felt stuck and tugged at the same time. I plopped on the far end of the rust-coloured couch and faced the fireplace. The firebox opening was as wide as my wingspan — if I had wings — so about 1.5 m, or 5 ft. Its hearth was just as deep. I loved the massive wood beam mantle supported by its equally sturdy jambs. And although I wasn't a huge fan of Mona's tin-can art, the intricate tin apron replicating fish scales with embossed trout cut-outs added a unique touch. To be fair, I wasn't sure if the credit went to Mona or someone she commissioned, but whoever created that apron should be commended. That fireplace was a sight to behold.

Then I flopped over to the other side of the couch just to see a different perspective. Through the wooden grid-paned window on the left wall, I could see the layers of variegated greens from the forest hanging above the river. Had I been taller I might have been able to see the rushing water, but being vertically challenged, I was resigned that this would be my view, which was better than a suburban brick building any day. The smaller window directly in front of me framed parts of the path and its colourful nasturtiums that lined the big pond. And next to that window, French doors opened up onto the large terrace. Through the twin doors, which we left wide open whenever we were home, I saw the terracotta tiles reach the knee-high wall that edged the big pond, then over on the far right-hand side a sliver of the pasture.

We owned this house nestled in this little piece of paradise and yet it didn't feel like ours yet. The first ten days kept us busy outside, either learning about the farm and all its water features or attending to official business in San Marcos. The inside of the house had simply been a place to grab a bite to eat and lay our weary heads.

I wanted to rearrange the furniture but most of the furniture was built in…except for the dining table that seemed to float like a bulky barge in the middle of the room directly in the path of the doorway. A humongous three-tiered wrought iron chandelier hung above it. If its sheer size wasn't impressive enough, its gothic style certainly was. I could understand why Rick and Mona felt the need to anchor the table directly beneath it. It made sense, but it was just too much. Dodging around the table, often bumping into one of the protruding corners — like some obstacle course testing our agility skills — was a pain in the ass. It was in the way. In the way of my serenity. Sitting there, feeling the vertical lines between my brows creasing into even deeper grooves, I realized I felt stuck and disconnected from our space all because of that honking big table and those uncomfortable straight-back wooden chairs.

We hadn't sat down at that table even once since we arrived. We either made ourselves comfortable on the couch and held our plates in our hands or sat on stools at the kitchen island. So I *d-r-a-g-g-e-d* that heavy son-of-a-table outside onto the terrace and kept dragging it another fifteen paces to the right. I stopped to catch my breath and came around to the opposite side of the table and bore down as I shoved it in a corner under our covered porch, then tucked the chairs in close so no one would bump into them. I figured if we ever had people over for dinner, we could drag it back in.

The living room area was transformed in an instant…less cluttered…less claustrophobic. Although it was no doubt perfect for Rick and Mona's purposes, I now felt unfettered from their presiding energy.

Freedom to make an imprint of my own.

Not to mention there was so much more room. I leaned against the bare wall across from the couch and imagined our pine dresser fitting nicely with our wide flat-screen TV on top. Perfect. The vision was coming into focus. I was having fun. I wanted to repaint the entire house now, too. My creative juices were flowing.

When we renovated our house in Canada, we took great pains to make sure there was a cohesive theme, that tiles worked with countertops and cabinets. That textures and colours struck the right balance. I didn't much care for the matching department-store-furniture look. Finding a sense of harmony between contemporary and that rustic feel had been my mission. Clutter makes me feel anxious, so I needed ways to keep my environment simple without looking too sparse or austere. It was less about the look and more about the *feel* that our space needed to evoke. I'd always had a hard time describing what I meant until I learned the word *hygge*. It's a Norwegian and Danish word that refers to a form of everyday togetherness. It's often defined as a cozy atmosphere that promotes well-being. Striking the right *hygge* balance was my creative problem to solve. And although I loved the eclectic feel of Cindy and Larry's home, I knew I couldn't pull that off.

Some people may have looked at this house and used the word *eclectic* and I suppose they wouldn't be wrong, but I would be more inclined to describe the inside as *frenetic*. It felt like someone looked at the flooring tile and said, "I really like these oversized terracotta squares with smaller diamond-shaped navy-blue accent tiles. Let's buy them." Then they saw a butter yellow counter tile and said, "Oh, I really like this," and decided to install it without really checking in to see if everything was working together. The grout was a weird army grey-green colour and the walls had a fleshy peach sponged effect. There was nothing wrong with any singular choice. Taste is subjective. It was the clash of all these choices together that was the problem for me.

We couldn't afford to rip everything out and start over. And we didn't buy this place to do what we had done in Canada. In fact, we bought an imperfect house so we could learn to relax despite its imperfections. To loosen our uptightness was an actual goal.

Kevin didn't necessarily care about what colour the walls were, but the gaps and rough finishes made his brow sweat just as much as bad colour schemes made mine furrow.

Nothing more was going to get done on this Sunday, though. I was just musing and dreaming. To be honest, I was happy for the diversion. I was happy not to have to speak Spanish or listen or decipher or interpret or translate. The pressure of being the one to understand all communication was exhausting. I was so tired I didn't even want to speak English. I just wanted to spend the day in my head. And that's exactly what I did.

Monday, September 3, 2012
You Can Take That to the Bank

There was no way we were going to tempt fate by being late. As instructed, we got to Samuel's office at 8:00 a.m. sharp. We were led to a different room this time, but it was as grim as the first.

Samuel started to chat with us while his sidekick, Anton, was gathering the documents. It seemed Samuel's English improved considerably over the weekend. He was all smiles and treated us like old friends. He explained with enough English words that the trout business was a lucrative one and he seemed excited to enlist us in the fish-farming cooperative. He said he'd be happy to visit our farm and help us get set up. He pointed out that our business plan projected favourable results, and we could do very well.

Anton then walked in with a package containing a detailed summary of income and expenses for a viable trout business, and the bill. It was obvious that a lot of work went into it so we didn't balk. *Out loud, anyway.* We thanked them for their kindness, paid the bill, and left.

We returned to the Banco Nacional with the accounting papers, which we hoped was the last piece of the puzzle we needed to open our accounts. We needed all our money in Costa Rica to be able to apply for residency. We prayed the rules hadn't changed since Friday, but we didn't bank on it. It wouldn't have surprised us if Valería sent us on what seemed like another expensive goose chase. But she didn't. She greeted us with a smile, apologized for the extra work we had to do, and promptly completed the transaction. Although saying *promptly* seems somewhat inaccurate. With the three hours we spent in the bank and the extra running around at Samuel's office on Friday and then again that morning, this transaction took approximately six hours. So not really *promptly* at all. And after paying our lawyer back home to sign all our paperwork, the fees at the Foreign Affairs office and the consulate before even stepping foot in Costa Rica, plus our new Costa Rican accountant, it cost us just over $500 to open two measly bank accounts. It was what it was, and we had to accept it and move on. We reminded ourselves we were only paying $150 a year in property taxes on a 37-acre farm (that's not a typo). We had to take the bad with the good...and there was plenty of good to keep us smiling.

Catalina

The school kids hadn't had any English instruction for the last two months. The previous teacher quit because it was too far for her to travel. She lived in Cartago, just outside San José. It must have taken her two hours to get to our little one-room school. That was quite the commute there and back.

The new English teacher was starting today, and Elizabeth was eager for me to meet her. As soon as I walked through the chain-linked gate, the kids ran towards me flailing their arms in the air and screaming out my name, "Anne! Anne! *Hola! Cómo esta?*" like I was some kind of celebrity. They were full of warm hugs and quick chatter. Those kids had a way of making me feel special.

The new teacher's name was Catalina. She was in her mid-twenties, and although technically young enough to be my daughter, we hit it off right away despite the age difference. During the lunch break, Elizabeth, Catalina, and I had a three-way conversation with Catalina in the middle serving as our translator. It was the first time I'd had a grown-up conversation with Elizabeth since starting school and the ice was now officially broken.

"I live in San Pablo but teach in Copey," Catalina shared.

"Is San Pablo far?" I wondered.

"You know where San Marcos is?"

"Yes, my husband and I were there this morning at the bank."

"Well, it's the next town after San Marcos, so not too far," she stated.

I hadn't seen an extra car parked outside the school and asked, "How did you get to Río Blanco?"

"I teach in Copey and my husband drives me there," she explained, then continued in English, then repeated herself in Spanish for Elizabeth's sake, "but now I'll be splitting my time between Copey and Río Blanco. I'll be in Copey Tuesdays, Wednesdays, and Fridays, then I'll come to Río Blanco on Mondays and Thursdays. Our car is okay to get to Copey, but not good to drive up here on the dirt road. I will walk up and down from Copey on those days."

"Wow, that's quite a hike carrying your laptop and books up that hill. It must take you at least forty-five minutes to walk all that way," I blurted.

"It's good exercise, I don't mind," she nodded with a buoyant smile.

I wondered how two teachers share the tiny one-room school while teaching separate subjects.

"I find a corner in the back of the room. I sit with Tamara and Kebin and teach them songs, show them videos on my laptop, get them to colour and repeat words after me while Elizabeth teaches the other kids. After forty-five minutes, we...how do you say...*cambiamos?*"

"Um, you change or switch," I half-guessed.

"Yes, we change. Tamara and Kebin sit down at their desks and continue with Elizabeth, and the Grade 2 students sit with me."

I was more than a little curious how they managed in such cramped quarters. *It must be so distracting.*

I offered to help Catalina instead of going straight home as I would have done normally. I was able to provide pronunciation tips when she asked.

"I learned English from a Spanish-speaking teacher. It's so good to have a native English speaker here!" she exclaimed. The irony was that my native tongue was French, but I took it as a compliment.

"I'm happy to help."

Catalina was kind and patient. She was the type of person who smiled with her eyes. It was her first day with these kids and it was clear she had a captive audience as they listened closely and repeated with gusto.

At the end of the day, as we were saying goodbye to the kids, Catalina packed up her things in her leather slingback satchel and put on her raincoat.

A forty-five-minute walk downhill...in the rain.

"Let me give you a ride down to Copey. I can pick you up on the days you come to Río Blanco and drive you back at the end of the school day," I offered. She could then hitch a ride with one of the high-school teachers going her way or wait for her husband.

"Oh, that's not necessary. It's not a problem for me to walk," she said, wearing a *I wouldn't dream of being such an imposition* expression.

"Well, actually, you'd be doing me a favour. Maybe I could speak Spanish with you. I need the practice," I nudged, selling her on the idea that it would be a fair exchange: a ride for Spanish lessons. And although that was true — I definitely needed the practice — I figured it would give us more time to get to know each other outside of the classroom. So far, most of my local friends were all under ten years old.

Self-serving, really.

Catalina smiled and accepted my offer.

Explosion!

In Rick and Mona's left-behind toaster oven that sat on top of our diminutive fridge, I slid a remnant nonstick-coated rectangular pan that I found in one of the kitchen cabinets. The pan was worn and no longer *nonstick*, discoloured with permanent scars from what seemed like years of abuse. It was a tight squeeze, but it was the only toaster oven we had until our container arrived. *And the only pan.* Since the toaster oven could only fit that one pan, I crammed everything in it: chicken, broccoli, carrots, and potatoes. Then I covered it with tin foil. Although the light went on, the heating elements weren't turning orange on the *bake* setting. I turned it to *broil* as a solution. A few minutes later, the door exploded off its hinges and shards of glass shattered everywhere. *Whoa!* I felt a bit shaken from the whole ordeal, but mostly I felt stupid.

Apparently, putting it on the broil setting is not the solution.

This kitchen had no oven, nor did it have a microwave. We had decided we didn't need either of those appliances. If Rick and Mona were able to do without, then so could we. We didn't want all the North American conveniences. We were determined to keep things simple. That toaster oven *was* our only means of cooking other than the portable propane stovetop with two burners — something you might use when you go camping. There was no point in buying a new toaster oven since ours was scheduled to arrive in a few weeks. We would just have to make do.

After we cleaned up the mess, I recovered our foiled dinner and finished cooking it over the stovetop. At least we had two propane burners. *Winning!*

River Rising

As if an exploding toaster oven inside the house wasn't exciting enough, there was a torrential rainstorm going on outside. The river was muddy brown and was rising fast.

We had only been there a few days when Nacho brought the threat of the river to our attention. "Did Rick tell you how high the river rises in the rainy season and how dangerous it is?"

"No, Rick didn't tell us anything about it," Kevin answered.

Nacho's face showed visible concern.

That's not good.

Nacho implored us not to get too close to the river when it was like this. As if no amount of caution was enough, Nacho emphasized by beating his right fist into his left hand, "*Muy, muy, forte... The river is loco, loco, loco...craazee...* You understand?"

We knew there was no winning over the fierce force of water. If we fell in, the current would drag us under.

A few days later, Roberto would reinforce the same warning, but with a much more subdued, self-restrained delivery. Roberto's resting face was serious so there was no need to invoke more drama. Knowing we had asked Rick outright about the river — on two occasions — we were a little perturbed. Rick had said, "It rains a lot in September and October." That was it.

Kevin and I stood on the narrow walkway, watching the chocolate-brown river get wilder. Broken tree limbs crashed against the rocks as the water swelled. The bending wind howled. We hoped the rain would subside and the river would calm down soon. It was unnerving but I kept telling myself that this place had been standing strong for decades. Surely, this was no different from what they experience every year.

Right?

We watched and waited.

Throughout the evening, we received phone calls from concerned neighbours. People we didn't know invited us to come stay with them if the river got too turbulent. What they meant was *if we got too scared*. In Spanglish, I thanked and assured them, "*Sí,* we're okay, *gracias.*" The kindness of strangers was a tremendous gift; we felt less isolated. The storm — outside our doors and inside my mind — calmed down.

Eventually.

Eighteen
Official Trout Farmers

Tuesday, September 4, 2012

Puma on the Prowl

In Costa Rica, dogs are considered outdoor animals, and few are allowed inside. They usually sleep under a carport near the house, or in a nearby shed, or in a back room away from the rest of the household. And that's only if they're small dogs. Big dogs have to fend for themselves out in the yard or farm. We saw dogs roaming everywhere all the time. They were healthy and carefree, not mangy nor mean. For us, it was hard to tell which ones were strays and which ones were people's pets out for a jaunt.

We had yet to hear stories about our neighbours' dogs wandering too far or going missing. If they did, they must have returned home before it was time to set any alarms.

When Martín arrived for work, he was visibly distraught. He rattled on and I was trying to follow what he was attempting to explain.

"What's he saying?" Kevin asked.

"There was a lot of barking and yelping outside his house last night and after calling out to Flexo and Pulga, only Flexo came home," I answered.

"So where is Pulga?" Kevin tried to piece together what Martín was saying.

"*Donde está Pulga*?" I asked Martín as the go-between.

"*No se*," Martín shook his head. "*Una puma*?" Martín imitated the swiping of a ferocious claw with his own hand.

This scary point punctuated how important it was to keep careful watch over Frankie, even in paradise. In Canada, we had to keep her safe from skunks and raccoons, which can be threatening in their own right, but our new backyard was home to a whole new level of danger. These big nocturnal cats usually prey on small animals like rabbits. And although seeing a puma would have been extraordinary, it was rare that they came so close to human dwellings. Having said that, we weren't exactly in the suburbs.

Stray dogs must have been an easy target and their demise due to stealthy predators probably happened more often than we imagined. But this tiny dog wasn't homeless. She was a family pet and never wandered too far. All it took, though, was one swift pounce and a puma could carry a small dog away in its mouth, leaving no trace. Frankie was a chunky monkey, but still not much bigger than a rabbit, so she would have been a succulent treat for any of these wild felines.

Yup, we're definitely keeping Frankie inside at night.

Wednesday, September 5, 2012
On Shaky Ground

Kevin and I drove down to San Isidro de El General, which was about an hour's drive from our place. We wanted to compare prices of clothes dryers and tools.

Driving south on the Pan-American Highway, we climbed further up into the mountains where the temperature dropped to 10°C (50°F). We reached the crest, then drove down the other side. By the time we reached San Isidro, a half hour after our descent, the temperature was 37°C (98°F)! I'd never before needed heating and air conditioning within a thirty-minute time span. We liked San Isidro, but man it was sizzling.

While we were in one of the shops, we heard a ringtone coming from Kevin's cargo pants pocket. That was unexpected. We did carry the flip phone on us for emergencies, but we hadn't used it since we got the SIM card. The only time we flipped it open was to check whether we could find at least three reception bars somewhere on our property. Anywhere. We rarely did. But San Isidro was more populated, and the signal must have been more reliable. We just figured if we ever did use the phone away from home, it would be for outgoing calls, not incoming.

With a quizzical expression, Kevin reached into his pocket and pulled out the folded device.

My curiosity was piqued. *Who the heck is calling us? Who has our cell number, for that matter?*

It was his mother. By Kevin's reaction, she sounded a bit frantic.

"Mum, slow down," he told her. "What's going on…? Oh really…? No, we hadn't heard… Yes, we're both fine. Promise. We're nowhere near that area. We're out shopping,"

I heard Kevin reassure his mum and after a few minutes he said goodbye, then looked at me and said, "Apparently there's been an earthquake in Guanacaste that measured seven-point-six on the Richter scale."

Guanacaste is located on the Pacific Coast in the northernmost area of Costa Rica. We had been there when we were travelling with Hanne and Hendrik. The earthquake happened at 8:40 a.m. Whatever quake we might have felt was disguised by the SUV shaking on the bumpy dirt road we were just driving on.

In one of the stores, a TV blasted the news, showing images from Playa Samara. One of the schools — debris everywhere — was badly damaged by the tremor. Later, we heard there had been three deaths due to heart attacks, but no other life-threatening casualties from the quake, which was remarkable.

Costa Rica is no stranger to earthquakes — they happen frequently — but usually they're not large enough to cause much destruction.

Little and often is a good thing.

This one was considered a big one and we found out about it from my mother-in-law in England. It appears this is a universal truth: the further you are from a disaster, the quicker you will receive news of it. The closer you are to a disaster — provided it doesn't affect you directly — the more oblivious you are to it.

We only paused long enough to take the call, then continued shopping.

Life simply goes on.

Thursday, September 6, 2012
Fill'em Up

It had been a little over two weeks since we landed in Costa Rica. All the grunt work on the retaining wall was complete and the ponds were ready to be filled with water. With boulders, chunky logs, and sandbags wedged between them, Kevin diverted some of the river water, allowing it to flow down the intake canal to the aqueduct system. Swiss Man would have been proud.

What a day!

Although we were celebrating this milestone, the sense of triumph was short-lived. As annoying as it was, enduring cosmetic blemishes didn't compare to the weight we would now have to carry. We had traded muddy craters that marred the landscape and vexed my aesthetic sensibilities for far bigger stresses. Adding river water to the ponds wasn't the hard part. Keeping the ponds clean and aerated so our trout business could thrive would be.

We were about to face the rainiest, dirtiest two months of the year. We would have to be extra diligent. It was anxiety-inducing thinking about everything that could go wrong. We had never done anything like this before, but we knew we had to take the plunge. No stalling. We would learn by doing. There was no other way.

Chasing what seemed like ethereal rainbows had been life changing. It allowed us to believe in something. It gave us hope and led us to this dream life.

Chasing and catching rainbows that shimmered below the surface of our ponds would be another matter — one of sacrifice.

We framed it as an adventure, but in truth, it was so much more than that. It was a journey of beginnings and endings.

Muchas Truchas

As part of the purchase agreement, Martín was expected to replace the fish he took out of the big pond when Rick left Costa Rica. Those fish were considered part of the farm's assets even though Rick wasn't coming back. However, we weren't sure if Rick had bothered to explain this detail to Martín when he announced he was selling the farm. For all we knew, maybe Martín assumed they were now a gift from Rick.

We felt hesitant to bring it up, but getting those fish back would be the catalyst to starting our rainbow trout business sooner rather than later. And even if we weren't thinking of starting a business, they were part of the purchase deal. It became a matter of principle.

We explained the situation to Nacho and he, in turn, explained it to Martín.

"*Sí sí, no problema. Las voy a traer mañana,*" Martín said to Nacho, and continued saying more while nodding like this wasn't fresh-off-the-press news.

Thank you, Rick.

"My father said he can bring the fish over tomorrow," Nacho translated. "He doesn't have any one-kilo fish right now, but he will fill your big pond with smaller *truchas,* but don't worry, you'll get more than Rick's two hundred. Probably about three hundred to three hundred and fifty. *Más o menos.* Some will be a bit smaller; some will be a bit bigger."

"Awesome. Thank you!" Kevin shook Nacho's hand with a huge smile.

The deal was to replace Rick's 200 trout that weighed 200 kg (440 lbs) back in the spring. So, 300–350 fish meant they weighed a little over 0.5 kg each (1 lb each). Kevin was happy with this outcome because we'd have about 150 more fish weighing 1 kg (2.2 lbs) in just a few short months, giving us a good head start. This first batch of fish would probably see us through the first year.

After visiting the INCOPESCA facility a week earlier, we had already decided we'd buy 700 fingerlings in November, at the end of the rainy season. At $0.08 per fingerling, we were prepared to invest a whopping $56. Although it was a laughable amount, the cost of feeding them would prove to be a lot more, so we didn't want to bite off more than we could chew. We still had no idea who would buy trout from us. Everything felt like a vague experiment. But knowing Martín was going to transfer the 300 trout the very next day made everything feel a lot more real.

Friday, September 7, 2012
Go Fish

Water was sloshing out of a big, black tank in the back of the army green Land Cruiser. Martín didn't bother hooking up the oxygenation machine. He would have needed it for a longer trip to ensure the trout's survival, but because it was such a short jaunt, he knew it wouldn't be an issue. With fishing nets, Martín, Nacho, and Kevin worked together to transfer a dozen trout from the tank to the pond. Then another dozen, and another. The trout were jumpy and slippery and weighed the nets down. There was no elegance to this manoeuvre; it was all about speed. *Swoop...glop...smack...splash...plunk. Swoop... glop...smack...splash...plunk. Swoop...glup...smack...splash...plunk.* The objective was to get the fish into the pond as quickly as possible to prevent too much trauma.

I don't know, it looks like the trout are pretty stressed out to me.

While they were out of the water, even for a few seconds, they were flipping and flopping, gasping for air.

It's stressing me out; I can barely breathe myself watching the process.

But with each splash, the trout plunked into the water and darted to the other side of the pond. Our big pond was at least three times the size of Martín's biggest pond and twice as deep, so they had lots of room to grow. There was enough room for at least 1,500 fully grown adult trout without crowding them. We were hoping the clean oxygenated water and the vastness of their new home would encourage a relaxing environment. They were short and thin — about the length and thickness of a wrench — but with the right nutrition they would be ready to eat in January. Feeding them fish pellets every morning and evening was added to our daily chores. Martín warned us not to feed them until the following morning. They were in shock from the day's ordeal; we needed to let their nervous systems calm down first. Since our ponds were natural, there were plenty of microorganisms and bugs to feed on, anyway.

We were officially trout farmers.

San Gerardo

After the trout were safely transferred into the big pond, Kevin and I invited Martín, Clara, and Nacho for a celebratory lunch in San Gerardo. We wanted to thank them for their hard work and kind help since we arrived.

San Gerardo was a little over a half hour away from where we lived, but still in the Dota mountains. From the Pan-American Highway, the dirt road that led down to one of its acclaimed resorts — The Trogón Lodge — wasn't too dissimilar to the road that wound down to Río Blanco.

Set in a valley with several trout ponds fed by a river, we wondered if we could draw inspiration from the resort. The difference between it and Hush Valley Lodge was that it had several cabins, a restaurant, and a large staff. They'd been in business for nearly twenty years at that point and the property was meticulously manicured — maybe a little too manicured for my liking — with many rest areas to sit and enjoy the views.

Clara appeared thrilled to see all the different plants. She especially loved the birds of paradise because Río Blanco was a smidge too high in altitude for them to grow, so they seemed particularly exotic to her.

Known for its tourism, San Gerardo attracted many visitors from all over the world, especially birdwatchers. As I walked around, I looked for new ideas to attract more birds to our property. The resplendent quetzal nested in our trees and if marketed correctly, I knew birdwatchers would come for a chance to glimpse one. But if we could attract other types of birds, too, then we could create a birdwatchers' haven.

While Clara and I meandered, Martín, Nacho, and Kevin studied structures and discussed ways of building decks and pergolas from the resources we had on our land. Infused with inspiration, Kevin and I imagined a grandiose project and let enthusiasm run amok.

As the five of us lunched together, we brainstormed ideas to elevate Hush Valley Lodge to a world-class destination and made it clear that we welcomed their suggestions. It was important to us that we conveyed how much we valued their opinion, because we did. Only two weeks in and it was obvious to us, if we were going to build something special in these remote mountains, that we couldn't do it alone.

We all beamed as the animated chatter continued.

Once the bouncing-off-the-wall ideas simmered down, I shifted the conversation from us to them. I asked about their family backgrounds, the adventures they had had when they were younger, and their hopes and dreams they held for their children.

Martín was raised near Providencia, a tiny village tucked in a valley between San Gerardo and Río Blanco. Reaching back into his childhood memories with fondness, Martín told us how the roads back then were barely roads at all and how he had to walk long distances to find work. The manner in which Nacho recounted sounded like one of those exaggerated *I walked barefoot uphill in the snow* kind of grandfather stories, except it rang true. Martín even walked up and down the mountain to date Clara, which he said took him several hours. Clara blushed.

How romantic!

Nacho commented that, although still a tiny village, Providencia was now popular for its rock-climbing competitions, mostly due to the efforts of another Canadian couple.

"And they run an English school and an adventure park, too," Nacho added.

Where was this information when I was looking for an English school for Jude?

As we were wrapping up and getting ready to head back home, it occurred to me that Martín, who was usually reserved and didn't show a lot of emotion, appeared stoked by the entire outing. Although always polite, Martín had been a little guarded with us until then. But on that day, he had been talkative in a way I hadn't seen before — smiling and laughing without inhibition. Every time Kevin attempted to speak Spanish, showing he was trying and willing to learn, Martín attempted to speak English. They would teach each other a few words and chuckle when pronunciation tripped them up. I felt a new level of acceptance emanating from Martín.

This excursion away from Río Blanco seemed to clinch it for him. We were in his good books.

What a great feeling!

Nineteen
Leaving the Rat Race

Saturday, September 8, 2012

Squatting in a Swamp

A lthough the days weren't hectic, we accomplished what seemed like some monumental task each day, and each task seemed to require hours of waiting, mental gymnastics, or both. It felt a lot like work. The days may not have been fast paced, but they had been taxing.

It was Saturday and we woke up without an agenda. It felt glorious. This was the feeling I dreamed about when we decided to leave the rat race. We didn't have to meet Martín, Nacho, and Clara in the carport to assign chores. We didn't have meetings with lawyers, bankers, or accountants. No vegetable garden to attend to; the beds were bare. No chicken coop to clean because we had no hens. No guests to host; the B&B wasn't open yet. Nothing was pressing. We could venture out as long as we were back in a few hours to let Frankie out and feed the fish — preferably before it started to rain.

"Hey, we should do something fun today," Kevin suggested as if he had just read my mind.

"Sure! Like what?"

"How about we take the four-wheeler for a spin up the other side of the mountain to Providencia? We can try to find that adventure park with the canopy ziplining rides and monkey bridges that Nacho mentioned yesterday," Kevin suggested.

He didn't have to convince me. "Great idea. I'm in."

Although the idea of selling trout and opening a B&B seemed like the best way to make money for us, we were still considering other business options. Our curiosity was piqued hearing Nacho talk about how a couple from Canada's Great White North, way up in the Yukon, moved to Costa Rica and created an adventure park, then an English school, then a yearly rock-climbing event.

So ambitious!

We had a lot of unused land, and the vertical topography would lend well to building some kind of eco-friendly amusement park. If we built something fun for everyone, maybe it would benefit the people of our area.

Bringing jobs without destroying the land gets rewarded in Costa Rica. By 1940, over 75% of the available land zoned for forestry was being used for either timber or agricultural production. After the country was nearly decimated by clear-cutting, the government was pressured in the 1990s to turn things around before it lost its culture and way of life to industrialization and gentrification. The government mandated that 30% of the land in Costa Rica be protected and due to this policy, secondary forests were now thriving. Hush Valley Lodge was located in a preserve and there were strict rules regarding which trees we were allowed to cut and which we weren't. Oh, and if we let our pasture grow and get unwieldy for more than five years, it would no longer be considered a pasture, and we wouldn't be permitted to cut it back. This was one reason we had to maintain it — at least until we knew for sure we didn't want pastureland.

Kevin filled the tank with gas, then checked the tire pressure, lights, and gauges. After we slathered sunscreen on our faces, I threw the tube in my knapsack along with our rain gear. We needed both.

Since our motorcycle helmets were en route with the rest of our stuff, we fastened Rick's old, musty, open-faced helmets we found in the garage. The four-wheeler was comfortable with plush seats and a solid backrest. It felt rugged yet luxurious. Rick didn't skimp out when he purchased this baby. Kevin drove while I sat behind him, relaxing and taking in the scenery.

Barking ferociously and snapping aggressively at our heels, two large dogs suddenly jumped out of the bushes and started chasing us. One managed to nip my ankle through my jeans.

Son of a bitch.

Startled, I instinctively booted him in the face. Kevin reacted quickly and accelerated faster than the dogs could keep up. We didn't account for such a hostile encounter. Our experience so far had been quite the opposite; every dog we had met until that day had been calm and docile. I did hear somewhere that dogs sometimes get feisty towards moving vehicles; however, most dogs lay in the middle of the road, and it took a bit of coaxing for them to move out of the way, forcing us to drive around them because they couldn't be bothered to get up. I sometimes wondered if they had a pulse.

As these dogs ate our dust, we reached Copey a few minutes later. At the second T-junction, instead of turning right as we normally did when we went to Santa María, we took a left. It was our first time going up this way. The rays shimmered through the layered foliage, creating swaying silhouettes while the frothy river lapped over rocks. The mossy carpet beneath the mature trees made it all the more enchanting.

Downright mystical.

We rode up and up and up on a narrow, gravel road — ideal for the four-wheeler. The panoramic views were breathtaking. A dense forest in the distance bordered velvety pastures where grazing cows dotted the rolling landscape.

Postcard perfect.

We rode for almost an hour until we found what looked like the adventure park; we saw the cables and platform for a possible zipline, but the gate was locked. After our experience ziplining in Monteverde, this park was much smaller, overgrown, and appeared abandoned.

Perhaps they close during the rainy season?

There was no one around to ask, so we kept going. The road zigzagged into a valley and we finally reached Providencia. It was a quiet place.

Like tumbleweed-rolling-in-the-streets kind of quiet.

It was summertime hot — about 28°C (83°F) — under a cloudless blue sky. I couldn't quite believe that we had been riding on *our* four-wheeler for the last hour exploring more of Costa Rica's countryside. We had a four-wheeler as our second vehicle...how cool was that? The idea that I didn't have to show up to my corporate job on Monday morning still felt surreal.

This is my life!

We stopped at a small general store — *the only store* — to buy a bottle of water to quench our thirst. We walked in, but no one was around. I called out, "*Con permiso?*" a few times. I learned it's the polite thing to say before entering someone's home. It means *with permission*. With no one around, it felt a bit like we were intruding.

After several minutes, a man sauntered through the front door and said quietly, "*Lo siento, estaba en mi cabina.*"

"What did he say?" Kevin asked.

"He's apologizing for not being in the store when we came in. He was in his cabin," I translated...filling in the blanks.

"You wouldn't see storekeepers leave their store unlocked and unattended back in Canada, eh?" Kevin winked.

The culture shock kept on shocking. I pumped for information about the other Canadian couple. "*Sabe dónde vive la pareja de Yukon?*"

The man looked at me quizzically.

Maybe I said it wrong? Is it my accent? Maybe Yukon is pronounced a different way?

I repeated but this time called the couple *gringos* and he lit up. He pointed in a vague direction, somewhere to the left, and said, "*Casa amarilla.*"

"What did he say?" Kevin asked.

"He said the Yukon couple lives in a yellow house over there to the left," I translated some more. This was how our interactions went. I butchered the Spanish language but managed to get by, the Tico or Tica would respond, and I would usually get the essence of what they said. I didn't get every word, but I got the gist. Then Kevin would ask me what they said so he could keep up with the conversations and I would paraphrase as best as I could.

I thanked the store owner, paid for our water, and we left. We hopped back onto our four-wheeler and rode in search of a yellow house, but none was found. No adventure park or Yukon couple were discovered on this quest, either.

Instead of backtracking, we decided to loop back home via the Pan-American Highway — it would be more direct. To confirm we were going the right way, we stopped and asked a random woman for directions. She nodded with a helpful *that way* point of the finger, just as vague with her directions as the store owner was with his. We were hoping we'd have more luck finding our way to the highway though.

As we rode out of the little village, the road steadily wound to higher altitude. Without warning, grey plumes rolled in and the air got nippy. Not much further up the road, it started to spit. We were usually the "we'll be fine" kind of people and took our chances, but we had seen how intense the rain could be. Kevin stopped so we could change into our rain gear before tackling the rest of the way to La Trinidad and back down to Río Blanco. We still had an hour or more ahead of us, depending on traffic.

"Well, this should be interesting. Are you ready to get wet?" Kevin asked rhetorically.

"Maybe we'll get lucky, and it'll just keep drizzling," I responded.

By the time we reached the Pan-American intersection, the temperature dropped considerably, and it was pouring. It was easy to balance on the chunky quad so I sat on my hands to keep them warm while keeping my head down and eyes closed to avoid the stinging droplets pelting down at a 45° angle.

I was starting to miss our stuff — our helmets had visors. Kevin wasn't so lucky; he was driving and had to keep his eyes open.

I hope he's keeping them open!

I felt the rain sloshing in my boots, and the water dripping off Kevin's back trickled down, pooling in the indents of my seat. It felt like I was squatting in a swamp. Even with our waterproof jackets, we were soaked to the bone.

When we got home, we stood outside under cover in front of the French doors, peeled off our drenched clothes, and hung them on the makeshift clothesline. Mother Nature duped us every morning with her glorious sunshine. We needed to learn to time our outings better. Rick was right…it rained a lot in September.

Can't wait to see what October brings.

Sunday, September 9, 2012
Grit

After we had found Rick's property online and during our thirst to research anything and everything about Costa Rica, Kevin stumbled upon a blog written by a woman named Stella. At the time, inspired by the pictures of the organic vegetable garden, he wanted to understand more about composting. Kevin's investigation led him down the internet rabbit hole, which brought him to an article Stella had written specifically about how red worms help with the decomposition process. The information was so interesting that Kevin kept on reading only to learn that Stella and her husband, Nick, who were from Seattle, Washington, packed up and began a new life in Costa Rica three years earlier than we had.

"Hon, you should read this woman's blog. You'd love it," he had pointed out.

I did. I pored over Stella's blog from beginning to end and loved it. I learned about their big adventure — from landing with only two suitcases each to looking for and finding the right property in Puriscal, and from living in a damp concrete shed to building their dream home. They didn't speak more than a handful of Spanish words, either. We were just at the dreaming stage at the time…we hadn't seen Rick's property yet, but the plane tickets were booked. Stella's words energized me and provided the inspiration I needed on those depressing days when I felt our wild idea of moving to Costa Rica might be too far-fetched.

I had gotten in touch with Stella back then, told her what we were preparing to do, and peppered her with questions. She always answered back with genuine interest. Now pen pals, Stella became my lifeline. Stella was generous with the good, the bad, and the ugly; she had nothing to lose by giving me the straight goods. And because she had nothing to gain from us moving to Costa Rica, I felt we could rely on her information. It was harder to trust Rick; he had a vested interest in us feeling positive about buying his property. This was not a Rick-specific issue; to me, this seemed true of anyone who was trying to sell…*anything.*

Through back-and-forth emails over time, we sent each other pictures of our renovated houses; Stella and Nick had just finished renovating their home in Seattle before they decided to up and move. Our lives shared parallel paths except they were three years ahead of us in the process. When I told her we were arriving in August, she invited us to visit once we had settled in.

So, about two weeks after landing in Costa Rica, I called Stella and made plans for us to drop in and finally meet in person.

When we arrived at Stella and Nick's front gate, we were greeted by two exuberant dogs.

"Hello! Welcome," cried a slim woman trying to catch up to the dogs. Her light brown shoulder-length hair floated in the wind. The man next to her towered over her as they walked toward us.

"Get down you two. Sorry. They get excited when people come to visit. Hi, I'm Stella and this is Nick."

"Hi, nice to meet you both," I replied by rote.

Although there was a sense of familiarity, we were strangers after all, and the greeting felt a bit clumsy. The mental indecisiveness of whether to hug or shake hands or just smile and turn our affections to the dogs tripped us up. We opted to do all three.

"Aren't you a good boy...yes, you are," Kevin said, patting one of the dogs.

Puriscal is lower in elevation than Río Blanco and the temperature is a lot warmer. Stella and Nick were wearing khaki shorts and sandals. Kevin and I were wearing long pants, sweaters, and hiking boots, and felt overdressed. In Southern Ontario, Canada, if it's cool in one town, you can anticipate that the temperature in another town two hours away could shift a degree or two, not ten. We weren't quite used to the altitude difference. It didn't take long for us to peel off our sweaters as we took in the gorgeous view that overlooked mountain peaks in the distance.

"Come on in," Nick ushered us into their newly built home. The long narrow bungalow with ultra-high vaulted ceilings boasted wall-to-wall floor-to-ceiling windows that opened up to the panoramic view. The concrete floor kept the room cool, and the open-concept layout created an airy feeling. The design was minimalist and functional, allowing the natural beauty of the outdoors to adorn the space. The windows had been rolled into the walls and out of sight, blurring the lines between the inside and the outside. And the *pièce de resistance* was the wrap-around terrace that jutted out over their property.

"WOW!" I blurted, without filter.

I glanced at Kevin, who was wearing the same amazed expression. Kevin followed Nick into the backyard to talk about mechanical engineering stuff while Stella and I stayed behind and chatted about how we were settling in so far, about the cultural differences, and about how happy they were for taking the leap but also how hard it had been.

"If I knew then what I know now, I don't think we would have landed here with just our suitcases and no plan," Stella mentioned. "I mean, we have no regrets, and everything is working out, but it's been tough at times. Not knowing the language is a disadvantage for sure and still three years later we're not much further along. I expected to pick it up more quickly."

"I get that," I said. "It's only been two weeks, but I somehow felt I'd be able to remember my high-school Spanish from thirty years ago. Or that my French would naturally pick up the slack. I even go to school almost every morning — "

"Haha. I read on your blog that you're now a first grader. That's awesome that you're willing to do that," Stella smiled.

"Yeah, but it feels like I'm doing way more colouring than learning new vocabulary." Stella chuckled.

As Stella and I soon meandered outside — the men in sight but beyond earshot — we drew the gap closer until we were all strolling over together toward a wide-open space.

"Over here is where we lived while the house was being built," Sadie pointed to a concrete structure with no windows. It was barely fit for animals but somehow, they made it work. It's astounding what people are willing to put up with to make a dream come true.

"And here is the garden," Stella continued. Plants were growing out of mounds of dirt and a little further was a closed-in structure with clear plastic wrapped around it.

"On your blog, you mention that you're experimenting with polyculture. How's that working out?" Kevin inquired.

"It's hit and miss. The idea is to grow different plants mixed together instead of the usual monoculture crop method," Stella described as she opened the door to the greenhouse.

"I read it's supposed to reduce the amount of weeding and helps with pest control," I inserted, looking for confirmation that my information was right.

"For sure, if you're strategic about placement you don't need any chemicals. I'm still learning. Part of the fun is filling in crops where there is empty space just to see what happens. I sometimes find it hard to know the difference between a seedling and a weed though. Polyculture definitely isn't for everyone. I'm getting used to the slightly chaotic feel of the beds. It always looks messy. But if you like tidy rows then this method would drive you crazy," Stella laughed.

As we walked through the tennis court-sized greenhouse and chatted, Stella picked vegetables — spinach, onions, tomatoes, radishes — and placed them in a wicker basket as if by instinct.

"For lunch, I made a vegetarian lasagna with our organic veggies," she put a tomato to her nose and inhaled its freshness.

"Mmm... Sounds delicious... Can't wait!" I enthused.

At their kitchen table, as we gorged on Stella's lasagna, Nick explained his driver's license ordeal and warned us to get our driver's license before our ninety-day visitor's visa expired. We learned our Canadian driver's license was only valid during those first ninety days.

"Somewhere in our research we read we had to wait until *after* the three months had lapsed," Kevin said.

"That's what I thought, too...but no," Nick replied. "If you wait to get your Costa Rican license after that period, then your Canadian license is considered invalid. And they won't issue a Costa Rican one in its place. And you'll have to go through the entire testing process in Spanish, no less."

Yikes! Good to know! Nick learned the hard way, so we don't have to.

They also had great advice about applying for temporary residency. They used ARCR, the same agency that we were using, and everything went smoothly for them. We felt encouraged.

After so many months of emailing one another, it was lovely to finally meet and exchange stories face to face. Their grit was impressive and helped keep everything in perspective when we felt things weren't going as smoothly as we would have liked. So far, we had it easy in comparison.

We left Stella and Nick's right after lunch. We were still new at gauging the weather patterns and wanted to be home before the rain started. Although it was a good plan, we ended up driving in the rain anyway.

As we drove down our driveway, we noticed the river and ponds looked like thick gravy. Kevin parked the SUV and ran. I knew he was heading up to check the first two ponds closest to the aqueduct opening. I was beginning to understand our new rhythm — he didn't have to explain. He was attending to river and pond business. That's what he did.

I went inside the house and let Frankie out; she had been cooped up for several hours and regardless of the rain, she needed to attend to her own business.

Kevin returned looking worried and said, "The grit and sand are up to here," bringing his hand to waist level to indicate just how much had collected in the sediment ponds. There was no way to prevent the river from coming in, no gate we could shut. All that dirty water was flowing from one pond down to the next through the canals; that was why they were so murky.

While I made dinner, Kevin was on high alert. With a flashlight, he checked the river and ponds every hour throughout the evening. He said it was impossible to see whether the trout were alive or not, but we couldn't run a trout business and face this kind of potential loss. It wasn't economically viable.

How did the Swiss guy who built the trout ponds twenty years ago manage it? How does Martín manage his three ponds? How does anyone make any money if they have to start over every time Mother Nature has a little fun?

There was nothing we could do about it at that moment, but I knew Kevin was ruminating. He was worried. Exhausted, he finally came to bed at 11:00 p.m. That was the latest he'd been up since we arrived. We were quickly learning a farmer's day was never done. And we were reminded that we also had grit.

In more ways than one.

Mudslide

Kevin was up and out before daybreak — before he even had his first cup of tea — an obvious clue that he was worried or overthinking something. As far as I was concerned, it was far too early and much too dark to be able to help him, so I rolled over and fell back to sleep.

It wasn't until the sky brightened that I woke up again. The periwinkle dawn suffused the room with the promise of yet another sunny morning. I got up and surveyed the situation out the window. I couldn't see Kevin anywhere.

After I showered and got dressed, I put the kettle on to boil — surely, he'd be ready for a cup of tea and breakfast soon. The porch roof prevented any direct sunlight from pouring in, but I could tell by the golden glow outside that the sun was now hovering over the treetops. As I opened the French doors to let Frankie out and the warm breeze in, I glimpsed something bright blue on the right-hand side. It was Kevin's fleece peeking through all the lemon and orange trees that bordered the big pond.

I saw him more clearly as he marched toward the house. He was wearing his black rubber boots, a head lamp, and his sweatpants were filthy.

He must have been shovelling out the sediment heap that had filled the upper ponds.

In my peripheral vision, I saw Nacho appear from the opposite direction.

It must be 7:00 a.m. Hmm, I wonder where Martín is?

Nacho reached Kevin and I could hear their muffled voices. I was curious so I put on my boots and joined them mid-conversation. They both acknowledged me with a quick smile but didn't stop.

"...last two hours cleaning out the two small sediment ponds up there. What a job!" Kevin was saying.

"Us too. Martín and I can't work today. Two of his ponds are full of sand. Most of his trout died last night. I need to help him dig all that sand out. Sorry."

"Oh no, what about the third pond?" I injected myself into the conversation.

"Luckily, not as much sand in that one. The trout in that pond survived."

Kevin was chewing on his cuticles as he was listening to Nacho. The wheels in his bald skull were turning. I could almost hear the gears grind. "Give me a minute to have some breakfast, then I'll come over and help you. I'll bring my shovel," Kevin said to Nacho with a handshake, then turned to me as he and I walked back to the house. "There's got to be a better way for us to control how much water flows into our ponds. This is crazy. I can't believe no one's solved this problem yet. Martín might be okay with losing his fish every time the rain comes, but I'm not."

Between the canal that ran from the river into the first sediment pond was a solid concrete barrier about the width of a single-car garage, give or take. At the bottom of the barrier, smack in the middle, was a rectangular cut-out portion with a metal grill. When the water flowed in, it brought in leaves and sediment and the grill served as a sieve in the same way a strainer catches pulp when you pour fresh-squeezed juice in a glass. It was this opening that was the culprit. The metal grill caught the leaves and bigger twigs, but not the finer sand and gritty sediment. And there was no way to stop the water from coming in unless we redirected the entire flow back into the river. Of course, that wasn't the solution.

Something had to be done. Leaving it wide open for another disaster to strike wasn't smart. After helping Martín and Nacho all morning, Kevin spent the afternoon tinkering in the garage and devising a solution to our problem. I left him to it.

With a piece of corrugated metal sheet that was possibly used for one of the sheds' roofs, Kevin built a gate. He built a mechanism similar to a guillotine. He attached the sheet of metal in such a way that it could slide up and down and we could adjust the height depending on how much water we wanted to let in. If we wanted the full water capacity to flow like we would in the summer months, all we had to do was leave the sheet up. If we wanted less water to flow in during the bad weather season, then we simply lowered the sheet down a notch or two. And if we didn't want any water coming into the canal, then we had to make sure the sheet was all the way down. There were two nails — one on each side — that fit into drilled holes to hold it in place. It wasn't fancy, but it worked like a charm.

Trout can survive up to twelve hours without oxygenated water. Depleting the oxygen was never a good idea, but neither was letting the ponds get dirty. There was a fine line between which was more important: oxygenated water or clean water. In the rainy season, it was a delicate dance between the two. Our ponds were much larger than Martín's, so they took a lot more time to shovel out the sand.

Being able to reduce or shut the water flow whenever we left the property gave us peace of mind that we wouldn't come home to this type of catastrophe again.

The rain had been relentless that afternoon. *Torrential* doesn't begin to describe what was going on outside. Everything was green with a punch of colour from all the flowers surrounding the big pond, and it would have felt cheerful if it weren't so miserable.

In our rain gear from head to toe, Kevin and I stood on the footpath watching the river gush at incredible speed. Huge logs careened by while one tree laid on top of the rocks near the bend.

Maybe it was struck by lightning?

Although the rain was finally subsiding, the force of the river and the howling of the wind were not. Everything was deafening; Kevin and I had to shout at each other to hear above the hurricane-like winds.

Nacho came by later to make sure that we were okay and to update us about why the river was so dirty.

"Martín and I walked up the river this afternoon," Nacho spoke in a loud voice. "We wanted to know what was causing the muddy water. We discovered it was a huge mudslide."

"Are mudslides normal? Is this something that happens every rainy season?" Kevin questioned.

"No. We think the big earthquake from a few days ago moved the ground," Nacho answered, shaking his hands back and forth to simulate a trembling motion. "It'll probably take a few days for the water to clear up. No problem."

He didn't seem worried.

Later, while we were preparing dinner, we received three phone calls from concerned neighbours. The first was from our friend Roberto, who was calling to make sure we were okay — and between cracklings — to invite us for lunch and a cheese-making tour on Thursday.

The second phone call, about fifteen minutes later, was from Vanessa — Sharon's mother, one of the students in my class. To my surprise, Vanessa spoke a bit of English. She called to see how we were doing and invited us to stay with her family if the river got too high. She also invited us to her husband Albarito's fortieth birthday party that was taking place the following Saturday, on September 15, which was another surprise. Not the party, but that we would be invited to join in on the celebration.

Two hours later, Clara called.

"*Todo bien?* Happy, happy, happy?"

"*Sí, sí, sí. Todo bien. Gracias. Buenas noches. Hasta mañana.*"

Just another day in paradise.

Twenty
Rainbow Connections

Tuesday, September 11, 2012
Rival

Without the use of a toaster oven until our belongings arrived from Canada, I was determined to master the round outdoor earthen oven. People commonly use outdoor ovens in Costa Rica, and we knew Rick used the one on the terrace fairly regularly. There was no reason I couldn't adapt.

The dry alder needed to burn until embers glowed and emitted a consistent radiant heat. I struck several matches one after another, and although the crumpled newspaper ignited with a hot flash and would scorch the alder shavings and sticks I had gathered from the forest, I couldn't get the flame to burn long enough. It snuffed itself out quickly. This was my mission. I had no other plans. I was focused as if my survival depended on it. As I whittled away the tinder, so did I whittle away the entire day until the rain came.

Although I tried to conquer my rival, it would be the first of many times that I would not succeed.

Wednesday, September 12, 2012
A Full Spectrum

It was a beautiful and hot day. By late afternoon, there was still not a cloud in sight.

Parked behind the one-room school in that sweet spot of the soccer field, I got out of the SUV, walked around to the passenger side, and sat where there was more elbow room. Overlooking the dips and rises of the lush landscape, I opened my laptop.

Peering out the window as I pondered what to write for my blog post, my jaw dropped. The most perfectly formed rainbow glistened directly in front of me. The arc cut through the green leaves and poured its prismatic colours deep into the valley like a waterfall. Each stripe — so sharp and vivid — pulsated, as if God was trying to speak through its luminosity. I was transfixed.

The weird thing was there weren't any obvious rain droplets in the sky for the sunlight to pass through and create the rainbow. The sky was bright blue as far as my eyes could see.

How is this happening?

In Canada, rainbows tend to be muted and incomplete. We're lucky to see more than a sliver. And they seem so far away.

I felt like I could walk right up to this one and touch it.

My heart pounded. The desire to write my visceral reaction and tell my family and friends about this wondrous sight was strong, but how could I possibly describe it without sounding like I had just slipped some acid into my tea? I'm sure I used one too many exclamation marks as it was.

I lingered long after I was done writing my post. I just sat there. Mesmerized. The arc didn't fade. In fact, I could have sworn it grew brighter...more intense.

No one was around. The school kids had all gone home hours ago. I was alone. It was as if this peculiar anomaly was just for me. I removed my librarian-style black-rimmed glasses and wiped away the wetness that was pooling on my bottom eyelids. I wasn't sure why I was crying.

Before leaving Canada, my life was a frantic mess. Pausing for tiny moments seemed impossible. That was on me. I never took the time. I trudged through the mire of one self-appointed obligation to another. Moments vanished into the hurried and unyielding hamster-wheel loop of parenting, household chores, and work. Those days grew into years. I slapped on a smile and juggled the proverbial balls in the air until I was too numb to notice that I had mastered both well. Wearing blinders, however, didn't fix the damage to my nervous system. Omr to my soul.

I used to ask God...no, *pleaded*...for a sign; to speak to me in a way that I could understand; to explain what my life purpose was. I would have been happy with some small gesture. Anything to feel connected to my higher power.

Why do I feel so lost? So stuck all the time? What's wrong with me? Why don't you speak to me?

That was before I understood God spoke in a myriad of ways...in the faintest of whispers...in the echoes of a canyon...in the movement of the breeze...or like now, in the pulsating colours beneath those trees. Connection was there for the taking. That was the great lesson.

I had learned this lesson when my first husband, Christopher, and I decided to walk across Canada with our big Husky dog, Samson. The outward adventure taught me how immense Canada is as we travelled across the provinces of Ontario, Manitoba, and Saskatchewan. A few weeks into our walk, on the edge of Lake Superior, a murder of crows circled above us. Although it felt a bit Alfred Hitchcock-ish with so many black birds flying in formation overhead, Christopher and I took notice. Instead of feeling dread, we felt comforted.

The next day we had met an artist from the Ojibwe tribe on the side of the road chiselling animal carvings out of soft pine. As we got closer, we saw bear, squirrel, rabbit, owl, eagle, wolf, and fox shapes spread across a large picnic table. And in his hand? A crow. We told him of our adventure and recounted what had happened to us the day before. He smiled sagely as he nodded, "Oh, that's a sign of Andek. ...Andek the crow thought he had no purpose, but found out that his purpose was to help others find or renew their purpose. You must be on the right path to have been visited by so many Andeks at one time on your journey."

A profound sense of spiritual connection had washed over us as we walked that entire day in complete silence. We also discovered we could have been travelling with an elephant and Manitobans driving teeny Datsons still would have stopped and offered us a lift. Kindness and generosity greeted us everywhere we went in that province. And it was across the Saskatchewan prairies where I was reminded how small I was in the grand scheme of life and yet how expansive I felt within its never-ending vastness. The breadbasket of Canada fed us grains of possibility. Phoenix was born nine months later in Regina.

I learned this lesson when we lived in a tent for nearly three months with two-year-old Phoenix. I learned how little we needed. I was taught how entertaining rocks and sticks could be for any child with an imagination.

I learned this lesson when we became camp-watchers of a heli-fishing resort in Northern British Columbia — Canada's westernmost province — a place accessible only by boat, float plane, or helicopter. I learned how when I removed myself from the noisy, overstimulating world for months at a time, I could be still enough to befriend a blue heron. There was a clarity of mind that happened; a natural, meditative state.

But over time, once back in suburbia and working in a corporate setting, it seems I suffered from amnesia. I had mistakenly believed that I'd never forget the messages or lessons in all those soul-affirming moments; that I'd never be lulled to sleep ever again.

We had been in Costa Rica for three weeks and life hadn't gotten any less stressful, but we had broken the stuck-in-a-rut cycle, that's for sure. There were too many new things to learn and wrap my head around to get complacent or bored. But perhaps, I was finally starting to decompress. Perhaps I was allowing more space between doing and being. I hadn't been intentional about it, but maybe it was happening anyway.

That day, I basked in the full spectrum of the experience and felt connected to God, to Mother Nature, and to the peace deep within myself.

Thursday, September 13, 2012
Cheese-Making Lesson

Our neighbours, Adriana and Roberto, invited us over for lunch. Since our arrival, we only saw them once in passing. They had just come back from being on holiday and promised to call so we could catch up properly. They seemed eager to hear how we were settling in. They asked about Jude and looked surprised when we told him he decided to stay in Canada.

We were used to turning left at the one-room school when we drove up to find an internet signal, but it was our first time venturing any further. We had noticed the rutted road next to the soccer field, but an imposing black security gate read *"PRIVADO, MANTENER CERRADO*!" Our brains automatically knew it meant *"PRIVATE, KEEP CLOSED*!" by the cap letters so we never dared to open it. We knew the road led to a few homes and farms, Abel's — Roberto's father — being one of them, but we had yet to see anyone drive in or out. And the shaded alley gave nothing away. Within a few metres the road swerved, leaving the rest of the landscape up to our imagination.

Does the road roll down? Does it slope up? Is the forest still dense or is the land clear-cut around that corner?

It was a mystery.

"When you come, there will be a few pasture gates. Please make sure to close them so the cows don't get out. We live in the round house. You can't miss it," Roberto had said.

Of course. Dairy farm. Pasture-raised cows. It's not a "keep out" gate, it's a "keep in" gate.

Even though Adriana and Roberto lived less than five minutes away as the crow flies, we weren't sure how long it would take to walk over. Striding up to our own entrance gate took us five minutes; then another five to walk down the hill, across the bridge, and up to Martín and Clara's restaurant; then, keeping the same momentum, five more minutes to get to the school. Not knowing what lay beyond the tall black gate, it could have been another fifteen minutes or more to get to their front door. To avoid arriving panting and sweaty, we decided to drive over.

I swivelled out of the SUV, opened the gate, Kevin drove through, and I made sure to close it. We followed the bend in the road, excited to uncover what lay ahead.

The SUV rocked back and forth in and out of potholes as it climbed the gradual incline. The forest was dense on both sides for a short while. We passed two modest houses. *Unassuming or abandoned?* It was hard to tell.

We continued on a little further until the forest ended and the pastureland spread across the hillside. Another gate. *Get out, open, drive through, close, get in.* On the left, we spied the dome-shaped house in the middle of the pasture. *So cute. Like a hobbit home in The Shire.* Then another gate.

And to think I was afraid I'd be arriving all sweaty had we walked over. All this getting in and out of the SUV is a full-body workout.

Roberto was helping his dad make cheese. The typical everyday cheese in Costa Rica is ivory white and has the consistency of tofu. It tasted bland to Kevin and me. Not our favourite. It nearly cured me of my cheese addiction. But Abel's cheese was sharper, almost like an old white cheddar.

As Roberto gave us a tour of the property, we noticed a man milking a cow.

"That's my brother over there."

We waved. His brother kept milking with one hand as he waved back.

"The calf beside the cow he's milking was born yesterday."

"Wow, look at those wide eyes. They could melt butter," Kevin observed.

"Ah yes, speaking of which, I make butter, too," Roberto announced. Sometimes his delivery was so dry that it was hard to tell if he was joking or if he was merely dispensing information. It didn't appear that he had the same anthropomorphic affection for animals as Kevin had. This was business; cows were not pets.

Roberto led us down to the cheese house where Abel made cheese mostly for restaurants in San José. Their customers catered to North American and European palates where they appreciated stronger-tasting cheese.

"Making cheese is part science and part art," Roberto demonstrated. "It has to do as much with pH levels and adding specific moulds at the right time and at the right temperature as it does with using your sense of sight, touch, and smell. Much like making coffee or wine."

The small room — not much larger than two side-by-side office cubicles — had large windows on every wall that overlooked the mountains. A far cry from any office environment I'd ever worked in. Stainless steel pots, bowls, and scales lined the stainless-steel countertops.

"When my brother is finished milking, he will bring the pail down here and pour it into one of these large pots. Once the milk is heated to 32°C, or 90°F, we add microbiotic cultures to make the milk more acidic. The temperature has to stay the same for at least a half hour. Then we add an enzyme that makes the milk curdle. We stir and wait, stir and wait, then separate the solid curds from the liquid whey. All cheeses follow the same process, but the taste comes from how much salt and brine and how much moisture is left or removed and so on. Like I said, it's a bit of an art. And one should not divulge all the secrets." Roberto threw us a sly smile.

Behind a heavy wooden door, a dark cool pantry-type closet with old wooden shelves were stacked with round wheels covered with cheesecloth.

"This is where the cheese is left to ripen for several weeks. Have you tried the Costa Rican cheese?" Roberto asked.

"Yes, it's a bit rubbery and doesn't have a strong taste," I chose my words carefully. I wasn't fond of it, but didn't want to insult the national cuisine. To a cheesemaker, no less.

"Yes, Costa Ricans don't like strong cheese. And they are too impatient to let it ripen. This is why it has the consistency that it does, and the mild taste. The longer a cheese sits and ripens, the more flavourful the cheese becomes. We let our cheese ripen for several weeks and depending on the customer, sometimes months." Roberto grabbed one of the large wheels, cut a big chunk, and wrapped it in a brown paper bag. "Here you go. Let me know how you like it."

"Thank you! Can't wait to try it," I said as I took the bag from him.

"Do you like smoked trout?"

"Love it," Kevin chimed in, speaking for the both of us.

"Come with me. We're done here. Adriana is waiting for us at the house. I'm sure lunch will be ready now." Roberto led us from the cheese house back to their hobbit-like home where we drank coffee — tea for Kevin — and ate delicious cheese with home-churned butter on fresh-made bread, with melt-in-your-mouth smoked trout on the side. None of the food spread before us came out of a can or a box with a list of ingredients the length of my arm. Adriana did not go to great lengths to make a fancy feast. No airs or pretenses. She was not concerned about the perfect presentation. She opened her home and welcomed us as if we were family. I was struck by the authenticity of the exchange.

Adriana practiced her English to accommodate us when we should have been the ones speaking Spanish. Every couple of sentences she'd turn to Roberto and rub her thumb over her fingers as if it would help retrieve the word she was looking for and say, *"Cómo se dice?"*

We chatted for hours this way — a melding of Spanish and English — but for the first time it felt easy and not taxing.

Roberto mentioned that the trout he smoked came from Abel's pond. He only had one small pond and only a few dozen fish. Not enough to run a trout business. He wondered if we might be interested in selling him some trout once we were up and running as he was looking to start a new venture separate from his father's cheese-making business.

Kevin and I were still figuring out how to be trout farmers and didn't know how we'd build a viable business, but we believed the path would somehow reveal itself. It really was a leap of faith. The business plan that Samuel and Anton prepared for us seemed fictional just ten days ago. We had no idea how we'd find customers. Then came Roberto.

Friday, September 14, 2012
The Walk of Lights

On the eve of Costa Rica's Independence Day, before the celebratory parades and lively parties, the custom is first to gather with your family and neighbours to pay homage to those who made independence from Spain possible. Our neighbours gathered in the community centre every year on this day and Clara asked if we'd like to join them this year. Any reason to experience more Costa Rican culture always seemed like a good idea, and the fact that it was an opportunity for us to meet people we hadn't met yet was a bonus.

In the small community centre, we stood side by side with our neighbours in a solemn stance. Kevin and I took our cues from what everyone else was doing and put our right hand on our hearts.

They sang Spanish anthems in flat, monotone voices. The sombre mood was punctuated by the rain pinging on the tin roof and the fluorescent light casting sharp shadows on everyone's faces.

I can't stand these blue lights; they make everyone look like cadavers and they give me a headache.

Some of the school kids recited poems. They stuttered and stumbled, and it was obvious they didn't understand what they were saying, but I gave them an A for effort. Sharon and Nicole were dressed in the traditional Costa Rican costume with blue skirts and white and red headbands called *campasinas* while they danced to folklore music. Sharon was all business; she was concentrating so hard on the choreography she didn't crack a smile. Meanwhile, free-spirited Nicole was smiling ear to ear. They were charming in their own way. They had obviously practiced a lot because they danced in perfect unison...*well, near perfect.*

Then, it was time to eat. The women had each made one of their special dishes: rice and beans, fried pork chops called *chalueta*, *papas*, plus different kinds of desserts. They also served a typical drink called *Dulce*, which is basically brown sugar and water.

The rain stopped just long enough for the walk of lights called *faroles*. The Costa Rican tradition is to make little houses out of cardboard or wood and attach them to a stick. They place a candle in the middle of the house, then walk up and down the streets singing forlorn patriotic songs. I was stunned that they handed some of these lanterns to the under-five-year-old kids. Paper plus fire equated to an accident waiting to happen in our bubble-wrapped North American culture, but here they thought nothing of it.

The candlelit houses symbolized a simpler time. They walked in the dark of night holding these glowing beacons, singing with gratitude for what they had: liberty, opportunity...*electricity!* For some, electricity was still a fairly new commodity.

Kevin and I were grateful to have been invited to bear witness to this cultural experience. We felt part of something special.

Saturday, September 15, 2012
Independence Day

They were preparing for quite a crowd. We noticed a large terrace with long tables and patio chairs under white tarps. Husking, shucking, chopping, dipping, tasting, stirring... tasting some more...the cooks were in the zone.

A woman greeted us, "*Soy Aurea, la mamá de Diego. Bienvenidos, mi casa es su casa.*" Although very welcoming, Diego's mother was not a sweet matronly madam, but rather a shrewd lawyer who exuded no-nonsense moxie. She immediately offered us a drink, pointing to a variety of alcoholic options. It was 9:00 a.m.

"*Solo limonada, por favor,*" I replied on behalf of Kevin and me.

Diego eyed us and with his arm extended, crossed the yard in long strides. Kevin was ready, he knew the drill. Handshakes were imminent.

Aurea came back with two lemonades and handed one to Kevin and the other to me. Diego introduced us, formally, to his mother and father, then his wife, María Fernanda...then his brother and his brother's wife and their daughter, then a cousin and an aunt. It was hard to keep track.

"*Hola... Hola... Hola... Hola... Hola... Hola.*"

Kevin and I smiled and nodded, striving to be gracious guests. Diego quickly switched to Spanish, and it was clear he was explaining who we were, what we were doing there in Costa Rica, how he met us, and how he invited us to take part in the festivities. Their eyes widened and their acceptance was made clear by them chiming, "*Muy bien, muy bien.*"

Diego was chatty and far more casual than at our first meeting. We had jumped from clients to friends in the space of two meetings.

To pass the time before we went to watch the parade, Diego guided us around his parents' property. As lawyers, they'd done well for themselves and would be considered rich based on the typical standard of living where most Costa Ricans live in modest homes with small rooms regardless of the number of family members. Diego's parents' house was tucked between Santa María and San Marcos, and was so unassuming from the front, it was easy to miss. However, the property itself was large with undulating plateaus.

As we walked down, then up, then down again, we came to a cozy casita. An older gentleman was tending to its adjacent garden.

"This is my uncle, Pedro. He's my mother's brother. He lives here," Diego said just as we approached the tiny house. "Let me introduce you to him."

"*Hola tío. Estos son mis amigos Anne y Kevin de Canadá,*" Diego introduced. I felt proud that I understood what Diego said. I understood that *tío* meant *uncle*. And that we were his friends from Canada. My ear was attuning to the language. Maybe I was learning more in my first-grade class than just colouring inside the lines after all. Maybe I was absorbing more vocabulary than I realized.

Kevin and I stood beside Diego and said, "*Hola*," as Pedro got up from his knees, wiped his dusty right hand on his already dirty shirt and extended it to Kevin's.

"*Con gusto.*"

"*Con gusto,*" Kevin repeated.

Diego continued in Spanish, and I understood enough to know that he was asking his uncle if he would be going to the parade. Pedro answered with many words, but he spoke too fast and mumbled his words, so it was hard for me to get everything he was saying. I did hear him say, "*No, demasiado caliente.*"

Turning to us, Diego filled in the blanks. "He says he's not interested in going to the Independence Day parade because it's too hot — but he'll be joining us later for lunch." Then he nodded to Pedro and said, "Okay, *hasta luego.*"

Pedro wasn't wrong — the sun was beating down and without a breeze, I could feel the heat on my bare arms and my jeans were feeling too heavy for this scorching temperature. Standing still chatting with Pedro made the heat seem even more intense.

As we snaked down to the rocky beach, Diego pointed to where his grandfather used to own a bar.

You mean that old shack in the middle of the river?

It was an interesting place to have a bar; you wouldn't want to be too drunk when rowing back to shore. Apparently, it was a hopping place back in the 60s. People would come from near and far just to drink there.

I imagined the room glowing from candles or kerosene lamps with patrons resting on furniture milled and built from local trees, listening to musicians strumming, drumming, and tickling the ivory keys in one of the corners. And maybe they'd be dancing and singing.

Was it a place alive with frivolity or somewhere to drown your sorrows? Maybe both?

It was sad to see it empty and abandoned. I wanted to pretend that all the old folks chatting with the bank tellers were sharing memories of this once beguiling place.

María Fernanda and Diego's niece, Natalia, were dressed in the same matching outfit: blue skirts, white blouses, and red sashes to match the Costa Rican flag. This was similar, but a little different to what Sharon and Nicole had worn the night before. Kevin and I were asked to wear a white T-shirt and blue jeans; Aurea gifted us with red bandanas to wrap around our necks. We were all set, too.

"It'll be hard to find a parking space. You can leave your SUV here and come with us," offered Diego. "Kevin, come sit up front with me. María Fernanda and Natalia will keep Anne company in the back."

We all climbed into Diego's car as instructed. Thank goodness Diego had turned on the ignition several minutes earlier and cranked the air conditioning, otherwise the leather seats baking in the hot sun would have seared my jeans right off my legs. And although we were a bit squished in the back seat, the slight discomfort was a fair exchange for the cool air blasting through the vents.

Diego's parents, brother, and the rest of the family followed in their own cars. We drove five minutes down to San Marcos. Diego was right. It felt like all nine thousand habitants from San Marcos, plus additional people from neighbouring towns, had converged onto a two-block radius. Diego eyed an open spot that faced one of the intersections where the parade would be passing by. Best seats in the house. Whether it was legal to park there, I didn't know, but I figured we were with a bunch of lawyers in a town where they carried clout.

It's good to have friends in high places.

We stood on the sidewalk, watching the parade where kids from regional schools marched in colourful costumes. Their slumped shoulders, slow shuffle, and drawn-out faces said it all.

"This activity is mandatory for these kids," Diego explained. "They've been practicing for months and bored of it all by now. They were probably up early this morning for a dress rehearsal, as well. I remember I had to do it when I was that age."

Although I was sure Diego was right that they'd been practicing — and I certainly couldn't do any better — it was hard to listen to the high-pitched flutes, off-key horns, and off-beat snare drums. The blazing sun was beating down, and clearly, beating them down.

After the parade, the crowd quickly dispersed, rushing to be first to get out of the congested streets, only to cause more traffic. Although it took five minutes to drive into San Marcos, it took over twenty minutes to get back to Diego's parents' house.

The bar was open and free flowing. The lineup to get a drink, however, was at a standstill. In the outdoor kitchen, smoking grills and huge steaming cauldrons released mouthwatering aromas of Costa Rican delights. Diego and María Fernanda were attentive and proudly told us what everything was, but I couldn't for the life of me remember any of the names except for *tamales* (corn paste with vegetables wrapped in banana leaves). Relatives and friends clustered in cliques under white canopies and Diego introduced us to everyone. I couldn't remember any names.

Our hands full with flimsy paper plates, making them precariously unsteady with the amount of food we had piled on them, along with zero gift of Spanish repartee, our crow's feet wrinkled as we smiled, projecting polite acknowledgment. Our goal was to make a beeline to one of the tables without offending anyone in the process.

Indiscernible lyrics serenaded us through the loudspeakers and Diego, in between chugs, translated each song. I learned from him that most Latin American songs are about getting drunk and losing a woman...or a dog...*or both*. And the tipsier Diego got, the funnier the interpretations. By the time we left, we felt like we were part of the family.

Albarito's Fortieth

We had met Albarito only the night before, so it seemed overly generous to be included in this milestone celebration. Albarito was Vanessa's husband and father to my school chum Sharon and her little brother, Thomas. The family lived directly across from the school so after driving back from Diego's parents' afternoon party, letting Frankie out, and feeding the fish, we walked over.

Wet hair combed back, no make-up, wrapped in a bathrobe, Vanessa greeted us at the front door. Grasping the terrycloth to make sure she was covered, she lowered her eyes and gave us a half smile. "*Bienbenidos.*" Pointing to her less-than-ready self, she giggled and explained that being on time in Costa Rica means you're early...*by an hour.* Our turn to feel embarrassed. "*Tranquilo, no problema,*" she said with assurance, then led us through the house to the backyard where there were six rows of long tables with plastic rental chairs under a white tarp.

The day's theme.

Two DJs were ensconced on a small platform; Latin American songs wept through loudspeakers. Kevin and I gave each other side glances and smirked, wondering if brokenhearted drunks had lost their women. Or dogs.

Because we failed to be fashionably late, we were one of the firsts to arrive. Vanessa introduced us to the only other couple, Rolando and Maritza, who were sitting at one of the long tables; then quickly scooted back in to finish getting ready.

We sat across from Rolando and Maritza to keep them company and because it would have been weird and impolite if we walked away and sat over on the other side of the patio on our own. Both in their mid-forties, they looked like couples do when they've been together a long time. It wasn't that they looked alike; rather, like they fit well together. Rolando had a shaved head and Maritza donned long chestnut waves, but each had a roundish frame with piercing brown eyes. And both radiated inviting smiles, although Rolando's was surrounded by a five o'clock shadow.

We were already pretty tired from our outing earlier in the day and I knew we both got a bit tongue-tied in forced situations, so I was prepared for a short visit. But I could tell Kevin liked this couple's energy. So did I.

Thankfully, Rolando spoke English, and we spent the evening exchanging stories. "We lived in the U.S. for a few years. That's where I learned English. I was a truck driver in New Jersey, but we came back to Santa María to enjoy a slower life," Rolando declared. "I grow coffee on our farm now."

Although Maritza understood a lot of the English conversation, she didn't speak more than a few words, so I took this opportunity to stretch my ever-expanding Spanish vocabulary.

I must have learned at least ten new words this week.

Like the loud buzzing song of cicadas, the surrounding chitchat competed with the music. I looked around and noticed the space was now packed. Although we acknowledged the familiar and not-so-familiar faces with a friendly nod, Kevin and I made no effort to mingle with the other guests. We were single-mindedly focused on our new friends. We spent three solid hours with Rolando and Maritza, then made plans to visit their coffee farm once the weather got a bit drier.

Although it was only 9:00 p.m., both Kevin and I were beat. We'd had a long day, so we wished Albarito a happy birthday one last time, thanked Vanessa for the great food and hospitality, and mustered a cursory wave to the other guests as we said goodnight. We didn't mean to be rude, but if we didn't make a clean break, we knew we'd be there another hour with all the cheek kisses and handshakes.

Sunday, September 16, 2012
Precious Sisters

Three-and-a-half weeks had passed, and we hadn't yet visited Sisters Gladys and Gloria. They had been so welcoming when we came to scope out the country and again when they opened their home and hearts to Kevin and Jude in February. We had told them we were looking to buy a property in Costa Rica, but we had failed to let them know we had found a farm in the mountains, that we had made an offer, and had closed the deal. We had landed and hadn't reached out yet. Our guilt was eating away at us. We decided to drive down to San José and drop in. If we had driven all the way there and they hadn't been home, that would have served us right. This was our first trip back to San José since we landed and if nothing else, we needed the practice of manoeuvering through its chaotic streets.

We rang the buzzer next to the wrought iron gate and the latch unlocked without us having to announce ourselves. The gate squeaked open as we walked into the courtyard and before we could take our first steps forward, the front door swung wide.

"*Dios mío!* Anne *y* Kevin! *Bienvenidos.* Welcome."

Sister Gladys stood in the entryway in her blue habit and sensible black shoes. She stretched out her arms and we both rushed over and leaned in for a hug.

Kevin and I sat in the front reception room of the daycare as Sister Gladys scuttled into the next room. It was Sunday and there were no children playing on the other side of the wall. While we waited for Sister Gladys to come back, Kevin removed his laptop from our knapsack. We thought that showing pictures of the farm would be easier than trying to explain ourselves.

Sister Gladys returned with two glasses of fruit juice and handed one to each of us. She sat down between us and said, "*Bueno.*" She placed her calloused hands on her lap. She was ready for our update. It felt as if she had been waiting to hear from us. We did our best to converse. My Spanish had improved somewhat since she last saw me. I understood more Spanish, that's for sure, but it was still a struggle to find things to talk about.

Curious, I asked, "Is Sister Gloria here?"

"*Pronto.*"

Since the meaning of *soon* in Costa Rica is a matter of interpretation and we were struggling to keep the conversation going, Kevin decided to start the slideshow. He set the laptop on the coffee table in front of us and pressed the *play* button.

A picture is worth a thousand words, as the cliché goes. And God knows my vocabulary has not reached a thousand words yet.

With every picture, Sister Gladys sighed and shook her head in disbelief, "*Precioso... Muy muy precioso.*"

After a half hour had passed, Sister Gloria came barrelling through the reception room wearing the identical blue habit and sensible black shoes. She threw her arms up in the air and praised God. We got up and squeezed her tight. She returned the bear hug.

Sister Gladys motioned for her sister to sit beside her on the green leather couch. To make room, I moved over to a side chair. Sister Gladys brought Sister Gloria up to speed, then asked Kevin to start the slideshow from the beginning.

"From the beginning?"

"*Sí, sí, sí.*"

How could Kevin refuse? It was a small penance for taking so long to visit.

With every image came the same singsong, but it was now in stereo. They would look at each picture with great enthusiasm, then chat to each other, question something, click the back button to see the previous picture, then nod their heads again in some unspoken agreement, sigh, then press the forward button. One hundred photos multiplied into a thousand views. At least that's how it felt. They giggled, bobbed their heads, and thanked God for providing us with this paradise.

"*Precioso... Muy muy precioso.*"

It was lovely to see them both again. So very, very precious.

Monday, September 17, 2012

Fire Challenge

The ongoing saga of trying to light a fire in the outdoor ceramic oven continued. Up until now, it had been in vain. I received advice from different people who all seemed to know better but when it came time for them to start the fire and show me how to keep it lit — which was my issue — they failed, too. You name it, there was a reason for its dysfunction:

"The arch of the dome is too high."

"The door is not wide enough."

"The chimney is too small."

"The chimney is too big."

"There shouldn't be a chimney."

I stopped asking. I would succeed on my own. With each new trick and new idea, I felt confident I'd overcome this ridiculous fire challenge. And so far, I had been overcome with merciless frustration to the point of crushing my spirit. I nearly caved once. I thought I might spray a little kerosene since it worked so well to keep the fire going in the huge hearth inside. However, considering the goal was to cook food in this oven, I surmised it would not be a healthy choice. I was afraid its strong stench would be trapped in the dome forever and everything I cooked in there would come out smelling and tasting of kerosene. I thought better of it.

I was using newspaper because that's what I was taught to use at Girl Guide camp when I was twelve; not to mention, it was always the go-to fire starter on any camping trip. But on this day — *Day 26* — I added prickly bits of straw, dried moss, and sawdust instead, *not newspaper*. The match spark ignited the tiny mound. Smouldering, a white cloud of smoke drifted upward.

"Com'on."

The red and orange glow radiated.

"That's it."

By instinct, I gently blew on it. As the straw and moss shrivelled and disintegrated, I added more, then with a ginger touch I placed slivers of kindling over top. A little at a time. I didn't rush the process.

"Please...*please!*" I implored under my breath.

The flame grew as I patiently piled on more tinder.

"There we go."

As focused as I was, I felt my cheeks lift and my lips curl with pride as the sustained flame flickered brightly. I looked around for Kevin, for Martín, for Clara...*anyone*...to share in this triumphant turning point. No one was around, except maybe for clapping angels, as I took a bow to the thunderous applause in my head.

Twenty-One
Life in the Middle of Nowhere

Tuesday, September 18, 2012
A Run-in with the Policía

The internet and cell phone reception in the schoolyard was dismal, at best. We were so hopeful it would do the trick, but we spent half our time searching for that elusive signal. The sweet spot wasn't as sweet as often as we would have liked.

We found a much more reliable connection in Copey. Although it was a bit of a nuisance to drive down the road, it was worth it, and it was better than having to drive all the way to Santa María.

We parked on one of the side streets, parallel to someone's house. We didn't think much of it. We were not in the way, and it was often raining later in the afternoons with few people around.

Kevin had racked his brain to figure out a way to use a Magic Jack, an internet device that allowed us to have a U.S. phone number, making our calls free anywhere in North America and much less expensive when he called England. These are the types of problems Kevin was born to solve. He lived for this stuff. Thrived, even.

It's certainly not my calling.

This is how it worked: I inserted the data card into my laptop; then, with a blue ethernet cable, we connected my laptop to Kevin's. Kevin plugged the Magic Jack into his laptop and plugged an old-fashioned landline phone into the Magic Jack device.

Cue the theme music of Mission Impossible.

I wrote my blog entries and emails in advance, then saved them into my drafts folder. Sometimes, I had as many as twenty messages keeping family and friends abreast of how we were doing. The data card was *very* slow, but it got the job done without the internet cutting out, which was great. I made sure I didn't have large files — no pictures to bog the system down.

I'm not entirely sure whether I was learning the meaning of patience or impatience.

While I was waiting for my emails to download and upload, Kevin was on the phone to his mother or one of his friends back in England. It made me smile to hear him try to end a conversation and hang up.

"Okay, talk soon, bye..." a quick pause. "Bye... Yeah...okay... Bye..." another last pause. Then, as if to make doubly sure he wasn't abruptly hanging up, there was a final, "Buh-bye."

Going down to Copey and rigging our devices up became our daily routine. Usually, Kevin and I went together, but he was less concerned about having to connect every single day. If I missed a day, I felt jittery. Not only because I wanted to contact my family and friends — I did — but I was also trying to build interest in our adventure through social media. We were opening our B&B in January, and I used Facebook as our sole means of advertising. The social media world, to me, felt fickle with a short attention span. If I didn't post regularly, it was easy to lose readership and potential business. I was determined to write something about our experiences as often as possible. *Daily, actually.* Luckily, living in our new pastoral setting provided constant fodder.

One day, I drove down on my own and parked in the usual spot. I had a lovely session: I sent my draft emails, uploaded the incoming ones, and updated my blog and our Facebook page. Just as I disconnected and was packing up my gear to head home, a police officer rode up on his motorcycle, got off, and leaned his heavy bike on its kickstand behind the SUV.

In my rearview mirror I saw the officer, in neon-yellow rain gear, take his notepad out and write something down. Then, he walked closer. He didn't seem in a hurry, which made it feel more intimidating somehow.

When he reached the driver-side window, I could *feel* his stern stare meet my Bambi-in-the-headlight gaze. The rain was torrential and the windows inside were fogged up, so the truth is I couldn't really see his eyes. I just imagined they'd be stern considering the scenario we were in. But I did see him point his finger downward, gesturing for me to roll down the window.

I turned the key and activated the electronic window button. *Mmmvsh.* I was alone in the remote mountains of Central America with a police officer questioning me in a language I didn't comfortably understand. I understood the gist that someone from the community had called wondering what I was doing, sitting in a black SUV, day after day after day. God help me if I said the wrong thing and made things worse.

I felt the blood drain from my face as I pointed to my laptop and data card. In my stilted Spanish, I explained that I lived in Río Blanco and we didn't have internet at home.

His serious demeanour changed into a hearty laugh.

A bit confused by his reaction, I stuttered when I told him I was leaving and promised never to return.

Ever!

His laughter simmered to a wide smile. He assured me with pantomime gestures that it was not a problem for me to be there. *"Regrese mañana, señora, sí, sí, regrese mañana, no problema!"* he kept repeating, emphasizing that it wasn't a problem for me to return tomorrow or any other day to connect to the internet. Dripping wet, he returned to his motorcycle, climbed on, and drove off.

Once my legs stopped feeling like wet noodles, I was able to see the humour in the whole exchange. Clearly influenced by Hollywood movies, I had to get over my preconceived notion of how being questioned by a police officer in Central America would go down. However, this little incident helped spur the desire to get internet at home that much quicker. Not to mention learn more Spanish, *pronto*!

Wednesday, September 19, 2012
Abel

It shook my suburban sensibilities a little when I saw people riding horses as normal everyday transportation. I love horses, but it took some getting used to.

I was pruning our thorny purple Guaria Morada tree when I noticed a man stride down our driveway on a horse like some cowboy in a Western movie. I squinted from the blinding sun. His large-brimmed hat cast a shadow over his face, making it impossible for me to recognize any defining features that might give me a hint of who this was.

I called over to Kevin, who was walking down the pasture hillside. He had been checking to make sure the second tank he had installed was functioning properly. Just as Kevin reached the driveway, the man swung his leg over his saddle and landed with a thud. He then tied the reins up to one of our spindly trees.

"Hello?" I called as I put my sheers down and met the man in front of our garage. Kevin was right behind me.

"Hi. I'm Abel, Roberto's father." He gave an awkward chuckle. "I knew Rick. And Elly, my wife, was very good friends with Mona. I guess you're the new kids in town?" He laughed again.

"Yes. We've been here just a few weeks. Nice to meet you. I'm Kevin and this is my wife, Anne."

"Yeah, Rick told me before he left that he sold the farm to a Canadian couple. I'm a cheesemaker, but I suppose you know that already. Roberto mentioned he gave you a tour of our little operation last week. Sorry I missed you. I was out of town."

Abel's speech cadence was stilted, as if he didn't get a chance to speak to a lot of people and he had fallen out of practice, so when he was faced with having to form and utter words out loud, they came out a little uneven or a bit laboured. But there was no shortage of storytelling skills. He spoke English with a Spanish accent, but he was easy to understand.

Abel's family was originally from the San José area, but as self-proclaimed hippies back in the early 80s, he and his young bride — they were only nineteen at the time — decided to move to the country and live off the land. They found work in Río Blanco as farm hands and did that for several years until eventually they managed to save enough money to buy the house and land from their aging employer. They bought a few cows, started a dairy farm, and supported their young family by making and selling cheese.

"I have two mares, and I do guided tours during tourist season, too," Abel added. "I can take you out for a ride someday. Horseback riding is a different way to see the area. You get to see places that you can't get to by foot or car."

"That's very kind of you," Kevin remarked, not wanting to commit. I could tell by his imperceptible hesitancy that he was being polite and hoped the offer would be forgotten. I knew Kevin wasn't thrilled with the idea of riding a horse. But it wasn't only the horse riding that Kevin was hesitant about — we had only just met Abel, and he wasn't sure if he wanted to be indebted to him so soon. Kevin liked to let things marinate... to allow people to show their true colours over time. Coming on this big life-changing adventure provided opportunities to embrace our strengths and qualities but also to face some of our well-ingrained character flaws. I wouldn't say treading cautiously was a flaw, but it was a character trait that was definitely well-ingrained in Kevin. It was hard for him to trust.

"Oh yes, I'd love to go some time. Thank you," my gregarious inflection balanced out Kevin's less enthusiastic tone. I actually did want to go. I loved horses and had taken a few riding classes. It had been a while, but it seemed like a great way to widen our community base. Gratefully accepting a neighbour's kind offer could help forge a deeper connection. And, at the very least, not put us in his bad books by insulting him. And always thinking about our B&B business, I thought it would be great to offer Abel's tour as a sightseeing experience.

As Abel mounted his horse to go home, he turned and looked directly at me. "Elly's visiting family in the U.S. right now but will come another time to meet you."

"Look forward to meeting her. Tell her to come over anytime," I called out.

Even though Abel didn't stay long, he stayed long enough for his horse to deposit a gift of fresh manure, which I promptly scooped up and added to our compost as soon as he was gone.

The gift that keeps on giving.

Thursday, September 20, 2012

How Much?

Without any income coming in yet, we were being careful how we spent our money. In the spirit of not wanting to be wasteful, we became frugal. Living out in the middle of nowhere away from the barrage of advertising trying to lure us into temptation also helped. However, we did need to buy some stuff regardless of how self-sufficient we planned to be.

One of the tires on the SUV had a puncture so Kevin replaced it with the spare. We wanted to get the damaged tire repaired as soon as possible to avoid driving on the smaller spare too long on the gravel roads, so we went into San Marcos. The tire repair shop charged us $2.60 to take the spare off, fix the puncture, and re-install the newly repaired tire.

In the hardware store, Kevin asked for some fuses, and he paid $0.06 each. To put things in perspective, they cost approximately $2.50 for just one fuse in Canada.

We went into the Vehicle Registration office to replace the four-wheeler's yearly sticker, and they didn't charge us a penny. Not a penny!

Since we were embracing more of a garden-to-table mentality, we rarely bought packaged foods since arriving in Costa Rica. That didn't always mean our garden, but it did mean buying our produce at local markets. Six large mangoes cost $2.80, each banana $0.06, five cucumbers added up to $2.00, and three huge pineapples were a mere $3.00. And that was just a fraction of what we bought. We walked away with four large bags full of fruits and vegetables for under $16.00. Back in Canada, one of those bags would have amounted to a small mortgage.

When we stopped at a nursery, we purchased three sweet mandarin trees. They would take three years to mature and produce any fruit, but we were already looking forward to plucking some fresh mandarins right off our own trees. Each tree set us back a whopping $4.00.

Worth the investment, I'd say.

Costa Rica was considered expensive compared to the other Central American countries. Its infrastructure was more developed with better healthcare, education, and road construction. But there was an added layer, too. If expats decided they wanted all the amenities and comforts they had back home, then the government was happy to ding their wallets. Plugging in a bunch of North American appliances — and draining more energy than the average Tico — would cost you. Affluent Ticos who lived the high life got hit, too. No matter who you were, if your energy consumption jumped over a certain threshold, the fees could triple. Learning this tidbit of information encouraged us to do everything we could to live as humble Ticos. As much as possible.

I became resolute that we would make do with the few kitchen appliances we had. We would not buy a new range with an oven and a four-burner stovetop. Nor would we replace the diminutive fridge. I would learn to prepare the right amount of food to avoid having leftovers. Adamant that I would cook the bulk of our meals from fresh ingredients and would not store extra portions even as we hosted guests, I refused to entertain the idea of buying a separate chest freezer. The tiny one in our small fridge would have to do. The dryer we bought was powered by propane gas, so it didn't make any demands on the grid. But even so, to conserve the propane, I dried our clothes on the line on dry, sunny days, and used the dryer for sheets and heavier items. Luckily, we lived at an altitude where we didn't have to rely on central heating or air conditioning, so in that regard we lived off the grid every day. We managed to keep our expenses low.

There was an emotional price to leaving everything that was familiar, and it was heftier than I had anticipated, but the simplicity of living in this paradise was priceless.

Friday, September 21, 2012
Lucky

Frankie had become quite bold exploring the property on her own, so we really had to watch her. She liked to wander up to the top of our property, where the river flowed into the sediment ponds. Each pond was lower than the previous, creating a small waterfall. The cascade was miniature compared to those at Niagara Falls, but the pressure of the water flowing over the edge was considerable. Any lightweight object or animal could easily be swept away.

Kevin went up to work on the sediment ponds with Frankie on his heels. I didn't think twice about it until I saw Kevin walking down with Frankie in his arms.

"What a madam, she is!" Kevin announced, sounding out of breath.

"What happened? Is she okay?"

"She will be. We'll need some towels."

I rushed inside and grabbed the first ones I saw in the cupboard. They were old ones left behind. Then ran back out.

"I noticed a clover patch on the other side of the canal and jumped over," Kevin relayed as he handed our sopping wet dog to me.

Kevin had a knack for zeroing in on the one-and-only four-leaf clover in a patch of hundreds. It was one of his intuitive tricks. He was so good at it that when we first met and went on walks, he would suddenly stop, bend down, and pick that one lucky clover. If I hadn't seen him pluck it out of the ground with my own eyes each time, I would have suspected that he had planted it there ahead of time to impress me. He would then present the little green stem to me as a romantic gesture like most other men present a bouquet of wildflowers. It happened so often that it became *our thing*. We even used it as our wedding theme: A simple image of a silver four-leaf clover, with the words *Lucky in Love* written underneath, adorned our invitations.

As I wrapped Frankie in the towel and rubbed her dry, Kevin continued, "Suddenly, I heard a quiet *plop*. I looked around and couldn't see Frankie anywhere."

Vertically challenged with a cinnamon-coloured coat, Frankie could play hide-and-seek in the thicket and win the game.

"I shouted out her name several times. Then started whistling. But nothing."

Whistling usually got her attention and brought her back instantly. I could imagine how frantic Kevin must have felt.

"After about a minute — *sixty very long seconds, I tell ya* — I saw Frankie's head pop up from under the waterfall. Her eyes were big round saucers. She looked terrified. Gasping for air and her stubby little legs frantically paddling."

"Did she manage to swim to the edge? How did she get out?"

"The sides of that sediment pond are too steep for her to climb out on her own so I just reached down, grabbed her collar, and plucked her out," Kevin said, shaking his head.

Trembling in my arms, she whimpered, begging for cuddles. I bathed her on a regular basis in warm water, but to my knowledge, Frankie's head had never been completely submerged. This ordeal must have been cold and scary for her. It had been scary for us, too, so the cuddles were as much for me as they were for her.

I wondered if this was just one of those lessons she had to learn. She was pretty precocious and could be quite stubborn, so I was betting this wouldn't be her last misadventure. I just hoped she would always be this lucky...with or without a four-leaf clover.

Saturday, September 22, 2012

Cranky Frankie

I came back from running errands and Frankie, who had been following Kevin around the property again, was covered in muck from head to tail and whining at the door. There was no way I was letting her in the house. With a little less patience and empathy than I had shown her the previous day, I gave her a bath in a small, round, yellow basin outside by the big pond. She was so filthy I had to replace the water three times. And she wasn't happy about it, either...the water was very cold. I was normally nice enough to mix in some hot water, but since I was caught in the pouring rain and getting soaking wet, I, too, was cranky.

This damn, unrelenting mud!

My only goal was to get her clean as quickly as possible so we could both go inside and get dry. The rainy season and the incessant mess it brought with it was starting to get on my nerves. I was beginning to understand the decision to leave pets outside. She gave me the cold shoulder for several hours afterwards.

Sunday, September 23, 2012
Surprise!

"I've booked the flight," Mum told me matter-of-factly. Even though she'd been living in an anglophone province for over thirty years, her French-Canadian accent was noticeable, even to my ear. And even though we spoke French to each other most of the time, we often slid into English where the words came more easily. For me, anyway.

Sitting in the office area of the house where the landline's cable was affixed to the wall socket, I made myself comfortable in the high-back leather chair that Rick and Mona left behind. I assumed, like most of my conversations with my mother, I'd have to concentrate. My mother had a habit of foregoing the lead-up to most of her stories. She expected everyone to know all the important details before she opened her mouth as if they were mind readers. There was usually a certain amount of reconnaissance required to get the full picture.

"Flight? Where are you going? Are you now flying down to Texas in January instead of driving because of Dad's health issues? How's he feeling by the way?"

In their retirement years, which started at age fifty-seven for Dad and fifty-five for Mum, my parents bought a fifth wheeler and spent January to April road-tripping across Canada and the United States. I don't remember when, but at some point, they rolled into one of the many trailer parks in Texas and liked a specific one so much they secured and leased a site. They left their trailer there year-round and migrated from cold Canada to this warm and sunny destination every winter. No longer having to tow their heavy house on wheels, driving their Ford F-150 was easier to manage and more economical on gas. But reaching his late seventies, I noticed that Dad was slowing down. He was suffering mysterious inflammation in his hands and feet causing numbness and he felt out of breath without any exertion. It was worrisome.

"No, not Texas. Dad won't be going," Mum said.

"He won't be going to Texas?" Following my mother's storytelling breadcrumbs required deduction skills equal to Sherlock Holmes at times. And the patience of a saint, which I did not possess.

"No, to Costa Rica."

"Costa Rica?" I repeated more out of surprise than confirmation. "You're coming to Costa Rica without Dad?"

My mother never travelled without my father, so I was sure I was misunderstanding her. If I kept calm and stayed the course by asking more questions, I would get to the bottom of it.

"Yes. Dad has trouble to breathe."

"Dad has trouble *breathing*," I corrected her gently. It always felt like I was being the language police with her for not getting verb conjugation or English expressions right, but this was something she asked of me. It took her a long time to remember that we wash our *hair* — singular, even though there are a lot of *them* — not *hairs*. "So you're thinking of coming here alone? When are you thinking of visiting?" I was wrapping the coiled phone cord around my index finger, then untwisting it.

"In January. I just bought my ticket."

We were opening the B&B the first week of January. I imagined myself busy with the casita booked and my mum underfoot. Where would she stay? Upstairs in the loft on the lower bunk bed? My mind was hiccupping, but I recovered and pressed on.

"*Okaaay*. Hmmm. I'll have to make sure one of us can pick you up at the airport. How long are you staying?"

"A month."

I felt a sharp pain, but I couldn't pinpoint where, exactly. In my temple? In my chest? In my neck? In the back of my throat as I choked on my response?

I was feeling blindsided since my mother had made these plans without discussing the details with me first. She had mentioned in passing when we first announced that we were moving to Costa Rica that she wanted to visit, and I had agreed that it would be nice, but we hadn't fleshed anything out. I didn't want to dismiss her or make her feel like she wasn't welcome. She was. It's just that in all my adult years we hadn't spent more than two hours at a time in the same room.

Mum and Dad did most things together. It was a package deal. They had different interests but none that kept them physically apart in distance or in time for very long. I couldn't remember the last time my mother and I occupied the same space, just the two of us, for more than fifteen minutes. Sure, I went to see them, but my visits would be limited to small talk upon arrival — the time it took to eat lunch or dinner — then without appearing rude or too eager, I would wrap things up as quickly as possible. I did the same when I dropped Phoenix and Jude off for their annual summer vacation with them. My parents didn't spend a lot of time with any of their grandchildren and these two weeks every summer were the only real bonding time my kids had with them, so I made a point of not lingering then either.

On the day trips, the invitation to stay overnight was offered but I would sooner drive back home. The thought of staying longer brought on anxiety. Two hours was the perfect amount of time to keep things on an acceptable superficial level. Keeping things light and non-confrontational was the goal. I needed the first two hours in the car to psych myself up and the last two hours to calm myself down from whatever guaranteed tizzy tailspin I'd have to bear.

Although I loved my parents very much, I would never have described our relationship as close. My mother's lack of maternal instinct — not prone to hugging tightly or showing much affection at all — perplexed me for most of my life. Admittedly, I possessed an intense need for overt signs of love and approval which might have been a little over the top for any parent. As for my father? The fact that his daughters had their own thoughts and feelings seemed to cause him deep irritation, leaving me to slink out of sight and seek attention elsewhere. I didn't start out that way. Apparently, when I was very young, my father was bewildered by my precocious nature and ability to make him laugh with my animated antics. He would leave the room and chuckle to avoid encouraging my silly behaviour, then return with a stern, "That's enough." I must have learned quickly the benefits of muting my innate spirit in his presence because I don't ever remember amusing him...*ever*.

Don't get me wrong, we were well cared for in terms of material goods and I do believe they loved us. But having children seemed to me like a business decision on both their parts rather than a true desire to have a family.

My two sisters and I enjoyed middle-class comforts, but we weren't spoiled — Mum and Dad were strict. There were rules we had to follow and lines we had better not cross. These were mostly presumed by my father's permanent frown lines that had ossified into a steely expression, leaving very little room for interpretation (full disclosure in the spirit of fairness: I have inherited that same perpetual creased brow as an adult, much to my dismay...and my children's). When talking was involved, it was a one-way street. Communication came *at* us. Any inquiry, rebuttal, or even light-hearted curiosity would be shut down with a firm and disapproving "tsuh tsuh." The mentality of their generation being that kids should be seen and not heard was alive and well in our family: do not question those in authority.

The Sound of Music*'s von Trapp rank-and-file expectations come to mind.*

So, when my mother blurted out that she intended to stay with us for a whole month... *Thirty-one days...!* I'm sure you can understand my sincere trepidations.

Sitting more upright in the swivel chair with both elbows pressed into the desk, I continued my interrogation. "A whole month, I see. And you're coming alone? Dad doesn't want to come?"

"No, he says a month is too long."

Agreed.

"I will have to take three planes and carry my own passport and tickets. This will be the first time I travel on my own without your father."

I had to give my mother credit. When she set her mind to do something, she had unwavering determination. Don't try to stop her. At seventy-four years old, she wasn't going to let the fact that my father didn't want to visit deter her from coming herself. I admired that. A lot. My heart softened in that moment.

She was reaching out and making an effort. I was curious. I had so many questions about my upbringing...her upbringing...my father's upbringing. This could be my chance to uncover parts of my family's background that lay under what seemed to be a cloak of secrecy. I imagined the truth of it all to be rather mundane and benign, but their refusal to talk about any of it only fueled my paranoia in the early days and my disassociation over time.

Although I suspected my mother's agenda was more about practicing the Spanish she had been learning than visiting us, it occurred to me that having her all to myself for such a long period of time might provide the opportunity to crack us both open.

"You're very brave, Mum. Good for you," I said reassuringly. "Kevin and I look forward to seeing you in a few months."

Twenty-Two
Promised Land

Monday, September 24, 2012

Cindy and Larry

Fifteen big bags of organic fertilizer were delivered. I couldn't wait to get my hands dirty and play in the garden, but it would have to wait until later. Rick and Mona's friends, Cindy and Larry, who lived in Santa María, called us the week before inviting us over for an afternoon visit.

We arrived in Santa María with the plan of hopping onto the internet before meeting up with Cindy and Larry. With so many cell phone towers nearby there was usually a good signal, but for some reason the connection was extremely slow even with full signal.

When Kevin tried to call England on the Magic Jack, it wouldn't connect at all.

I only managed to write a few words on Facebook and upload my blog entries. I couldn't download or send any emails.

So frustrating.

Twenty minutes later, we packed it in. My addiction to internet connectivity was waning. Don't get me wrong, I was still an addict, but a recovering one. The more I spent my day *unplugged*, the fewer cravings I had. I could go without it for longer stretches.

It was time to go meet Cindy and Larry anyway. Cindy had instructed us to meet them beside the park in the centre of town and to look for a blue Nissan.

We were parked in front of the town church, which was on the east side of the park. The park occupied one-square block. In one corner, swings, monkey bars, and a slide kept active kids entertained while interspersed benches — along winding paths that crisscrossed the entire green space — welcomed whoever needed a rest. There was even a band shelter. We hadn't seen it used for concerts yet and I wondered if it had been relegated to a hangout spot for adolescents. Mature trees would provide refuge from the searing sun during the dry hot months and from drizzle during the wet season.

After packing up our things, looking westward through this mini forest, we spotted a blue car.

"Hey, I think that might be them," Kevin pointed.

We couldn't tell if it was a Nissan, nor could we make out if there were people in the car, but we were hedging our bets. Kevin put the SUV into first gear and did a slow U-turn...then shifted into second. He never got out of second gear. That's how short the distance was.

As Kevin turned left, then left again, he parked on the right side of the street, facing south again. The blue car, indeed a Nissan, brushed against the park side curb and faced north. From our vantage point, we could see shadowy figures inside it. We waited a minute until two occupants emerged. The thin, well-toned woman — with a Marilyn Monroe wavy blonde bob — had a youthful bounce in her step. From afar, she could have been mistaken for a teenager. The man beside her wasn't much taller than Kevin and his spry steps kept up with her easily. Wire-rimmed glasses reflected the sun, adding a certain sparkle to his oval face. Despite a thick bristly moustache, it was no match for his even wider smile. His buttoned-down shirt tucked into his belted cargo pants and his full head of chalky white hair, combed with a side part, reminded me of my dad.

As they came closer, they both threw us an easy-going wave. We waved back.

"Hey, we recognize that SUV. You must be Anne and Kevin. I'm Cindy and this is Larry."

From up close, Cindy's freckled face exuded a childlike sweetness. A kind of innocence. I loved her vibe instantly.

"Yes, hello. Nice to meet you both," Kevin said, shaking Larry's hand.

"*Pura Vida*, as they say. Welcome to Costa Rica! You're going to love it here," Larry grinned with a degree of certainty.

"Well so far, it's been great. We're happy to be here and happy to meet you. Rick had mentioned he had good friends that we should meet. We're so glad you reached out," I replied. "Do you live in town?"

"We live five minutes by car, straight up this road," Cindy said, pointing south. "We usually walk everywhere. We're just borrowing this car from a friend for a couple of days so we can run a few errands in San José. We have a doctor's appointment tomorrow for a hearing test. We're at that age."

"How 'bout you kids follow us up to our place. Better than standing around here sweating our asses off," Larry chortled.

At forty-seven, it was odd to hear the term *kids* being used when referring to Kevin and me. But I guess considering there was a good twenty-year age gap between him and us, his perspective was different.

No matter how old I get, when my mother calls me on my birthday and repeats my age in disbelief, she always — and I do mean always — ends with an exaggerated half-joking, half-serious moan, "My baaabeee!" I expect to hear her say it 'till the day she dies!

"Sounds great, lead the way," Kevin motioned.

Most of the houses on this road were built of concrete and painted pastel yellow, green, or terracotta. Others were plain white. No yard to speak of — it would take anyone only a few steps to reach the front door from the sidewalk. The properties were close to each other and sometimes separated by chain-link fences. It was the closest to a suburb we'd seen in this region.

Cindy and Larry's house, however, was tucked away on a hillside. Their long driveway zigzagged up a large front yard. Trees, tall grass, and flowers grew on either side of a short bridge that crossed over a babbling brook. From this spot, I had to crane my neck to see their log home. It was like stumbling onto a secluded cottage somewhere in northern Ontario, Canada.

Another little haven tucked away, promising respite from the world's troubles.

Manoeuvering around the mini switchbacks, Kevin kept the SUV in all-wheel drive until he reached the end of their driveway and pulled up on the emergency brake. I imagined Cindy and Larry having to hike this incline with heavy grocery bags.

No wonder they're so fit.

"Wow, how lovely," I marvelled to myself as I shut the passenger door apparently loud enough that others could hear.

"Com'on in..." Larry said with a you-haven't-seen-anything-yet Cheshire-cat grin.

It's amazing how much a person can say with so few words. Well...it's amazing how much I can infer.

We entered one by one. It was as quaint as any cabin with its quintessential horizontal logs stacked on top of one another, but a *cabin* it was not. The large-scale gable windows in the living room soared past the second-floor loft and looked out over green foliage and mountain peaks. Shafts of light gleamed through the panes, brightening up what would have been a sombre space with the oppressive dark wood. I don't know if it was their sheer size, their particular shape, or the glow streaming in, but they conjured a church-like quality. Bold original paintings covered the walls while the shelves and tabletops showcased gold and silver artifacts from Middle Eastern countries. I noticed an intricate coffee carafe that could have been hiding Aladdin's genie. The child in me wanted to rub it and find out. But the adult that I was refrained. Their modern dusty blue sectional contrasted with the hand-carved antique furniture and old-world charm. It was eclectic in all the best ways. I was intrigued. There were stories in these mementos, I was sure of it, and I was hoping they were willing to share them with us.

"Sit down. Make yourselves at home," Larry suggested.

"Can I get you some coffee, tea, soda...juice?" Cindy offered. After taking our order, she scuttled off behind a swinging door, into the kitchen I presumed.

"How long have you been in Costa Rica?" Kevin asked Larry.

"Nearly five years. We're originally from Phoenix, Arizona. Our daughter, Samantha, still lives there with her partner, RJ. We love living here, but we sure do miss her. We're always happy when she visits or when we go back there."

"I just left my two kids, Phoenix and Jude, back in Canada. It hasn't even been a month yet and I miss them. I'm sure it'll be better once we get internet in the house and we can chat more regularly," I said.

"How old are they?" asked Larry.

"Twenty-two and sixteen. Jude, my son, decided at the last minute to stay in Canada and finish school there."

"It's hard to leave your social network at that age," Larry said, then asked, "How are you settling in?"

"We love it here so far. We're still finding our way around and learning new things about the farm every day," Kevin answered.

"We love that farm, the most beautiful property in Costa Rica. Such a gem. We were so disappointed when Rick told us he had sold it. We were hoping it wasn't to a conglomerate who was going to turn it into some suck-the-land-dry money-making project development. We were thrilled to hear that he had sold it to a couple who wanted to keep things as they are. To people who appreciate its natural beauty. That's what we wanted to hear."

"I'm glad you approve," Kevin chuckled. Larry and I laughed, too. "What brought you to Costa Rica?" Kevin followed up.

"Our intention was to retire in Mexico, actually. We were all set. Everything was decided. Then a friend of ours persuaded us to come visit Santa María first. Just to have a look. We did and the rest is history. We scrapped the Mexico idea and *bingo!* We moved here instead and haven't looked back," Larry explained with some verve in his voice.

"Do you speak Spanish?" I wondered, hoping they would be a good resource when we needed help.

"No. Well, a little. We should know more for people who have lived here five years, but it's hard to learn a new language at our age. I mean, we get by. We try."

Okay, so maybe they won't be our go-to Spanish teachers. Next question.

Keeping the conversation flowing, Kevin shifted and commented, "This is such a great house."

"We were lucky to find this place. We don't own it, we rent. And we hope our landlord never wants to sell it. It's perfect for us."

Cindy came through the swinging door holding a tray full of goodies. She handed us our drinks and served us some lemon squares while Larry continued talking.

"I'm an architect. Retired now, but I'm always dabbling. I worked at a bunch of firms in the States, but I didn't like where architecture was going. Boxes with no character. Anything to save a buck. I'd had enough so we packed up and relocated to Saudi Arabia for two years, then to Egypt where I managed an architecture business for six years." Larry paused and took a bite out of his dessert.

"Looks like you collected some wonderful souvenirs," Kevin said, looking around the room.

"Yes, they're nice reminders of our time there," Cindy mentioned. "Years ago now. Samantha was just a little girl back then. It certainly was eye opening, y'know?"

"I bet," I agreed and sipped my coffee. "One of my sisters lived in Riyadh for nine years with her husband. They just moved back to Canada this year."

"We hated Riyadh. Armpit of the world. Couldn't get out of there fast enough," Larry jeered.

"But Cairo was fantastic," Cindy pressed, offsetting Larry's bluntness.

I got the impression Larry didn't mince his words and Cindy was the type of woman who managed to weave silk with kind words. They were both endearing, each in their own way.

"Is that stained-glass art something you bought along your travels? It's beautiful," I pointed out.

When we first came in, I had been mesmerized by the light sparkling through the translucent cobalt blue that framed three delicate iris flowers with mauve petals and lime green stems. Exquisite in its simplicity. I had wanted to know where it came from and whether the iris was a symbol of a particular place with some enchanting story attached to it.

"Oh no, I made that," Cindy giggled. "It's a hobby of mine. I draw the sketch, cut the glass, and solder the lead. It can be fun but it's mostly frustrating. I'm not always good at cutting the pieces in the shapes I want. I'm getting better with practice though."

"That's fantastic! What other talents are you hiding?" my pitch raised a full octave with delight.

Cindy smiled, stood up, and motioned, "Come with me."

Kevin and I got up and followed her outside. Larry was close behind. Their backyard, which was the size of a postage stamp compared to the front of the house, was dedicated to growing herbs and vegetables.

"Larry built these for me because digging in the dirt on my hands and knees was killing my back," Cindy said, placing one of her alabaster hands on the waist-high raised beds.

"I just hammered a few planks of wood together and *bingo!* No big deal," Larry dismissed his effort and skill with a shrug.

"Such a great idea," I looked at Kevin to see if he agreed. I knew he did. It reinforced our plan of transforming the big concrete cylindrical tanks in the hatchery into a greenhouse.

If we fill the tanks up with soil and compost, get rid of the dark tin roof and replace it with clear plastic, it'll be perfect.

In their small, contained space, there was a lot to see. Kevin studied the way Larry had constructed the wooden boxes and how he had positioned the posts that supported the clear plastic sheet that sheltered the plants from getting soaked. It didn't seem permanent — installed only for the rainy season. Larry and Kevin broke away and had a conversation about structural stuff while I listened to Cindy. I could tell she was excited to impart the knowledge she'd acquired. It had been a journey for her.

"I hadn't gardened much before arriving in Costa Rica... It's all been trial and error, that's for sure, but there's nothing like growing your own food," her blonde curls bobbed and swayed as she talked. When she spoke about her failures, she chuckled in a nothing-ventured-nothing-gained sort of way. And when she spoke about the successes — no matter how trivial — she beamed with pride.

Cindy was interesting and our conversation felt effortless; however, I started to get antsy. My sixth sense told me it was time to wrap things up. I wasn't sure what time it was, but it seemed like we'd been there for a while, and I didn't want to overstay our welcome. For Cindy and Larry's sake, yes, but mostly for my own.

As a social introvert, I like meeting and getting to know people; I enjoy deep conversations. I have a lot of friends and I'm grateful for each one. That's the social part of me. But I also crave a lot of quiet and alone time. Too much external stimuli quickly drains my energy. Over the years, I've discovered I have to pace myself. I understand now that I need to fully recharge my battery before meeting up with friends or taking part in any large gathering. There's a certain point — somewhere at the two- to three-hour mark — where my body says *enough*. When I was younger, I used to ignore the empty-tank signs, and I would push my natural boundary. Not good. I'd get all air heady and exhibited mildly inappropriate behaviour. Well, not so much inappropriate but definitely awkward. I became less engaged and more robotic. My usual rambling chatter would switch to curt one-word responses. Then, when I just couldn't bear it any longer, I would get up in the middle of a conversation and say, "I have to go. Bye," leaving the other person in mid-sentence. It felt like if I didn't escape at that precise moment, my wiring would malfunction, and steam would blow out of my ears. I'm more aware of my inner workings now and know my limits. I usually manage to bow out more gracefully.

It helps that Kevin suffered from a similar impediment. For example, Kevin preferred not to carpool because he liked to be in control of when he leaves any situation without having to rely on someone else for a ride. I can appreciate that. And though no one could accuse him of not being affable, he was generally more anti-social than me and got bored easily. He was grateful to have a pet at home; it gave him the perfect reason to extricate himself sooner. He played that card often because it wasn't a lie. Pets do require their humans to be responsible and thoughtful. And Kevin was *the* most responsible and thoughtful in this regard. He tried to never be away for longer than two or three hours at a time. And with the added liability of rain, river, and sediment, all the more reason to keep visits brief in Costa Rica. Our trout were counting on us now, too.

Not a minute later, Kevin tapped me gently on the shoulder and said, "I'm sorry to interrupt, but it's getting late. We should get back to let Frankie out and feed the fish."

Bingo!

As we were getting ready to leave, Cindy cut some fresh dill, fennel, and thyme for us to take home.

"Thank you so much!" I inhaled the sweet aroma. "Next time, we'll have you over to Hush Valley Lodge."

Tuesday, September 25, 2012
A Day of Running Errands

Rick had promised that his power of attorney, Nathalie, would help us change over the ownership of the utility bills from his name to ours and help us sort out better internet connection. Getting high-speed internet to the house was still a priority. Having to write my blog posts ahead of time, then drive down to Copey and connect, was getting old… fast. It made for a fun story when we first got there, but the inconvenience was starting to wear thin. Not to mention, we had to ensure we had a good connection before we opened the B&B. Business would be conducted exclusively online. That's how we would market and how we would correspond with potential guests. We needed to be responsive and email back right away…not days later. I was happy for the slower pace, but I was hardwired to provide the best customer service possible. And I wanted good reviews.

Although we were eager, there was nothing we could do until Nathalie returned from her trip in France. We knew she would be gone for about a month and that she left days before we arrived, so we assumed she'd be back soon, but decided we'd wait to hear from her.

Nathalie called the previous day and arranged for us to meet at eight in the morning. That was the whole conversation. There was no preamble. No cheerful chat. I suppose she was merely following through with her legal duty to Rick. We were probably a thorn in her side. An obligation. I usually make friends easily, so I feel self-conscious when I sense someone isn't interested in being friends.

Not everyone has to like me but don't tell that to my people-pleasing inner child.

Much like the Cindy and Larry scenario in Santa María, Nathalie told me to meet her at the town square but in San Marcos. Same logistics: one-square block but with a grander church, a grassy park but with fewer trees, a large white gazebo but no playground, and meandering paths from all sides but with fewer chances to sit and rest as the benches seemed sparser. Every rural town we'd seen was designed in a similar way.

Kevin had no trouble finding a parking space. Nathalie said she'd be on her dark blue four-wheeler. The streets weren't busy for a Friday morning so it would be easy to spot her. Besides, she would recognize Rick's black SUV. We figured if we didn't find her, she'd find us.

Nathalie's four-wheeler engine thrummed as she pulled up behind us. From the passenger side window, I saw her remove her helmet and secure it on the back rack. I felt a bit anxious.

"I think that's her," I said.

Kevin and I stepped out and walked to the back of the SUV. Kevin was at a loss not knowing the protocol when meeting a woman on her own, without a man to shake hands with. Nathalie took the reins on this matter. Her lean boyish physique and ultra-short hair made her look as tough as she sounded on the phone, but to my surprise she moved in and gave us each a loose hug.

"*Pura Vida,*" her greeting sounded more terse than welcoming.

"Hi."

"You like it here so far? Rains a lot, huh? Ready to move back yet?"

Rather than sweet or funny, the edge in her tone cut through. Even her French lilt couldn't disguise it. We didn't know much about Nathalie except for what Rick and Nacho told us. She was a sole proprietor of a carpentry business and built houses for a living. According to Nacho she managed a crew of unreliable workers in an industry where women weren't taken seriously. She'd had to be smarter and more focused. She had to tune out the naysayers. She'd also seen her share of expats who became friends come and go, too, so I assumed she had little interest in getting too close or letting her guard down. There may have been a few reasons she came across as crusty.

Kevin didn't suffer rude people to any degree though, and I could see he objected to her sour attitude, but we needed her, so I also felt his restraint. He liked conflict about as much as I did, which was not one bit. He swallowed his objection and carried on. "We're managing well enough. No plans to leave anytime soon." Although polite, Kevin didn't add any warmth in his delivery. He wanted to dispense with the small talk and get on to the business at hand.

We walked straight to the ICE office with quiet purpose. Although we were following Nathalie who walked at a quick clip, we knew where we were going. We'd been there a month and knew where things were located, *mostly*. We needed her help, but we didn't need her help to guide us to the ICE office. We had been there weeks ago with Milagro when she helped us with the data card.

Nathalie was an expat like us, but the difference was that she landed thirty years earlier. She was more Costa Rican than French by this point. And it was obvious from all the nods she received on the way to the ICE building that she had made her mark.

As we entered the office, having gone through the usual security check, Nathalie looked around and seemed pleased to see a particular clerk sitting at his desk. "I like this guy; he's a straight shooter. He doesn't say *yes* unless he means it. I don't know if you've noticed yet but it's common for Ticos to agree or simply say *yes* when they mean *no* because they're afraid to offend you. They don't like confrontation. It's infuriating."

Nathalie didn't bother grabbing a ticket. She didn't bother sitting down either. There were only three people waiting to be served, unlike the last couple of times we'd been there. With a flick of the head, she acknowledged the clerk and walked right up to his desk. The people sitting down didn't appear to care that she had just butted in. It felt like an unspoken acceptance...deference. After decades of proving herself, perhaps she had earned some respect. Or maybe they were a little afraid of her. It was hard to tell.

Nathalie did all the fast talking as we stood there beside her, smiling but not uttering a word — not too dissimilar to obedient children waiting for their mother to finish her adult duties with the promise of ice cream if they behaved. I noticed her tone seemed gentler...kinder. Her hard shell had softened somewhat.

After the clerk's long Spanish explanation, Nathalie revealed a genuine smile. "He doesn't think there'll be any problem providing ADSL service to the house. Some of your neighbours in Río Blanco now have it, but he won't be able to confirm it until he sends out his technicians to assess the situation."

"That sounds promising," I said.

"ADSL is much faster than the data card you're using right now. It will be so much better, for sure."

"Will it be fast enough to video chat?" I asked.

"It should be. It's pretty fast."

"How much will it cost?" Kevin wanted to understand the damage it would cause to our wallet.

Nathalie turned to the clerk, asked him in Spanish, and the clerk mumbled something back.

"Fifteen dollars per month for unlimited use," she confirmed, looking at us.

I'll take that over ice cream!

Then Nathalie inquired about changing the phone bill from Rick's name to our name. Nathalie confirmed that the property had been sold, that she was Rick's power of attorney, and that we were the new owners. After another speedy exchange, Nathalie looked deflated.

"I was worried this would be the case. He said you can't have a landline phone in your name until your temporary residency is approved," she explained.

Now what? That could take between eighteen to twenty-two months after we apply.

Nathalie negotiated with the clerk to keep the phone line contract open under Rick's name and we would continue paying the monthly bill until we could prove our residency status. He gave a nod as if taking orders from a boss. Nathalie's clout came in handy, and I was grateful to have her in our corner. Had we gone in on our own, things may have gone down very differently.

When we were done at the ICE office, Nathalie took us to the blood clinic. Although the clinic was among the other buildings in the town core, it was hiding in plain sight. I'm sure we must have walked by it a hundred times by then and yet we'd never noticed it before. The front door opened into what we would consider a mall. There were only five stores in this mall and the blood clinic was one of them. If I'd had to ask for directions, I don't think I would have ever found it. I appreciated having Nathalie as our guide more and more.

To apply for a driver's license in Costa Rica, the ministry of transportation needed to have official proof of our blood type in case we got into an accident. Printed right on the license, first responders would have that information handy in life-threatening situations.

For a developing country, Costa Rica has one up on Canada. What a smart idea.

Once our blood had been drawn into little vials, we had to go to a different clinic on the opposite end of town to get a medical: blood pressure, reflexes, respiratory, weight, height, and finally an eye test. This requirement seemed a bit far-fetched, but Nathalie informed us that we couldn't apply for a driver's license without a clean bill of health. There was a nominal fee attached to this service; it wasn't free.

"Lots of Costa Ricans drive without a license because they can't be bothered to take time off work only to be told that nothing's wrong with them and then have to pay for the privilege. Certainly in these rural parts," Nathalie explained.

Another opportunity for the government to cash in, I imagine.

We passed our medical tests without incident, thank goodness. We now had everything we needed, but going to San José and sitting through the application process would be an adventure for another day.

Nathalie then led us to what she claimed was the best butcher shop. It was located a block further than where we had parked. So, from the medical clinic it was...clear across town. Had we known we'd be getting such an in-depth tour of San Marcos, we might have been more strategic in the order of each task. It wasn't raining yet so I chalked it up to getting more physical exercise.

Which is never a bad thing.

We didn't ask Nathalie about a butcher shop. This was an errand she needed to run herself. We couldn't attest to whether it was *the best*, but since we were there, we got in line and bought hamburger meat.

"Need anything else?" Nathalie asked.

"I've been wanting to buy an English/Spanish dictionary. Where would I find one around here?"

"The *librería* is right next to where you had your blood work done," she said.

"The *librería*?"

"Yes, I know, it sounds like *library* but in Spanish it means bookstore," she translated with a get-with-the-program annoyance in her voice.

And just when I thought we were getting along.

Nathalie indulged me, though, and walked us back to the bookstore where I bought a pocket dictionary.

All the back-and-forth, walking up and down streets and back alleys, going in and out of stops had made me notice that something had shifted. The culture shock must have been waning because the stores didn't seem as dingy or odd as they first did. We were no longer fazed by the corner store that sold shoes for your feet, shoes for your car, and shoes for your horse's hooves...all under one roof.

Wednesday, September 26, 2012
Eggscellent Idea

On our way back from San Marcos the day before, we stopped at the animal feed store in Santa María where we nearly bought eight egg-laying hens. We learned that hens didn't lay eggs every single day but produced one every twenty-five hours or so as long as they were happy, healthy, and got lots of sunshine. Eight hens averaged five eggs daily. That was thirty-five eggs for Kevin and me to eat each week. We loved eggs, but that was an awful lot of eggs just for the two of us. Consumption would increase once we had guests staying at the lodge, but we needed to know that we had a way of generating a little bit of income with the excess even if it only paid for the feed and wood chips.

Before buying the hens, we decided to wait and ask our neighbours if they wanted to buy eggs from us or make some kind of exchange.

"I'm sure you'll have no trouble selling your eggs or exchanging for something else. No one in Río Blanco sells free-range eggs that I know of," Nathalie encouraged us.

So, we bought the feed, the vitamins, and the wood chips for the bedding but would decide on how many hens to buy once we talked to our neighbours. Maybe we could create a bartering system? Eggs for butter with Roberto, eggs for cheese with Abel, and eggs for homemade pastries with Vanessa. There was no market in Río Blanco, but if our neighbours were willing to exchange their goods, what a great community project that would be.

Thursday, September 27, 2012

Bunch of Bovines

We were on our way to Santa María to meet Rolando and Maritza, the couple we had met at Albarito's birthday party. As we reached the top of our driveway, we were greeted by six reddish-brown female jersey cows all pressed against each other on the other side of our wooden gate.

We'd been warned to keep our gate closed because on occasion cows from nearby farms would get through a broken fence and roam, sometimes finding their way onto our property. Knowing this, every time we left the property, I diligently got out of the SUV, opened the gate, Kevin drove through, then I closed it again.

I hadn't seen any roaming cows in our area and closing the gate was feeling rather tedious. The day before, I left the gate open for about an hour after coming back from school because I knew we would soon be going out again. I now realized that cows do, in fact, roam unexpectedly.

I got out and shooed the wide-eyed cows away, waving my arms in the air like a lunatic. I'm a suburban girl and this particular situation had never cropped up before. Although docile and coy — batting those long eyelashes at me — these cows were big and had horns, too. As I approached the gate, they started to back away and scatter down the hill. They left a few parting gifts, which I was careful not to step in. I made a mental note to pick up the patties when we got back.

God bless country living.

Friday, September 28, 2012

So, So Close

We'd been without high-speed internet for over a month. The ICE clerk had warned us that although the farm seemed to be located on the cusp of the boundary limit from the hub, it might not be close enough; and if it was, it could still be a problem because it was in a valley. Perhaps naïvely, we believed high-speed internet access in the country was becoming steadily more available with more internet companies competing for business, so a solution would be found one way or another.

The ICE technicians came to check whether the house was close enough to the main hub to receive a good connection. The technicians came in, took out their gadgets — everything looking first-world official — checked our phone line, and after fifteen excruciating minutes, they came to the conclusion that the distance from our house to the internet hub in Copey was not an issue. But we weren't celebrating just yet. They were pretty sure our phone line had deteriorated and needed replacing. They told us that a different crew would have to be dispatched sometime the following week to assess the situation. At least, that's what I understood.

So, the good news was high-speed ADSL internet coming right to our house was possible. The bad news was we had to wait a little while longer, and at worst we'd have to replace the phone line.

Saturday, September 29, 2012

Kevin's Heaven

While we were visiting with Rolando and Maritza the day before, they had mentioned they were going to San José to do a bulk shop at one of those big box warehouse superstores. And when Kevin's eyes lit up, they asked if we'd like to join them.

Kevin couldn't wait to compare it with the one back home. Going shopping was considered a fun date night for Kevin. Me? Not so much, but one must make concessions in any relationship.

We left our SUV in Santa María and piled into Rolando's truck. The store was located in the heart of the city where truck, car, and motorcycle drivers alike competed for the most marginal space on the road, cutting the other off from a sudden left shift to a swift diagonal right like in a game of checkers. The drivers would jerk and weave, stop then go. The motorcyclists were the most cavalier though — they squeezed between vehicles that were brushing against each other as it was.

What the — ? Are you kidding me? Oh dear. Oh no!

Watching the spectacle kept me alert and curious. One rider had the audacity to grab Rolando's side mirror and flip it inward toward the window to make more room as he squeaked by. *How rude*, I thought, until Rolando smiled and gave the rider an acknowledging wave.

Is this why side mirrors fold inward? There's an actual practical reason, especially in busy cities with unruly traffic? Huh.

Street vendors selling fruit, candy, phone chargers, puppets — you name it — also did their part by walking in the middle of the road or blocking intersections. Pure bedlam. I wondered if I would ever muster the nerve to drive in the thick of this city where streets had no names or where amber traffic lights and faded painted lines were mere pretenses of road rules. We had been living up on a mountaintop — far away from pollution and traffic hubbub — for only a month and my senses had already become accustomed to a much slower pace where driving at 40 km/hr was considered too fast by the locals. The frenzied intensity of the city intimidated me like a schoolyard bully threatening to pounce on me. The coward in me was alive and well. I was grateful that big burly Rolando drove, kept his cool, and got us to our destination safe and sound. He didn't seem stressed in the least.

As soon as we walked through the warehouse doors, Rolando led us straight to the customer service desk to apply for a membership, which cost $35 per year — half the price of the membership we paid in Canada.

"Sweet!" Kevin exclaimed. He liked the difference already.

After arranging a meet-up time with Rolando and Maritza, we split up. I followed Kevin as he immersed himself in the supermarket hunt-and-gather sport.

I don't enjoy shopping as a general rule, but least of all in crowded stores. I get claustrophobic and feel an undercurrent of anxiety. It was only September, and the shelves overflowed with Christmas paraphernalia — floor to ceiling. People thoughtlessly parked their buggies and obstructed the already crammed aisles. It was too much for me to handle when I was in Canada — I avoided stepping into this kind of hell at all costs. The Costa Rican experience, distinct only by the name on the marquee, was no different to me.

While I tried not to have a panic attack, Kevin was in heaven. He read each label to see which brand offered the best deal.

"This one's cheaper," I noticed.

"Well, not really; in price, yes, but not if you calculate it per gram per pack," he pointed out.

There was a decent selection of the usual sundries. Some things were more expensive than back home, but a lot of things were either similarly priced or cheaper as Kevin surmised from his in-depth research. I wouldn't be able to tell one way or another because I never paid much attention to the prices back home. Usually, my goal was to get out of the stores as quickly as possible. With that in mind, I beelined to the items I needed and put them in the cart. I'm a bit of a brand loyalist that way. Once I find a product I like, I stick to it. Trust and reliability are what I count on. If it happens to be more expensive by a few cents or dollars, so be it.

Just get me out of here.

We purchased the largest format of laundry detergent, forty-eight rolls of biodegradable septic-tank-friendly toilet paper, and wooden clothes pegs. Okay, I admit I felt my heart skip a few beats when I zeroed in on the wooden clothes pegs. The plastic ones we had at home were useless and we'd not been able to find wooden ones in the smaller stores in our area. We also splurged and bought some old sharp Cheddar cheese, which was impossible to find locally. Roberto made delicious cheese, but not Cheddar, which for me brought an immediate sense of comfort like a warm embrace. Mostly though, we stocked up on necessities that, based on the fullness of our cart, should have lasted a lifetime.

I hoped that we wouldn't have to do another big shop like this for quite a while. I preferred buying what we needed as and when we needed it while supporting our local community at the same time. Not to mention, our pocket-sized fridge had limited space, and its Lilliputian freezer had even less. Having said that, I was grateful to Kevin for trying to save us money. It was hard to find fault with that — we were on a shoestring budget, after all. And seeing the gleam of satisfaction in his soft brown eyes, as if we had just come back from one of our date nights, made me smile.

Sunday, September 30, 2012
First Attempt at Baking Bread

Thirteen days had passed since my first successful attempt at keeping a sustained fire going in the outside wood oven. I got busy with other things so I hadn't been honing my skills but decided I would try and make bread.

I hoped I hadn't lost my touch. I managed to build a raging fire again within minutes and with a bit of tending, it blazed for over a half hour. I closed the door to keep the heat in.

In the kitchen, I started on the dough. It rose quicker than I expected. I thought at high altitudes it took longer to rise, but perhaps it was the reverse. Anyway, I punched it down and let it rise a second time. In the meantime, I opened the door to the outside wood oven and pushed the ash and hot embers to the back, then placed the round clump of dough on the wire rack from the exploding toaster oven. I had saved the rack, figuring it might come in handy.

"Leave the bread in there with the door closed for about an hour," Martín had suggested in Spanish.

It had been a while since I'd baked bread from scratch, and I had no idea how hot the oven actually was. Without a thermometer, who knew if it ever reached 180°C (350°F)? But waiting for perfect conditions seemed futile, so I was making the most with what I had in the moment and hoping for the best.

An hour later, I checked on the bread and it was almost as flat as a pancake. Although a thin plume of smoke came out of the chimney, the oven had cooled down without the constant blazing inferno.

Outcome: Rival – 1, Anne – 0.

Not being one to accept complete defeat, I scooped the flattened gooey dough, fried it up in a pan, and made bannock bread instead. Or a version of it, anyway. Bannock bread calls for baking soda instead of yeast, that's why it doesn't rise the way a yeast loaf does. I learned to make bannock bread in 1992 when I was camping for two-and-a-half months in British Columbia where all I had was an open fire to cook over.

The texture was thick and heavy but tasty enough with melted butter and maple syrup. Maple syrup makes everything better.

Redemption Outcome: Anne – 0.5, Maple Syrup – 100!

Monday, October 1, 2012
Forty Days and Forty Nights

In September 2011, we had come on a scouting expedition seeking to break out of suburbia's shackles, looking for an adventure that promised more freedom.

Freedom to call the shots. Freedom to live our best life.

After our two-week road trip was over, returning to San José to catch our flight home, we had driven through the Dota mountain range. Hanne and Hendrik — our dear travelling companions — Kevin, and I had gotten out of our rental to take in the view one last time. It felt like such an inconsequential moment at first. But as we stood on top of the world and saw a double rainbow stretching from the depth of one valley over a summit and spilling into the next valley, it felt like a sign. I admit I longed to attach some significance to it. It had to mean something. I felt stuck in suburbia and desperate for change. The trip itself hadn't provided us with any tangible clues that this was the place we belonged, but that double rainbow in all its vibrant glory had given me hope — if only a glimmer.

Then, a few days later, when Kevin had found the farm on some obscure realty website, that was the end of one life as we knew it and the beginning of a completely new one. Kevin didn't know it at the time. I didn't know it at the time. It was as though the train of life we were riding on caught up to a railway switch on the track and the hand of God pulled the level.

There we were a year later, living in the land of double rainbows. It had been forty days and forty nights since we had set foot in our very own Promised Land, and it felt symbolic.

As I mused over the significance of our transformation phase, the phone rang. It was our shipping broker. Our container had arrived in Limón — the shipping port on the northeast side of the country — and had gotten the all-clear at customs. Our stuff would be delivered the next morning. I could only hope our belongings had survived the long voyage without too much damage. It could rain all it wanted because we'd be busy unpacking for the next several days.

But hopefully, not for forty.

Part III
Real, Raw, and Remote

Twenty-Three
Pura Vida

October 2012

Bracing Ourselves

We had been warned that October was the wettest month and as if on cue, on the first of the month, it rained the entire night. The rhythmic drumming on the tin roof might have lulled Kevin and I to sleep, but we were kept awake by the hissing wind and diagonal sheets of rain smacking against the windowpane. A steady stream of bright flashes strobed through the all-too-sheer lime green curtains just seconds before thunder clapped above our heads. It felt like the bedroom had shapeshifted into our very own private disco club. The raucous continued until morning without interruption.

On that sleepless night, we braced ourselves and hoped we'd get through the month without any major catastrophe. While Kevin laid awake worrying about the river, the ponds, and the trout, I ruminated over what effect non-stop rain, for days on end, would have on my mental health.

Back in Southern Ontario, Canada — when it rained in the autumn — the skies usually became a dull granite grey and stayed that way for the entire day...sometimes *the entire week*. The cool, dreary atmosphere brought a certain kind of melancholy. It made me want to wrap myself in a plush blanket, sip hot tea, and read a book or watch mildly entertaining romantic comedies. The heavy doom clouds rarely dissipated quickly, making it harder to snap out of the gloomy mood that harboured in my being. It seemed as though I was in waiting mode on those days, like sitting at a red light and waiting for my life to turn green. I lacked my usual get-up-and-go spirit. As an introvert, I've always enjoyed quiet introspection, but too many grey days in a row would bring on a despondent temperament whereas sunshine would imbue me with a more buoyant frame of mind.

In the wee hours, as I lay under the covers listening to the cacophony outside, I pacified my fears knowing that even in October, seeing the sun first thing every morning felt guaranteed on our mountaintop paradise. More importantly, the rain clouds were rarely ominous — their iridescent sterling hue provided a bright and cheerful respite from the doldrums I had been used to back in Canada. In Costa Rica, rainy days weren't synonymous with malaise...from what I had experienced so far, they were merely synonymous with mud.

And I have big black rubber boots so no excuses for not going outside and living my best life.

Our Stuff Arrives

We were doing just fine without most of our stuff. It's amazing what you think you need but don't. Having said that, I couldn't wait to wear my own motorcycle helmet instead of the second-hand visorless one Rick had left behind. I also looked forward to making soups and smoothies in my industrial-strength blender and using our toaster oven, finally replacing the one that had exploded only twelve days into our adventure. Although we had been managing without any kind of oven since that fateful night, it felt good knowing we wouldn't have to do without for much longer. Having picture frames of our family, our favourite cotton bed sheets and cozy blankets, and a few select decorative items from the old house in Canada would help make this one feel more homey...more permanent. While I longed for my books, my Liverpool-fan husband missed following his favourite soccer team on our wide-screen TV. Getting that hooked up to a satellite dish would provide not only endless sports entertainment for him, but we could stretch our evenings out and watch a movie or a sitcom. Kevin was pining for his tools, of course — there were several projects where he could have used one tool or another to finish a job better or more quickly. He was relieved that they would soon be delivered.

Kevin had written to Emilio, the manager of the shipping company, to warn him about the tricky landscape. This company was located in San José so we couldn't assume Emilio had ever been this far into the mountains. Since our shuttle van experience with Minor, we couldn't assume *anything*. Kevin had gone over these details in emails and on the phone. He had several conversations to the point that it was starting to feel like he was harping.

"You'll need to send *two* smaller trucks rather than one big one. A large truck won't make it around some of the sharp turns and might not be able to cross the river," Kevin had explained.

Emilio assured Kevin he'd done this before and not to worry.

The morning after the stormy night, we received a call from Emilio. He mentioned that our container had been processed without incident and a crew would be on our doorstep at seven the next morning to deliver our belongings.

At 6:30 a.m. the next day, we were pleasantly surprised when Emilio called to say that his men were on their way and should arrive on time, as scheduled. Why surprised? Well, *Costa Rica*, that's why.

We were ready by 7:00 a.m. waiting for Martín and Nacho to show up. We had asked them to switch their daily grass-cutting and fence-fixing duties to help unload the trucks instead. It would be a race against the rain and the more hands and strong backs we had to help out, the faster it would go.

We were dumbfounded when we saw a white pick-up truck boot down the driveway. We knew it didn't belong to Martín and Nacho didn't have his own vehicle. Besides, they always walked over to our place.

This can't be good.

The driver stepped out and walked over to Kevin and shook his hand. "*El camino…* blah blah…*más grande…*blah blah…*río…*blah blah blah," the driver said in Spanish.

Kevin didn't need me to translate. Kevin may not have understood each and every word the driver had said but he understood enough to know that the one truck containing our boxes couldn't cross the river because it was too big. His exasperated look as he rolled his lips in tight and closed his eyes said it all. Kevin was pissed. But he swallowed his anger and didn't take it out on the driver. He knew better to argue with the man who was holding the keys to our stuff.

Just across the river. So close!

The only way to get our stuff from across the river to the house was to unload everything from the big truck onto the 4x4 pick-up's flatbed. Kevin, Martín, Nacho, and the three guys from the shipping company got to work.

As the men went back and forth — what seemed like a hundred times — and stacked the boxes haphazardly on our driveway, I checked the inventory list against the corresponding numbered boxes. If a box was missing or damaged, this was the time to bring it to the crew's attention.

While there were six of them doing the heavy lifting, there was only one of me tackling the sea of large and small cardboard boxes strewn everywhere. As I crossed the boxes off my list, I moved them to the garage where I organized them with their labels facing out and arranged them with easy access in mind. Although my account management skills kicked into high gear, I hadn't felt *this* rushed in a while. There was a fine line between making sure I carefully accounted for each box and hustling to beat the rain.

Not thrilled about the extra work and time involved due to the colossal misunderstanding about the number of trucks needed, our saving grace was that the crew had arrived first thing in the morning. Seeing as it was the wettest month in Costa Rica, we were prepared for a narrow window of sunshine. When it started to spit at around noon, we scrambled to pile the cardboard boxes under the carport so they wouldn't get wet. But the rain stopped within a few minutes, and it stayed dry until mid-afternoon.

It wasn't the first time the gods governing the weather had my back on moving day. I was reminded of a time in the late 90s when I had hoped for a sunny day.

As a single mother, I had purchased my first home, and the move-in date was scheduled for November 28. It had been cold and damp for much of the week leading up to that Saturday, but on moving day, it was freakishly sunny and hot, reaching 25°C (77°F) compared to the usual daily average of 7°C (44°F) for that time of the year in Southern Ontario. I remember I was wearing blue jeans, a white T-shirt, and running shoes. No jacket was needed. No cumbersome boots.

Having just left my abusive first husband, this townhouse symbolized a fresh start. It was one of those pre-construction homes bought directly from the builder and there was still a lot of construction going on. I bought it when the first of the four-phase plan was being sold and the kids and I happened to be the fourth family to move into the complex.

The trendy-at-the-time but impractical straw-coloured carpet I had chosen had just been installed. I had worried all week that it would get ruined on day one with all the rain we'd been having. Luckily, I was able to move our furniture, boxes, and clothes without any evidence of us traipsing in and out of the townhouse a hundred times.

The following Saturday a few more families moved in, but they weren't so fortunate. The weather was cold, rainy, and there were mucky red clay puddles everywhere. I watched our new neighbours endure the miserable mess from our clean, cozy home.

It's possible that I might have been wrapped in a plush blanket, sipping hot tea, feeling mildly entertained.

After paying Martín and Nacho and thanking them and the shipping company crew for their help, Kevin lugged a few boxes at a time up to our open concept living room/kitchen area. As I unpacked our belongings, I transferred the stuff we inherited from Rick and Mona into some of the empty boxes. The items that I deemed useful would go in the guesthouse and the rest I'd give away to Clara. I figured that some of it might be handy for their restaurant or the community centre.

While I sorted through our things inside the house, Kevin was busy unpacking and arranging his tools in the garage.

Bit by bit, it was feeling more like home.

License to Drive

We had heard from a few people, including Stella's husband Nick, that we should get our driver's licenses before our ninety-day visitor's visa expired. If we waited until after it expired, the process would get more complicated.

And who needs more complication?

Adriana offered to come with us to San José and help us get our Costa Rican driver's licenses. As a former student of the University of Costa Rica, she knew San José well and how to get around the city. This kind of help alone was worth it to us.

Once we reached the Ministry of Transportation, Adriana took over like a protective parent would support her daunted children. She asked all the right people the right questions and, thanks to her, we managed to skip the long lineup that we no doubt assumed we would have needed to stand in.

"This lineup is for people who are *renovando* their licenses. People who have license already, yes, and have to y'know, get again every year. We need to go over here," she described as we passed by.

Having a native speaker escort us around was a godsend. Since we weren't renewing our licenses — we were starting from scratch — we needed to go straight to the windowed booth where a wide-eyed bald man with a jaundice-looking complexion was perched on a swivel chair like Tweety bird in his cage.

Tweety checked our documents, and he babbled to Adriana who turned to us and said, "You need more copies of our *pasaportes*."

Adriana did an about-face and we followed. We found a photocopy centre at the far end of the building, and with photocopies in hand we made our way back to the booth. Tweety verified that our documents were in order before telling us to proceed to the waiting room on his right. Another person manned the door and checked our documents again. So many checkpoints, you would have thought we were entering the Pentagon.

In a high-ceiling, windowless, warehouse-looking room, six rows of ten people sat on plastic chairs under slow whirling fans that failed to circulate the air. The place was packed, and it felt stuffy and hot. The doorman kept tabs on how many seats were available and only allowed the exact number of people in, so no one would be left standing. Once there were three empty chairs at the back of the room, he let us in.

Adriana, Kevin, and I shuffled to our seats in the last row. When the person sitting in the first seat of the first row got up to be served, everyone else got up in unison and moved one chair over. The doorman let one person in who promptly sat in the chair next to me. It was orderly and no one seemed to question this assembly-line method.

The government agencies, we noticed, often had large waiting rooms with seats. There was a reason for that…a little over an hour and a half later, we finally reached the first row and another twenty minutes passed before we got served. I looked behind us and the room was as full as when we arrived. It felt like the human version of a refillable Pez candy dispenser.

Kevin was called up and Adriana followed him around an opaque wall. I sat alone — not counting the other fifty-nine individuals — waiting for my turn.

A few minutes later, I was walking around the same solid barrier that kept those who were waiting from those who were being served. I assumed this was for privacy reasons, but it could have just as easily been put there to create the mystique of authority. I couldn't be sure; I was still getting used to the cultural nuances.

The long, functional fluorescent lights above each of the six cubicles hummed imperceptibly yet I could feel it thrum in my bones. The space was much brighter than the waiting area and people's voices carried over the high partitions though I couldn't make out what was being said. There were only six government staff dealing with individuals needing a driver's license. We would have happily gone to a service bureau closer to Río Blanco, but San José *was* the closest. I'm sure we weren't the only people who had travelled a fair distance to get licenses.

Based on the crowd in the waiting room and the lineup wrapping around the building outside, they might consider tripling the staff headcount.

I handed my passport and Ontario driver's license to a plump woman whose name tag read "*Ramona*." The black roots poking through the ginger dye job she had gotten done likely over a month ago seemed more of a fashion statement than a lack of time or a money constraint. Ramona had one of those natural smiles and her friendly manner made me feel at ease in a nerve-wracking situation. Her long, manicured nails clicked quickly on the keyboard as she entered the necessary data from my paperwork. But then the tapping slowed down. Remember the passport incident? Ramona showed the same concerned look as the airline agent had when he scrutinized my passport and told me I would not be allowed to board the plane.

My passport was only eight months old — the expiry date wasn't the problem. I had originally planned to renew my passport using my married name, but since the plane ticket had been issued in my maiden name, I was told I had no choice but to renew my passport with my maiden name again — *for ten more years*. My Ontario driver's license, however, had my married name on it. I could see the consternation in Ramona's face as she perused my ID.

"*No es el mismo nombre*," Ramona said, pointing to the name discrepancy.

The fact my ID didn't have the same last name was the problem. She needed proof that I was the same person. The fact that both pieces of identification had my picture on them with the same birth date was not enough.

In case I'm the evil twin, I suppose.

I suddenly remembered I had two social insurance cards, one with my maiden name on it and one with my married name, and of course, both have the same number. I had gone to the trouble of changing this government ID to my married name, but never bothered to get rid of the social insurance card with my maiden name on it. So, I dug them out of my wallet.

"This is the *mismo número* for both *nombres*," I explained in my broken Spanish. I underlined the number and the two last names with my index finger. Then pointed to the pictures on my passport and driver's license to make the point crystal clear that there was only one of me.

Ramona's eyes lit up.

"*Un momento, por favor,*" she nodded.

Ramona got up with a bounce and stepped out of sight behind the dark green fabric wall while I sat waiting for the impending judgement. I wondered if Adriana and Kevin were still in their cubicle. I wanted to get up and find Adriana, but didn't, afraid my aimless wandering would be seen as suspicious. So I sat, glued to my chair, and waited. Although I felt alone and unsupported in that moment, I also felt like a badass solving the ongoing glitches my government-issued documents kept throwing at me.

Ramona came back ten minutes later with a big wide smile.

"*Bueno, todo bien, sí, no problema,*" she nodded her head, confirming my two social insurance cards could be used as proof that I was one and the same person.

Woohoo!

If they hadn't been able to give me a Costa Rican driver's license due to this name debacle, I wouldn't have been allowed to drive at all after the ninety-day visitor's visa period — goodbye independence and freedom — unless I took a written driver's test... *in Spanish*. I'd have had to wait until I knew the language better. So yes, it was a big deal, and yes, I was thrilled.

Ramona concluded our transaction by giving me a receipt. I slid the paper into my wallet and thanked her. I refrained from asking too many questions because I had been there long enough, and I figured Adriana would be able to guide me through the next steps. I soon learned there were quite a few more.

When I met up with Adriana and Kevin outside, Adriana explained that we had to go to the bank down the road a few blocks and pay for the licenses. Another bank, another line, another hour. Then we had to come back and show a different clerk the bank receipts. Once that was done, we had to stand in another line to get our pictures taken and our fingerprints stamped and imprinted on a white card. Although getting our licenses was supposed to be a step towards independence and freedom, it felt like we were being processed for prison.

The last step was to sign our names in a thick manual logbook. Signing my married name came so naturally to me that I had to stop, take a pause, and remember to sign my maiden name. Studying my passport to see how I had signed my last name, I made sure to loop the *B* the same way, so it matched. It felt so awkward; like I had lost all dexterity and a part of myself along the way.

I assumed my first husband's last name — a nice, easy-to-pronounce English name — in my early twenties only to switch back to my hard-to-pronounce — for most English speakers — French maiden name when we divorced eleven years later. Then in my forties, I assumed Kevin's last name when we married — another no-nonsense English name. I have friends who know me with one last name, other friends with another. It's embarrassing. Some might say I suffer from a form of identity crisis.

I've never been a fan of my last name. In Québec, it's as easy to pronounce and as popular as Smith or Jones. There's one on every corner. In fact, a friend of mine in high school was also Anne Beaudoin. I once received a math test with 95% written at the top next to a congratulatory *Bravo!* As much as I had wished it was my mark, I knew the teacher had handed me the wrong paper even though it had the right name.

In English-speaking Canada, my last name gets butchered. Having all five vowels smooshed between consonants causes tongue gymnastics. Consonants at the end of most French words don't get pronounced, which is a difficult concept to grasp for the English. And there are sounds that simply don't exist in the English language, which adds to the challenge. Even Kevin used to introduce me as Anne Bababa to his friends. I was happy to drop my maiden name and its heritage like a hot rock. Who needs the hassle of having to spell it every single time?

But, in Costa Rica, married to Kevin, I was still being forced to use my maiden name. There seemed to be a lesson in there somewhere; to embrace who I was and where I came from.

Once the fanfare was over and done with, we received two licenses each. One allowed us to drive a passenger vehicle like a car or an SUV and the other allowed us to ride a motorcycle. Although we had no intention of riding around on motorcycles, four-wheelers fell under the same category so we needed to have a valid motorcycle license to drive a four-wheeler. Luckily, both Kevin and I had the classification "M" on our licenses at the time and the clerk had been satisfied that it stood for *Motocicleta*.

Slowly but surely, we were crossing things off our long to-do list. So many tasks seemed monumental, time-sucking, and fraught with the possibility of things going pear-shaped in ways that could change the trajectory of how we wanted to live our life as legal Costa Rican residents. And yet, good fortune seemed to be on our side each and every time. The glitches were there to remind us what *could* go wrong, but the resolutions encouraged us to trust the process. Having those two licenses in my possession cemented my belief that we could do this. That I could do this. I felt brave and untethered.

Independent and free.

High-Speed Internet: A Good Day

The second crew of ICE technicians came to have a look at our phone line. After fifteen minutes of poking around, they confirmed our line was fine; there was no need to replace it for the time being. This was fabulous news. Why we needed two separate teams to get that answer was beyond me, but I was learning logic played little to no role in such matters. I just went with the flow of the good news.

One of the ICE service guys tried to make a call on his cell phone but couldn't get a signal. He wondered if this was usual. I explained in Spanglish — with a little sign language thrown in — that there was never any cell phone signal in the house and only sometimes a signal way up on the property. He cocked his head and frowned in that Winnie-the-Pooh *think think think* kind of way. He then asked if he could use our landline to make a call to ICE headquarters to finalize the internet start-up connection.

Of course, anything to get this puppy up and running.

A few minutes later, we had ADSL high-speed internet in the comfort of our own home. No more SUV stakeouts outside people's homes in Copey.

It was a good day, to say the least.

Video Chat

Everything was falling into place nicely. Now that we had internet at home, we had the ability to video chat, which I did with Phoenix and then again with Jude a while later. I can't express just how much I needed that. It made all the difference to be able to see their faces and have a casual conversation. I didn't feel quite so far away. It was as if I could reach through the computer screen and touch them. I honestly don't know how the pilgrims, pioneers, and everyone before the internet managed to travel such great distances, leaving everyone they loved behind for a better life without any contact other than some handwritten letters twice a year. We had it easy, and still, I struggled.

Costa Rica, Baby

Seven weeks had passed since we arrived. To celebrate, we went to San José to apply for temporary residency. As expected, it took all day.

We arrived at ARCR (the English-speaking agency that helps expats secure residency status) at the appointed time. Large picture windows let the natural light bounce off the crisp white walls. While phones rang and printers chugged, muffled voices murmured in the background. The office environment was buzzing with activity and had a North American fast-paced urban energy that I hadn't felt since arriving in Costa Rica. It felt like things were getting done and yet the loose papers and file folders wrapped with elastic bands piled high on every desk suggested perhaps not as fast as one would hope.

We met with the office manager, Bob, and handed him our documents. He was surprised we had everything in order. I couldn't help but wonder just how many people moved there without having done their homework. Based on his reaction, I guess quite a few. Considering all the stress and headaches we went through sending for original documents, waiting for them to arrive — some from England — getting our paperwork signed by our lawyer, then Foreign Affairs, then the Costa Rican consulate, all within short time restrictions, I just couldn't imagine trying to sort it all out from there. Being able to communicate in our native tongue certainly made things a whole lot easier.

After Bob explained in a snappy salesman-y way how their service and fee structure worked, he handed our documents to his assistant, turned to us, and said, "You're in good hands. Sofía will take care of you. Good luck." Then, just like that, he walked away.

We sat with Sofía for a while and answered her questions as she filled out a plethora of forms. "Okay, looks like you're applying for *Rentista* status...not a problem... The benefit of using our services means we take care of everything... We even appoint a lawyer to your case... If you'll please follow me," Sofía got up and beckoned without taking a breath.

We walked up a flight of stairs and through a narrow corridor. There was a 1930s Sam Spade detective novel vibe with the stark white walls and black doors. When we reached one of the doors, which had the lawyer's name hand-painted in gold calligraphy on the frosted picture frame window, Sofía walked right in. And so did we. The office was large enough to dwarf the solitary desk in the middle of the space. A man sat behind a stack of papers and folders as high as the ones I had noticed downstairs. I realized then just how trendy it was to relocate to Costa Rica. Apparently we weren't the only ones with this bright idea.

Sofía introduced us to Victor — the thirty-something lawyer appointed to our case — and handed him our bulky folder with our original documents and completed forms.

After looking over our file, Victor seemed satisfied. "Next step is to have your pictures taken. Come with me," Victor stepped around his desk in his wrinkled grey pinstripe suit and, as if by instinct, adjusted his yellow tie, then pulled a marbled button through the top slit of his jacket. As we stood eye to eye, the three of us smiled at one another in some non-verbal understanding that we would follow him.

While leading us down the street, our dark-haired lawyer tried to engage us in small talk by asking us how we were enjoying Costa Rica so far, what brought us there, and how he would love to visit Canada one day. His friendly manner put us at ease until he opened the door to the hole-in-the-wall photography studio — the space was no larger than a walk-in closet. Victor rambled a few quick words in Spanish to the man behind the counter and then said, "Meet me back in my office when you're done. Don't worry, this man will take care of you. You know the way back?"

Kevin and I nodded.

After Kevin and I both took turns having our pictures taken, we paid the photographer $14 for twelve pictures. While we were gone, Victor's assistant, Dolores, had organized and typed up the legal documents. By the time we returned to the office an hour later, they were ready for us to sign an invoice for $1,100 USD per person for services rendered. The cost included everything that had to do with the entire immigration process.

Surely we were done. We had paid and after more than two hours of being at ARCR, we were ready to go home. But no, not so fast.

Dolores had to walk us to the Banco Nacional de Costa Rica a few blocks away.

Banks are always a few blocks away and apparently necessary in every payment transaction we make.

Part of the process was to have the bank write a letter stating we had the approved amount of money to qualify for residency status by acquiring certificates of deposits. In our case, as *Rentistas*, we needed $30,000 USD per year for the following four years to qualify. This bank task took a little over two hours. I could tell even the bank teller felt the paper trail of bureaucracy was ridiculous. Multiple copies of each receipt, stamped and initialled, got slipped under cashier trays, stacked in three different small square cubbies, stapled to the originals, then filed in manila folders.

I wonder how many trees are lost in the process.

Then, every piece of information that was gathered on paper was entered on some data sheet and saved on the computer. The teller had several tabs open and kept jumping from one tab to another, typing a number or name or address or some important information and copying it onto another page. The bank's software system seemed particularly slow, too, which only added to the teller's frustration.

"*Lo siento*," she repeated, apologizing every couple of minutes.

Kevin and I smiled back because there was no point getting upset.

Costa Rica, baby!

We decided to be Zen about it, but what a waste of time for Dolores. For some unknown reason, the rules stipulated that she must wait with us, but she didn't seem the least bit put out. Peering through her bifocal glasses that perched on the end of her nose, she sat in the waiting area and knitted a light blue baby garment. She came prepared for the wait.

Smart lady.

When we were done at the Banco Nacional de Costa Rica, Dolores walked us back to the office and mentioned there was a backlog in the system and that we shouldn't expect anything to be finalized anytime soon.

"It can take between eighteen to twenty-two months before you get your official *cedula* — the document that indicates permanent residency," she warned us. "Carry this with you."

Dolores handed us each a little white card with our names and a serial number. "This is your *comprobante*. It's proof of your open file with *Migración*. It's now your ID. You can show this card instead of your passport at all police checkpoints and government agencies. I'll email you to let you know how things are developing. Don't worry. Pura Vida." She nodded again with a pursed smile.

Pura Vida: Enjoy life to its fullest, embrace optimism, and appreciate the moment. Pure and simple. Costa Rica's mantra.

And that was that. We were in the system. No longer tourists. *Pura Vida*, indeed.

Twenty-Four
Bettys and Property Fixes

An Eggscellent Decision

Having done my research, I was confident there were enough people in our village who wanted fresh eggs and were willing to buy or trade. Roberto agreed to exchange his hand-churned butter. Abel would trade his cheese. Another neighbour was willing to exchange fresh-pressed apple juice. Vanessa needed eggs for the dessert business she was setting up so she said she'd exchange some of her homemade desserts for a few dozen, and Elizabeth would purchase eggs for the kids at school. Clara said she'd buy some, too.

Kevin and I decided to buy ten Rhode Island hens. This breed had the usual brown and white body with a red cap on its head. What I didn't realize was how soft chicken feathers were. I had never thought of hens as being soft before.

Being a farmer was teaching me things I took for granted in suburbia. For instance, the farmer's point of view — around there anyway — was that animals were meant to serve. It was plain economics. Their single purpose in life was to be or to produce — *food*. You shouldn't get too emotionally attached. As a farmer, it was important to treat cattle and broods with respect and kindness, but it was just as important to remember the animal kingdom hierarchy. A good farmer loved her animals and endeavoured to take good care of them, but she never crossed the line of anthropomorphizing them. Giving pet names to your food was a waste of time. Kevin and I understood the rationale; it's imprudent to love animals as though they're part of the family when their days leading up to the butcher's block are numbered. But as much as Kevin and I were willing to embrace the farmer's ethos, admittedly our suburban mentality was hard to shake.

Kevin and I had this great idea of giving each of our hens a name based on the female characters from the long-running English TV show *Coronation Street*.

"Let's see, there's Dierdre, Rita, Vera, Liz, Audrey, Gail, Sally, Eileen, Fiz, and... Betty," I said as I counted on my fingers.

But it became obvious we couldn't tell any of them apart, so we gave up...but not entirely. We ended up referring to the brood, one and all, as *Betty*.

I coaxed our Bettys outside as they seemed to prefer lounging inside their coop. Once they were all out, I closed the sliding door that led to the back pen so they couldn't come back in. I shovelled the wood shavings into my blue yard container, then hosed everything down. Chickens don't have any sense of decorum — they are not clean animals in the least — but I was amazed their nests weren't more disgusting.

Once I finished up, their coop was transformed into a 5-star hen hotel — the only thing missing were little chocolate mints.

Being the hens' maid had its reward. After doing the rounds the next morning, Kevin opened the hen house and found an egg in one of the nests. He handed it to me as if it were a crown jewel. I was giddy with excitement because it felt rather magical. The egg was small, and we weren't sure if it was just the size of eggs these hens laid, the fact they weren't all pumped up with hormones, or if the first eggs were trial size. We were new at this, and time would tell. We hoped the rest of the Bettys would follow suit.

Two days later, there were two eggs. Within ten days, our productive hens were each laying one egg a day. We were told with ten hens, we should average six or seven eggs daily, so we wondered if it was a fluke that all our Bettys were consistently laying daily. It wasn't. It was amazing. I was convinced it was because when we put them to bed every night, we told them how much we loved them and thanked them for providing us with so many.

We might suck at being detached farmers, but we're eggscellent at appreciating our brood.

Betty Bites Back

Frankie was curious about these loud hens. She followed me down every day to their outdoor enclosure. One day, I opened the gate to refill their water basin and Frankie managed to squirm her way into the pen. I was concerned about her harming the hens and yelled at her to get out, but she didn't listen. She was having too much fun barking at them. She'd bound forward, showing some audacity, then bounced back with uncertainty.

Most of the hens flapped to the other side of the enclosure, screeching and huddling on top of each other. One of the Bettys, however, strutted right up to my wild hound, squawked loudly, and pecked Frankie right between the eyes with her yellow beak. That Betty stood her ground and showed zero fear. Frankie, on the other hand, was stunned. She backed away and left the coop. She skulked back to the house feeling, no doubt, cut down to size, which was pretty humiliating for a Miniature Dachshund, I imagine.

That'll teach her.

November 2012
Inspired Foodie

It's strange how quickly we can take things for granted. When we first arrived, I was thrilled to see there was an orchard on the property. Although to be fair, it could hardly be called an orchard. It was more like a handful of trees that stood on elevated banks on either side of the driveway — up near the entrance. Driving back and forth every single day on the gravel path that cut through this grove, one would think I'd be reminded of its potential and be more curious about its yield. My excuse was that we had so many other things on our long to-do list, tending to these trees in the first two months landed at the very bottom of it. The scraggly trees needed a good pruning, which meant devoting time to a new project. I suppose I didn't hold much hope that the fruit they produced was going to be good enough to eat. I figured it was all just bird food.

Early in November, in my black rubber boots and an empty bucket in hand, I finally walked up to the orchard and inspected the situation. Considering I hadn't noticed any blossoms blooming, imagine my delight when I saw the peach, plum, and avocado trees — as sad as they looked — abundant with fruit.

I picked a dozen soft pink peaches and purple plums and snapped five hard bright green avocados. It was an amazing feeling to be so close to our food, knowing it was just there. As I lugged my nearly full bucket back to the house, I stopped and plucked about twenty golden berries from a small shrub. I wasn't sure if this berry was becoming my all-time favourite because it tasted so good — the flavour had the sweet notes of orange, mango, and pineapple with a tiny twist of green grape tartness — or because it grew in the cutest, almost translucent paper-like lantern. Tearing the casing to get to that juicy yellow berry was half the fun. Either way, this shrub was prolific and was a gift that kept on giving.

I wasn't sure what I would do with my loot, but when I spied the rhubarb in the garden, I cut a few long stalks, too.

Facing the mound sprawled on the kitchen counter, I found a recipe online and made a crumble with flour, Roberto's fresh butter, and a bit of raw sugar with a dash of vanilla extract. This had been my first crack at making dessert since...

I don't know when.

I hardly ever baked in Canada. I rarely had the time and never felt inspired. I'd often heard from people who baked that baking was a creative activity. I consider myself naturally creative, but when I thought of baking, I imagined careful measurements and measuring meant math...and math didn't feel creative to me in the least.

I'm not the Anne who got 95% on her math test. I'm the other Anne who barely passed.

Math was a painful exercise designed to stress me out, which was probably why I had avoided baking my whole life. But how could I resist, surrounded by all this organic goodness from our own orchard, not to mention all the blackberries in our pasture?

So many blackberry bushes!

We talked to Martín about chopping the blackberry bushes right down and making sure the grass was cut short. Based on Costa Rica's reforestation law, if we allowed the pasture to get overgrown, after five years, it would be considered a secondary forest and we would no longer have permission to clear it, even though we owned the land.

We had no definite plans for the pasture, but we had over 15 acres of it and wanted to keep our options open. Of course, that was a lot of maintenance and hard work for one person to keep the grass cut short with a machete or a weed whacker.

Time is money.

Martín's daughter Nicole had been gifted a huge white horse and called him Paloma, which was an unusual name since *paloma* meant *pigeon*. Sadly, Martín didn't have enough property for Paloma to roam and he would have had to be tied up outside their house when not being ridden. Knowing it was unfair for a large animal that required space to be condemned to standing in one spot for hours on end, Martín had decided to sell the horse. However, when Nicole became inconsolable on hearing his plan, Martín thought better of it. He asked Rick if he could keep her horse in the pasture. Rick had no qualms; having a horse in a pasture he never used was no bother, and we were fine with that agreement when we bought the property. It was lovely to see Paloma there. Sometimes, he'd trot over to the fence for a gentle bridge-of-the-nose pat, but mostly he scampered away and hid from view.

However, one grazing horse was not enough to keep the grass from growing out of control — especially during the rainy season. Martín suggested we get a few cows to help Paloma out. Although we weren't looking to own cattle, we learned that there were farmers who had cows but not enough land for their cows to graze.

"El granjero de arriba está buscando el pasto para sus vacas...um...cómo se dice...man... up... cows...need..." Martín, looking for the right English words, gestured that there was a farmer living above our property, higher up on the mountain, who was looking for pasture for his cows. "I ask him, *sí*?"

"Sí, gracias, Martín."

We figured as long as we weren't responsible for the cows, then we were happy to make the trade. Free land for the farmers for free grazing machines.

A few days later, Martín found us three cows and assured us that within a few weeks, they would graze the pasture bare. In a good way. And although the cows did nibble on the thorny blackberry bushes, nibbling wouldn't be enough to get rid of these hardy plants. Our land was covered with them — so many that we had considered selling blackberries like many people in this region did. When we found out how low the return on time investment would be, it just wasn't worth the backbreaking work for us. Just 1 kg (2.2 lbs) of blackberries yielded less than $1.50. It would cost us more in wages for the time spent picking — no profit would be made.

Although the majority of the bushes had to be cleared out, we decided to keep a small patch and give it to Martín to maintain and use as he pleased. During the picking season he collected them and made fresh juice for his restaurant and sold the rest. We didn't care how he used them; all we asked in exchange was half a bucket of berries for our own use.

Cooking with fresh ingredients was a pleasure and easy to get used to, even with only our small toaster oven and two stovetop burners. I tried several different recipes and felt encouraged we would be able to provide our future guests with simple but delicious options.

Experimenting with baking, making jams and pies, taught me how much fun math could be.

Spring Cleaning in November

Since landing in Costa Rica, I'd been concentrating on my Spanish studies and getting involved with our community. I'd been keeping up with daily household chores, but Kevin was doing most of the hard manual labour. I didn't realize just how burnt out I was from the hustle and bustle of my life in Canada. My job alone wasn't to blame. I had spent too many years in an abusive first marriage, which led to raising my children on my own. I had worked my whole adult life often as the principal wage earner. I went from being single to being in relationships that didn't work out. My footing rarely felt sure. By forty-seven, I had accumulated a lifetime's worth of stress, and I hadn't really dealt with it. A two-week vacation wasn't the antidote for calming my nervous system — it wasn't enough time to exhale and let my shoulders relax. I needed time to flounder... to be lazy and not have an agenda. But finally, after two months had gone by, I sensed a change in my energy. I was motivated to do more around the farm. I was ready to roll up my sleeves and carry some of the grunt work.

I cleaned out the casita where our guests would be lodging. I sorted the dishes, separating what I considered to be less-than-optimal items from the good stuff. I organized a box of kitchen utensils and linens to give to Clara and the rest I threw away. I sorted the pots and pans, too. I vacuumed up the cobwebs near the ceiling where it appeared no one had bothered to clean in quite some time. I emptied the wardrobes of all the useless bits of junk that was stored in there: rusty old nails, pieces of wood, an incomplete deck of cards, and a pair of prescription glasses.

I found an oil lantern, which was not so useless, but it was dirty and needed polishing. Then I washed all the linens and made sure the casita would have new cotton sheets and warm duvet covers. There was no rush; I plodded. Had I known how to whistle, I would have whistled a tune absent-mindedly as I worked.

I still needed to buy paint to freshen up the walls and kitchen cabinets and Kevin would eventually replace the homemade tin-can and beer-cap creations that were precariously hanging from the ceiling with new light fixtures. These details mattered to me, but until then, our little guesthouse was looking a lot more inviting.

As the transformation of the casita came together, I exhaled, and I felt my shoulders drop.

Twenty-Five
English Teacher...Who, Me?

The Call

S eidy, the co-founder of the Copey Learning Center, had heard through the grapevine that some English-speaking Canadian had moved to Río Blanco and was attending school with the elementary kids. News travelled fast in these parts.

Nathalie called on Seidy's behalf to ask whether I might be interested in volunteering. I'd never considered myself teacher material — that was my sister Lyne's calling — and I had no idea if I had it in me, but I was willing to meet Seidy to discuss it. One benefit I could see was it would allow me to meet more people in the larger area of Copey. Maybe I'd meet the lady who called the police on me.

I'm not bitter.

Being of Service Somehow, Some Way

Nathalie was waiting for me in Copey on her dark blue four-wheeler and before I could stop the SUV, she rode away slowly to indicate there was no need for me to get out or for us to have any conversation. I followed her to Seidy's house where Seidy was waiting on her front porch. I got out of the SUV and perfunctory introductions were made. Seidy volleyed between speaking speedy Spanish with Nathalie and ponderous English with me. Then, just like that, Nathalie turned to me and mentioned, "Good luck, we'll talk soon, I'm sure," and left.

"Please come in," Seidy gestured as she widened the front door — and her smile — then waved me to keep my shoes on. Her black hair pulled into a tight bun made her look stricter than her kind sparkly eyes through her black-rimmed glasses would suggest.

Seidy's English was good, but I sensed she was a bit shy to speak in front of me.

"Hi, I'm Angela. Nice to meet you," introduced a demure twenty-something woman sitting on the couch. "I'm a Peace Corps volunteer." Then she went on to explain how Seidy and her older sister had opened the centre three years earlier. The sisters believed if the children of the community could speak English, it would open more opportunities for them...like better jobs. Growing up in such a remote place had its drawbacks and not being exposed to higher education was one of them. And although the kids of Copey learned English in class, if they were enrolled in Seidy's program, they got an extra hour and a half each day after school, or seven-and-a-half hours more a week. Kids there received more English practice than most other students in Costa Rica.

Smoothing out a prim floral dress against her thighs and over her knees, Angela continued, "The parents pay a nominal fee for the kids to attend these classes. The teachers, however, don't get paid...it's all done on a volunteer basis. The fees fund the electric and phone bills, rent for the building, expenses for host families, field trips, and teaching materials...stuff like that."

"Wow, that's amazing. And are you one of the teachers?" I asked.

"Yes, I've been teaching here the last two years, but my Peace Corps placement is coming to an end. I've accepted a paid position near San José so I'm not leaving Costa Rica just yet, but I'll be too far to help out at the centre. Seidy has requested another Peace Corps volunteer, but she hasn't heard back if and when someone will be assigned to this post. She's now desperate to find a replacement before I leave in three weeks," she explained.

"*Three weeks*? Wow! That's not long at all. How many classes a week are there?"

"The centre is open five days a week and we teach every grade," Angela replied as she swooped her mousy brown hair over her right ear. Her flawless complexion radiated a certain kind of innocence. She was by no means a child, but her round smiley face gave her a youthful appearance.

"And you teach all those classes?" I wondered, feeling impressed and daunted at the same time.

"No, but I do teach a lot of the classes. We've been recruiting volunteers from the States, Canada, and England for extra support. They volunteer their time, and the centre provides a host family with room and board. The idea is that the volunteers get a true cultural experience in exchange. It's been working well so far, but we've hit a bit of a snag lately. We ultimately like the volunteers to agree to stay for at least three months, it's too disruptive if it's less. Longer is always better, but people have lives and are reluctant to commit to something too long term, especially when they're not getting paid," Angela divulged.

"What credentials are required as a volunteer teacher?" I inquired.

"Of course, we prefer candidates with some kind of teaching experience. They don't have to have a degree, but some kind of certificate like TEFL is helpful."

"What's TEFL?"

"It stands for Teaching English as a Foreign Language," she answered.

"I don't have any of those credentials. I'm not sure how I can help."

"But you are a native English speaker and part of our community now, which is even better," Seidy said with a tone of delight and a pinch of expectation.

How ironic that my native tongue is French.

"My husband and I just relocated from Canada, and I've been focusing on learning Spanish and setting up our trout and B&B businesses. Honestly, I'm not sure if I'll have the time. And I don't know if I'd even have the patience to teach young kids."

"Some parents are so gung-ho that they take the evening class. I teach that class, too. Maybe you could come to one and see how you feel," Angela pressed, softening her already angelic eyes. She made it hard to say no.

Copey seemed like such a sleepy village. Every time Kevin and I drove through it to get to Santa Mariá, it felt as quiet as a ghost town. I hadn't noticed there was even a centre let alone all this activity coming from it.

I was flattered to be considered and rationalized that meshing into this community would give me a chance to expand my network. It would also help demystify our presence. Kevin and I wanted to infiltrate our new surroundings, not as spies but as advocates. Wasn't that one of the things that was missing in our suburban life…a sense of connection with our neighbours? Maybe I could be of service somehow, some way.

Challenge Accepted

After shadowing Angela, I agreed to teach the adult class twice a week. I left the younger grades to the professionals or to those with saintly patience. It was definitely not my forte and although it was easy to get swept up in the moment and want to say yes to everything, the reality was there was only so much I could take on.

Although the kids' classes stopped for the summer holidays at the end of November, the adult classes continued with only a week off at Christmas.

My adult class ranged anywhere from six to twelve students with several different skill levels. Some were university-educated; others barely had their Grade 6. Some had enough English vocabulary to carry a simple conversation and others were dazed and confused. And it wasn't necessarily those with university degrees that were more advanced, either. Some adults didn't understand the grammar rules in Spanish, and they didn't know what I meant when I said *subject* or *verb*. It wasn't without its challenges. There was no curriculum for me to follow so I made things up as I went along. It felt a lot like Forrest Gump's box of chocolates...no one knew what they were going to get from one class to another, including me.

Adriana, Nacho, and Paola all signed up and I drove them down to class from Río Blanco, which meant they were always on time, but many of the students would stroll in late, still chatting on their phones or they'd strike up a conversation in Spanish catching up on gossip, disrupting the flow of the class. It reached a point where I instated the rule that I would lock the front door to the centre fifteen minutes after start time.

"If you're more than fifteen minutes late, I won't let you in," I warned them.

I don't think they took me seriously until the next week when the door was locked. Those who arrived on time were surprised I was enforcing the rule and seemed impressed that I meant what I said and wasn't backing down.

Don't waste my time.

The class did shrink to a consistent eight students, and I looked forward to teaching those two-hour classes, twice a week. One woman, Rosa, meek as a church mouse, came to class religiously. She had a hard time grasping the language and most people would have quit, but not Rosa. She did her homework and showed up. Her progress was so slow even I wondered how she was still invested in learning, but I had all the time in the world for people like Rosa.

Recruiting Volunteers

Since I only agreed to teach the adult class, Seidy was looking for English native-speakers to come to Copey as volunteer teachers for the younger grades. With Angela leaving at the end of the school year, which meant at the end of the month, Seidy was looking to find one or two volunteers to start when classes resumed in early February, after the summer break. When school reopened, so did the centre. She advertised on Dave's Café and TEFL websites, which seemed to attract a lot of applicants in their twenties — from people with teaching degrees to people just looking for a cool experience.

I offered to help Seidy; I read some of the emails that were flooding in and reviewed the applications. Seidy did the same on her end, then we met to narrow the list down. The next step was to video chat with our top three candidates. I could definitely help with this process and offered to take on the task. Seidy seemed relieved.

Little did I know how labour-intensive my new task was going to be. I contacted all applicants to thank them for their inquiry — that alone was time-consuming. Keeping track of who'd been contacted, who had questions, and who required a reply took up all of my spare time. Then I emailed back and forth with the candidates who appeared enthusiastic, qualified, and ready to start in February. I made arrangements to video chat with them individually. I needed a calendar to keep track of all these appointments and it started to feel an awful lot like a full-time job. But Seidy and I were becoming good friends, and it was for a good cause, so I pressed on.

The process was tedious.

I video chatted with each candidate, and it became clear some applicants were better suited for what we were looking for than others. Face-to-face interviews revealed a different side that couldn't be seen by reading resumés and writing emails. I had a list with names, and I checked *yes* or *no* beside their name. When I thought he or she was a great fit, I warned them I had other interviews but would get back to them by the end of the week. They said, "Great."

After I was all done, I met with Seidy and gave her the rundown of what transpired and which applicants I recommended. Seidy took a few days to look over my recommendations then either agreed or disagreed with me, and I contacted the lucky candidates in a timely manner. But guess what? The candidates I got back to had since made other plans. It had only been a week. They had decided they'd rather do something else or realized they didn't have enough money, or some personal matter had cropped up unexpectedly. I was gutted.

Over time, I learned this outcome was pretty common. I went through the process several times and I got to the point where I asked Seidy for permission to accept candidates right on the spot. In fact, my whole focus was just getting someone...*anyone*...committed to this volunteer post. The qualification requirements went from absolutely needing someone with a teaching degree or TEFL certificate who could develop a curriculum to anyone who was reasonably interested, with little experience but willing to learn... and teach. I went from a cool *we'll let you know* attitude to a desperate *please say yes and mean it* mentality. It was draining. I had other things to do that needed my attention. Kevin was trying to be supportive, but I could sense he was fed up. I spent way more time helping Seidy than I was helping him on the farm.

Finally, I lined up two volunteers to start in early February. I was thrilled. Seidy was thrilled. Kevin was thrilled. We were all thrilled! All we could do was hope for the best and wait and see if they'd show up.

I had other things to think about...packing for my trip home to Canada, for instance.

Waking up the Activist

Meanwhile, the one-room school that had been undergoing renovations for the past three years was close to being done. But yet again, they'd run out of money. They might not have been able to finish for another year at the rate they were going. Although the banging had stopped, Clara continued to cook in that dark, dingy closet and the kids were eating at their desks still.

There must be something I could do to help speed things along.

Kevin and I couldn't afford to fork over a bunch of cash, so I started brainstorming ideas. I decided that when I was back in Canada, I'd try to fundraise. I had donated to many different causes over the years. I had also participated in large events to raise money, like cycling for the Heart and Stroke Foundation and paddling in a dragon boat race in support of the SickKids Foundation. However, I'd never asked people for money for a cause that touched my friends and neighbours at such a personal, grassroots level. I didn't even know if it was legal to do so. I wanted to make sure everything was above board and everyone who donated would know where the money was going to and how it would be spent. The school was not an official non-profit organization so I couldn't offer income tax receipts. I wasn't sure how this was going to work; it wasn't like me to have my hand out, but those kids deserved a finished dining room. I was no Mother Teresa, but this cause was waking up the activist in me.

Twenty-Six
A Foreigner in Two Lands

Flying Back to Canada

My homesickness had not entirely lifted. It was not really homesickness at all...it was specifically *missing-my-children* sickness. It hung over me and sometimes knocked me off my feet.

Kevin sensed this a few weeks earlier and suggested I go back to Canada for a visit. We had to buy a return ticket when we flew down to Costa Rica. The Costa Rican government welcomed us in but also wanted to know that we planned to leave — a common practice. So we bought a ninety-day open-ended ticket so we had some flexibility with dates. I booked my flight for the second week in November.

Buzzing with excitement, I dialled Phoenix first, then Jude. Although happy knowing the trip was set — I had hinted that a visit was being planned — their reactions felt flat.

"That's great, Mum. Can't wait. Sorry, I'm just getting ready for work. I have to go but we'll talk soon. Love you."

And Jude was playing a shoot 'em up video game and was definitely distracted. "Awesome... Nooo, get out of there... Does Phoenix know? Ah damn..." Jude said as though he was talking to two separate people at once.

"Yes, I just called her. You sound busy," I replied.

"Yeah, sorry, you caught me... Oh you son-of-a..."

"No problem. Just wanted to give you a heads-up. See you soon. Love you."

I won't lie, I wanted whoops and happy dances. I got neither. For me, it felt like I was announcing that I was coming back from an immeasurable distance and incalculable time away — as if I were flying back from being on the moon or something. Their life in Canada hadn't changed a great deal once I left. They settled in and life had moved on. I was not on the moon but in Costa Rica. And it had only been three months. We video chatted regularly, so it wasn't like they hadn't seen or heard from me. I wasn't lost at sea. The truth is we had been more in touch since I had moved to Costa Rica than we had been when we lived under the same roof.

Once I had spoken to the kids, I made rapid-fire phone calls to sort out my accommodations and set a few dates in the calendar.

I contacted Kevin's sister, Kaz, and asked her if I could stay with her. Making Burlington, Ontario, Canada my homebase would be the most convenient way to see the kids as often as possible.

"Of course, I'm happy to collect you at the airport, too. The good news is I'll be leaving early the next morning on business, so you'll have the apartment all to yourself for the first week. Remind me to give you a set of keys. The bad news is I won't be around to ferry you around," Kaz told me in her distinctive English-from-England lilt. Even after years of living in Canada, accents die hard.

"That's great, thanks. And no problem. Once in Burlington, I'll rent a car. I'll need one to get around and do my rounds. I have a lot of people to see and things to do while I'm there. I wasn't expecting you to be my taxi driver."

After putting the receiver back down on its cradle from my call with Kaz, I picked it up again and dialled my parents' number to let them know about my plans. "I'll be with you in time to celebrate my birthday."

"My *babeee* is going to be forty-eight years old!" my mum fake-cried into the phone as she did every single year. Since I was the youngest, she liked to pretend that it was impossible that her baby was getting older. I found this ironic since she seemed in such a hurry for me to grow up and move out of the house, but I let her have her fun. And even though I may have rolled my eyes at Mum's comment, I did look forward to seeing her and Dad.

Then I made appointments to meet with Jude's teachers so I could introduce myself and get caught up on his progress. I also contacted our bank manager and set up a meeting to close some of our accounts. It would be a busy couple of weeks.

In preparation for my Southern-Ontario-in-November trip, I gathered some of my cold-weather clothes and my never-unpacked fashionable leather shoes from the boxes stored up in the loft and started filling my suitcase. I looked forward to wearing something other than my big black rubber rain boots.

A Stranger in My Own Land

The Toronto, Canada airport was a ghost town. It was so empty of people that when I sneezed, I heard an echo. I'd flown many times, and I'd never experienced anything like it. There was an eerie, apocalyptic feeling about it. It was 10:45 p.m., not 2:00 a.m.

I was one of the first to disembark from the plane and didn't waste any time. I walked with purpose down the long corridor and to get an edge over the other passengers behind me, I took the stairs instead of standing still on the escalators. Something propelled me forward. I wanted to get in line as quickly as possible and get through customs. Except there was no line. There were eight available customs officers for me to choose from and I approached the closest one. I breezed on through, picked up my suitcase from the rolling carousel, and walked out of the sliding doors. The sprawling *Arrivals* lobby was just as deserted except for one person standing right in front of me...

Jude!

I hugged him so tight I nearly asphyxiated him.

"What are you doing here? Are you alone? Where's Kaz?" I asked, trying to make sense of him being at the airport since he didn't have his driver's license yet.

"Phoenix called Kaz to let her know that we wanted to surprise you. We know how early Kaz likes to go to bed and since your flight delays meant you were coming in so much later, we figured she'd be fine with it and she was. She was really grateful, actually, so it worked out," Jude explained as we walked outside. The nip from the November wind was a fast reminder of why I wanted to leave cold Canada.

While Jude came into the airport to greet me, Phoenix waited in the car by the curb to avoid paying for parking. As she was keeping watch for security officers who didn't tolerate idlers, she must have spotted us in the rearview mirror because she got out of the car and ran up to me with her arms flung wide open. It had only been three months, but we hugged as if it had been three years.

From an expedition to the moon.

It wasn't until I was outside the airport that I realized just how much my life had changed in such a short period of time. I still felt like a foreigner in Costa Rica and in my lowest moments I had longed to be surrounded by familiar sights, sounds, and smells. Oddly enough though, within five minutes of being in my native land, I could sense that I was just as much a stranger there. I felt a deep inner stirring, as though the life as I knew it was motoring along with or without me; a feeling that I didn't quite belong in Canada anymore...like I didn't quite belong anywhere.

The nip got nippier, so I quickly shoved my suitcases in the trunk and hopped in the passenger seat. The three of us gabbed the entire hour and caught up until we arrived at Kaz's apartment building in Burlington.

It was almost midnight. I was beat. We made plans to see each other the next day and the day after that and the one after that.

I waved the kids off and, feeling a bit guilty for the lateness of my arrival, I buzzed up for Kaz to let me into her building. As I reached the seventh floor, I walked up to 710 and heard the door unlock. After a quick whispered chat, Kaz handed me extra keys and went back to bed while I settled on the pull-out couch in the living room. This was my home for the next two weeks.

Phoenix, Jude, and I hung out as often as their work and school schedules allowed. I squeezed in every minute there was, just like squeezing all the juice out of an orange — not wasting one drop. One Saturday, the three of us sat together and binge-watched almost a whole season of *Modern Family*.

The laughter.

I'll never forget that sweet bonding time.

Sweet Charity

Speaking of *sweet*... Three weeks before leaving Costa Rica, I had posted on social media that I was raising money to help pay for the continuation of the new kitchen that was being added to our one-room school. So many people had reached out to me pledging their support. I had felt encouraged, but I also knew that what people say and what they do can be different. I didn't want to pressure anyone, and I needn't have worried. When I met up with my friends and former coworkers, I never once had to ask or find a way to slide the topic into the conversation as a reminder. Each one was quick to bring up my fundraising efforts and doled out their cash just as quickly.

"Hey Anne, I have some money to give you for the kitchen you're building. Don't leave without coming by my office. My wallet is in my purse. I love what you're doing," one of my former colleagues said from inside one of the boardrooms as I passed by.

I poked my head halfway through the boardroom doorway and saw that she was alone, maybe waiting for other people to join her. "Well, just to be clear, I'm not personally building the addition, I'm just raising money so the school can buy more materials and keep paying the labourers. But thank you, I'll come find you for sure."

"Yes, whatever. It's a great cause no matter who's doing the work. I love that you're doing this. So grassroots of you. So inspiring," she replied, unconcerned about the details.

Many people told me they were reading my blog and enjoyed keeping up with the updates of our adventure. They claimed they knew Elizabeth and my fellow classmates from all my stories. Compelled to help me assist my new community, they gave like it was no big deal...like they were doing some small insignificant thing. *If they only knew.*

I managed to raise over $800 USD for the school. I couldn't believe it. I couldn't believe the overwhelming support my family and friends showed me.

I had escaped suburbia and the corporate grind, feeling that my spiritual cup was utterly empty. Three months later I returned, and it was my suburban family, my suburban friends, and my suburban coworkers who filled my cup until it was overflowing. I couldn't have done it without their sweet charity.

This trip was everything.

First Day Back in Río Blanco

Something had shifted in me while I was away. Surrounded by the rushing river, the splashing trout, and Frankie's wet welcome-home kisses, the feeling of being a stranger in a strange land had diminished. These were the sights, sounds, and smells that now felt familiar — I was home.

And how quickly I got back into the swing of things. While Kevin did his morning rounds, I started the fire in the fireplace and prepared our tea and cereal. After breakfast, Kevin led me around the property, showing me everything he and Nacho had accomplished while I was in Canada.

First, they had built fences around the property, which was a huge job in and of itself. But they also cleaned out the hatchery — which was an even bigger job. The solid corrugated tin sheets on the roof kept the space dark, which was fine for hatching eggs once upon a time and useful for hiding the mess that was left behind, but our plans were to use the long-forgotten round concrete cylinders as raised garden beds. But before we could get started on that, we'd have to remove most of the tin roof. While I was away, that was what Kevin and Nacho did. They took off half the roof and added a clear taut plastic sheet that kept the rain out but let the sunlight in. It looked so much brighter now. And all the scraps of wood that were piled on top of one another had been removed. Kevin sawed them into smaller pieces and stacked them in the kindling pile under the carport. The hatchery was ready to be transformed into a greenhouse.

I loved meandering up and down our property. I loved seeing our progress in such a short time. I loved breathing the clean air. What I didn't love was seeing how overgrown my vegetable garden was. It was obvious what my first task of the day would be: weeding.

As I crouched on my hands and knees, with my small spade, I worked my way from one garden bed to the next. The carrots were growing well and so was a leafy green, which we learned through the wonders of the internet was called *mizuna*. It looked a little bit like a type of arugula with wider leaves and it had a bit of a cabbage bite to it. My tomato plants were really growing well, too. I picked a beautifully ripe one... It was small, but really tasty.

After grounding myself in my garden, I picked up where I left off two-and-a-half weeks earlier and got on with my other chores. I put a first coat of paint on the outdoor shower walls and then a second coat everywhere else in the casita.

It was nice to be back and feel productive.

An Emotional Affair

Catalina was the only person who knew about my fundraising efforts. I wasn't sure how much money I'd be able to raise for the kitchen and didn't want to spread false hope. Or maybe I didn't want the pressure.

What if I don't raise a penny?

I sent Catalina a message just before I left Canada to let her know that I had received enough money to finish the kitchen and to ask her advice on how to proceed. The cultural nuances were still new to me, and I didn't want to make any assumptions or offend anyone.

Catalina was thrilled to hear the news and said she would set up a meeting for the following Monday with the Río Blanco school board, which consisted of Elizabeth, Adriana, Vanessa, Martín, and a few other parents whom I'd yet to meet. She would explain that I had something to share with them but wouldn't mention anything else to not spoil the surprise.

Spreading the Good News

My letter to the school board, which Catalina was nice enough to translate into Spanish, explained that my trip to Canada was primarily focused on seeing my children and parents but also on raising money to finish the school kitchen.

Since I didn't want my poor Spanish accent having me stutter and sputter, getting in the way of being understood, I had asked Catalina if she would read the letter on my behalf. I felt relieved when she had agreed to help me out, but unfortunately, something came up at the last minute and she was unable to make it to the meeting. I was too nervous to get up in front of these people and read the letter myself. I hadn't practiced. I hadn't prepared myself mentally to take on the task. I'm not sure why I felt so nervous facing the school board — our neighbours and friends. This was good news! But I felt paralyzed. I didn't want to botch it up. I pulled Adriana aside and put her on the spot.

"Adrí, could you *please* read this for me?" I pleaded as I handed her the piece of paper.

"*Sí*, okay. *No problema*." She took the paper from me and started reading to herself. I could see her eyes land on certain words as she brought her hand to her mouth as people do when they're shocked or amazed. After reading the entire letter she looked at me and said, "Really?"

"Yes, really. Could you read it to the group for me?" I asked again.

As parents and board members straggled into the unfinished kitchen chatting to one another, Adriana encouraged them to grab a seat in the chairs that had been brought over from the community centre and asked them to quiet down.

"*Por favor amigos y amigas. Con permiso...*" she started. She had something important to share. The room came to a hush.

After each paragraph, Adriana had to stop reading because there was so much excitement and so many questions. Adriana politely asked them to wait until she read the whole letter, or she would never get through it. They all laughed, then listened intently — biting their lips, shaking their heads in disbelief, and twirling their scarves as a means to calm themselves down. Although I was the one getting all the thanks, I was merely the face behind all those who responded to my plea for help and I had Adriana make that point clear.

The board members couldn't believe perfect strangers would dig into their pockets to help a community they'd never seen, for people they'd never met. The committee asked me to relay back to my family, friends, and former coworkers how much it appreciated everyone's generosity; but more importantly, the spark of hope such kindness ignited. That right there was what touched their hearts to the core. Then came the tears — theirs and mine — hugs, sheer joy, and excitement.

We talked for over two hours prioritizing what items were most important and we made a wish list. The committee had almost a grand to work with and although in these parts it was considered a lot of money, it didn't go as far as one might think. But every bit helped and based on their expressed gratitude you'd have thought it was a million dollars.

We made a plan; we'd use the money to parge the crumbling wall, get cabinet doors made, install countertops, and buy a glass pane for the front door to let the sunlight in. The money would pay for materials and labour. Clara would finally be able to get out of that dingy closet and the kids would have a clean, bright place to eat their lunch.

Success.

Twenty-Seven
The Winds of Change

December 2012

December was the beginning of summer in Costa Rica, also known as the dry season. And as if by the snap of God's fingers, the wind picked up and blew away the clouds from the Pacific side over the Continental Divide and across the Atlantic Ocean, exposing a smooth expanse of blue without even the slightest wisp in the sky. What was once in soft focus now had a crispness to its edges, like when you've needed a new prescription for some time and you finally put on your new glasses.

The river flow dropped and got more transparent. The water swept over and around the boulders rather than swallowing them up. The river was finally playing nice and sharing the riverbed rather than consuming it. It was starting to feel like how I remembered it when we visited the property for the first time.

As I drove down to Santa María to meet Catalina and Adriana for a coffee date, I noticed that the tall green bushes growing on both sides of the road seemed to have bloomed overnight with bright purple flowers.

"These flowers are called Catalinas," Catalina said.

"That will be easy for me to remember."

"When you start to see the first flower in late November, it's a sign that the rain will soon stop. It's a sign of hope," she explained.

"Ah, your birthday is in late November. Makes sense that your parents named you

Catalina. You were a sign of hope," I suggested.

"I think they just liked the name. My parents are not that *poéticos*."

Adriana and I laughed.

"So now that there are so many Catalinas everywhere, does that mean summer has truly started? Just like that? No more rain until the end of April or May?" I asked.

"Yes, that's how it usually works. The kids are off school from December to early February. Many people take time off and go to the beach or travel to see family and friends. Just like in Canada and the United States when the schools close during July and August. Everything slows down here, too. Unless you're a farmer of course or in the hospitality business. Then this is their busy time. But at least everyone gets to enjoy the hot, sunny weather," Catalina divulged with Adriana nodding in agreement.

"Back in Canada, my friends are drinking hot chocolate and watching snow fall. I don't like cold winter months or the pressure the Christmas season brings. I was so busy escaping all that, I didn't really think about how weird it would feel to celebrate Christmas in a hot climate. It's hard for me to get into a festive mood. I have no desire to put up a Christmas tree or decorate."

"Ah, *sí*, in Canada Christmas is about cold and snow. Here, people know Christmas is around the corner when the wind comes," Catalina shared as she fanned her hands back and forth towards her face. Her eyes were closed for a brief moment and the corners of her mouth curled with anticipated delight.

"The wind?"

"*Sí*. December is the windiest month. When the wind comes, people...*cómo se dice*...um...*asocian* — "

"Associate?" I guessed.

"Yes, associate. People associate it with Christmas coming soon."

"Do you eat turkey and stuffing?"

"No," Adriana shook her head. "Well, maybe some people... The rich Ticos who like to copy North Americans, *sí*. They watch movies and see the turkey, potatoes, and how do you say...*relleno?*" Adriana rubbed her thumb against her index and middle finger as if it would help her remember, then looked at us for support.

"Stuffing," Catalina translated. *Thank goodness for Catalina, I would not have known that one.*

"Most Ticos, especially the people who live in small villages or in beach towns... they follow Costa Rican traditions," Catalina added.

"So what do you prepare? What's considered traditional?"

They gave each other a knowing look, then in unison, belted out, "*Tamales!*"

"I've heard of *tamales*, but I have no idea what they are. I don't think I've ever had one," I admitted.

"What? You have never had a *tamale*? We will change that, *sí*?" Adriana interrogated affectionately, although it felt less like a question and more like a directive.

"Sure, I'm happy to try one, where can I buy them?"

"It's not only tradition to eat *tamales* at Christmas but it's tradition to *make* them. Every family makes them a little differently," Catalina smiled.

"Roberto and I will be making ours next weekend. Please, you come to our home, and we will teach you how to make them. We will teach you a new Christmas tradition. The Tico way," Adriana beamed with pride.

New Christmas Tradition

"*Hola*, Anne. Come in. Are you ready to roll up your sleeves?" Roberto said with a smirk. Roberto had a dry wit with flat delivery, and it was sometimes hard to tell whether he was serious or whether he was teasing.

"*Sí, señor*. I'm here for my *tamale*-making lesson. What should I do first?"

"Ah, first, you must wash your hands," Roberto directed me to the kitchen sink and handed me a bar of soap.

It was a long and involved process. Adriana demonstrated how to clean the banana leaves one by one. Then we had to chop, shred, and dice pork, carrots, onions, parsley, and olives. Roberto also showed me how to make a corn-type gooey paste called *masa*.

Traditionally, the women (mothers, aunts, cousins, daughters, etc.) gather under one roof and assemble the *tamales*...hundreds and hundreds of them. The matriarch oversees the production, making sure everyone is at her post and is doing a good job. If they run out of ingredients, she's there to replenish the bowls.

"There are as many *tamale* recipes as there are families, so the matriarch is usually pretty strict about how the women make *her* batch," Roberto described with some emphasis.

I learned the first one in line adds a spoonful of *masa* on a clean banana leaf, then hands it to the second one in line who adds one tiny morsel of pork (not two morsels, *only one*), then passes it on to the third where she adds one piece of carrot, and so on. The last person in line folds the banana leaf into a neat square and ties it up with string. Depending on the size of the cauldron, a batch of ten or twenty *tamales* get boiled for an hour over an outdoor fire pit. While the first batch is cooking, the assembly line continues, and the *tamales* pile up. When they're done, the family members divide the bundle among themselves. They share in the making of the *tamales* as well as the bounty.

"Although most Ticos are not rich, they are generous, and they like to invite family and friends over for parties during the holidays. They can afford to do this by making hundreds of *tamales* with small portions of each ingredient. An ingredient like pork, for instance, is expensive, but by only adding a tiny piece of meat per *tamale*, they can stretch it further," said Roberto. He seemed to be taking the teacher role to heart as he dropped our first batch in the boiling water. "Sometimes people have more than one pot so they can cook more *tamales* at one time. But we only use one."

"Yes, we are only making eighty," Adriana confirmed.

"Eighty? That sounds like a lot to me! How long do they last in the fridge?"

"About a week," Roberto replied.

"You're going to eat eighty *tamales* in one week? You're going to have to give a lot away, I think."

"Well, forty for you and Kevin and forty for Adriana and me. So not so much." Roberto dismissed this number as though it was a mere handful.

Forty! I thought I was going to try ONE.

I was grateful Adriana and Roberto taught me how to make *tamales,* but the social aspect was definitely the best part.

Four Months and Counting

Four months had passed since we arrived in Costa Rica. A great deal of work had been done on the farm. Some vanity had been lost. Some sanity had been found. A little Spanish had been learned. A little English had been taught. And many new friends had been made. I'd say we were integrating into our community well, which is not always easy in small, rural villages.

I found myself taking the time to appreciate my surroundings, such as noticing the clear skies, bright moon, and starry nights. The air was thinner up in the mountains, but I loved that it was so clean. No light pollution. No noise pollution.

No pollution.

I lived more in the moment, probably because I didn't have appointments and meetings booked three months in advance nor was every minute of my day scheduled. I had time to breathe...actually breathe.

I was learning to let go of my preconceived ideas of how things *should* be and accepting what *was.* I didn't hyperventilate if my house wasn't spotless when friends turned up unannounced.

Well...not as much as before.

I was learning to relax.

I was learning to cook with simple, fresh ingredients and managing to make flavourful meals. I was also learning that I didn't miss the variety and conveniences available in Canada, but when we ever moved back, I'd try not to take the variety and conveniences for granted or judge them as trivial. The minimalist lifestyle that I was latching on to in this new environment felt good. It felt right.

There are pros and cons to every situation and the universal rule that we can't have it all resonated especially true this time of year. Although I didn't miss the cold weather or commuting on snow-covered roads, I did miss — I never thought I'd say this — a cold, white Christmas. It just wasn't the same in a warm climate and I wasn't sure I'd ever get used to it. Some traditions ran deeper than even I could have imagined...deeper than *tamales* could cure.

Access to technology was my lifeline between two worlds. The fact that I could write my blog, post my entries, and have people follow our adventure every day was amazing to me. That I could click a little green button and within seconds be video chatting astounded me. I was even more appreciative that I no longer had to drive down to Copey for that connection. The internet made it possible for me to live so far away without suffering serious bouts of depression. For that, I was truly grateful. We did have the best of both worlds.

All this reflection after only four months. What would I glean after a year or two, or five? How would living this adventure transform me? Deepen me? Broaden me? What would I gain? What would I lose? How would I ever be able to put a value on this experience?

Twenty-Eight
Long-Standing Wounds

January 2013–January 2015

The winds had finally died down, and the rainbow trout were ready to catch and eat.

Happy New Year to us!

We were looking forward to seeing how this next year would unfold. We had given ourselves four months to ramp up, market on social media, and have the B&B opened for business. Our first guests were booked and arriving within a few days.

My blog readers were starting to reach out, letting us know that they couldn't wait to visit and see our paradise property for themselves. My mother was the first to make good on this promise when she had sprung the news back in September that she had bought her plane ticket to spend a month with us come January. Costa Rica would be her first solo flight without my dad, and she told me every chance she got on our video chats how excited she was. She would add a new fact about her travel plans or describe some new apparel she had bought for her trip.

And as time so often does, it crept up on us. January had arrived and so soon would my mother.

My parents had travelled a great deal over the years. They were no strangers to flying and visiting interesting places together. Rather than self-guided meandering road trips like I enjoy, they took a particular shine to organized bus tours and cruises. And when it came to booking flights, acquiring boarding passes, filling out the customs form, holding on to passports, hailing taxis, paying the restaurant tab, and finding their way around from one appointed meeting place to another, my father took charge of all those logistics. Not that my mother was incapable of doing those things on her own, just that certain expectations had naturally developed over the span of their long marriage, and I don't think she questioned them all that much. Nor do I think my father trusted that my mother could manage to keep track of such important details. I believe my father thought he was smarter and more capable, pure and simple.

Born during the Great Depression as part of the Traditionalist Generation, my folks prospered in an era of economic growth. Their work ethic was strong, their desire for stability was profound, and their need to uphold a sense of conformity was not subtle. As young adults, my thin father slicked his jet-black hair with Brylcreem like all the other guys who copied the Elvis trend, and my mother donned the popular cat eyeglasses and wore poodle skirts or capri pants with saddle shoes. In short, they were not trailblazers. As they followed social decorum closely, the typical gender roles of that time were cast and moulded in their final form like handprints in wet cement — solid when preserved yet ever so fragile if cracked.

Through the decades, my father's physical build became more rotund but he still combed his thick greying hair back as he always had. I'd only known my father to have one hair style. He never jumped on the perm bandwagon like some of my friends' dads. As a company man, he wore suits and ties. His casual wear of checkered buttoned-down shirts and ironed khaki pants were saved for weekends only. He did own a pair of jeans, but even those were pressed. I don't think my dad ever owned a pair of pants with rips or frayed hems, or socks with holes. And if he did, they must have been quickly discarded. Even his "dirty" work clothes were spotless.

My mother didn't purchase fashion magazines — a needless expense for her — when she could easily peruse new trends at her every-six-weeks hair salon appointment. And for as long as I've been alive, I've known Mum to exercise. Self-motivated and self-disciplined, she never went to a gym or bothered with fitness shows. Instead, she exercised behind closed doors after Dad had gone to work. I only knew about this routine of hers because as a very young child, while my older sisters were in school and I was still at home, I would go looking for her when the TV show I was watching was over.

As a bona-fide Gen X-er, I'm a product of sitting through back-to-back children's TV shows in our unfinished basement. I was first exposed to francophone programs like *Chez Hélène*, *Bobino et Bobinette*, and *Sol et Gobelet*. Then, to fill up more of my time and to keep me quiet, the channel was switched over to the iconic Canadian-produced TV programs *Mr. Dressup* — the Canadian version of *Mr. Rogers* — and *The Friendly*

Giant. But my favourite was the ever-popular U.S. show *Sesame Street*. These Anglo shows, along with Saturday morning cartoons like *The Flintstones* and *The Jetsons*, were my first real introduction to the English language, which served me well later on the playground. Square-eyed and glued to its mesmerizing glow, I loved TV. It was the most fun babysitter ever, but still, I was young and sometimes I got that sinking feeling that I had been abandoned in the bowels of our big house, especially when a boring adult commercial snapped me out of my stance. So, I'd go looking for Mum.

With my hands holding on to the railing and my little pudgy legs climbing what seemed like very high steps, I'd reach the main floor. When I didn't find her in the kitchen or the laundry room, I'd make my way up to the upper level of our house where all the bedrooms were. The master bedroom's door would be opened a crack, just enough for me to peek in. In her light blue velour tracksuit, my mother would be counting under her breath.

Un...deux...trois...

Sometimes she'd see me and invite me in, and I'd watch her stretch or squat or lunge. Most of the time, she just guided me straight back downstairs to the TV and found another children's show for me to watch. So while she was exercising, I was learning the art of sitting for long periods of time in front of a different kind of dopamine activator.

To this day, after she's walked her daily 5 km (3 mi), Mum exercises behind closed doors. Next to people ten years younger than her, she's often the fittest person in the room. I wish I had inherited THAT self-discipline gene.

Where my parents were permissive with TV-watching activities, they were much stricter in other areas, possessing high expectations of their three daughters. As self-regulated and responsible humans, my parents taught both my sisters and me to think things through carefully...not to be impulsive and embarrass ourselves; but more importantly, not to embarrass *them*. They droned into us that each decision we would make in life would be met with consequences...sometimes long-lasting. No half-hatched plan would do. And once we shared our plan even with one single person, then it would be out there, and we would have to follow through. That was the unspoken Beaudoin law.

There is no room for error so make sure your plan, whatever it might be, is foolproof and stands the test of time would have made an apt family motto. Although a lesson that stuck with me, it didn't come by way of gentle coaching. It often came across as stern and unforgiving, with a scolding finger shaking at us. Their uncertainty in our ability to navigate life was tantamount to believing in our inevitable failure.

Over time, and after a few therapy sessions, I realized that was not the case. I was a sensitive soul and what I took as criticism was concern over our ability to take ownership of our future. Their intent was to mitigate their own worry by making sure they prepared us for the world. It wasn't until I became a parent myself that I truly understood that point.

At forty-seven, Kevin and I had outweighed the possible consequences of moving to a developing country. Was there room for error? You bet. But we were going to do it anyway.

Back in April, when we had invited my parents over for a weekend visit, there was a three-fold reason: The first was a means to celebrate my father's seventy-sixth birthday. The second was to show off our newly renovated home since they had only seen it in mid-chaos, and we didn't know when they'd get the chance to see it completely finished. And the third was to tell them about our plans to sell our house and move to Costa Rica. On the third point, I expected resistance and a whole lot of questions. But the twelve-year-old me learned my lessons well, and I was ready.

My parents had arrived in their pristine sage green Ford Freestyle. Dad was at the wheel — he always drove. With his belly-forward stance and knees permanently bent at a 45° angle, my dad carried their one small suitcase and followed my mum into the house. Mum, who was always expressive in an extroverted way, *oooh'd* and *awww'd* as she walked in the door. Dad was the strong, silent type. It was always harder to know what he was thinking.

After the two-hour house tour — our house wasn't that big, but we had to explain what we had done and why to satisfy their insatiable need to understand our decision-making process — we broke the news like ripping off a Band-Aid.

"Oh? What about this beautiful house?" my mother had asked. "I thought you were going to live here forever… All the renovations you've done… I can't believe it. What a shame."

"Well, things change," I had replied, trying to hold back my snarl.

To avoid a barrage of sniping questions, Kevin and I had prepared a slideshow.

A picture is worth a thousand words, as the cliché goes.

Inviting Mum and Dad to make themselves comfortable in the living room, we projected onto our large flat-screen TV — that hung above the fieldstone fireplace's wooden mantle — a few dozen pictures of the Costa Rican property. We explained how we intended to raise rainbow trout and run a hospitality business in the remote mountains of Costa Rica, in a village with less than seventy-five people.

In retrospect, I see how that might have sounded a bit crazy.

But to my utter surprise, seeming impressed with our well-thought-out plan, Mum's earlier disappointment turned to sudden excitement. Changing her tune, she was convinced that this move was a great idea.

"Wow, so beautiful. So many ponds. Very good idea to rent out the little house. Nice that everything you need is all there. You're the perfect age to do this sort of thing. Not too young, not too old. Better to do it before it's too late. I'm sure your house will sell quickly. I'm going to pray you sell it for a million dollars," she had prattled on with unrestrained approval.

My dad wasn't unsupportive, but he kept his thoughts and feelings close to his chest. Announcements of big lifestyle changes weren't exactly uncommon in our family. If not this daughter, then another was living in some faraway land.

My eldest sister, Lucie, had lived eleven years in the far north of Canada with her husband, Tim, and their four children. They spent most of those years on the shores of Great Bear Lake in the tiny settlement of Déline, but in 1990, when their youngest was only a month old, they moved from the Northwest Territories to the northern tip of Baffin Island in Nunavut — 644 km (400 mi) *above* the Arctic Circle!

Mittimatalik, also known as Pond Inlet, is sunless between November and February. The long, extremely cold winters feel longer still by this polar night. Amazingly, the thousand or so locals go about their business by star and moonlight during these four months where the average low hovers close to −40°C (−40°F).

That's the average!

Déline, which is pretty darn cold in its own right, felt like the tropics in comparison.

Living near the eastern entrance of the Northwest Passage and surrounded by glaciers, Lucie had mentioned how in the month of April, when the sun stretches across the sky for twelve hours a day and the air warms up to a balmy −25°C (−13°F), she would bundle up the kids and they would travel by snowmobile to the nearest iceberg for a picnic. Tim, at the helm, would tow a long, flat wooden sled behind the snowmobile where my nephew and two older nieces sat between my sister who snuggled her four-month-old under her parka.

Imagine the station wagon version of snowmobiles.

Although, calling it a *picnic* was a stretch and far more indicative of Lucie's ability to spin any challenge into an inviting adventure. The reality was she could only pack hot chocolate and cookies because anything else would freeze. Regardless of the subzero temperature or the lack of a more substantive meal, the kids would have fun climbing up the floating mass and sliding down its slick white surface on sealskins.

By contrast, the middle child, Lyne, had been living in Riyadh, Saudi Arabia, with her young daughter and fighter pilot instructor husband Eric for nearly a decade. They were about to move back to Canada when we broke the news that we were uprooting.

Riyadh couldn't have been more opposite to Lucie's experience. Its population was cresting six million, making it the most populous city in Saudi Arabia at the time and the third most populous in the Middle East. Situated in the middle of a desert where dust storms were common, Riyadh was known for its long, oppressively hot summers and short, mild winters. The average high in August reached 43°C (110°F). And if the temperature wasn't a hot enough topic, the political climate regarding women's rights was on everyone's lips.

Women had to wear abayas and hijabs in public. And they were not allowed to drive. Lyne once described how she and Eric had gone motorbiking in the barren desert, far away from prying eyes. She had never ridden a motorcycle prior to moving to Riyadh but the chance of driving any kind of motor vehicle enticed her to learn. By wearing full-body gear from neck to toe and a face helmet with a tinted visor that camouflaged her gender, she felt it was safe to bend the rules in no-man's land. The risks were calculated, but dangerous, nonetheless.

Both my sisters are hardcore to the bone — independent and brave.

When we described our upcoming adventure, Dad probably thought, *Costa Rica... Lush mountains...perfect climate...pfff!*

But he didn't say a word. He just nodded knowingly. That nod could have meant a number of things. It could have meant he thought we were fools. It could have meant he wished he was as cool as us and had taken more risks when he was younger. Or maybe he was wondering why his daughters were compelled to live so far away.

I'll never know. He didn't say.

As you can imagine, family reunions where we all spent time together in the same room were few and far between. Trying to get us in the same province was a challenge. What we sisters knew of each other came down to a bad case of broken telephone, mostly. What we told Mum was relayed back to Dad and the other two sisters...sometimes only one. Mum would forget who she told what and life would move on, often leaving one of us out of the loop.

Why didn't we just reach out to one another directly? Well, I suppose it's easy to forget that long-distance phone charges back then used to add up by the minute. Lengthy conversations were prohibitive, even short ones were expensive. So Mum would call us on occasion, and as the hub of information, she dispersed our news and updates. It's hard to remember a time when texting and free video chats weren't a thing.

It's fair to say that my family's geographical separation didn't help with the emotional disconnection I felt. I'm pretty sure my sisters felt it, too. But we three apples didn't fall far from the parental tree and the subject was rarely brought up.

Flying Solo

Over the ensuing months, at every turn, before we ever landed in Costa Rica, Mum mentioned how much she was looking forward to visiting, but I knew Dad was struggling with respiratory issues and he felt it wasn't a good time for him to be flying anywhere. The high altitude was his biggest concern; he worried it would slow him down and hinder his enjoyment.

I thought that was that. The decision had been made. The Grand Poobah had spoken. They would wait until my father felt better.

But no.

In her mid-seventies, my slender featherweight mother had decided to fly on her own for the first time. She figured she and Dad could visit together when he felt up to it, but she wasn't about to miss out on this opportunity. Mum's decision to travel on her own probably concerned my dad — his ego might have been bruised a little too — but I imagine *Who's going to make me dinner for the next month?* might have been the heaviest question weighing on his mind as he lounged in his poofy recliner working on his crossword puzzles.

I expected my mother's first solo flight to be a direct one. Baby steps. However, her journey would consist of three planes and two layovers, starting from McAllen, Texas — where they lived in a trailer park during the winter months with a gaggle of other snowbirds — to Houston. The George Bush Intercontinental Airport may have only ranked twelfth on the list of busiest airports in the United States back then, but it was huge. Mum would have to disembark and find her way to her connecting flight on her own. Then, she'd have to repeat the process in Nicaragua. Would the directional signs be bilingual? I prayed they would. As long as she managed to find the correct gate, the final leg of her trip would be straightforward. The Juan Santamaría Airport in Costa Rica was not big and it was fairly simple to navigate because the choices of where to go were limited. Just follow everyone else.

Although a gutsy, optimistic woman with fierce determination, my mother had confessed that she was feeling apprehensive.

No kidding! Who planned this trip?

Kevin and I stood outside the arrival doors with all the other families, friends, and shuttle drivers holding up signs with names. Looking to earn a buck, taxi drivers were crammed in there, too, ready to holler at disoriented tourists. We watched the travellers file out the sliding door and eventually saw Mum march out in her signature taut gait with her head held high looking straight ahead as she rolled her suitcases behind her. I was relieved to see that she was looking spry.

Mum was amusing to watch. She was all business, no eye contact with anyone, oozing a strong *I'm not buying what you're selling, leave me alone* vibe. Part of this posturing was her way of repelling unwanted advancements from people she deemed unsavoury individuals, but it was also her natural disposition. Before anyone had a chance to ask her a question she would answer, "*Not interested*," not just to those she had judged as unsavoury but to anyone in her path. Sometimes she would blurt out, "*Not interested*," to people who weren't even looking at her. This no-nonsense trait crossed over into other parts of her life which made getting close to family and friends difficult. My hypothesis is that my mother built this impenetrable wall as a safety mechanism — as a means to hold on to a shred of autonomy — and it became her default setting.

As Mum scanned the crowd, I spotted her glancing in our direction and waved to get her attention. With an acknowledging smile, she forged through the cluster of slowpokes in front of her.

We hugged without squeezing. Mum was never much of a hugger; she tended to cup her hands as she touched my shoulders ever so slightly with the tips of her fingers as though afraid of crushing something.

Crushing what? My spirit?

The gap between us had always been more than a physical one.

Kevin grabbed my mother's luggage and rolled it through the multi-story parking garage while I held on to my own heavy emotional baggage.

Mum had succeeded. She had arrived safe and sound in Costa Rica without my father leading the way. Mum beamed with pride in the back seat. She sat behind Kevin, who was driving, so that I could turn my head without getting a painful kink in my neck while I talked to her from the front passenger seat. From the airport, driving back to Río Blanco through San José in rush-hour traffic as the sun was setting, I expected the journey home would be slow, but I sensed my mother had lots of energy and was eager to share stories of her new solo experience.

"How did all your flights go? Did you have any problems?" I asked. I knew these questions were equal to winding up the Energizer Bunny. It would keep her going for a while.

"Dad dropped me off at McAllen Airport. There was no problem in McAllen, but when I got off in Houston...the airport was so big... I had no idea where I had to go, and I was afraid I would get lost and miss my next flight. How do people know where they're supposed to go? I asked a woman if she knew where I had to go... She was very nice, but she didn't work at the airport, so she didn't know... She told me to look on the big board... But that didn't help because it told me the gate number but not where the gate was... I just kept asking people until I found someone who could tell me. I never have to think about it when I'm with Dad... I just follow him...he always knows. But I figured it out. I'm smart, eh? Good thing I'm not shy.

"Then, we landed at Managua Airport...it was very clean. I thought I would practice my Spanish, but they spoke too fast...I didn't understand anything anyone said... Why do they talk so fast? They should slow down or speak English for people who don't understand. I have been studying Spanish for years, but I can't understand when people talk to me... It must be a different Spanish or maybe a different accent... I was a bit nervous, but I held my purse very close to me and everything was okay. No one bothered me..."

As my mum recounted her journey step by step, I cringed when her prejudices slipped out unconsciously. For someone who had travelled as much as she had, it amazed me how bubble wrapped she still was. There was an arrogance that seeped out of my mother's pores, which triggered me. I struggled to reconcile her uninvestigated, *laissez-faire* discriminations. Influenced by and comfortable with Western societal norms, she didn't seem to question life in general or question what made people tick specifically. From her white, suburban, middle-class plateau, if people didn't behave a certain way... *like her*...they were viewed through a myopic lens of misunderstanding.

As I judged my mother for not asking questions about what made the people around her tick, I had perpetuated the same crime. I had not bothered to inquire about *her story* all these years. I didn't know what she dreamt about as a kid. I didn't know what it meant for her to be the fourth of five children living in working-class Pointe-Saint-Charles, Québec. I had heard peripheral stories — sweeping generalizations — but I didn't know if she had had a good childhood; if she was happy with the path she took in life; if she had any regrets; if being a mother was what she wanted for herself, or if she simply fell into it as a matter of societal expectation...and if she had any particular fears. I didn't know any of that. Her manner was so matter of fact and practical, I guess I accepted that we just didn't talk about stuff like that.

Lalalalala.

We arrived home in the dark and Mum was excited; animated in a way I hadn't seen her before. She was looking forward to seeing our property in the light of day. After Kevin and I hauled her suitcases up the narrow ladder-like staircase to the loft where she would be sleeping, I realized I was looking forward to seeing my mother in the light of day. Who was my mother without my father? I wondered if she herself knew the answer to that question. I had a month to mine for answers. I would go down into the deep unexplored cavern of my mother's childhood memories and if I plucked up enough courage, I would question her about my own childhood, share my own recollections... and reveal my fractured soul.

At first, a month seemed like an excruciatingly long time, but suddenly, it felt like it might not be long enough.

Walks and Talks

My mother was in great shape. Although a little older and nearly half her height, Mum reminded me of Jane Fonda especially when the actress wore her hair short. I can't quite put my finger on why, but Mum took pride in her appearance and exuded a similar air of confidence. Physically speaking, I mean — that's as far as the comparison goes. I wouldn't say my mother shared any of Ms. Fonda's activist or feminist traits. But, like Ms. Fonda — or what the tabloids would have us believe — Mum followed her own strict exercise routine, and she certainly wouldn't let any vacation hinder that discipline. I guess my mother was an activist for herself in that regard.

Mum and I were up early and out the door every morning for our daily walk — up and down the rocky, dirt roads. Mum was used to walking 5 km (3 mi), but always on flat streets at sea level. Although she loved the magnificent views up in the mountains, she found these hikes much more challenging.

When we first arrived, walking up and down our trails and dirt roads was hard for me, too. I huffed and puffed and needed many breaks. But I guess my body was growing accustomed to it because it didn't feel as strenuous as it once did. It's true I had lost twenty pounds in the first three months; I attribute the loss to reducing my consumption of processed foods and being physically active. Walking up and down our property was more exercise than I had been doing at the gym three times a week, let alone all the digging and lifting and lugging and squatting and lunging. My new habits couldn't have looked more different from my sedentary lifestyle back in Canada.

In the beginning, on these walks, I posed gentle questions. I didn't want to pry open a door that had been kept shut tight my entire life too forcefully only for it to slam back in my face. I wasn't sure how she would take my prodding. But Mum was surprisingly receptive and seemed to welcome the opportunity to share her thoughts and feelings.

"It must feel a bit strange not having Dad around… I know you met at your neighbourhood tennis club, but can you tell me a little bit about how you felt when you first met Dad? Was it love at first sight?" I asked, almost in interview fashion.

I can't be sure, but I think she blushed a little.

"*Oui, c'est vrai.* In the summertime, I spent a lot of time at the tennis club in Verdun. It was a popular place for teenagers back then and I made lots of friends there. I met your dad in the summer of 1955…I turned seventeen that August…just before I entered my last year at boarding school. Dad was a very good player. And so handsome. I really liked him and when September came, I was sad that we would only see each other during the holidays," she reminisced.

"Wasn't he allowed to visit?"

"No. It was too far. But your father used to write me beautiful letters. He was such a good writer…good with languages…so smart…" she swooned.

"Our mail was distributed in the cafeteria after lunch, and I couldn't wait to receive his letters. Every Friday, without fail, an open letter would be handed to me," her eyes glistened as she recollected the event as though it had happened the day before. She continued, "Each letter was read by Mother Superior before we were allowed to read it ourselves. Dad knew this so his letters were very *innocent*. Then one day, Mother Superior asked me to tell my gentleman friend not to send letters during Lent. I was so upset that when I left the cafeteria that day I started to cry. My teacher asked me what was wrong and when I told her she said, 'It's only forty days,' as if to say it wasn't that long. But to me, it felt like an eternity..."

We walked, she talked, and I listened.

"...So halfway through Lent, Grand-maman phoned your dad and said that if he wanted to write to me, she would hand-deliver the letter next time she visited."

"Ah... Bypassing Mother Superior's spying eyes... Sneaky... Was it romantic?" I chuckled.

"Oh, yes. I hid it in my little cedar box where I kept other mementos and when no one was looking I would take it out and read it over and over and over again. It made me feel less lonely. I was sure he was *the one*."

It was strange for me to see my mother so wistful, but I was enjoying how soft and sensitive she was as she described this teenage scenario.

"I remember that cedar box. Do you still have all his letters?" I wondered.

"Of course. They mean so much to me," Mum replied.

Her sentimentality touched me. I hadn't seen this side of her before. She was so open. It was as if I had been holding a blurry Polaroid all this time and what it took was exposure to the light for the image of my mother to become clear.

Knowing that my dad pursued my mother and waited for her shed a new perspective on their bond. It warmed my heart to learn that their relationship had started out as a love story, not just a pragmatic decision. Weaving their beginning into the fabric of our family dynamic was one of the missing threads I needed to understand the many layers and textures that make up my DNA.

Two Canadian kids growing together and doing the best that they can.

Our morning walks became a ritual of sharing, learning about one another, and being real. Sometimes my inquiries were benign, sometimes they were more pointed and sharp. Mum didn't always have answers because some of my questions delved into areas she had never considered. She would sometimes answer a question from the day before, having had the time to mull things over. I was thrilled that she was willing to go into the mine with me...two canaries exploring its depth. I felt like we were *both* digging deep and every day we found nuggets of pure gold.

One day, it was her turn to probe. Mum revealed her bewilderment about her daughters not calling her more often. She wondered why we weren't closer.

Oh, I don't know, maybe bragging about how you strapped our milk bottle to our crib railing like some gadget you'd see on a hamster cage has something to do with it? The pride that emanates when you tell how this little invention of yours made it so you didn't have to hold your newborns lacks a certain maternal connection. The practicality is what you seem to latch on to. Your unwavering goal to raise independent daughters, and your belief that holding back affection was the way, might have backfired.

"I used to talk to my mother every day," she said.

I could almost detect a sigh. A longing.

"What? You spoke to Grand-maman *every day*? Really? What did you talk about?"

"I don't know. We just chatted about our day, I suppose. I was very close to her. And I miss her so much, even forty years later," Mum expressed with anguish in her voice.

The only time I had seen any signs of vulnerability in my mother was when I was fifteen. I had opened the door to the laundry room and found my mother staring at my father's white dress shirt splayed on the ironing board. I noticed wet streaks down her face. She wasn't sobbing. It felt more like I walked in on some sort of quiet desperation. I had never seen her cry before — not even when she lost two toes in a lawn mowing accident... She wouldn't cry... She wouldn't limp... No one would know her pain.

Feeling paralyzed, not knowing what to do, I had awkwardly asked if she was okay. She said that she was fine as she gripped the steaming iron in one hand and dabbed her cheeks with the other, as if the vapour had caused her eyes to leak. Ever the austere stoic.

I had backed away like a skillful ninja and shut the door behind me. We never talked about that moment... Sweeping things like that under the carpet was our family's mode of operation.

Nothing to see here.

And yet, there I stood years later listening to Mum lament her disappointment at not having the same close relationship with her daughters that she had had with her mother. As she reminisced, her grief was palpable.

"Grand-maman was so healthy and vibrant. We all believed Grand-papa would die first and then she would be free to travel and see the world. They had the money, but Grand-papa liked to stay home and never wanted to go anywhere... The day she died was such a shock," Mum shared.

"I remember the day you got the call. A car accident. She and her cousin were on their way home from I don't know where. Grand-maman was driving and somehow had veered onto what she thought was the on-ramp except it was the off-ramp and that's when they were in a head-on collision. You had rushed to the hospital to see her."

"How do you remember all that? You were only six."

"Well, because it made a huge impression on me. I remember the urgency you felt to be by her side. You dropped everything. You weren't worried about chores or making dinner or anything like that. Your only focus was to be with your mother."

"Of course that was my focus. I was so worried."

"Yes, I understand, and it makes sense, but I had never seen you devastated before. Or since, really. I know how close you are with your brothers and sisters. I know your side of the family is fun and has that *joie de vivre*. I've never seen you have any disagreements; it always seems like one big, loud party when you get together," I said.

"Yes, it's true. We do have fun, even now."

"So what happened? You and Dad didn't raise us girls that way. We weren't allowed to cry or get angry. We weren't even allowed to laugh too loud. There was no fun in our house growing up. What was that all about?"

"I know. Dad loved to come around to our place because it was so relaxed compared to his house. And he had a lot of fun, too. Great sense of humour. He got along well with your aunts and uncles. We used to sing and play board games and Grand-maman had food ready to serve no matter what time, day or night. There was an open-door policy and everyone was welcomed. So that's the man I saw. A man who wanted what I had at home with my family. But when he became a father, something changed. He became very serious and strict just like his parents were. They were so poor and he never wanted to be poor like that ever again so he worked really hard to provide for our family. And when your dad is stressed and tired, he gets impatient and...*marabou* — "

"Grumpy," I translated without missing a beat.

"Yes, grumpy."

An understatement, but we'll go with that.

"Didn't it bother you?" I pressed.

"Well, yes, but what could I do? He was the man and — "

"You were being a dutiful wife. It was a different generation and all that. I understand."

"Well, it was."

The conversation was sliding, and I could feel myself getting impatient and grumpy. *I come by those traits honestly. Thanks, Dad!*

I felt the need to curb my self-righteous judgement and end the interrogation. I caught myself and simply nodded in agreement.

A few days later, on another one of our walks, I blurted with genuine curiosity, "Tell me something... What made you decide to come here for a month when we've rarely spent more than a couple of hours at a time with each other since I moved out of the house at twenty-two?"

I was dying to know her thought process. She did take a minute to think about it, then replied, "I don't know."

"I love your honesty. Do you want to know what I think?"

"Sure."

"I think you've been learning Spanish for the last couple of years and you thought this would be a great opportunity to immerse yourself. I don't think you decided to stay with me, your daughter, for a month. I think you thought, *How convenient that Anne and Kevin live in a Spanish-speaking country, I'll stay with them for a month so I can practice.* It served your purpose," I suggested. There was no anger in my tone.

I was expecting her to shut down or refute my hypothesis, but she didn't.

"Of course, I wanted to see you and Kevin. But you know what? You're absolutely right. I'm so determined to learn Spanish... And I'd never been to Costa Rica before. When your dad said he couldn't travel this year, I guess I thought this was my chance to concentrate on learning Spanish. I know he would never come for more than a week. But a week is not enough to practice and get good. I figured a month here would be better. I just decided to come for a month because it was good for me. I didn't think to ask if it was fine with you. I'm so sorry."

Mum was contrite as she replayed the scenario in her mind. I wasn't prepared for that.

My outer shell cracked open, and my insides felt like mush. I had never heard my mother say "I'm sorry" without being facetious; not in a self-evaluating, wanting-to-be-a-better-person kind of way. The fact that she recognized her motives and was able to admit them to me was groundbreaking. I don't think I ever felt more hope with the prospect of mending long-standing family wounds.

"I'm so happy you're here, Mum. Really. These morning walks are wonderful and thank you for being open to hearing some hard truths. I'm sure it's not easy. I really appreciate your willingness to learn and grow with me. I love you."

Twenty-Nine
Hush Valley Lodge

Business up and Running:
First B&B Guests

We were officially open for business, and I wish I could say it felt great. But it felt terrifying. Like, *what the hell do I think I'm doing* kind of paralyzing doubt. We already had a few bookings through word of mouth, and we were getting a lot of inquiries from my marketing efforts on Facebook. We were off to a good start, so why the trepidation?

I wasn't an entrepreneur at heart. I'd always been a cog in a big wheel. Now it all came down to Kevin and me. Well, when it came to the B&B...mostly me. He had enough to do with everything else farm related. But there we were. There I was.

Shit or get off the pot.

We were expecting a Canadian couple with their two young children; there was a lot to do. I had received an email before Christmas from a former colleague. We had worked side by side on the same team for a couple of years and became friends. Christine reached out saying that one of her friends was going to be in Costa Rica with her husband and her two young boys, both under six years of age, asking if we could host them.

Well, yes, of course.

I was so nervous, but pumped, too. I got into the zone and Mum was a huge help. I washed the sheets and dish towels, and Mum ironed whatever was wrinkled. She cleaned, dusted, and vacuumed the entire casita. I made the beds, stocked the cupboard with extra toilet paper and soap, and cut some fresh flowers and arranged them in a glass vase. I filled a stainless-steel container with tea bags, another container with fresh coffee, and a third with sugar. Then I arranged them neatly on the kitchen counter.

While I was prepping the vegetables for dinner, Kevin and Mum were outside catching fish. Our guests, Fiona and Doug, were running late and we had to make sure we caught the fish before the sun went down. Fiona had requested the trout dinner for her and Doug, and hamburgers for their young sons.

At about 4:00 p.m., the phone rang. It was Fiona. They drove down the right road, but as the terrain got sketchier, they started to feel hesitant, so they turned back to La Trinidad. I told them to hang tight; I drove up to meet them and guided them back down.

As soon as we got home, Kevin gave the family a quick tour of the property before the sun set. Meanwhile, I started dinner.

Mum looked on, a bit surprised, I think. She'd never seen me in action before. I was focused — wanting everything to be as perfect as possible. I stuffed the rainbow trout with fresh lemons and rosemary from our garden. I poured a little olive oil over the fish and sprinkled dill and a dash of salt and pepper. I wrapped them in tin foil, ready to cook on the BBQ. An organic salad — lettuce, tomatoes, green and red peppers — was served up with homemade honey mustard vinaigrette. Roasted potatoes and carrots were added as side dishes. Although the burgers were plain and hard to get wrong, the added menu item requiring their own cooking time had me scrambling. There were many moving parts in our hot kitchen, but I kept my cool...on the outside. On the inside, I was freaking out.

What if I overcook the vegetables? What if I undercook the trout? I'm not a chef... I don't even like cooking... What am I doing? Who the hell do I think I am thinking I can get away with this?

After Kevin was done with the tour, our guests settled into the casita and waited for me to deliver their dinner. As a business model, we decided that we would not have our B&B guests dine with us in the main house but rather let them enjoy a home-cooked meal in the privacy of their own space, away from all the dirty pots and pans. Also, with the fact that we had to get up early to do farm chores and we loved our downtime in the evening, it seemed like the obvious choice.

And let's be real, I'm an introvert, I can't handle too many people in my space.

The casita was not far from the main house, but there were several uneven steps to navigate. Mum opened the door, and I walked out, tray in hand with wrapped platters carefully arranged like a Jenga tower. I manoeuvred with great concentration to avoid tripping and smashing the tray of food on the ground. With my hands full, I reached the door to the casita. I couldn't knock on the door to announce my arrival.

Awkward. Note to self.

I heard hushed but stern reprimands. Feet shuffling. Something clanging. A family of four in our snug casita. Our first guests.

"Knock, knock," I shouted, hoping my voice would cut through the high-pitched whines of tired, hungry kids. "Hello?"

Fiona opened the door a few seconds later. I entered, careful not to stumble over the shoes scattered on the floor and set the heavy tray down on the counter.

My face felt flushed from the relief that I had made it through the mental and physical obstacle course. I heard the muffled words, *"Bon appetit,"* and assumed they came out of my mouth. They might have thanked me; I can't be sure. That moment is a blur.

About an hour later, a little more composed, I went down to retrieve the tray of dirty dishes, and I replaced it with a wicker basket of fresh eggs, homemade bread, marmalade, blackberry jam, Roberto's churned butter, and delicious fresh-pressed apple juice. They had everything they needed to make their own breakfast — at their convenience — in the morning. As bedtime entertainment for the kids, I handed them an old DVD of the animated movie *Cars*. Their eyes opened wide with excitement. One of their favourites, I was told. I felt like I got bonus points for that little touch.

It was a good first run for us. This self-employment gig was hard work but satisfying.

A week after their three-day stay, we received an email from Fiona:

January 14, 2013
Hi Anne and Kevin,

Doug and I would like to thank you again for the stay at your lodge. This is our last night in Costa Rica, and we've been looking back on this trip, and the stay at Hush Valley Lodge was definitely one of the highlights! It was something different we wouldn't have thought to do, which made it more memorable. Your casita is so charming and sweet, definitely a very nice place to stay for someone who wants a getaway in paradise! The food and hospitality were also top-notch. With the kids, it was a bit harder for us to fully enjoy than if we were on our own, but it was still a great experience for all — the kids still talk about it!

We are very impressed with you being able to just jump in and go for it with this move! Looks like you have made a great decision. I will recommend your lodge to anyone I know coming to Costa Rica. We are leaving tomorrow to go back to the cold and chaos. We wish you all the best with your business, keep enjoying the Pura Vida, and I'm sure we'll meet again.

Fiona, Doug, and the boys

I was overwhelmed with the positive feedback and felt encouraged. Shortly after, we signed up as hosts on a popular travel website and it didn't take long for our calendar to fill up with bookings and our guestbook with more kind and positive reviews.

Kevin, imbued with an entrepreneurial spirit, had built his own business from scratch in England and had succeeded. He wasn't fazed by any of this. With my employee mindset, the decision to pack up and step away from the security of a regular paycheque forced me to become a businesswoman by default.

No small step, I assure you.

I'm So Glad We Had This Time Together

I had spent more uninterrupted time with my mother than I had in the previous two decades...possibly three. Besides our daily walks, she tagged along with me when I did my errands in Santa María and San Marcos. And I made sure I introduced her to our new neighbours and friends along the way.

While Kevin stayed behind looking after things on the farm, Mum and I bussed over to the Caribbean side for a few days and strolled the beach village of Puerto Viejo. I wanted to give her a different perspective from our views and climate. She loved it. All of it. But mostly, we stayed close to home.

After dinner, she would video chat with Dad and debrief him on her day. She would talk to him about what new person she had met, what new animal she had seen, what new flower she had smelled... She would describe everything with a childlike sense of wonder. Uncensored. Free. But, inevitably, when she droned on too long about the same views and the same flowers or repeated stories that were too darn similar to what she had told him the day before, I would hear Dad get impatient with her.

"You've told me this already," he'd say with some irritation in his voice.

Typical.

Before I knew it, a month had flown by. It was time to drive Mum to the airport where she would repeat her flights and layovers in reverse, with Dad waiting on the other end. He would no doubt be happy to see her, but I suspect even happier to finally have home-cooked meals again.

We encountered little traffic, and the roads were clear for the first hour. We hit a cloudy patch, but we got to the airport with time to spare.

Kevin parked. He and I walked Mum into the terminal to guide her through the process of paying the exit tariff, filling out the customs form, obtaining her boarding pass, and getting her luggage checked. I wanted to see her get through security without any hiccups before we left the building.

As we said goodbye, I wrapped my arms around my thin, fit mother. She leaned in with arms outstretched and pressed her palms against my back, holding me close. Lingering longer than usual, she squeezed a little tighter. It was the hug I had yearned for since I was a child.

When Mum pulled away, she thanked me. They were not hollow words, but ones of real appreciation. There was a soulful resonance in my mother's voice, and I noticed her eyes were glassy as though she was holding back tears. It took forty-eight years to harden my heart and an instant to melt the resentment away.

I couldn't have been more grateful for the time we spent together and for Mum's willingness to shed some light on the shadowy crevices of her and Dad's childhoods and my upbringing. Although digging, drilling, and blasting to clear the toxic fumes was risky, it was worth it.

This canary not only survived a month in the mired mines — she came out a little more whole.

Finding Our Stride

Over the following weeks, the stress levels diminished; Kevin and I both had a better grasp of what we were doing...what worked for us...what didn't...and where we drew the line.

For one, we had given up on the fishing rods we bought in Canada and instead had replicated Martín's basic blocks of wood with fishing line wrapped securely around them and fish food paste as bait placed on a hook. Nothing fancy. No reel, no handle to crank, no feathery lures to tangle with. Fishing rods, as it turned out, were more trouble than they were worth when you handed them to people who didn't have a clue how to use them; they were causing frustration and taking quite a beating.

The rods were, not the people.

As for my housekeeping duties, I had a better understanding of how long I needed to allot to each step. I made sure I had enough time between our guests' departures and arrivals, so the turnover didn't cause me stress. I didn't move there to run myself ragged. Between teaching twice a week and having to create individual lessons, and doing my farm chores and raising trout, time was like a fugitive running from the law. It was fleeting. As much as we needed income to survive, I vowed that I wouldn't let this adventure turn into drudgery. Freedom had little to do with money. It was about slowing down and being present. Giving myself the permission to say *no* when I didn't feel compelled to deplete my energy was the epitome of freedom.

I was gaining more confidence in my cooking skills, in general. Speaking of which, I changed the way I served meals. At first, I was thinking how a restaurateur might think...cook individual meals based on unique preferences. Oh boy, it became painfully obvious our kitchen wasn't equipped to accommodate this kind of offering. This is what I had to work with:

1. One small toaster oven, where anything and everything that needed baking went into;
2. one crock pot/slow cooker;
3. one propane hob with only two burners (think camping stove);
4. one Vitamix blender;
5. one BBQ, which I never touched — that was Kevin's domain, and we didn't use it all that much;
6. and a fridge that only a mother could love.

That was it — we didn't even have a microwave. It was an exercise in preparation, organization, and perfect timing to achieve the best taste, temperature, and great service. The only way to succeed was to scale back.

My project management skills came in handy. I created a simple menu and didn't deviate from it. Once guests had booked their dates for their stay, I would reach out to them and share our menu selection. I asked them to decide what they wanted to order and to let me know before they arrived. To manage expectations, I explained that I prepared one meal that we all would eat (like you would at home). Kevin and I would eat whatever they chose. This allowed me to stock the fridge with what I needed. I made everything from scratch — nothing was ever cooked from frozen.

I still delivered the meals to our guests in the casita though, but I stopped collecting their dishes. They could either wash those themselves or bring them up in the morning for me to wash. And I had the breakfast basket neatly placed on the counter when they arrived, and they could do as they pleased with the contents. This way I didn't have the extra burden of bringing it down after dinner. I knew when the rainy season arrived, I would want to make as few back-and-forth trips as possible.

We also decided that having young children running around on the property was too nerve-wracking. Although we made it clear that adult supervision was one hundred percent mandatory (we were not babysitters), it was hard to enforce this rule without sounding like a curmudgeon or a nag. It was not until young children visited that we realized that what made this place so spectacular was also what made it dangerous: steep hills, narrow trails with sudden drop-offs, rickety bridges, slippery rocks, and all the water features — rivers, ponds, and waterfalls. The local children were used to the environment; however, we didn't want to risk injuries with our B&B guests. Also, our paradise setting promised serenity and relaxation, which was nearly impossible to achieve when young children were vying for their parents' attention. If our guests were looking for an amusement park, Hush Valley Lodge wasn't it. Marketing works best when you understand your audience. So our new rule was *no kids under twelve*.

We tweaked as we learned, always looking for ways to improve our routine and service. We found our stride by trial and error.

Trailblazing

While we were busy hosting our guests — staying close to the house in case they needed anything — Martín was clearing one of the old trails above our pasture. We owned 37 acres and the manicured portion with the ponds took up less than 10 of those acres. There were approximately 12 acres of pastureland and another 15 of dense secondary forest. The manicured portion, where the house and ponds were, was tucked at the base of the valley's bowl. The river separated our property from our neighbour's property. A dense forest with a steep cliff was our view of that side. No one overlooked us. It might as well have been considered our property. The other side of our property sloped steadily, reaching plateaus, then more steep banks. We had done a peripheral exploration by foot, but to reach the very top, we had always taken the four-wheeler up the dirt road. We didn't realize there were trails up there until Martín told us about them. Since Rick and Mona didn't take advantage of hiking the property, I suppose keeping the trails well-maintained wasn't a priority for them. After fifteen years of growth, the trails became impassable.

Martín chopped the overgrowth by hand using a machete, every day for two weeks. *My back hurts just thinking about it.*

What a fabulous trail. It was wide enough to ride up on the four-wheeler, which would allow us to lug building materials up and down more easily. The clearing revealed obvious lookout points, too, which was a nice surprise. Eventually, we could add benches so people who hiked up could rest, appreciate the expansive view of mountains and valleys beyond our property, and listen to the sweet sounds of chirping birds.

When I say "people" could rest, I mean me. When Mum was here and we would walk up and down the gravel roads, I felt like I was kicking ass. But I guess Mum was setting the pace, and keeping up with her was not such a big deal. But boy, Martín's pace is a different story. He walks up without even the slightest bend in his spine. It doesn't matter how vertical the slope is. In stark comparison, I'm hunched over holding my waist, and my knees are about to buckle under my shaky frame.

Martín knew this mountain well; he was a great guide.

"*Mira...danta,*" he said, showing us a three-toe indent that belonged to a tapir, also known as *danta* in these parts.

Huge in stature — adult males can reach up to 2.5 m (8 ft) — these creatures are shy, herbivorous mammals that keep to themselves deep in the forest or hard-to-reach swamps. They don't pose much danger to humans unless you find yourself between them and their offspring. In that scenario, yes, they might charge at you. But although dantas can storm squarely with gusto, their large cumbersome hippopotamus-shaped bodies make it hard for them to be nimble. Lucky for us, swerving on a dime doesn't work for them. Just take a few steps to the right or left and get out of their way.

Dantas have broad-hooved toes with four toes on their front feet. Their hind feet only have three, which create an outline that looks a lot like Mickey Mouse's head wearing a birthday hat. The middle toe tip extends longer than the other two on either side.

When no one was looking, I drew in two wide eyes and a goofy smile in the muddy footprint with my walking stick.

Just adding a little magic to my hike. I think Mickey would approve.

According to Martín, wild mountain goats and boars were living on our property, too. I wouldn't have believed it except that there was a raw, farm-like stench that would sometimes whiff towards my unsuspecting nostrils.

As we were meandering, our guard down, Martín sniffed the air and spotted something ahead. He took a few deliberate steps forward, then crouched. Kevin and I froze in place, waiting for Martín to unravel the mystery. He looked over his shoulder and signalled for us to come closer with a swift head tilt. Intrigued, we followed his silent command and tiptoed closer. As we hunched over him and peered down, he pointed to sheeny long, dark-brown segments of excrement curved into a large mound. I wrinkled my nose at the pungent smell.

"De que animal?" I asked.

"De puma."

Fresh puma poop! On our property! Martín's eyes nearly popped out of their sockets while he grinned mischievously. I wasn't sure whether to be concerned or to shrug it off.

We knew pumas lurked in the shadows. One attacked and disembowelled Martín's small dog in the fall. At night, we were mindful to secure our Bettys in their coop and keep Frankie in the house but never worried too much about predatory creatures during the day. Pumas are nocturnal cats. The freshness of the scat and it being only mid-afternoon felt alarming to me. Martín assured us that it was *no problema* and gestured that if we made noise, the puma would leave the area.

The rest of the hike remained calm and uneventful; however, I couldn't help but be a little paranoid that a large wild feline, hidden in the foliage high above our heads, was ready to pounce on us. As if I had developed a bad twitch, my eyes darted up every couple of seconds.

On the way down the mountain, Martín took us on what I inferred was a shortcut — a different trail he hadn't cleared yet. Martín told us he would get to it next. More nooks and crannies to discover.

I was eternally grateful for my walking stick at this point. I was no longer taking it for granted as a superfluous tool to draw silly pictures in the muck. In some places, the slope was perpendicular to the pasture below. With uneven terrain amid thick brush and prickly blackberry brambles, each step felt perilous, but my sturdy stick kept me steady.

We'd been gone barely an hour, but I was exhausted; completely and utterly shattered. While Kevin and Martín talked about other possible trails that could be created, I lumbered to the terrace and sat in one of our Adirondack chairs to catch my breath for a minute and…

ZzzzZzzzZzzz.

The Fork Incident

After working all morning cleaning the living room skylight, Kevin and I took a break. It was a beautiful February day with a lovely breeze, so we decided to eat our lunch on the edge of the pond and soak up some sun.

The French doors opened onto the large terracotta-tiled terrace, which ended with a knee-high terracotta-tiled wall capped with a concrete surface wide enough to sit on. This short wall served as a barrier between the terrace area and the large pond, so no one fell in, especially at night in the dark. While we were sitting there, Frankie wanted to join us on the ledge, so she jumped up and snuggled between us.

As we ate, I noticed Frankie's bum was hanging precariously over the edge and I worried she would fall into the pond, so I nudged her over with my elbow. This tiny manoeuvre had my fork flying off my plate and into the 1.5 m- (5 ft-) deep pond. I saved Frankie but lost my fork in the process.

Kevin — always up for a challenge — wanted to retrieve it. He went back and forth from the garage to the old shed to the carport looking for the right farm tool. He tried scooping it out with a hoe, then with two different types of rakes. Nothing worked. Not one to take defeat sitting down, he decided the only way to rescue that fork without draining the pond was to go in after it.

There's a reason we didn't swim in our ponds — the water was only 14°C (57°F) even in the sunniest, warmest month of the year!

Determined, Kevin changed into his bathing trunks. He deliberated on how to proceed and decided using his toes to grasp the fork was the best option. He inhaled to prepare himself. As he lowered himself into the frigid water, his face contorted. He shuffled closer to where the fork landed and wiggled his toes as they grappled for the stainless-steel utensil. Some fish came to investigate but quickly dashed away. Kevin stretched over to one side, then over to the other, reaching out further. No luck. I could see his frustration mounting. Next thing I knew, he was diving in headfirst, attempting to glimpse anything shiny in the sediment below. He resurfaced, teeth chattering.

Nope, nada.

"How cold is the water, Kevin?" I shouted, trying not to laugh.

"IT'S FORKING FREEZING!"

After about fifteen minutes of being in the cold water, Kevin's lily-white English skin was turning blue. He told me his hands and toes felt completely numb. And to add insult to injury, Kevin's many attempts had stirred up the silt, making it impossible to see anything at all. As he pulled himself out of the pond and dried off, he begrudgingly stopped the search.

Later, once the sediment settled, the glistening fork prongs appeared. They seemed to be arrogantly waving at Kevin, as if to taunt him further.

Kevin's competitive spirit showed, and I *knew* he was not about to let a simple fork and cold water conspire to beat him. His pride wouldn't let them. The sun was setting, so the second round of this match would have to wait until the next day.

No Forkin' Way

Kevin didn't sleep a wink; he was busy problem-solving. I could almost hear the gears turning as he lay beside me in bed. Inspiration struck early in the morning and as soon as he finished his chores, he was off to hack a bamboo branch.

By rummaging in the garage, Kevin found a thin piece of metal wire and formed a loop. Then, with duct tape, he attached it to the end of the long bamboo branch. He tested it on one of our other forks to make sure the loop was big enough to slide around the handle, but not so big that the prong portion would slip through. Once Kevin made a few minor adjustments, he was ready to scoop out the rogue fork from the pond.

Kevin took his handy-dandy gadget, submerged it, and tried to gently glide the loop around the handle. All this was done with unshakable concentration. Slowly… *ever so slowly,* on the third attempt, he managed to hook it, and he carefully pulled it up.

Ta-da!

Kevin was victorious. There was no *forkin'* way he was going to lose this challenge… of that, you could be sure!

Now for the Weather Report

Kevin had bought a digital weather gadget in Canada that measured the temperatures inside the house and outside, humidity in the air, wind speed, wind chill, and rainfall. After six months of overseeing more important tasks, he finally got around to unpacking the box and installing it.

I don't consider myself a gadget kind of gal, and I'm pretty sure my initial reaction was, "What do we need that for?" but it turns out it was pretty useful. The idea was that we would document and compare the temperature throughout the year, from year to year. Not only would this help us get an accurate reading of what each year was like for our own sake, but it would help our guests determine if our climate was right for them. I planned on updating our website with a chart at the end of every month.

Many people stay away from southern destinations because they feel they'll be roasting on a beach, and sweating their buns off is not for them. Due to all the microclimates, you can, in fact, enjoy this beautiful country and stay away from the sweltering heat if you choose your destination wisely.

After our February visit the prior year, I added Santa María to my cell phone weather app and I would check it every day. It consistently said *rain and thunderstorms*, which was completely inaccurate, especially during the summer months. Thank goodness I knew better because I'd have never considered visiting let alone living in such a wet location all year round. My reporting of the weather from our property would be accurate.

I checked the weather gadget daily and kept a daily log. This data represents one day, but within a degree or two, this was what every day in February looked like:

7:00 a.m.: 10°C (50°F), Feels like: 10°C (50°F), Blue skies
1:00 p.m.: 28°C (82°F), Feels like: 28°C (82°F), Blue skies

These temperatures were not hard to take. This time of year in Canada, I was usually suffering from Seasonal Affective Disorder, but there were no signs of any symptoms whatsoever.

Changing my circumstances and living according to my personal needs seemed to have been the right medicine.

Cool Nights

February brought clear blue skies during the day as well as a starry firmament at night. While the hot sun offered us a perfect summer's day, the temperature dipped considerably at night without any cloud cover. It was not unusual to wake up to 10°C (50°F), but lately it had been dropping to 5°C (41°F). We noticed a thin layer of frost on the grass replacing the early morning dew.

Brrr.

Tearing ourselves away from the warmth of our cozy duvet and facing the bone-chilling air was a challenge. One could argue that staying in bed until eight was the better choice. However, there's no such thing as sleeping in when you're a farmer.

At 5:30 a.m., Kevin layered up with a heavy fleece, toque, and gloves — you'd think we were back in the Great White North. As the dawn was on the cusp of breaking, he checked on the river, the pond gates, the fences, the pasture, and determined if any trees might need felling. He assessed what needed doing and made a priority list for Matín, then he fed the fish.

Meanwhile, seeing the vapour from my breath linger in the air, I postponed slinking out of bed a good half hour after Kevin braved the chilly elements. It wasn't much warmer but at least the pinky purple sky held the promise that the sun would soon peek over the tall trees. I got dressed as quickly as possible. I put the kettle on and started the fire in our massive fireplace. While I caught up on emails and organized my day, I wrapped my hands around a hot mug and sipped my tea in front of the glowing hearth. The irony was that the temperature would rise to a fabulous 25°C (77°F) by 9:00 a.m. Every day was the same: shivering at dawn only to strip down to our T-shirts three hours later.

Experiencing winter and summer conditions in a three-hour window typifies how it went down in the remote mountains of Costa Rica. Well, this is how it went in our particular microclimate on our particular mountain. If you travelled higher up or further down, it would be a different story. Someone else's story.

Thirty
Hair-Raising Adventures

April Showers Come Early

We arrived in Costa Rica during the rainy season, so we quickly got used to wet afternoons with lush green landscapes on all sides. Late November became drier, but it was often still cloudy. By December, the winds shifted and moved all the dark clouds away and it rarely rained.

Just as I drove our early-March guests back to the bus stop in Santa María, it started to spit. I was happy with the prospects of some precipitation but didn't hold out much hope for any significant amount of rain.

Boy, was I wrong. The clouds got thicker and darker, and it rained all day. I could almost hear the dehydrated earth gulp every drop to quench its thirst.

I loved the sunshine, no question, but rain served its purpose, and it was just as important for the health of our farm. By March, the grass was a brassy yellow colour, and the soil cracked from lack of moisture even though I watered the flowerbeds regularly.

It rained all through the night, which bode well for the water table and river flow. We had a lightning show to boot.

The rainy season doesn't officially start until late April, and when it does, it's a slow ramp-up from month to month until it comes down at its worst in October. We had yet to experience a full year, so for now, everything was still considered *firsts*. Neighbours told us things, but stories seemed to differ. Some people were prone to exaggerate, others to downplay. We just had to be patient and experience it for ourselves.

By October, we would be praying for the rain to stop. But on this March day, we were relieved and grateful for the early shower.

Praise

We left Canada on a wing and a prayer seven months earlier. We followed our tug and did as much homework as we could to prepare — but really, how could we have predicted how it would all turn out? We dug deep and hoped for the best. If it all went sideways, at least we could say we tried.

I'm an introvert, so I wasn't sure how I would deal with different personalities landing on our doorstep, how I would manage complaints, or if I would have the energy to interact with strangers. We had never done this B&B thing before. I think the upfront correspondence helped our guests and me understand what to expect. I was better prepared to receive the ones I profiled as needier. And they probably felt more comfortable knowing what they could expect from a remote mountain experience compared to one in a beach village.

Most of our guests were lovely. I don't have any horror stories to share, but we did bond with some guests more than others. Some people leave an imprint. Ingrid and Allan were one of those couples.

Since these were still early days of being hosts, you can imagine how affirming it was to read their feedback in our guestbook:

March 9, 2013
Dear Anne and Kevin,

For us, the magic of our stay with you already began when the taxi deposited us outside the church in Copey. Already smitten with the quiet, secluded, but pretty nature of the village, there was Anne to take us to Hush Valley Lodge. The drive, which was great, did not prepare us for the beauty of your driveway, up and over the hill, around the curve to the vista that was going to be our home for three days. Or so we thought. So taken were we with everything about Hush Valley Lodge, we stayed five days.

What did we do here? Well, we discovered the casita offers the best napping environment we have ever enjoyed. It is a very cheerful cabin. We can hear the river right beside us, just the right amount. There is just the right amount of light coming in and dancing around.

We also had the best showers ever; perched outdoors right beside the river, a little shower turret on our little casita castle.

As readers, we were very happy with the comfortable furniture inside and out and the good lighting. And it wasn't just comfortable: it was all so damn attractive.

Hush Valley Lodge is great for lazy people who just want to move their chairs around the property during the day to enjoy different views. But for those of us who like a little activity, it is great, too. Thank you for having a place where we could put on our hiking boots and go for good walks. As you know, I went way up a couple of times on your trails and further up on the road, which was itself picturesque. The vistas were awesome, the walks down a great reward.

Usually after some sort of exhausting activity, we would make coffee. Well, of course, it's great coffee and for those of us who are kinda needy about having our good cup of coffee every day, it was really something, which we looked forward to.

It was also very nice during our lazy evenings to have access to a TV with all its channels.

Thank you so much Anne for your delicious meals and your bread! OMG! We really appreciated that we had the option to feed ourselves or be fed. That really worked for us. And thank you for being EVER READY with the wine... you clued in right away we were those kinds of people. And thank your Bettys for those eggs. Man, we forgot how lovely fresh eggs are. And Kevin, thank you for sharing your interest and passion with us. We learned a lot from you and are so impressed with what you have accomplished with this property. It is an amazing piece of property; thank goodness it's got someone like you and Anne to take care of it. Here's a place for people to recoup, fix themselves, for lovers, for artists, and for people like Allan and me. We are very lucky we found you. Thank you so much for your wonderful hospitality.

Ingrid and Allan
Ontario, Canada

The Great Wall

Our house sat firmly on a huge rock high above the riverbed, but the constant flowing water eroded the riverbank, which was a concern, especially during the rainy season. We had experienced the wildness of the river and when it slammed the side of the bank, it took chunks of dirt away. So, Kevin decided to build a retaining wall to prevent any further damage the torrent might create.

The river was at its lowest and had receded from the edge of the bank, leaving part of the bedrock exposed. For a week, Kevin spent a few hours a day collecting dusty rocks from the sun-drenched border. But the bigger and heavier rocks that he needed were submerged in the middle of the river. It was strenuous work and wading through knee-high water slowed him down further.

"Take a break, hon," I implored when I saw the strain on his red face.

"I can't. I'm determined to get the wall done before the rain comes next month," he said without stopping.

But at this rate, not for lack of trying, I just couldn't see how he would meet the weather-imposed deadline. After dinner, when he had a chance to relax, he would stretch and complain that his neck, shoulders, and back ached. Although he was not building the Great Wall of China, doing it all on his own, it might as well have been. On the seventh day of this dogged boot camp challenge, Kevin relented and rested.

On the eighth day? Kevin hired Martín and Mateo — another neighbour — to help. *Hallelujah!*

Standing in the river, Kevin pulled out one bulging rock at a time and heaved it onto the dry bank where he had piled the other rocks from the week before. From there, Mateo carried them closer to the huge boulder under the house. Then, like a jigsaw puzzle, Martín stacked the rough, irregular shapes and trowelled wet cement mix between the gaps. I swear, some of these rocks weighed more than a baby hippo; they were massive and cumbersome. Mateo was skinny and looked like the slightest gust of wind could blow him over but looks can be deceiving...he was as strong as an ox. We'd never seen anything like it. Don't get me wrong, Kevin and Martín were both strong and certainly held their own, but Mateo sometimes lugged two of these baby hippos under his scrawny arms. There was no huffing or puffing, no grunting or squawking. Like a machine, there was no stopping him. Kevin and Martín could barely keep up. Competitive by nature and not wanting to lose face, Kevin pushed himself to stay on pace.

These guys were on fire! A few days later, the retaining structure spanned the width of a fire truck and reached the height of its extended ladder.

What a Great Wall.

We definitely felt safer knowing the foundation wouldn't collapse under the steady pressure of the flowing river. Kevin's muscles, on the other hand, were so sore, he collapsed on the couch and didn't move for three days.

Dying to Be Healthy

After seven months, we continued to discover new and amazing things on our farm. We investigated the possibilities of growing blueberries since they are so healthy and our climate would, in theory, be perfect. When growing berries in a hospitable environment, they are easy to maintain. Martín had pointed out trees with beautiful blue-coloured berries and had told us they were edible. At first glance they looked like blueberries, but smaller. Kevin and I popped a berry in our mouth for a taste.

Delicious!

"My throat is a bit itchy," Kevin cleared his throat.

"Mine, too," I noticed a weird tingly sensation.

But because they were so tasty, we ignored the mild irritation and munched on a few more. The tingle developed into a full-blown sandpaper scratch, making it hard to swallow. Our tongues were feeling swollen and pasty, too.

After a bit of internet research, Kevin learned that these were not blueberries, but rather *elderberries*.

"Elderberries have many medicinal benefits.... They are full of antioxidants... They lower bad cholesterol, improve vision, boost the immune system, improve heart health, and fight against coughs, colds, and flu, as well as bacterial and viral infections," Kevin read the list out loud.

It's the miracle berry, apparently.

There's a whole lot of good in this tiny, purply blue berry, but another tidbit of information Kevin discovered is that these berries must be cooked before they are eaten.

"Raw elderberries contain a chemical similar to cyanide, which can cause an itchy sensation. If eaten in large quantities, one could get sick, even die," Kevin looked up from his laptop with an "uh-oh" expression.

Not sure whether to panic or not, we decided we'd wait until morning to see if we were feeling worse. That was a calculated risk but neither of us felt we had eaten enough to harm us. We hoped. If we were dead in the morning, we would have been wrong. As it turns out, the small amount of poisonous berries we consumed didn't kill us after all... *Phew*. Phoenix and Jude were coming to visit soon and death would have caused a grave inconvenience.

The Dog Came Back the Very Next Day

In pitch darkness, I walked down to the hatchery beyond the chicken coop to dump our food waste in our large compost container. I could have waited until the morning, but I was now used to extending some of my outdoor chores beyond daytime hours. Kevin did his rounds every night, raking the leaves off the aqueduct grate, and checking to make sure the river flow reached the ponds. Living in the forest where wild things lived was becoming second nature and our guard was down. The light emanating through the windows of our home served as a beacon of safety. At least, in my mind. Over time, when nothing bad happens, it's human nature to get complacent and forget what dangers lurk in the shadows. And I think this is a good thing. Who wants to be on high alert every minute of the day?

How exhausting.

I was wearing headgear with a miner's light shining from my forehead, keeping my hands free to carry my bins and to open the compost lid. As I turned around to walk back, I saw a pair of amber eyes glaring back at me. After my heart had jumped into my throat and had settled back down — ever so slightly — I steadied myself and shone the light back onto the owner of the glowing eyes. The animal bolted towards me and jumped up. It was Feliz.

I think I just peed myself.

I was resolute with the decision of not having any more dogs... Well, pets in general. I loved our Frankie, but dogs are like children, except they never grow up. They always need you, which creates some limitations regarding the freedom to travel as and when we want. Of course, they provide many unexpected lessons, too. In my case, having dogs helped me relax; my house simply couldn't be as spick-and-span clean as I tended to want it.

Frankie had short hair, so she was pretty easy to groom, but there was still hair on our couch. If we didn't dry her right away after she'd been out in the rain, muddy paw prints across the floor were inevitable. I'd learned to be *somewhat* good with it. Pets also provide unconditional companionship and love. They are masters at tugging at my heartstrings. I never thought I'd fall for it.

Such a sucker.

In Costa Rica, there were many stray dogs. They were friendly — the majority seemed healthy and happy. They roamed...that's what they did. People fed them and gave them a stroke of affection now and then. And sometimes scraps of food. It seemed like a good life for them.

Feliz was a small brown and black mixed breed. He had the gentlest eyes and demeanour. He was just one of those really happy-go-lucky kinds of dogs (*Feliz* means "happy").

There was a woman in Copey who took in stray dogs, had them fixed, and tried to educate the folks on how to properly take care of their pets. It was a hard, long road as the concept was so foreign in this culture. Feliz's owner, who lived in La Trinidad 5 km (3 mi) from Río Blanco, didn't seem bothered one way or another whether his dog stayed or strayed.

Feliz had been hanging around Martín's place a lot since we'd moved there. In fact, in the early days we thought he belonged to Martín. He followed Martín onto our property most mornings and kept him company while he worked.

During the past couple of weeks our little friend took up residence under our covered porch, just outside our French doors. We weren't sure why this was his new habit, but he was no bother and too sweet to shoo away.

Feliz was such a calm, appreciative creature. He rarely barked. He never whined or scratched at the door. Even when our French doors were wide open, he never crossed the threshold. Although he was a free agent, we fed him, brushed him, and applied flea and tick solution on his neck to help kill the nasty critters. Although we wouldn't allow him in the house, he was welcome to hang out for as long as it suited him. We didn't want to get too attached as he wasn't ours and at any given moment, he may choose to move on. For me, it was the perfect relationship. I got to love Feliz freely without feeling obligated to him. The give-and-take seemed pure.

Frankie and Feliz got along; she sometimes got aggressive and territorial with other dogs, but she never displayed any of those tendencies with him. So, for as long as Feliz was with us, we were happy to consider him part of the family.

Suckered in again.

Thirty-One
A Week with the Kids

It had been four months since I had last seen Phoenix and Jude in the flesh. Sure, we video chatted, but that wasn't the same.

I had bought their plane tickets a few weeks after I had visited them back in November, knowing we all needed something to look forward to. March Break seemed like the perfect time for Jude to come down without missing any school and Phoenix had told me she was able to book time off work and join him.

By this time — whether for residency type appointments, bulk shopping, visiting Sister Gladys, or picking up and dropping off friends and family at the airport — Kevin and I had driven to San José and back again several times. Although we didn't drive into the city that often, it was often enough that the journey had now become almost second nature.

There was a time when I thought I'd never attempt driving in the city on my own. Unruly motorcyclists weaving in and out traffic and oblivious drivers crossing over unmarked lanes without signalling or checking their rearview mirrors was enough to convince me to stay squarely planted in the passenger seat, preferably with my eyes closed. But with a little help from our GPS, I grew more confident with the idea and decided I would pick up the kids from the airport on my own while Kevin stayed home.

I must have been a bit dazed from the anticipation of seeing Phoenix and Jude because I don't remember any of it. I wish I could give you a good story about how brave I was, but to be honest, it's all a blur. I drove through the grimy city where the streets have no names without any road rage coming at me. I don't remember feeling any anxiety. I know I didn't get lost because I made it to the airport without incident. I remember chatting up a storm with Phoenix and Jude on the way back. They were excited to finally be on holiday.

There is a six-year spread between Phoenix and Jude, so they rarely hung out together. They had different personalities with different aptitudes. They didn't mind each other's company, but I always got the feeling they forgot they each had a sibling. They lived ten minutes away from one another in Burlington yet made no effort to see each other or even call. When Jude had dropped the bomb that he wouldn't be moving to Costa Rica, I felt comforted knowing he and Phoenix would be living nearby. I just assumed they would seek each other out to commiserate over their shared experience of having a mother who moved out of the country, leaving them both behind.

That was not the case. Just like the role my own mother played, I became the hub. I video chatted with Phoenix and told her what Jude was up to. I video chatted with Jude and updated him on Phoenix's life.

"Oh, that's cool," was often their reply. I detected no animosity or bitterness, but they never seemed to get past the aloof stage either.

Where did I go wrong?

I do remember hoping — as we were listening to one-hit wonders from the 80s on the radio and boogied in our seats — this trip would bring them closer...create a deeper bond.

Knowing Kevin wouldn't want them encroaching on his space in the main house, I set them up in the casita. I had made the entire week unavailable for B&B guests to book. Keeping Kevin away from them was an equally important goal. I wanted Phoenix and Jude to have a nice, relaxing time, which would have been impossible with all of us crammed under the same roof. This was not rocket science. I knew their dynamic.

Spending a week together in the casita, just the two of them, might be good for them. They can stay up and sleep in as late as they want and not be disturbed by our early morning routine.

There were card games, books, and a TV to keep them entertained. I stocked the fridge with drinks and snacks, giving them some autonomy from having to come up to the house every time they felt peckish.

Phoenix and Jude had both mentioned that they wanted a relaxing vacation, so I didn't make any touristy plans. They said they were happy to explore the property and follow me on my errands. The three of us either hung out together or I'd spend time with each of them one-on-one. Every day was slow and full of doing nothing in particular.

Although I desperately tried to stay present and enjoy the dreamlike quality of our meandering days, I felt each minute trickle like sand in an hourglass.

Where's the pause button?

Making Moments Matter

Although I didn't go out of my way to plan special excursions, I was afraid that the first four days of blissfully slothing around the casita and roaming our finite trails were creeping into boredom territory.

When I was delivering eggs to Adriana, she mentioned there was a rock-climbing festival in Providencia.

"The festival happens every year. Many people from the world came...no, um, *come...* to climb the big rocks," Adriana corrected her grammar mid-sentence. Her English was improving and I secretly felt proud of her progress. Attending the adult classes in Copey seemed to be helping.

The last time I was in Providencia, it was deserted. Kevin and I did not find the couple we were looking for who owned an adventure park, and we got caught in a downpour while riding the four-wheeler on the way back home. That swampy butt experience seemed like eons ago.

Since both Phoenix and Jude loved rock climbing and bouldering — the one thing they *did* have in common — I figured it would be fun to go to Providencia and feel its vibrant energy. We're the kind of family who loves road trips, and I knew this one promised inspiring views, too.

As much as I was tempted to hoard every single moment with the kids to myself, I thought it would be nice for Phoenix and Jude to have someone closer to their age to chat with, so I invited Nacho to come along.

"I haven't been there in more than four years. I would love to go with you guys. I'm not working tomorrow so it's perfect," Nacho sounded genuinely happy to tag along. I did not detect any hesitation or a sense of obligation in his voice.

"Great! We'll pick you up at ten in front of the restaurant," I said, then placed the receiver back in the landline's cradle.

The next day, I packed my black knapsack with a few cold drinks, some snacks, and beach towels. Nacho was sitting on a well-worn bench, leaning against the shuttered wooden building. He knew by now that I did not run on Tico time...ten o'clock meant ten o'clock. And I appreciated that he didn't make me wait.

As we gave Nacho an acknowledging smile, Phoenix got out from the front passenger side and flicked the lever to slide the front seat forward. Nacho ducked as he squeezed himself into the small opening and climbed in the back with Jude. Nacho was used to this inconvenience from when I picked him, Paola, and Adriana up to go down to Copey for English class. He didn't seem to mind. Our SUV was far more comfortable than Martín's Land Cruiser. Good suspension and padded seats made all the difference. *But seriously, who thinks an SUV without rear passenger doors is a good idea?*

Phoenix and Jude had already met Nacho earlier in the week so there was no stiff small talk or awkward silence. It didn't take long for our chatter to mingle with the music coming from the stereo. I noticed that many of the potholes had been filled, and the gravel had been spread more evenly since Kevin and I had driven up this way, which made for an even smoother ride.

It was the dry season and the chance of rain spoiling our day was almost nonexistent. The panorama was as spectacular as ever. The *oohs* and *ahhs* ringing in surround sound was a dead giveaway.

It never gets old. Even for Nacho who's lived here his whole life.

During the hour-and-a-half trip, I stopped a few times along the way so Phoenix could capture the stunning landscape with her Canon.

When we rolled into town, there was no sign of any festival. No banners. No cars parked on the side of the road or in a field as one would expect at a large festival. No kiosks or food trucks or pop-up markets. No hubbub at all. It was the same ghost town as before. There was zero evidence anything was happening that weekend. Maybe we'd arrived too early. Or too late. We weren't sure what to make of it.

"If you keep going straight, we'll get to a place where there are big rocks. Maybe that's where the climbers are?" Nacho leaned forward between the two front seats and pointed beyond the tree line.

Trying to stay positive and salvage whatever we could of our shattered expectations, Phoenix, Jude, and I agreed to check it out. From where we were sitting though — as if we had reached the end of the world — the road ahead seemed to drop off suddenly. But trusting Nacho, I put the SUV in first gear and drove. It wasn't until we were closer to the edge that I realized the road swerved around the mountainside. I zigzagged down the switchbacks.

The bottom of the valley was as devoid of activity as it had been up top. Tall trees and scraggly bushes fringed the dirt road. The thick foliage seemed impenetrable.

"Park here," Nacho instructed.

The small patch of crushed weeds was large enough to park the SUV without being in the way of passing cars but also so inconsequential that I would have missed it entirely if Nacho hadn't flagged it.

We got out of the vehicle and stood there, looking around blankly.

"Follow me," Nacho grinned as he flung my knapsack over his shoulder and walked down a well-trodden path — obvious to the naked eye only once you knew where to look.

As we weaved through the trail, the forest cleared and revealed peppery megaliths with razor-smooth edges on some facings and jagged ones on others. They jutted 25 m

(82 ft) or so out of the ground, maybe higher. In some sections, it felt like we were trekking in a canyon's narrow gorge.

"Wow, impressive!" Phoenix pressed down on her camera's shutter button. *Click, click-click...click.*

As we peered around a corner, the hallmark reward of a long journey unveiled itself to us: a roaring waterfall sparkling in the midday sun with an aquamarine plunge pool at its base. Tucked out of sight and earshot, this enchanting oasis must have been one of Providencia's best-kept secrets. No signs, no paid parking lots, and no lineups giving us the slightest hint it was there.

Getting to live as the locals do is one of the best parts of being an expat. You get to take paths less travelled. Not only is there a sense of adventure in that but a sense of freedom from that tourist feeling, too.

Mouth gaping, we stood still for a few moments watching the white frothy torrent blast over the cliff. The splash settled quickly in the basin below where the water then rippled gently forward. Like an infinity pool, the overflow eventually cascaded over a natural dam and created mini rapids farther downstream. The stark contrast between the invigorating force of the chute and the soothing serenity of the small lake reinforced life's sweet equilibrium. It was the perfect spot for a picnic.

Phoenix and Nacho didn't waste any time. They kicked off their shoes and peeled off their socks and started rock-hopping over to the other side of the shimmering river.

Jude, not much of a follower, hung back and assessed the situation more analytically. Keeping his hiking boots on, he climbed onto one of the slick logs that had fallen into the water and steadied himself. Like a tightrope performer, his outstretched arms swung up and down as he took one measured step after another. Then once he reached the end, he reset his concentration and jumped onto another half-submerged limb.

Young and agile, I wasn't worried about any of them. They appeared comfortable with their surroundings and confident in their abilities.

As the three of them navigated slippery rock surfaces or mossy felled trunks under the intense sun, I relaxed on a flat, grey stone under the forest's dense canopy where leaves fluttered breezily in the shade. I took it all in.

Rather than backtracking, Nacho rolled up his pants to his knees and walked through the frigid river. The water reached halfway up Nacho's calves; it was shallower than I had imagined. Phoenix, not to be outdone by a boy, followed close behind. Their bodies wobbled. Their laughter echoed. I anticipated that one of them would lose their footing in the pebbly sand and fall in, but both managed to get to my side without getting soaked.

After Jude was done being a lumberjack, he tried to climb one of the imposing boulders. He came back looking defeated.

"It's pretty slick. It's like the rock is sweating and it's really hard to grip. I would need chalk...and my climbing shoes. A good reason to come back," he smiled at me as he wiped the moisture from his hands on his khaki shorts.

Before packing up and heading back home, we took the mandatory selfies — with the waterfall as our backdrop — imprinting this day on our hearts and souls.

We had forgotten all about the festival. We left without seeing any climbers.

Providencia never seems to give me the experience I'm looking for and yet manages to make the simplest moments matter.

Slowing Down Time

The day before Phoenix and Jude were due to fly back home, I spent that morning making blackberry jam while they hung out in the kitchen with me.

After lunch, the kids and I drove down to Santa María. Since it was Sunday, most stores were closed, but we got ourselves milkshakes at the coffee shop and sat in the park for a while. Phoenix snapped pictures of us and captured what would one day be sweet memories.

While I started dinner, Phoenix and Kevin chatted on the couch and Jude went for one last hike before it got dark.

It was a full day without being hectic. It was our last night together and I activated the imaginary slow-motion button and tried to savour every last minute we had with each other. I knew I'd miss my kids when we decided to pack up and move to Costa Rica, but never in a million years could I have imagined how much.

Thirty-Two
Life in Paradise

I received a Facebook message from Phoenix telling me they had arrived home — after a twelve-hour layover in Miami — to snow and cold temperatures. I was glad to hear that they were back in Canada safe and sound....and sad they were so far away again. Having them there for a week was like a dream, but it was time to get back to reality.

Laundry beckoned. I cleaned out the casita and got it ready for the next B&B guests. I reorganized all the cupboards in our kitchen and defrosted the freezer, too.

Kevin worked with Martín to prepare the pond next to the hatchery. Our baby rainbow trout were growing bigger and needed to be transferred from the concrete container.

Just another day in paradise.

Found and Lost

Our friendly stray dog, Feliz, had been visiting consistently for several weeks and he'd become a bit of a fixture around Hush Valley Lodge. Except, we hadn't seen him for the last four or five days. No one had seen him. Everyone thought he'd been with another neighbour. So, we were all a little worried for him. We hoped he had gone back home to his owner in La Trinidad or had found a family somewhere who was showing him some kindness.

I know better than to get attached to a stray. They roam...that's what they do.

The community prayed he wasn't injured in the forest in need of help. There are dangers in the jungle and not knowing if he was okay was the hardest. He was such a sweet guy; I missed him.

But don't tell anyone I said that.

Holy Week Traditions

Costa Rica is predominantly Catholic and Easter is celebrated for an entire week. The kids don't have school, the shops are closed for most of the week, and people spend their time visiting family. If they're strict about it, they go to church every evening and only eat fish, no red meat. However, the younger generation seemed to be straying from the flock. The people I spoke to said they believed in God or something bigger than themselves but could do without church dogma. Even so, *Semana Santa* is their most sacred holiday, even more so than Christmas, and religious or not, traditions die hard.

Martín and Clara opened their restaurant every day during Holy Week. Because they needed to prepare for the anticipated crowds, they both took the week off from working on our property. Martín had told us that what they earned in that one week equalled what they made the rest of the year.

Holy mackerel! ...Or trout in this case.

Let It Rain

Another beautiful day.

"I think it's going to rain... I can feel it in the air," Kevin boldly blurted his weather forecast as I was reading on the terrace. I looked up and saw no indication whatsoever, not a wisp of a cloud in the sky.

An hour later, we walked over to Martín and Clara's restaurant to deliver some fresh eggs as a Holy Week gift. The place was packed.

We didn't go to eat, just to socialize. I played a bean bag game with the younger kids, we talked with Nacho and Paola, then mingled with a few of our neighbours. Martín was running around in the blazing sun, paying attention to all his customers, and cleaning the fish they had caught. Clara was busy in the kitchen frying up the trout. This gorgeous day was great for business. When Martín saw us, he stopped what he was doing and came right over to say hello. Although he worked for us on our farm, he was the king of his domain and he beamed with pride.

About an hour later, we headed home. As we walked down our driveway, a light mist cooled us off. It felt divine. Then the wind picked up and dark nimbus clouds hovered overhead. The rain came within minutes. They were true and proper water droplets — none of this light *gato de pelo* stuff. And it poured for an hour. I could hear the grass, trees, and flowers say, "*Aaaaahhhhh*!" It was our second, real proper rainfall since late November, the first being a fluke in early March. The rainy season didn't officially start until late April, but we were not complaining. Let it rain!

Kevin's gut feeling was right again.

Lost and Found

Kevin and I were lounging inside after a long, hard day. It started to rain as the sun was setting. We were settling into the evening when we heard a noise outside. It sounded like something bumped into one of the Adirondack chairs.

Kevin opened the door and flashed a light.

"Feliz!"

We were thrilled to see him. He was soaking wet and hungry. We promptly brought him inside — which went against *all* the rules with strays — and fed him. It felt like a celebration. I couldn't tell you just how happy we were to see that he was no worse for wear. After we showered him with affection, we took him outside where, with a full belly, he curled up and fell asleep on the little mat under the chair. Everything was right with the world again.

Smouldering Smoke

Wasps. *Everywhere!*

When we walked up and down the path to the left of the big pond, on our way to the chicken coop, wasps buzzed around our heads and ankles. At first it was just the odd one. But over the course of a few weeks, the numbers multiplied.

Had they been bees, we might have been more accommodating; I find bees less annoying, in general. Wasps, however, are a nuisance. They were getting problematic with guests, too. It's hard to enjoy the serenity of the place when you're spending half your time swatting these relentless predators. We made sure to have fresh lemons on hand in case anyone got stung — the acidity of the lemon juice neutralizes the pain. It's a great life hack to know, but even without the inconvenience to our guests, we were getting tired of the invasion ourselves.

"Martín, do you know why there are so many *avispas* and where they might be coming from?" I wondered if Rick and Mona experienced the same problem when they lived there.

Indicating he had no idea, Martín shrugged. Then he took his machete out of its sheath and marched up the path. He stopped at the cluster of trees and started stabbing tree trunks with intentional force, but one after another, the bark resisted the jabs.

When Martín struck one of the bigger trees through a gnarly knot, the hollow centre swallowed the silver blade all the way to the black handle like you'd see at a magic show.

Where'd it go?

Kevin and I had been keeping our distance, giving Martín a wide berth, but even from where we stood, we could hear a low vibrating hum amplify to an angry rumble. The thrust disturbed whatever slumbering occupants huddled inside. When Martín wiggled and pulled out his machete blade from the sliced trunk, a swarm of wasps raged out of the thin slit. Dropping his weapon, Martín covered his head with his forearms, turned, and ran. Kevin and I ran even faster.

Mystery solved.

Martín explained that the wasps would disperse and leave their nest within a few days. Once they had moved on, he'd chop down the dead tree and cut the trunk into smaller pieces with the chainsaw. It was the perfect type of tree to make charcoal.

Over on the other side of the river, on our neighbour's property, there was a small clearing. That same neighbour tried to sell us that pie-shaped piece of land because even though we had to cross the river, we had easier access to it than he did. It was unusable to him. Nice try, but why would we pay for a sliver of land that we didn't need but also we felt confident would never be developed? We enjoyed the natural landscape without the responsibility of having to take care of it. We had enough on our plate.

Martín decided that this clearing was the perfect spot to reduce the dead tree to charcoal. It would be close to water, away from any buildings, and easy to keep an eye on it without it being in the way. We were all about safety, so we agreed it was a good plan.

Martín and Kevin lugged the chopped logs to the other side of the river. Digging two deep trenches, they then piled the logs on top of each other and covered them with earth, leaving a tunnel opening at one end. Using a bit of gasoline, Martín set the logs inside alight. The opening was then covered up. Smoke seeped through the mound, but no flames. It was a controlled underground fire and Martín, Kevin, and I monitored it regularly.

After two weeks of smouldering, Martín checked to see if the coals had cooled down. Once he was satisfied they had, he cleared the earth away and sieved the larger pieces of charcoal, then shovelled them into two or three recycled fish food bags.

Charcoal is an excellent fire starter for BBQs, smokers, and outdoor bread ovens.

I won't hold my breath on the latter.

Martín knew people who would be willing to buy charcoal from us and we were happy to make a buck or two in the process. It wasn't going to make us rich but learning how to live off our land — or the neighbour's, in this case — was just as rewarding.

We didn't set out to become charcoal suppliers — it was a byproduct of ridding ourselves of the dead tree and any surviving yellowjackets that might have been spiteful enough to rebuild their wretched factory so close to the house.

Rage of Fire

While Martín stacked the bags of charcoal under the carport, Kevin and I went into town. We were only gone a couple of hours. Upon our return, after closing the gate and driving past our tiny orchard, we noticed thick plumes of smoke billowing from our little valley.

How odd.

As we followed the long, winding driveway and got closer to the house, we saw our carport in flames and Martín frantically dowsing the fire with a watering can...*A WATERING CAN*...and our limp garden hose, which had little to no pressure. No time to process what was happening, the fire raged. Eyes wide as saucers, Martín's face was pale from panic. Adrenaline kicked in and Kevin jumped out of the SUV to help him. I ran to the back of the house and grabbed a stack of empty white large pails — the ones we used to store fish food or transfer fish from the pond to the gutting area. Since I was too stunned to think logically, my flight response kicked in; my body was carrying me, my hands clasped the handles, and my legs moved me forward. I filled the pails in the channel and the men carried and splashed the water as fast as they could. They came back with the empty pails, and I would refill them. They were doing the work of twenty men. Time vacillated between wild frenzy and slow motion.

Martín was exhausted by this time, but he kept going. And although the pails were a vast improvement, they were...*PAILS!* And not to put too fine a point on it, their efficacy paled in comparison to a firefighter's gushing hose.

After twenty long minutes of nonstop back-and-forth drenching the inferno, we were able to finally catch our breaths and assess the damage.

The back windows of the carport had shattered. The plastic skylight and the back walls were nonexistent. The woodpile was charred.

Great...more charcoal.

But the most shocking was how close the fire had gotten to the four-wheeler. Oh, and the propane tank next to the dryer. If Martín hadn't been there to prevent the fire from spreading closer, the four-wheeler — that had just been filled with gas that same morning — and propane tank would have exploded, destroying anyone near along with the entire structure. If shrapnel had landed on the house, who knows how much more serious this could have been? Not to mention what could have happened to Martín.

Wiping his sweaty brow with a sooty bandana, Martín inhaled deeply. I think that was the moment the magnitude of what had just happened hit him. His thin but strong frame suddenly appeared frail. Martín wore a dazed expression and wobbled.

"*Todo bien, Martín? Necesita hospital?*" I asked, worried he might collapse.

"*No, no. Voy a mi casa.*" Martín put his hands in a prayer position and brought them next to his left cheek and closed his eyes. He was going to go home and sleep. I hoped that would help calm his nerves.

Martín shook Kevin's hand and croaked out, "Thank you." And walked off.

The fact that Martín was fighting the blaze on his own with a measly watering can before we got there made me shudder. I felt sick to my stomach just thinking about it. Trust me, the wreckage was bad enough without adding "*what ifs*" to my swirling thoughts.

The left side of the four-wheeler looked like a scene from the movie *Aliens* — the bright yellow plastic bodywork had melted, leaving the frame completely raw and exposed. I laughed when I saw Kevin put the key in the ignition and turned it to see if it would start. I laughed even harder from sheer delirium when it did start.

How is it even possible?

Who was I to question the gifts of the gods? Although I couldn't believe my eyes, the proof was right there in front of me.

"Woohoo! It runs, which means it's just cosmetic. We'll just need to order the parts and rebuild the body."

Just?

Kevin sounded more optimistic than I would have expected. Maybe he was still in shock. One look at the molted mess would have any reasonable person question the feasibility of performing such extensive plastic surgery. But I was too tired to argue or cast doubt on his confidence. If anyone could do it, it was my very own MacGyver.

Once we were 100 percent sure no tenacious embers were lurking beneath the rubble, we took a break. We showered. We fed ourselves, Frankie, and the fish. Kevin did his rounds. We got things done, but our foggy minds were preoccupied.

"I think we should stop in on Martín. See how he's doing and find out what happened," Kevin suggested.

As we approached the front stoop of the small olive-green house, we heard more than a few mumbling voices on the other side. Some high-pitched, some baritone. Some fast, others steadier. Clanging of... I didn't know what. The family was home.

When Kevin wrapped his knuckles on the wooden door, the nattering stopped. Then there were clomping of heavy footsteps and scampering of lighter ones. Quiet. A few seconds later, the door swung open.

"*Oh Anne*! *Kevin*! *Cómo están*?" Clara clutched at her chest with dismay.

"*Todo bien... Gracias.* Martín?" I shifted the attention to the man who saved the day.

Clara stepped aside and invited us into the dusky living room. As our butts sank into the bloated grey couch, she lamented how horrible she felt, thanked the good Lord for his mercy that no one was hurt, and mentioned something about how Martín was worried that we would fire him. Clara then scurried out of the room as people do when they remember that they left the stove on and soup is boiling over.

Moments later, like an apparition, a lanky silhouette entered from the bright kitchen. It was hard to make out who it was. Our eyes were still adjusting to the dim light. As the figure got closer and loomed over us with hunched shoulders, we saw Martín with downcast eyes.

After making sure Martín was physically and emotionally okay, Kevin smiled, trying to assuage Martín's fears that we weren't angry.

"*Qué pasó* today?" Kevin was simply looking for answers of what had happened.

Careful not to bang his shins, Martín wedged his long legs between the coffee table and the bulky chair that was crammed at a 90° angle from the oversized couch. He sat down and searched for the right words — Spanish words that I might understand. He didn't stammer, but his delivery was measured.

Martín explained that after we had left to run our errands, he finished stacking the bags of charcoal neatly — one on top of the other next to the dry woodpile — then cut the grass around the casita. When his shift was done, he put the weed whacker and other tools away, then came home. Just another ordinary day.

No sooner than he had set his machete down, took his boots off, and removed his cell phone and keys from his pocket, Martín noticed an ominous cloud from his living room window. Curious, he slipped his rubber boots back on and stood on the porch to have a better look. It wasn't a dark rain cloud, it was smoke. It was hard to tell where it was coming from exactly. People burned their garbage out there all the time, but the smoke was black, not the same thin grey wispy smoke from burning household trash. Thoughts scrambled, he rushed over and checked on the property without letting anyone know where he was going.

The dry woodpile was engulfed in flames by the time Martín got there. He tried using the hose, but the pressure wasn't strong enough. He panicked. He had left his phone on the kitchen table. There was no way of alerting anyone to come help him and he didn't want to waste precious time running back home. He grabbed the watering can from under the workbench, ran to the canal closest to the house, filled it up with water, ran back, and chucked it at the fire. He kept doing this. Back and forth. It seemed pointless. It felt hopeless, but he couldn't...wouldn't...stop.

Then we arrived.

"Ask him how he thinks this happened," Kevin turned to me looking for a translator.

"He says that there must have been a piece of wood that was still hot when he collected the charcoal, and he missed it."

"*Lo siento*! Sorry, sorry, sorry! *Es todo mi culpa*." Martín shook his head while scratching his chin stubble. Guilt-ridden, he believed the fire was all his fault.

We told him not to worry and to take some time off. This was the type of trauma that could cause a person to second-guess their knowledge and skills. And it certainly was not worth having a heart attack over. We believed Martín just needed a little time to rest, de-stress, and recover.

As luck would have it, we didn't have any guests booked for the next couple of weeks, but to ensure we would have the time to deal with the mess without the pressure of hosting and having to explain what had happened, I made sure our B&B calendar was set to *unavailable*. While Martín was taking a break, we tried to ignore the eyesore between the house and casita. Cleaning up the carport would have to wait. Kevin's priority was to ensure the pump for our water hose was working efficiently. The hose had been a garden tool, nothing more. The water was gravity-fed and at first, we didn't mind that there was no pressure; as long as the water trickled to the garden beds, we were happy. Having the river, flowing canals, ponds, natural springs, and a waterfall all around us, it's embarrassing to admit that fire didn't seem like much of a threat. It wasn't even on our radar. We took it for granted that it couldn't touch us. Clearly, we were wrong. All it took was a little cinder to spark mayhem.

Three days after the fire, Martín showed up, still contrite but ready to work. Together, he and Kevin cleared the debris. By the time noon rolled around, they were sweeping away the finest layer of white ash. The customary handshake should have come next but instead, I saw two comrades hug it out.

Aside from Martín or anyone else getting hurt — or worse — this scary event could have destroyed more than our material goods. Unchecked suspicion could have created a rift between close-knit neighbours. Martín could have lied. We could have blamed him. Tempers could have flared. Distrust could have shaken the bedrock of our friendship and working relationship. But none of those things happened.

We learned it wasn't the nature of the challenge that was important, but how we faced it. I think Martín was surprised by our reaction and goodwill towards him. He seemed relieved we didn't fire him. I know we were relieved that he didn't quit. We needed him as much as he needed us. Probably more.

Kevin and I had witnessed the force of water and now the rage of fire. Mother Nature usually wins. We got lucky this time.

Very lucky.

Upholsterer

Doing his research on the Bombardier dealership website, Kevin got prices for the four-wheeler parts we'd have to replace. Two new seats and a backrest from the dealership would cost us over $1,500!

"We'll have to buy most of the other parts from the dealership, we don't have much choice, but I bet we could get a much better deal if we take the seats to a local guy," Kevin said.

I was all for saving money, but I also wondered if the quality would be any good. We rode the four-wheeler daily. I didn't want wonky stitching or material that felt uncomfortable or that would wear out quickly. If Kevin was going to go through the trouble of rebuilding it to look like new, there was no point in him doing a slapdash job on the seats.

Eight months into this journey, I had let go of much of my suburban sensibility, but not entirely. Not in this case. I half-heartedly agreed to look for a local upholsterer, but I wasn't convinced we'd find someone who could provide that high-quality, off-the-assembly-line manufactured look.

Kevin had asked around and I think it was one of the guys at the hardware store in San Marcos who scrawled a phone number on a piece of paper and recommended we call Pedro. Although my Spanish was improving, I still felt anxious speaking on the phone. I felt more at ease knowing I could read body language. I think I subconsciously read people's lips, too, which made it easier to understand what they were saying. On the phone, I had to decipher each word without any visual cues. Having said that, it no longer took fifteen minutes of mental preparation to calm my nerves and dial.

A few days after that phone call, carrying the four-wheeler seats and backrest under our arms, Kevin and I stood in a room of a house in San Marcos. The place was in shambles. Dozens of car seats ready for a facelift filled the small space. Fabric scraps and bits of thread lay scattered on the floor. The seats weren't stacked in cubbies or tagged with a number to identify which ones belonged to which customer; no, they were piled haphazardly one on top of another, from floor to ceiling. The disarray fueled my skepticism.

How does this guy keep track of everything? What if our seats get misplaced or mixed up with someone else's?

Pedro's friendly manner put me more at ease. He apologized for the clutter and explained that with so many old vehicles on the road, seats got worn over time and needed to be mended or replaced. Made sense. He started repairing seats as a hobby on the side. He hadn't expected that it would keep him so busy. This hobby of his had flourished into what seemed to be a full-fledged business. And although it was obvious to us that he had outgrown the tiny spare room in his house and that it was time to consider finding a larger location, Pedro seemed oblivious.

I muddled through the language barrier and showed Pedro our mangled seats.

"*Fuego?*" Pedro had seen fire damage before. We nodded.

After inspecting what was left of our singed seats, he asked us to wait a minute.

He came back with fabric swatches. He flipped through them as if he knew exactly the sample he was looking for. No dawdling. He landed on a textured vinyl square that felt like leather and looked identical to the original black seat covers. Then he combed through different pieces of spongy material and recommended a high-density foam for the cushions. Without having to ask, Pedro then produced a sample of his work. The neat row of stitching was impeccable; more precise than my off-the-assembly-line expectations.

"*Cuanto por todo*?" I asked.

He scribbled some calculations on the back of a notebook. For the main seat, the back seat, and the backrest to be completely refurbished, he quoted us $140.

Kevin was right. Shopping local saved us a bundle.

Pedro told us to come back in a week. The rebuilding of our four-wheeler was officially in progress.

In a Fog

What's the difference between fog and a cloud? Well, they are both formed when water vapour condenses into tiny droplets in the air. But fog *only* forms at low altitudes. It's basically a cloud that touches the ground. It forms when the air near the ground cools enough to turn its water vapour into liquid water or ice. Clouds, on the other hand, can form at many different altitudes. So, at the risk of stating the obvious, clouds are a regular occurrence in the Cloud Forest...*or so you'd think*.

Our property was technically located in a Cloud Forest and being at a high altitude we should have been familiar with dense clouds that looked like what we would visually describe as *fog*. Truth is, we weren't. I don't know why our valley was exempt, but we rarely experienced heavy clouds, or what looked like fog. One night in May, however, the clouds rolled in, creating a thick soupy white mist. Strangely, it wasn't cold or damp. It had a surreal netherworld feeling — quiet and serene.

I felt the *hush* of the valley that night.

Noticeable Scars

I read on Paola's Facebook timeline there was a forest fire near La Cima. It had been burning all day, apparently.

What? Really?

We couldn't see anything from our farm, but I felt a surge of PTSD from the carport fire run through my veins. I needed to get a closer look.

I needed to understand the implications. Did we need to evacuate? Did I need to cancel upcoming B&B bookings? Would our garden hose, with its maximum pressure, save us?

As I drove down to Copey, I saw the intense orange flames raging against the periwinkle night sky. It was spreading before my eyes. I'd only ever seen news coverage of forest fires. This was my first time being up close and personal.

The townspeople were gathered outside their homes chatting to each other, but there was no sense of panic. Two yellow fire trucks were parked on the side of the road and the firemen were just standing around looking nonchalantly at the scene above. They seemed resigned; there was nothing they could do. Not only was there no access to get to the fire, but the trucks also didn't carry enough water to make a drop of difference. One way to put out this fire was by helicopters dumping water from the air, but I was told it was unlikely the Costa Rican government would spend that kind of money unless it was a national emergency. Another way was a good dose of rain.

There had been a forest fire ten years ago in the same spot...what bad luck for the community. There was no word yet on how it started, but quite a few farmers burned their garbage on their land. There was no garbage pick-up in remote rural areas so unless you collected it and disposed of it in the receptacles provided in the larger towns like we did, there was no other way to get rid of it. It was illegal to burn garbage on your property due to the danger during the dry season, but there was always someone who pushed the common-sense envelope.

Mid-April is officially the start of the wet season and every time it would start to rain I'd think, *Here we go, the rainy season has arrived.* But by mid-May that year, it had been fairly dry with negligible rainfall. Farmers had hoped for a good dousing even before the fire, but now we were all doubling down with actual prayers. I was assured if the rain didn't come, the fire would simply burn until it reached a deep ditch at the bottom of the mountain where it met the river and would extinguish on its own. I was told not to worry.

The fire raged for three days before the rain put out the blaze, but not without leaving noticeable scars on the mountainside.

As part of the healing process — for the forest and for our hearts — the community made plans to come together and plant new trees.

Winter Garden

The old hatchery was starting to look like a winter greenhouse. After Kevin filled the bottom of the concrete containers with logs and rocks, he and I shovelled sand halfway. Kevin lugged several heavy bags of compost, which we bought from a farmer in Copey, and dumped some in each container. Our own compost heap was cooking well, so I dug into it and sprinkled some of the rich, nutritious soil for an extra boost. I loved the fact that we had our own compost… Soon we wouldn't have to buy someone else's mixture.

I planted my seedlings: tomatoes, lettuce, red peppers, and squash. I watered, waited, and hoped for the best.

Wrong Place at the Wrong Time

Feliz had gone missing a few months back and we had been frantic. Well since reappearing, he'd been prancing through our neighbourhood in his easy-going fashion. This dog was the friendliest, sweetest dog; he wouldn't hurt a fly. He was affectionate but not demanding. He was happy with however much love and kindness you could spare.

Feliz came one night in June and Kevin fed him. It was raining at the time so after eating his dinner, he curled up on the dry mat under the chair outside. We made sure he was comfortable and said goodnight. Business as usual.

Kevin came in, sat on the couch, and snuggled up to Frankie, his face up against hers. She couldn't be bothered to lift her head. She gave his bald head a lick and rolled over.

"What a charmed life you lead. We should have called you *Princess*," he said.

Feliz was always gone by the time we got up and started our day. Doing his rounds, we supposed…probably getting breakfast at Martín and Clara's place and lunch at Vanessa and Albarito's. This was his routine. This was the life of our little tramp. We reminded ourselves not to get too attached, but we couldn't help it. *Everyone* loved Feliz.

The following morning, I had gotten an early start on the laundry and was stuffing sheets into the propane-fueled dryer located under the carport. Kevin was waiting for Martín to go over the daily chores. It was unusual for Martín to arrive late, but when he did, it normally had to do with the river causing havoc with his ponds. But it hadn't rained that much overnight. The river seemed clean and calm.

We didn't overthink it.

Twenty minutes had passed when Martín emerged from the river trail that wound between the road and our property — a shortcut he used frequently. A listless Martín shuffled across the ankle-high grass. As he got closer, I noticed two dark bull's eyes in the middle of his pant legs. Maybe from kneeling on the ground? When he got closer still, his bloodshot eyes had me worried.

He had found Feliz's limp body in front of their house.

What?

"*Muerto.*" Martín pantomimed digging a grave. No wonder his jeans were filthy.

Feliz wasn't old and didn't appear sick. How could he be dead? He was prancing around the property the day before and had settled under our chair for the night.

When you can't speak the language it's easy to remove yourself from the village gossip — all the better for us, as far as we were concerned. We got along with everyone, we didn't take sides, and we certainly didn't want to get caught up in familial or neighbourhood drama. As our Spanish improved and we became more involved within our community, we started to understand the relationship dynamics between certain families. It was hard to keep our heads buried in the sand forever.

"It doesn't make sense that Feliz *just died*. No signs of being attacked. Something's not adding up," I turned to Kevin, stunned and confused. He nodded, just as stunned and confused.

I pressed Martín for more information.

This was the theory: One of the neighbours, whom we had yet to meet, had a vendetta against Martín's family. They were angry about something someone did or said and were getting back at them through their dogs. Martín added that one of Bryan's dogs, Noa, had been poisoned a few nights earlier. We hadn't heard. Martín believed a piece of meat had been laced with rat poison and left near Bryan's gate — who lived next door to his parents — in hopes of killing his bigger dog. Kai was a beautiful large Vizsla, but he had a habit of yelping incessantly when people walked by the gate. A good guard dog. His barks never bothered us because of the distance between our properties, but perhaps these other neighbours who lived in closer proximity were fed up. Martín said Feliz might have eaten something poisonous that was intended for Kai...the old *wrong place at the wrong time* scenario.

Unfortunately, the custom in Costa Rica — from what other Tico friends had told us — is to avoid and deflect conflict. Instead of confronting the person who has offended them, they preferred to vent to everyone else about it or deal with things in a backhanded way, especially in rural out-of-the-way communities where family feuds can run generations deep. With a sense of self-righteousness, keeping the torch of injustice burning, it's easier to hold a grudge than to resolve the problem. I'd heard of this type of small-town mentality before. It doesn't matter if you are in Canada, England, the U.S., or any other country, for there's a good chance you'll encounter it. But this kind of vindictiveness was over the top and foreign to Kevin and me; we didn't operate that way. It hurt my heart.

Martín was late because he had wanted to bury Feliz in his backyard before the rest of his family woke up.

Martín was visibly upset and Kevin and I, still in shock, were too distracted to get on with our day as though nothing had happened. It seemed callous. Kevin and I set our list of chores aside and asked if Martín would show us Feliz's resting place.

We followed Martín back through the river trail, crossed over the bridge, then turned left on the rugged unpaved road and hiked up the steep incline until we reached the heavy chain-linked gate in front of Martín's humble home. Martín pointed to where he had found Feliz, then led us around to the back of the house.

I hadn't seen his backyard before that day. The small, square, level plot housed a couple of old wooden sheds in the far corner. Weeds were taking over whatever lawn might have once grown there. Smack in the centre, a rectangular-ish mound of loose dirt marred the lot like a Band-Aid on a fresh gaping wound. It was impossible not to notice it. There had been no stealthy or covert plan on Martín's part. Hiding the crime, if that's what he was hoping for, had failed. He would not be able to keep the secret from his family for long.

Beyond the perimeter of that shabby patch of land, unobstructed views of peaks and valleys undulated as far as our eyes could see.

I knew Martín and Clara's house was close to the cliff. There was some talk that they might have needed to move because their mountainside was eroding, and the house could get swept away in a landslide. From the front yard, this concern was less obvious; however, seeing how precariously close the house truly was to the edge of the abyss was alarming.

How do they sleep at night?

My nervous system didn't know how to respond: freeze or flee? There were so many questions I wanted to ask Martín, mostly about what they were doing to find a new place to live! But it wasn't the time.

In a spontaneous blur, I had clipped an assortment of flowers from our garden. I was holding on to them that whole time — squeezing the stems so tightly my hands were stained lime green. As Kevin and I stood over Feliz's grave, I laid the droopy posies onto it. The tears rolled down my cheeks like a leaky faucet that wouldn't stop dripping.

It appears I had become attached after all.

The Elusive Quetzal

Although considered one of the more elusive birds, Kevin and I saw a quetzal three times in the span of a few short weeks. I started to think I should walk around with a video camera attached to a helmet so I could capture these sightings. Being face to face with a quetzal and seeing it in all its glory was exhilarating. His plumage of many colours never got old. Gorgeous.

I could see why birdwatchers from all over the world came to this region for a chance to get a glimpse. Some leave, never spotting it. Friends who had lived there their whole lives hadn't seen one. So we counted ourselves lucky.

Thirty-Three
Little Rainbow Trout Business

It had been two-and-a-half months since the carport fire and two-and-a-half months of waiting for the plastic parts to reassemble our four-wheeler. After doing careful research, Kevin had ordered all the parts we needed. However, most things — that aren't fruit or coffee — are imported from other countries. And when things are imported, they usually arrive on a slow boat from China or the U.S. or sometimes even Canada. Early in July, Kevin received an email informing him that the parts had arrived.

While we had prayed for rain in March, April, and May, June more than made up for it. Although we still had sunny mornings, it rained every afternoon, which meant Kevin was on guard, assessing the river level and the amount of water coming into the aqueduct system. We were ramping up and getting ready for the worst the season would bring.

However, we learned that the weather in early July tends to be less rainy than the other wet-season months and to benefit from this reprieve, the schools shut down for a two-week break, just like the schools in North America do at Christmas time. It's a great time to visit Costa Rica as a tourist as well. There's an uplifting feeling in the air.

In between our B&B guests' arrivals and departures, we had a couple of free days. Knowing we could expect the sunshine to last most of the day, we made plans to drive down to San José to pick up the new parts for the four-wheeler. It was always safer to drive on dry roads and Kevin would worry less about the trout while we were out.

When we arrived at the Bombardier building, we told the receptionist we were looking for Xavier, the guy Kevin had been dealing with and who should have been expecting us. The receptionist asked us to wait a moment and paged the sales rep. While we were waiting, we looked at all the shiny new all-terrain vehicles and motorcycles. Kevin and I both had motorcycles at one point in our lives, so it was nice to browse and see what new models were being sold, but the inventory was scant. It didn't take long to complete the showroom tour. We found our way back to the reception desk, trying to make our presence felt, making sure we hadn't been forgotten. Eventually, after several minutes, she picked up the phone and paged Xavier again. Several more minutes passed when a short middle-aged man approached us.

"Hello. You must be Señor Lawrence. Nice to meet you," Xavier announced in perfect English as he shook Kevin's hand. "My colleague will be right down to help load the parts into your vehicle. Where are you parked?"

"Down the street a little bit, we couldn't find anywhere closer," Kevin replied.

"Go get it and park next to the building," Xavier marched out the door and pointed to a space with a sign that clearly read *"No Estacionar,"* which meant *"No Parking."*

"Right here? Are you sure?"

"Sí, don't worry, *Pura Vida."*

We went and got the SUV and Kevin parked it where he was instructed. After only a few short minutes, Xavier and his colleague came out with the two largest parts. Kevin and I took them out of their boxes to reduce the space in the back of the SUV. They brought down four more parts.

Great! Let's keep this pace going. At this rate, we'll be home by lunchtime.

But they did not keep up the pace. In fact, they disappeared.

Where'd they go? Is it something we said?

Kevin and I stood outside in the no-parking zone with the trunk door open waiting for all the other parts. But none were forthcoming.

What the heck?

"Can you go inside and see what's happening?" Kevin begged.

Just as I was heading inside, Xavier came outside and said his colleague had gone for a coffee break, but he wouldn't be much longer.

Pardon?

We learned that there was a company birthday party or some kind of celebration going on, which the other guy decided was more important than finishing what he was doing for us.

We couldn't believe someone would stop in the middle of a task and go on a break while the customer was still waiting. The definition of *customer service* sure was different from what we had been used to in Canada.

Kevin and I looked at each other, shook our heads, and said, "Costa Rica, baby."

An hour later, we were still waiting. We're pretty patient people, but this was bordering on ridiculous. I went in to see what the heck was going on. Kevin didn't care at this point; he had had enough. He removed the parts from the SUV and repacked them in their cardboard boxes.

When Xavier emerged and saw that Kevin had repacked the parts, he tried to convince us he could get the other parts down and packed in our vehicle in only a few minutes. We knew, however, that getting the parts in the SUV was only the first hurdle. Going through our list of parts and checking everything off, getting the invoice printed, double checking it, then standing in the lineup to pay (crossing fingers the cashier wasn't on *her* break) would take more time than we had. We couldn't risk it. It was getting late, and we had to get back to feed the fish.

We opted to leave everything behind and come back the following week. We loved many things about Costa Rica, but not everything. We tried hard not to have an arrogant attitude when we encountered this kind of behaviour, but there were times we were tested beyond normal limits.

But we breathed it out and remembered ninety percent of the time, we lived in paradise.

A New Beginning

A week later, we were up early and off to San José again to pick up the parts for the four-wheeler.

Xavier was expecting us.

All the parts were lined up, leaning against the wall of the dealership. We could tell Xavier was proud of his effort. Whether he did it all on his own, we didn't know, but we were grateful.

Kevin checked each and every part and ticked it off the list. We were on a roll until everything came to a screeching halt. There were two parts missing. Xavier was panicking. I could see the fear in his eyes. They were saying, "Oh no, this can't be happening, Mr. Lawrence wrote me twice to have me confirm all the parts were ready. And I told him they were."

Kevin and I waited patiently while he ran around and looked for the parts. Then Xavier, triumphantly holding two small kraft boxes with his arms stretched above his head as if he had, like Rocky, just climbed all seventy-two steps to the Philadelphia Museum of Art, shouted across the dealership, "I got 'em!"

We were relieved but not more than Xavier was.

Kevin had a new project to tackle. The carport had been restored and soon the four-wheeler would be resurrected from the ashes, almost as if the fire had never happened.

From the Ashes

On July 23, our eleventh month anniversary of living in Costa Rica, Kevin presented me with the four-wheeler's transformation.

Kevin spent two days stripping the quad bare and then rebuilding it...without a manual to follow, I might add. It looked better than it did before the fire. All sparkly and new.

It was Kevin's first time doing this sort of thing and although frustrating at times, he enjoyed the challenge. His competitive nature wouldn't let him quit.

I, on the other hand, wouldn't have known where to begin. One look at the carcass and I immediately saw it as too complicated. Not redeemable. I would have surrendered and gone without a four-wheeler.

Thank God for Kevin.

Selling Trout to Roberto

When we first bought our property, we weren't exactly sure how or if we could create a viable trout business. Swiss Man, who owned and built this farm, was responsible for making it one of the first commercial trout farms in the area. He hatched the eggs in the hatchery, grew the trout in the ponds, and sold the fish raw, dried, and canned. He also ran a small restaurant on the property. Enough corroborating stories had us believe that people from all over the country would drive and line up for a chance to dine at one of his tables. He was kind of a big deal in these parts, and it was his success years ago that encouraged other mountain-dwelling habitants to give trout farming a try. And over time, many of the *ma and pa* operations made enough to get by and feed their families as trout farmers. However, there were few large commercial farms in the surrounding area. There was one off the Pan-American Highway and it had all the newest processing machinery. Apparently, they supplied many restaurants in San José.

We were not the least bit interested in running a big operation; however, if we could find a way to cash in as a small boutique or artisan business, that would suit us nicely. We had a few fish left over from our original batch; some were weighing in at 1.5 kg (3.3 lbs). That was a lot of fish on two dinner plates.

Roberto helped his father, Abel, make cheese during the week, and to make room for the new cheese, he would pack up the older riper cheese that was ready to sell in his car. Every Friday, he and Adriana would drive down to San José and hand-deliver the blocks of cheese to their customers, primarily restaurant owners. These same restaurant owners were also asking him if he could supply smoked trout. Smoked trout was becoming more popular, and the demand was increasing.

Abel's farm wasn't set up for trout farming. He only had one small pond, so it wasn't an obvious leap for Roberto. He decided to buy a batch from the commercial farm up on the Pan-American Highway, but it was a bit of a trek to go back and forth. This was a trial business while he was still working for his father. He needed to be efficient and not add too many more hours to his already long day.

One day, Roberto came by to deliver fresh-churned butter in exchange for a dozen eggs and asked if we would consider selling him some of our trout. We were neighbours — it would be convenient for both of us.

How fortuitous.

We could make a bit of money and perhaps start a nice partnership helping each other out. Roberto spoke English so communication was easy. And we considered him a friend and trusted that he was sincere in wanting to see us prosper.

We had been looking into getting a smoker to provide options for our guests (not to mention we loved smoked trout ourselves) so we thought maybe we could help Roberto with production as well. These were early days, but we could see the opportunity before us.

Maybe those numbers the accountant predicted back in September weren't so far-fetched after all.

A Trial Run

As a trial run, Roberto asked us to catch sixteen trout.

First, we tried catching them with a net. We threw fish food close to the edge of the pond and dipped the long handle, gliding it through the water where the fish sprinted to feed, but that didn't work as well as we had hoped. They were too fast and the resistance of the water made it difficult to scoop them up quickly. We abandoned that idea in favour of using our trusty line and hook. It worked much better. Kevin did the fishing, and I followed him with the net. We caught sixteen as requested, which translated to 17 kg (37.5 lbs). It wasn't much, but it was a start.

Once I had gutted and cleaned the trout, Roberto, with his serious business game face, inspected them thoroughly. With a wide smile, he told us he was satisfied with the size and rainbow colour of this bunch. The gleaming prism effect sealed the deal.

We were officially in the trout business.

Trout and Their Enemies

There was good money to be made raising and selling trout, but there was a cost too. The cost of the fingerlings, for one; the cost of the food to feed them for a year; the cost of the time to grind the food based on fish size; and the cost of the wire surrounding the ponds to deter the solitary great blue heron that stood on its long skinny legs on the bank, extending its slender neck and spearing the trout with its sharp, dagger-like beak. The worst part was that the Great Blue didn't eat every fish it maimed; it was lucky to strike a few, but not lucky enough to catch the writhing trout every time. In the mornings, we often found a dead fish or two floating on the surface of the pond. The crime scene revealed piercing stab wounds.

The great blue heron was my all-time favourite bird. I even wrote a song about one once. But with all the maiming, the illusion of its grace and majesty faded quickly. Becoming a trout farmer was all it took to soon relegate it as my least favourite.

The thin wire around the ponds tacked on wooden sticks didn't look good. I hated that we had to add this extra layer of protection. It was a simple solution and a practical one, but it did nothing for my sense of aesthetics. But our duty to protect our investment trumped good style.

Damn it.

The heron wasn't the trout's only enemy. Otters would swim up from the river and slink into the ponds late at night. Otters didn't come alone though; they brought their extended family. They were much better hunters than the heron. They dove right in and feasted until they were full. Otters? In Costa Rica? It never occurred to us. No one ever mentioned they would be a problem. I used to think otters were so cute and playful. Becoming a trout farmer was all it took to see them as a menace.

Kevin decided that the wire we had around the ponds would do a better job if it were electrified. Sending a punishing zap to intruders might help our cause. The intent wasn't to kill any of the animals. We didn't want to hurt them. That wasn't the point. We simply needed them to go find a different turf to flex their natural instincts. And it worked for the most part. After installing the electric fence, there were fewer incidences of cold, bloody murder. This was a good thing. But we could only do so much. Mother Nature was fierce and relentless, whether it be from the elements or from the wild things we shared our space with.

There was a broad-winged hawk that used to perch up on a dead tree trunk that looked like a ship's crow's nest, high above the big pond. It provided the perfect angle. As I drank my coffee under the covered porch, I'd observe the hawk watch the shadowy silhouettes swim. I'd keep still to see what she'd do next, but I knew what she'd do next. I just didn't know *when* she would do it. If I got up from my chair, I'd surely miss it. Most days, it was a game of patience that could last more than an hour. Then, without warning, she would swoop down with her golden talons spread wide, skim the water, and with clockwork precision, snatch one of the trout straight out of the pond. Never losing momentum, the hawk would glide back up to altitude and fly away with her catch.

I never minded sharing our trout with the hawk. Witnessing her tactics provided a weird kind of entertainment. Besides, barring putting a net across all the ponds, which just wasn't viable, there was no way of preventing the hawk from helping herself to a meal. And it wasn't a daily occurrence; she wasn't greedy like the others seemed to be.

Kevin and I learned that we had to account for some unexpected losses like we would in any other business: A third of our stock went to our B&B guests and personal consumption; a third went to Roberto and other clients; and a third as an offering to Mother Nature. It turns out, she never took as much as a third, but it was good practice to factor the damage she could bring. We were always grateful when she was feeling generous and refrained from taking more.

The B&B

We shut down the B&B business from mid-September to mid-November not only for safety reasons with the river rising and its torrential swells, but we didn't want the responsibility of keeping our guests entertained in such miserable weather. I can't tell you how many guests came unprepared — even with all the warnings — and packed only flip-flops and shorts for their cool mountain stay. Not to mention, working the trout and B&B businesses was hard work. A two-month rest from having to make meals and clean the casita was a welcomed break.

I also learned that many people plan their winter getaways in September and October. Not being swamped with hosting duties allowed me to attend to the emails that were filling up my inbox. I spent a lot of time making sure Hush Valley Lodge was the right fit for those showing interest in staying with us. In some cases, by the time the guests arrived months later in the dry season, I felt like we were friends.

Ungrateful Workers

I remember when we first travelled to Costa Rica that Ran, who ran the hotel with his sister in Monteverde, had warned us about the possible complications that could arise when having people work for you.

We had a worker, Raoul, who we had hired to relieve Martín from the back-breaking weed-whacking chore. Raoul was a hard worker when he showed up. He didn't have a car so I would often pick him up in Copey and drive him home to ensure he'd come to work. We had discussed the terms and conditions of his employment and made sure Martín explained them in Spanish so there was no confusion. We paid his hourly wage in cash. Raoul seemed happy and accepted the terms. He needed the work, and we needed the help. This was not meant to be a long-term position, but if things worked out then we were open to that eventuality. Martín wasn't getting any younger.

Raoul was quiet and shy. He didn't understand one word of English, nor did he catch on to my Spanish attempts even with all the pantomime. I often had to ask Martín for help. Sometimes I felt like Raoul knew more than he let on but I could never be sure.

One day, he cut himself with his machete. Machetes were a staple tool, hanging from men's belt loops like gunslinging cowboys wore their holsters on their hips in the Wild West. And Raoul happened to be an expert machete wielder. Even Martín said there was no one more skilled in the machete department than Raoul. So this is why Raoul preferred using his machete over strapping on the heavy weed whacker to his back. We had no preference as long as the work got done in the same amount of time. The day Raoul cut his shin, I suggested I drive him to the hospital to get his wound looked at. He resisted. When I asked him why, that was when he told me he didn't have medical insurance. But all residents have medical insurance, it's a national privilege.

But Raoul wasn't Costa Rican. He was Nicaraguan. He was in the country illegally. *Oh, damn.*

Raoul was bleeding and the gash seemed serious enough to need stitches. Insurance or not, he needed medical attention.

We paid the bill.

That was a mistake.

While we thought we were being kind bosses, Raoul figured if we could afford to pay his medical bill he could get more out of us. The bill was about $40. It didn't break the bank.

When Martín's back was feeling better and the grass was growing slower in the summer months, we warned Raoul that his work was coming to an end, for now, and that we'd like him to resume work in a few months when the grass was growing again, if he was still available. We never gave him a guarantee that we would have work nor did he ever give us a guarantee that he would be available to work for us. We were taking things on a week-by-week basis.

But Raoul turned on us. He wanted us to pay severance, even though the terms were that we paid a higher wage *now*, but that would exclude any severance later. We would give him two weeks' notice, and we did. He only worked five months for us, so the severance would have been negligible, but that wasn't the point. We had a deal. He agreed to it. We were being taken advantage of. I didn't come out and say we wouldn't give him severance. I politely but firmly reminded him of our agreement. Then Martín chimed in, and by then I understood Spanish well enough that I got more than just the gist — that Raoul had managed to screw up any opportunity of ever working for us again. That we would have been happy to hire him when the need arose, that he could have had a sweet gig with bosses who were more than fair, who went out of their way to pick him up and drive him home, who gave him avocados and lemons and sometimes even trout and even paid for his medical bill.

Raoul just stared blankly at Martín.

It was hard to read what was going on in his mind. Martín then threw in a reminder that Raoul was living in Costa Rica illegally. How much leverage did he think he had? He didn't come at Raoul in a threatening way, this tone was more like *hey, man, com'on, think about what you're doing* kind of appeal to mitigate any repercussions. And although I didn't let on that I understood as much as I did, I felt we had been vindicated. And that Martín was a true friend and advocate.

We had no idea if Raoul would show up the following Monday. But he did.

Before giving Raoul his notice, Kevin and I had talked about it and agreed that we'd give him a little extra to thank him for his services and to entice him to want to come back when we needed help again. Raoul's demand for severance didn't impress us but we didn't want to be petty, so we decided to give him the bonus anyway, to keep the peace if nothing else. He knew where we lived, and we didn't want him to stir up trouble.

Two weeks later, we handed Raoul an envelope with the wages we owed him plus the bonus, and we had him sign a release form that our contract had been fulfilled. Martín advised this would be a good idea to serve as proof of the mutual understanding. We had the release form translated into Grade 6 Spanish so that there was no room for misinterpretation on anyone's part. We had Martín sign as a witness to ensure we had everything covered in case Raoul denied it was his signature later on. It all felt so legalese and bad but necessary.

Raoul's face tilted downward as he inspected the contents of the envelope. I wasn't sure if his expression showed disappointment or shame. Raoul turned and walked away in his big black rubber boots, machete hanging from this belt loop, and shoulders slumped. I had not offered to drive him home that day. Okay, maybe I was holding on to some pettiness after all.

You could be the best boss in the country but if you didn't cover your ass, trouble could find you. We had been so lucky with Martín and Clara. Introducing new workers was going to open us up to certain vulnerabilities. The experience with Raoul stopped us from wanting to grow our businesses any more than we had done so far. We wanted to avoid needing more workers on the property.

Just Ticking Along

Despite our business challenges and the never-ending ones with Mother Nature, after living at Hush Valley Lodge in our little Río Blanco community for two years, things were humming along seamlessly.

Kevin and I sat on the community's board of directors as treasurers. We, the outsiders, were elected to hold on to the money for safekeeping. It was either a testament that we had proved ourselves as trustworthy or their deep-seated distrust of each other.

We discovered in the early days with Feliz's poisoning that family feuds ran long and deep in this remote rural *cantón*. Betrayals and conflicts that happened three generations back were still causing rifts among neighbours. When we first arrived, there had been some protection by not knowing the language. We were immune to the badmouthing because we were strangers, and they weren't about to air their dirty laundry with us. And the fact that we didn't understand what they were saying kept us safe from gossip.

In the beginning, we were neutral out of ignorance. Then as we became more entrenched in the community and understood Spanish a little more, we remained neutral by choice.

"I'm sorry you feel so-and-so has wronged you, they've done nothing wrong to us and our experience has been positive so far so I will not speak badly about them," I would say, trying to shut down the conversation.

I thought this might rub people the wrong way; that they might feel as though if we weren't taking their side, they would think we were taking the other person's side.

We weren't taking any sides.

We were allowing everyone to show their true colours and we got closer to those who held our values and distanced ourselves from those who didn't.

We got along with everyone. Very few issues arose and when they did, they were usually minor misunderstandings. We would address our concerns with the person in question, not go around the situation. Considering both Kevin and I avoided conflict like the plague as a rule, in this environment, we seemed more willing to resolve any clash straight on. We wanted to clear the wound as soon as possible to avoid infection and bad feelings festering. The community had embraced us as their own, but we were still outsiders. We would always be gringos.

Thirty-Four
The Beginning of the End

2014–2017

The Reality

It's no secret that Kevin and I loved our Hush Valley Lodge property, our businesses, and the community that so warmly embraced us. But the truth is, even paradise wasn't perfect.

Feeling besieged by the concrete jungle, disconnected from nature, and stuck in the unyielding grind, we left suburbia. We felt confined and wanted to break free as if freedom would be more docile and submissive.

How naïve.

There was a great cost to freedom. Not only in a monetary sense, but the cost in letting go of my infantile fantasy that freedom is served on a plate of peace, harmony, and ease. No, freedom demands retribution. It demands a good hard look at what defines you.

The wet and dry seasons led and followed each other in close embrace like two well-practiced Tango partners. Kevin and I learned to anticipate the woes and boons that each season brought. And yet, that didn't stop us from praying for rain at the end of April, always feeling like we were on the brink of a drought. By November, we were pleading for mercy when it felt the rain would never cease. We became savvier with the weather patterns, but we never entirely trusted the rhythm of Mother Nature's dance.

Although Kevin had accomplished many projects, I think he was getting bored. The improvements to the farm were obvious yet too numerous to list. There's no doubt the value of the property had gone up from his ingenuity and handiwork, not just by our flourishing and viable businesses. Unless we injected significant capital to expand our vision by building more casitas or more outdoor pergolas or some larger retreat infrastructure, there wasn't much more for Kevin to do except maintain what we already had.

As one year turned into another, and then another, Kevin and I went about our day-to-day lives more separately than together. We never argued or discussed our dissatisfaction with the life we were living or with each other. We had always been good at stewing in our own personal thoughts but struggled with communicating them out loud to one another.

The first two-and-a-half years had us facing ourselves and tested our resolve. We got better at confronting the environmental challenges, but the inner work hit us hard and tested our relationship. Outwardly, things were going well. We were successful entrepreneurs in Costa Rica. We were living in the land of rainbows. What possible dissatisfaction could either of us have? How could we air any complaint?

We had each found our niches within each business but like an inflatable mattress that sprung a slow leak, our inner monologues seeped out imperceptibly over time through our behaviour toward each other until we both felt deflated.

On Christmas Day 2014, we were having our traditional trout dinner at Martín and Clara's restaurant. I'm not sure if doing something three years in a row constitutes a tradition, but it felt like one. I couldn't imagine celebrating Christmas any other way for as long as we lived in Río Blanco.

As we were sitting in the open-air restaurant at one of the rustic tables in mismatched chairs, Kevin looked at me with some hesitation, then said, "I love it here, but I think I'm done. I feel like maybe we should start thinking about selling and either move back to Canada or find a new adventure."

It didn't take long for me to wrap my head around his suggestion — a nanosecond, in fact. I was done, too. He was simply brave enough to utter the words first.

Well, neither of us felt *completely* done, but we knew it wouldn't be easy to sell the farm, and we'd probably have to be patient. We figured by the time we did sell we'd be so done we'd be fried like the dinner on our plates.

Reason #1

Being so far away from Phoenix and Jude didn't fall on Kevin's radar, but it sure did on mine. I knew when we made the decision to leave Canada that I would miss them, of course, but it never occurred to me that it would strike the marrow of my existence, exposing a maternal pang that even I couldn't explain. A different part of my mama gene was cracked open by the distance. It had been good for us to be away from each other. I wasn't pining. I wasn't crying my eyes out every night. Nor were my kids, for that matter. We were three independent beings finding our way, in our own way. But I couldn't shake the profound sense of longing to be closer. A clear understanding of what it meant to have each other bore even deeper into my heart and soul.

My children were nowhere near ready to have kids of their own, but the idea that one day I might be a grandmother sealed the deal that there was no way I was going to live this far away forever. Someone once told me having learned the same lesson, "It's okay if my kids move away from me, but I will never again move away from them." I didn't understand the difference at the time, but it resonated loudly having now lived the subtlety.

Reason #2

The news of my father's ill health became a concern and weighed on my mind, although I didn't talk about it much. Dad showed visible signs of slowing down. It was getting harder for him to keep up with my mother, which meant going for their evening walks became a chore rather than a pleasurable routine. He suffered from more aches and pains and got crankier by the day. I noticed he started to shake when pouring himself a drink. His rounded shoulders hunched further forward, and his knees bent as though his legs were about to buckle under him. He would lean on the counter to hold himself steady. He was never a big burly man or particularly tall, but when I had hugged him during one of my visits, I couldn't help but notice his shrunken stature. This undeniable frailty, I'm sure for my dad, would have stung. When I video chatted with my mother every Sunday, he would sometimes pop his head across the screen to say hello, but he never stuck around. He was getting quieter.

A good life lived with nothing left to say.

My father wasn't on death's door, but it was as though he was counting the years, not expecting too many more...and not making any great effort to prolong them. I felt too far away to be of any real support to my mother. Now that we had had our breakthrough, that we had grown emotionally closer since her month-long stay with us, I felt being physically closer was the next step.

Reason #3

I missed having four seasons that visibly changed. I missed the spring crocuses emerging from the stubborn winter frost and the sun's promise that warmer temperatures were ahead. I missed the long days of summer that stretched into late evenings, where one could catch up with friends on a patio sipping wine and lingering. Then, with the oppressive August heat beating me down, I always welcomed the cool, crisp autumn with its change of colours and its brisk procession to short, sombre days. Literally, but also metaphorically, there's a sense of death but in a restorative kind of way — not like everything is over, but like everything is over for now. An invitation to rest and to go inward in preparation for winter. Although I love this part of the year, it only lasts a couple of weeks. It often feels like we go from shorts and T-shirt weather directly to parkas and toques. Although Southern Ontario is much milder than many other parts of Canada — some years we don't even get snow — there's still an intrinsic sense of hibernation. And it seems to last forever.

Unless you're a winter sports enthusiast, then it doesn't last long enough. I don't fall in that category though.

One of the many reasons I wanted to move to a warmer climate was because it didn't seem to make sense to spend half my life shaking my angry fist at the cold winter months. Six months of complaining and whining for heat.

Not cool.

It took living in paradise, where the temperatures were ideal all year round, to realize that the climate I was used to, the traditions that grew out of the cycles, were more ingrained in my bones than I could have imagined. I never dreamed that I would miss winter. Not in a million years! But it didn't surprise me that I was missing the quintessential four seasons. I couldn't divorce winter and stay married to the seasonal sequence. It didn't work that way.

Reason #4

As for Kevin, he didn't miss much about Canada, except for a good night's sleep. Although our businesses were thriving — both the trout farming and the B&B were doubling year over year — he still worried about not making enough money.

As the trout business grew, so did the financial risks. More trout...more ponds... more risk...meant more worry. But it wasn't just the financial aspect; Kevin worried about the river and the natural spring drying up in the summer season and he worried about the river flooding us out during the rainy season. He worried about the trout constantly: Is the water clean enough? Aerated enough? Protected from the herons and otters enough? He was diligent to a fault.

Kevin worried enough for the both of us. The mental load must have been exhausting.

Reason #5

One of the attractions of moving to Costa Rica was that we were so eager to visit surrounding countries, but there was no getting away as farmers. Not if you had livestock, not if you couldn't afford to hire someone to take care of things while you were away and even if you could, not if you felt like no one else could do as good a job as you.

Kevin wasn't wired to delegate and relinquish control. I left the farm regularly to deliver eggs or drive down to Copey to teach or run errands in town. Rarely did we leave the farm together. When we left the country, we went solo. Someone had to stay behind to take care of things. How can we ever explore Peru or Chile or anywhere together?

So close and yet so far.

Selling Up: Our First Prospective Buyers

On January 6, 2015, twelve days after Kevin put the idea of selling out into the ether, we hosted B&B guests, Jess and Neil. They were a lovely white-haired couple from Arizona in their late sixties or early seventies. They were so raptured by the property at the end of Kevin's three-hour tour that Neil blurted, "I guess you'd never consider selling with all the work you've done?"

How serendipitous. Is this a sign? Not once have we been asked that question before.

Not quite sure how to respond, Kevin looked at me before answering Neil to make sure we were still on the same page; to make sure all our conversations in the last few days since that Christmas Day declaration was not just an empty pact. It was the moment of truth. I smiled and gave him a quick nod.

This was the moment where we would speak the words out loud to someone else.

"As a matter of fact...you're the first people to know... But we have decided to sell," Kevin uttered the words. Our intent crystallized.

Jess and Neil couldn't believe it. They said they wanted to buy it. We laughed. They were serious. Here we thought it would take months to sell.

After Jess and Neil went home, we stayed in touch. We continued hosting guests while they wrote saying they had been telling everyone they knew about Hush Valley Lodge. Knowing that they couldn't afford to buy our property on their own, they were trying to rally another couple into sharing the dream and investing half. There was only one house, but there was a lot of land to build more homes. Jess and Neil were retired so their vision was different from ours. They wanted a holiday home much like Rick and Mona.

Days of correspondence stretched into weeks...then months. The initial excitement that we might have sold our paradise home to the very first people we mentioned it to

— like kismet — and the relief that we might not have to go through the marketing process, waned.

One day in May, I received an email from Jess saying that good friends of theirs, Melanie and Garth, were intrigued with their proposal. They wanted to see for themselves what the hype was all about. Our adrenaline was pumping again.

We hosted Melanie and Garth a couple weeks later. They were suitably impressed. They wanted in. Kevin and I thought we were one step closer.

The flurry of correspondence that ensued after Melanie and Garth left was encouraging. All the right sentiments. Money and timelines had been discussed. Nothing was set in stone, but there was no reason to think we weren't moving forward and making a deal.

Until the emails slowed.

Kevin and I were confused. They seemed so stoked. But we didn't want to seem pushy or appear desperate, so we shifted our attention.

Marketing 101

The idea of selling and moving back to Canada was embedded in our minds and hearts. We were ready. We needed to cast a wider net and not get attached to people's intentions. This was affecting our future; we couldn't move forward until we sold the property, it wasn't personal. We had to stop hoping that the Arizona couples would buy it.

With our new mindset, we staged the house and took pictures. Kevin took care of finding international real estate sites and I took charge of writing the promotional copy. Just like Rick, we chose to advertise outside of Costa Rica. And, just like Rick, we kept the news that we were putting the property on the market from our community. We had already encountered bumps in the road and we thought it was best to lay low until we had a real deal. Signed and delivered.

Selling up consumed every thought from that day forward. We continued to do our chores, attend community events, and visit friends as though everything was normal. We lived our life in a sublime paradise setting yet with each passing day, we felt more trapped.

Newfound Hope

Fed up with the rain, feeling more cranky than usual, longing to be back in Canada with Phoenix and Jude and closer to Mum and Dad, I hit a low point. We had had a few inquiries on the property, but those fizzled quickly.

But then, on November 10, the day before my fifty-first birthday, I received an email from Tiff. Her note was full of specific questions and looking for details that no one had yet asked for. She and her husband, Clint, were looking to sell their own business in the United States and relocate. She had no idea, but her enthusiasm for my blog and interest in the property was the best possible birthday gift. It lifted my spirits in a way that gave me newfound hope.

Tiff and I wrote to each other regularly for the following two months, turning a property inquiry into a fast-forming friendship. By the time Tiff and Clint came to visit the property in late January 2016, it felt like we had known each other for years.

Tiff and Clint were smitten by the property and loved how we integrated into the community. They were eager. They were committed to purchasing the property, but everything hinged on selling their business back home.

Kevin and I wanted them to purchase the property. Of course, for selfish reasons, but also their desire to take over what we had started was palpable. But we also couldn't hold the sale for them. It was first come, first serve. We were rooting for Tiff and Clint, but we were rooting for us more. The sooner we could make a deal, the better.

Buyers Wanted

Over the following excruciating two-and-a-half years, Tiff and Clint visited five times. Meanwhile, we responded to dozens of inquiries from potential buyers and considered a few offers. But no deal was sealed.

We put on a brave face. We bought more trout and grew that business. But we halted any projects that required any monetary investment. We didn't want to put more money into the farm that didn't add significant value to the property. What we learned through this selling process was that every interested party we spoke with described completely different visions of what they would want to do with the property. Adding or removing anything could be detrimental in the long run.

Although Tiff's emails filled my inbox less frequently, when I did get an update, she reinforced their continued longing to buy Hush Valley Lodge. This was a double-edged sword that pierced my soul every time. She gave every indication that they were working diligently towards finalizing a deal. She and Clint hadn't anticipated that selling their business would be such a challenge.

Kevin and I felt their pain. It was real and raw.

We didn't think it would be easy to sell the property. We knew Rick had the property on the market for a couple of years before we bought it.

It was remote, which was the beauty of it. It was remote, which was also its downfall.

Rick had mentioned that he had had a few nibbles on the property and some low-ball offers that he refused to entertain, but he didn't make it sound like he was flooded with the same interest we had been experiencing. We, on the other hand, had been in negotiations with several people simultaneously. Sometimes the tension escalated and gripped us to the point of heart palpitations, keeping us on the edge of our seats like some unexpected plot twist in a movie.

The emotional rollercoaster ride had our stomachs in our throats and more than a few times I wanted to throw up. It was mentally and emotionally taxing.

Then, out of the blue, we heard from Jess. Her email revealed that she and Neil were still thinking of Hush Valley Lodge and looking for ways to purchase.

Don't toy with us, Jess!

It had been nearly two years since they had first contemplated the notion. The issue was that they could not live in Costa Rica full time and asked us if we would consider staying on as managers if they bought the property. We would not. We were not selling because we needed financial backing, we were selling to get back to Canada. And if I had access to a pair of magic red shoes, I would have clicked my heels three times by now because by this time, in my mind, there was no place like home.

We had two sets of people who had thrown their hats in the ring. In one corner: a couple wanted to live in Costa Rica but needed a way to raise more funds. In the other corner: a couple who apparently might have the funds but required boots on the ground to ensure continued stewardship of the land and businesses that we had created.

Hmmm.

"What do you think of me introducing Tiff to Jess? Instead of pitting them against each other to see who knocks the other out of this deal, why don't we bring them together?" I mused out loud.

Kevin was open to any brainstorming ideas that might get the property sold. This was one of my better pitches. "Do it!"

I sent an email to Tiff explaining the Jess-and-Neil situation. I sent an email to Jess explaining the Tiff-and-Clint situation. Both couples were intrigued and agreed to contact each other to chat.

We were throwing spaghetti on the wall to see if it would stick. We didn't have any expectations that it would.

A week later, we heard that Tiff and Clint were flying out to Arizona to meet Jess and Neil in person.

Things then started to move fast. Melanie and Garth were back in the picture. And another person, Darren, jumped on the bandwagon to complete the group.

You can't make this stuff up.

A verbal commitment was made. We had a deal...in principle: closing in early July.

Oops, slight delay...make that late July.

Just a minor snag...early August, yes.

No. Late August.

Going... Going... Sold!

Of the seven in the group of co-owners, Tiff and Clint were the only ones thinking of living on the property full time. They would move into the main house and run the day-to-day trout and B&B businesses, just as we had done. Appointed as proxies for their joint investment partnership with Jess, Neil, Melanie, Garth, and Darren, Tiff and Clint flew down on their own and signed the legal paperwork on everyone's behalf.

Unlike Rick, who said he would meet us in Río Blanco and show us the ropes, but didn't, we spent the following week bringing them up to speed on our whole operation. We taught them how to care for the fish, how the pond gates worked, and everything to do with B&B bookings. I shared my routine on how I got the casita ready between guests. We wanted to impart whatever wisdom we had gained during the five years we had been there. I filled a blue binder of contact names and numbers of people to call for every possible circumstance I could think of. I created a hefty manual of important information explaining government rules, where to pay property taxes, where to get the vehicle emissions test done, banking and internet processes, and so on. If we could answer questions or make something easier for them, we were happy to do it. We provided a launching point but knew they'd eventually find their own way of doing things that worked best for them. We introduced Martín and Clara to their new bosses, fulfilled our obligations regarding their severance pay, and officially severed their contract with us to ensure Tiff and Clint (and the other co-owners) were entering into a fresh agreement with no debts.

When Tiff and Clint arrived, we were hosting our last guests of the season. While Carrie and Stu were our last guests...ever...they were Tiff and Clint's first guests. Carrie and Stu witnessed the changing of the guards, so to speak.

It had been a long and trying selling process and we were ready to wrap things up. The community threw us a farewell party, which was the perfect occasion to make introductions to the other neighbours.

Welcome home, Tiff and Clint.

Little did we know that the rollercoaster ride we had been on for the last two-and-a-half years and thought was coming to an end had just reached the top and we were in for a few loop-de-loops.

Thirty-Five
Checked out but Can't Leave

Storm's a Brewin'

On August 31, 2017, a tropical storm was brewing in the Atlantic. Between saying goodbye to Martín and Clara and their kids, Adriana and Roberto, Catalina, Vanessa and Albarito and their kids, Abel and Elly, Cindy and Larry, Sister Gladys, and everyone we embraced as part of our Costa Rican family, we watched the news. We ran last-minute errands, then we came home and watched the news. While we packed, news updates blared through the house.

We wouldn't have thought much about it, living so far from the expected landfall, except we were flying out of San José in three days and our layover was in Miami, Florida. The storm fluctuated in intensity between Category 2 and 3. Although it was swirling closer towards the coast, there were no reports of imminent danger. No flights had been cancelled.

We were flying out on September 3, 2017. No cause for worry yet.

The Last Goodbye

We had Juan, a taxi driver from San Marcos, drive us to the airport.

Juan kept his car immaculately clean and dressed in a crisp, dark suit. He took his livelihood seriously and was a consummate professional. His good reputation preceded him, and he was the go-to guy among all our expat friends when they needed a ride to the airport. Kevin and I had met him a few times. Not only did we like his calm energy, but we knew we could count on him to be on time.

When I called Juan to arrange the pick-up, I had suggested, just to be on the safe side, that we give ourselves extra time to account for unexpected yet typical slowdowns. He assured me that it wouldn't be necessary to leave so early but that he was happy to show up at whatever time we wanted if it meant it would alleviate any stress.

My kind of guy.

But as it was early Sunday morning and still dark, traffic was not an issue. Without speeding, the usual two-hour drive took less than an hour and a half. The consummate professional was right.

When we arrived at the airport, Juan got out and helped us with our bags. I thought I detected a subtle self-satisfied smirk forming in the corner of his mouth as he glanced at his watch. But Juan was too polite and kind to rub in my face all the spare time we had. He might have quipped that we could catch up on some sleep while waiting for our flight, but he just shook Kevin's hand and wished us a safe trip home.

"*Muchas gracias*," we said as Kevin handed Juan cash for the fare. A lump formed in my throat, preventing any more words from squeaking out. Kevin held back tears by turning away and grabbing one of the suitcases.

Although we weren't buddies with Juan, he was part of the fabric of our life in Río Blanco. And in that moment, I understood this was truly our very last goodbye. Juan's kindness was the finishing thread being looped and knotted in an emotional tapestry that took five years to weave. And as final as it all felt, I knew I wouldn't be able to appreciate the whole picture until we walked away and allowed distance to bring it into perspective.

The Run-Around

Even though we had time to squander, we didn't dawdle. We'd rather be waiting on the other side of the security gate. But we weren't stressed.

My passport is valid for five more years.

We strolled down the wide echo-y hallway, Kevin pushing the metal luggage cart in front of us. We found the American Airlines check-in counter and dragged our suitcases and knapsacks on the flat scale to be weighed, then paid the fee.

The acne-faced check-in attendant, Ricardo, handed over our boarding passes with a youthful white smile. Brushing his blond emo-cut bangs out of his eyes, he said in English with a slight lisp, "I need to see the dog's documentation."

No problem.

Kevin handed over the vet's signed declaration that Frankie had received her rabies shot and was fit to fly. We were just as prepared as ever; this wasn't our first rodeo, and we were feeling confident.

"Thank you," Ricardo perused the stapled papers, then looked up. "Do you have the government exportation document? I'll need that, too."

Excuse me? Exportation what?

"Our vet didn't give us that form."

"I'm sorry, your dog cannot fly without this document."

Big problem.

"We researched what we needed. We brought our dog in from Canada. Nowhere did it say we needed this exportation document. Not even for the U.S. Maybe it's for a different country?" I proposed. He looked young and maybe he wasn't familiar with all the airline rules yet.

"This document isn't for Canada or the U.S....it's a Costa Rica regulation. Your pet needs this document to prove she's healthy to fly *out* of Costa Rica."

"Our vet never warned us about this document. What do we do now?" Kevin asked.

"Hmm... Let me see what I can do. I'll see if there's an official in the airport that maybe can sign it since you have all the other documents saying she's healthy. It shouldn't be a problem."

Ricardo switched to Spanish and made several phone calls.

"You have to go to the customs area," Ricardo glanced up from the receiver. We nodded in agreement.

Since no lineups forming yet, he volunteered to lead the way. We followed with all our luggage and with Frankie snug in her collapsible crate. Ricardo told us to wait for him, opened the door and disappeared, then reappeared a few minutes later.

"Sorry, nothing can be done at the airport, a vet must fill out all the paperwork from the department of agriculture. You will have to find a vet near the airport."

"What time do clinics open on Sundays?"

"Usually...noon," Ricardo winced as he gave us the bad news.

Ricardo offered to find phone numbers for vets in the area for us to call, but we no longer had a cell phone. We gave it to Tiff and Clint because it was an old flip phone that we knew we would never use in Canada and because it had all our Río Blanco contacts. It was more useful to them than to us.

Until this very moment.

Ricardo then offered to call for us and see if he could confirm an appointment, somewhere...and give us an address. All we'd need to do is get a taxi driver to escort us there. Ricardo was going well beyond the call of duty. He was sweet and we could tell he wanted to help us. But vet clinics didn't open until noon, so we'd miss our flight.

Ricardo typed frantically on his keyboard. His serious facial expression had us worried until, with jazz hands, he waved excitedly.

"I can reschedule your flight to tomorrow at 6:55 a.m."

Two layovers. Not ideal, but beggars can't be choosers.

Ricardo handed us the name and address of a vet and wished us luck.

We decided to move our luggage and Frankie up to the second level and camp out in the airport café where there was free internet access. We settled in.

We took turns watching our stuff while the other went to the washroom or to buy a beverage. We walked Frankie outside the terminal, got her bowl out, and gave her some water and a bit of food. She didn't complain once.

I didn't waste any time to reach Tiff via email to let her know what was happening. I could only hope she'd be checking her messages sooner than later. I asked her if she could Google other possible vets near the airport in case she might find one that was open earlier.

It was a long shot, but Tiff responded within seconds. What a star!

After several attempts, she got a hold of a vet that was open but fully booked. Tiff explained our situation and the vet had said we were welcome to wait around in her office in case one of her clients didn't show up. We could either wait at the airport — which started to feel hopeless and like nothing was being resolved, making us feel even more antsy — or we could wait at the vet's, with a slight possibility of Frankie being seen. The latter option felt like a step forward. We were feeling lucky. So, we dragged our four suitcases, our very heavy knapsack and Frankie, and headed to the taxi line.

One of the taxi drivers sped forward and rolled down his front passenger window.

"*Hola*, I'm Alonzo. You need ride?" he spoke English enough to get by.

"We need to get to City Mall," Kevin said to him.

"No problem... Ten minutes... Five-dollar ride."

"Okay... Let's go!"

While Alonzo was driving us to our destination, Kevin thought a local taxi driver might be a treasure trove of information and have a pocketful of contacts. So he asked Alonzo if he knew of any vets that would be open. Alonzo immediately called a friend or a family member, not sure, spoke Spanish a mile a minute into his phone, then hung up.

"There's a vet clinic not too far from here. It's open."

"Can you take us there instead?"

Off we flew. Alonzo read the room correctly and understood this was an important mission to us. He might not have had the professional acumen that Juan had, he might have been a little rough around the edges, but Alonzo stepped up to the task and stepped on the accelerator pedal.

He was on the case.

A few minutes later we reached a strip mall. I stayed in the car with all our belongings and Frankie. Alonzo and Kevin hopped out of the car and checked whether the vet could see Frankie. A minute later, Alonzo came out to retrieve me and Frankie. Things were looking up.

Alonzo said he would wait. There was no discussion of how much this would cost, but by this point, it was the last thing on our minds.

Kevin and I entered the large agricultural building and in my still-broken Spanish, I explained the situation to the cashier. We were told that it was not a matter of a vet being able to simply sign and stamp a form. A vet had to examine the dog, fill out the form, then send it to the government agency that prepared the final document. It required several different government departments' stamps. So, it didn't matter which vet we were going to see that day, the outcome would be the same. This process could be hastened, and it *could* be possible to get the official document by the following morning — the soonest being 9:30 a.m. — which, let's face it, meant 1:30 p.m. Tico time, if we were lucky.

Our flight was leaving at 6:55 a.m. We had to reschedule yet again.

Although the skies above were blue, we knew from reading the ticker tape on the airport TV screens that the tropical storm was picking up steam.

Sigh.

The cashier suggested that the vet check the current documents to make sure we had everything in order just in case something was missing. She would review them before calling us in. Kevin handed the vet-signed documents to the cashier, then we waited.

Although we took our small knapsack that contained our wallets, passports, and other important documents, Alonzo was sitting in his cab with our four big suitcases — out of sight from where we were standing. Alonzo seemed like a really nice guy, but I couldn't help myself, I kept peeking to make sure he hadn't absconded with our stuff.

Let's not add insult to injury to this exasperating day.

But he was still there.

I went out and apologized to him for the amount of time it was taking.

"No problema, señora, no problema."

Again, there was no mention of how much this was going to cost us, but I couldn't worry about that. I was sleep deprived, hungry, and a little punch drunk. Having Alonzo hang around, even for moral support, brought me a little comfort. I went back inside and waited some more with Kevin.

The vet came out and said she could see Frankie.

"Hola, my name is Raquel. I reviewed the documents. Sorry, but Frankie cannot fly before September 17," she said.

"W...w...why not?" I stuttered.

Raquel explained that an animal cannot fly within the first month of having its rabies shot. Frankie had hers on August 16. Even if the government agency expedited the exportation document, we'd still have to wait two weeks before being allowed to fly with her.

As stunned as I was, I felt resigned. It seemed par for the course. One last Costa Rica *hoorah* before sending us home.

I thought Kevin was going to have a coronary infarction. I'm not sure if he blamed me for not doing my due diligence when I took Frankie to our San Marcos vet, but he was beside himself with frustration.

After five years, my Spanish was pretty good, but I still misinterpreted things now and then. Since I had given the vet in San Marcos our departure dates well ahead of time, I assumed the timing of Frankie's shots was in line with flight regulations. It didn't feel like it was my fault, but maybe it was. Maybe I should have asked more questions. Maybe I was projecting, and I was blaming myself. Maybe Kevin was beside himself because this day sucked. Because it did.

We were no longer talking about staying an extra night or two in San José, waiting for quick paperwork. We now had to be there for another two weeks.

TWO weeks!

"Just when we thought we were out, Costa Rica pulled us back in," I said, squeezing my two fists and pulling my arms into my chest like Michael Corleone.

We're Baaack!

We paid Alonzo to drive us back to Hush Valley Lodge. Imagine Tiff and Clint's surprise when we showed up.

A few drinks might have been consumed while trying to explain the day's events.

We were guests now, staying in the casita, watching the new owners take charge of things. No question, it felt weird. As I was online letting everyone back in Canada know that we had been delayed, my email inbox pinged. It was an Airbnb review from Carrie and Stu, our last guests. It read:

> Anne and Kevin were the best hosts we have ever had the pleasure to stay with! What they have done to the property shows the love and dedication they have put into making Hush Valley Lodge what it is today. The Dota region is such a special place and staying there gives you a much more real Costa Rican experience than the bigger tourist areas of the country. Make sure to do the coffee tour because it will forever change how you view coffee and the process that goes into it. I highly recommend everyone to stay here. It is such a surreal experience staying in this hidden gem and enjoying the breathtaking property. Getting to catch your own trout and have the most delicious meals brought to your own cozy casita is an unmatchable experience. Take the hikes and

explore the property because it is too superb to miss! We hope to come back one day and experience this magical paradise with the new owners, Tiff and Clint. We know the beauty and charm that Kevin and Anne have put into the place will carry over into good hands. Now it's time for the new owners to have this place change their lives for the better as it did for Anne and Kevin! If we could give it ten stars, we would. A truly unique unforgettable experience you will not forget!

I cried.

Hurricane Irma

A massive earthquake shook the southern part of Mexico and there was a tsunami warning for the Pacific Coast all the way down to Costa Rica. But from where we sat, there was no evidence of any turbulent weather — there were clear blue skies, there was no wind, and it was warm.

I spent one morning taking advantage of the perfect weather by lounging and reading in the multi-coloured hammock that hung between two trees right next to the casita.

I didn't do enough of that when I lived here full time.

Kevin couldn't help himself — he needed to stay busy and enjoyed helping around the farm.

Although we stayed away from our devices during the day, in the evenings, Kevin and I were glued to the TV, watching the news for weather updates. The effects of the tsunami produced mega waves for good surfing in Tamarindo and further down the coast, but nothing more pernicious. Hurricane Irma, however, was picking up steam. She was clocking in, so far in 2017, as the strongest in terms of wind speed...worldwide. Her force was causing catastrophic damage in Cuba, the Virgin Islands, Haiti, and Puerto Rico. The devastation was insurmountable. It was sad and scary beyond measure. We worried that although all was well in paradise, our flights might be cancelled if Irma, who was heading straight for Florida, didn't weaken or change course. Irma would diminish in strength one day only to intensify the next. She gave us hope only to crush it unapologetically. Irma was the perfect metaphor to describe what the last two-and-a-half years felt like for us trying to sell Hush Valley Lodge. We were kept on the edge of our seats the whole time.

By September 10, Irma was still angry and showing no signs of mercy. How long could she rage on like this? Wasn't she tuckered out by now?

As we continued to monitor the situation, we heard back from the vet in San José. Kevin drove down and picked up Frankie's exportation documents on September 15

351

— Independence Day.

This coincidence was not lost on me. I could only pray it was a good sign. I remembered when we flew Frankie down to Costa Rica from Canada and I had joked that hers was a one-way ticket due to the trouble we had had with the airline. Maybe the travel gods took it to heart.

If anything else prevented her from boarding, the joke would have gone too far.

Home Stretch

Clint was kind enough to get up in the middle of the night to drive us and we had the gall to ask him if he would come into the airport with us to make sure we were able to check in. Kevin and I were both anxious. Considering our track record, Clint understood.

The check-in attendant — no name tag — was calm and expressionless. Maybe we were just overly sensitive, but it seemed to take an exceptionally long time to get the tags for our luggage printed. Standing around waiting to hear if everything was okay felt torturous. We hated that Clint had to stand around for this.

"Vet and exportation document, please."

No expression. More waiting.

Then, as the nameless man handed us our boarding passes, he mentioned that he made sure our luggage would go directly to Toronto, Canada. We didn't have to pick them up in Miami.

"It's too much work with a dog. Enjoy your flight."

We thanked him with more gratitude than he could ever understand. Then, we turned to Clint and thanked him with a hug. We had no more words.

At 5:47 a.m., on Sunday, September 17, 2017, we were sitting at Gate 10, waiting for our first flight back to Canada, with Frankie sequestered in her crate.

This was it. For real.

The skies were clear for takeoff. Even in Florida. Hurricane Irma had dissipated over Missouri four days earlier. The flight couldn't have gone smoother.

It had been a thrilling ride.

All of it.

The days were sometimes long, but the years all too short.

I highly recommend chasing rainbows.

Afterword

There are many people, events, and experiences that didn't make it into this book. Not because they weren't significant—they were.

One of the most rewarding experiences was becoming a volunteer teacher. Meeting Seidy, who championed and fulfilled her dream of creating the Copey Learning Center, was a turning point in making me feel like I belonged in this small rural community. And one of the most important ventures to come out of my short stint as its volunteer recruiter is the "Friends of Copey" fundraising initiative that was set up by Arthur Broady in 2013. He continues to spearhead the recruiting process, enlisting boots-on-the-ground volunteer teachers who make a difference each and every day while raising funds for much-needed scholastic materials. Arthur also created a sponsorship program where two students per year are awarded a trip to the U.S. Not only do Arthur and his tireless support system merit a thankful mention, but they deserve an entire book dedicated to their decade-long commitment. And at the time of writing this book, Arthur showed no signs of slowing down. He is an inspiration to so many. I feel blessed and honoured to have been there at the inception of such a worthy cause. I was merely a seed; Arthur has proven to be an oak. The students of Copey are fortunate beyond measure to have him in their corner.

I also wish I could have injected more hair-raising adventures, because there were many — too many to count. Or how we rescued baby bulls from neighbouring dairy farms and how Kevin bottle-fed them until they were strong enough to digest solid food. As adults, they grazed in our organic pasture to minimize Martín's weed-whacking efforts.

I thought for sure we'd be able to slaughter them for food, but we couldn't. I became a pescatarian after this experience.

I certainly could have written more about how we grew our business from a measly 300-ish trout to a whopping 15,000 by our fifth year. We went from catching each fish individually with a baited hook to dragging a large net the width of the big pond to capture hundreds of trout at a time. That imaginary business plan became a reality. Roberto continued to be our best and favourite client, but we did acquire another customer who bought far larger quantities. And he wanted smaller trout, and he wanted them alive, not dead and gutted. We had to adjust how we caught the fish and learn to transfer them into his big, oxygenated tanks in the most efficient way. Still grassroots, but we were always evolving. You should have seen the scale apparatus Kevin built. It looked like a big cross with one 20 L- (5 gal-) pail of water on one side, which weighed approximately 20 kg (44 lbs), and a hook on the other where we'd balance another pail full of fish. When the crossbar was level, we knew how much the pail of fish weighed. Business was booming. We had plans to increase the operation to 30,000 trout had we continued. We worked hard and there was always something to do as a farmer's day is never done. I gained a new appreciation for all farmers.

And although I alluded to the blissful serenity that surrounded the exciting fun storytelling moments, one simply cannot truly know how restorative it was for me to be given the gift of time. I like to keep busy and feel productive, but learning to slow down was a worthwhile lesson. Living a simple life also taught me to embrace a more minimalistic approach with my wardrobe, the size of my home, and all the stuff I don't want to accumulate.

But the Hush Valley Lodge experience wouldn't have been so memorable without the people. I wish I could have acknowledged every one of the friends I grew to love and cherish. And although I touched on the B&B, I could have easily filled pages upon pages of the guests we hosted. We met travellers from all over the world who chose to stay in our rustic casita. They braved the rutted roads and took a chance on our remote paradise. Their appreciation for our vision and the work we were doing fueled us. Reading review after review of how much they enjoyed their stay infused us with confidence that we were getting a few things right and urged us to keep our standards high.

Choosing what to keep in and what to leave out of this book...well, that's what editors are for. Blame them.

Since selling the property, much has happened. Moving back to Canada created a reverse culture shock. It took some time to adjust to the fast pace of suburban life again.

Kevin and I divorced amicably.

Phoenix, Jude, and I moved in together for the first two years, which was healing. We see each other often. I will never move that far away from them again.

To add to my many life adventures, in 2018, I walked parts of the Camino de Santiago de Compostela from Portugal to Spain. On that trip, I met up with Hanne and Hendrik, the Belgian travellers Kevin and I met during our 2011 Costa Rica scouting trip. When they heard I was going to be in Portugal, they changed their scheduled holiday plans and made a special effort to meet me in Porto. Seeing them was the highlight of that trip.

As life goes on, so does death. In 2014, we were saddened by the loss of Sister Gladys's driver, Jorge. We had formed a friendship with him during our many visits. Then in 2016, Sister Gladys called to let us know that Sister Gloria had passed away. These deaths were hard-hitting. There were losses back home, too. A dear friend in Canada had spent several weeks in the hospital and had succumbed to pneumonia and other complications. I wasn't there to visit during her battle or to say goodbye. I already felt stuck while we were trying to sell the property, but I really felt the shackles of distance even more at that time. Later, in 2017, shortly after returning to Canada, my father was diagnosed with ALS. While he lived valiantly with this terrible affliction, he surrendered and passed away on Sunday, June 21, 2020, which happened to be my parents' sixty-second wedding anniversary and Father's Day. As if he waited for the perfect day, Dad left his mark in a poignant way, never to be forgotten. As if we ever could be. I was relieved that I was back home to help support my mother and sisters during a difficult time. It would have been so much harder had I been living abroad. More recently, our dear friend, Clara, passed away in May 2024. My heart broke upon hearing this sad news and the feelings of being so far away surged in reverse. I wished I had been there to share in this immense sorrow and had been there to comfort my Río Blanco family in person.

At eighty-six, my mother continues to follow her health regimens and will surely outlive us all. Since her month-long visit to Costa Rica, she and I have nurtured a loving mother-daughter relationship. We talk on FaceTime once a week and I try to visit as often as I can.

And in a strange twist of fate, as I write this, I'm working on a contract at the same company I left to move to Costa Rica.

I'm forever grateful for our Costa Rica adventure. No regrets.

Acknowledgments

Phoenix and Jude... My soul soars because of you. Thank you for all your love, support, and understanding. No one could love you more!

Para mis amigos de Río Blanco, Copey, Santa María, San Marcos, Tinamaste, San José y Puerto Viejo...muchas gracias por hacernos sentir como en familia.

To the rest of my family and friends...no words can express my gratitude for all your kindness, encouragement, and support while I wrote this book. But most especially you, Steven. It means the world to me!

To Kevin, thank you for an adventure of a lifetime.

My heartfelt gratitude goes out to my first editor, Katherine Armstrong. Kate, you elevated Part I to the point of enticing my publisher to sit up and take notice. Part I set the tone for the rest of the book, it was my compass. Thank you.

And to Lindsay R.A. Dierking of The Awakened Press, it's hard to find the words to express how thankful I am that you took a chance on me. Your unyielding support and understanding during the arduous creative process knows no bounds. I look forward to riding this ride again with you and your stellar team of magic-makers when I write my next book.

About the Author

Anne Beaudoin

Desperate to escape a soul-draining suburban lifestyle, Canadian writer and author Anne Beaudoin dared to chase a dream. Settling in the remote mountains of Costa Rica, Anne immersed herself as an expat where she wrote and maintained a five-year blog and shared her adventures of becoming a trout farmer and bed-and-breakfast host with armchair seekers and fellow travellers alike.

Anne is a graduate of the Sheridan College Creative Writing Program and a co-songwriter of "Great Blue" on Alise Marlane's Stillness Hold On album. Between life's many adventures, she has worked mainly in the graphic design field. When she is not writing, Anne loves family game nights, hiking, and transforming a vintage 1984 Dodge Ram Roadtrek II — affectionately called Stan — into an awesome road-tripping van.

www.ingramcontent.com/pod-product-compliance
Lightning Source LLC
Chambersburg PA
CBHW061552120626
46550CB00004B/1464